Burson and Walls offer students of Lewis
and Schaeffer a rare treat:
fresh insights into the commonalities
and dissonances between these influential thinkers,
climaxed by a compelling, holistic agenda for apologetics
in the next millennium.
BRUCE L. EDWARDS
Author of *A Rhetoric of Reading:
C. S. Lewis's Defense of Western Literacy*

A thorough and perceptive assessment of two Christian
apologists who, despite sharing much
in common, display contrasting styles of argument.
GILBERT MEILAENDER
Valparaiso University

C.S. LEWIS
&FRANCIS
SCHAEFFER

Lessons for a New Century
from the Most Influential
Apologists of Our Time

SCOTT R. BURSON &
JERRY L. WALLS

InterVarsity Press
Downers Grove, Illinois

InterVarsity Press
P.O. Box 1400, Downers Grove, IL 60515
World Wide Web: www.ivpress.com
E-mail: mail@ivpress.com

InterVarsity Press® is the book-publishing division of InterVarsity Christian Fellowship/USA®, a student movement active on campus at hundreds of universities, colleges and schools of nursing in the United States of America, and a member movement of the International Fellowship of Evangelical Students. For information about local and regional activities, write Public Relations Dept., InterVarsity Christian Fellowship/USA, 6400 Schroeder Rd., P.O. Box 7895, Madison, WI 53707-7895.

All Scripture quotations, unless otherwise indicated, are taken from the Holy Bible, New International Version®. NIV®. *Copyright ©1973, 1978, 1984 by International Bible Society. Used by permission of Zondervan Publishing House. All rights reserved.*

The diagram on page ninety-six is from Escape from Reason. *Copyright © 1968, Inter-Varsity Fellowship, England. Reprinted with permission from InterVarsity Press, Downers Grove, IL 60515.*

ISBN 0-8308-1935-5

Printed in the United States of America ∞

Library of Congress Cataloging-in-Publication Data
Burson, Scott R.
    C.S. Lewis & Francis Schaeffer: lessons for a new century from
  the most influential apologists of our time / Scott R. Burson &
Jerry L. Walls.
        p. cm.
    Includes bibliographical references.
    ISBN 0-8308-1935-5 (alk. paper)
    1. Apologetics—History—20th century. 2. Lewis, C. S. (Clive
Staples), 1898-1963. 3. Schaeffer, Francis A. (Francis August)
I. Walls, Jerry L. II. Title III. Title: C.S. Lewis and Francis
Schaeffer.
BT1117.B87 1998   97-43691
239'.092'2—DC21   CIP

21 20 19 18 17 16 15 14 13 12 11 10 9 8 7 6 5 4

16 15 14 13 12 11 10 09 08 07 06 05 04 03 02 01 00

To Susie, Ashley, Lindsey and Ryan Burson,
whose lives are compelling proof that God is good.

To Bob and Marilyn Uhrig, Pete and Jan Edgington,
Jack and Joyce Kellenberger, John and Melinda Walls, and Joe and Tammy Walls:
personal parts of my cumulative case that Christianity is true.

Acknowledgments

First and foremost, we want to thank our families for their patience during many months of late nights at the office. Without their sacrifice, this book would never have come to fruition.

We are also indebted to a number of colleagues and organizations. The Asbury Seminary Communications Department—Fred Cramer, Alan Creech, Cathy Deon, Wendell Esbenshade and Michele Sparks—offered ongoing support. Ben Witherington III believed in this project and encouraged the publisher to pursue it. Research assistant Scott Haire meticulously checked hundreds of citations for accuracy. Linda Henson generously shared her extensive L'Abri tape library. The Francis Schaeffer Institute supplied important electronic and print resources. The Lexington L'Abri Committee provided access to the 1996 Lexington L'Abri Conference. Jerram Barrs, Lane Dennis, Os Guinness, Dick Keyes and James Sire all supplied many valuable insights into the life and ministry of Francis Schaeffer. Edith and Frank Schaeffer both wrote helpful and gracious letters in response to our inquiries.

Chris Mitchell and Marjorie Mead of the Wade Center provided helpful assistance during the research phase of this book. Wayne Martindale furnished gracious accommodations and stimulating conversation during a trip to Wheaton. Bruce Edwards offered many choice insights into the thought of Lewis during one of his helpful summer workshops. The members of the L'Abri and Mere Lewis electronic mailing lists provided provocative threads of discussion. The students of the C. S. Lewis Seminar at Asbury Seminary have over the years enriched our understanding of the Oxford don. Finally, IVP senior editor Rodney Clapp provided sage editorial advice and exhibited exemplary patience when it became clear that this project was going to take longer than originally planned.

To be ignorant and simple now—not to be able to meet the enemies on their own ground—would be to throw down our weapons, and to betray our uneducated brethren who have, under God, no defence but us against the intellectual attacks of the heathen. Good philosophy must exist, if for no other reason, because bad philosophy needs to be answered.[1]

C. S. LEWIS

The Christian is to resist the spirit of the world. But when we say this, we must understand that the world-spirit does not always take the same form. So the Christian must resist the spirit of the world *in the form it takes in his own generation*. If he does not do this, he is not resisting the spirit of the world at all.[2]

FRANCIS SCHAEFFER

Many, *many* evangelicals—including some of the most prominent evangelical intellectual leaders—were first inspired to serious Christian thought about culture by Schaeffer's pioneering books *Escape from Reason* and *The God Who Is There* (1968). It is perhaps fair to say, however, that one author's books indisputably affected American evangelicals during this period more than did Francis Schaeffer's. . . . And that author was neither American nor quintessentially evangelical. I mean, of course, C. S. Lewis.[3]

JOHN STACKHOUSE

When Worlds Collide

Paleo-orthodoxy in a Postmodern Age

A FEW YEARS AGO MICHAEL CRICHTON AND STEVEN SPIELBERG captured the imagination of the world with the blockbuster film *Jurassic Park.* Through genetic engineering and state-of-the-art technology a tropical island is transformed into an amusement park with actual, living dinosaurs. But dreams of a prehistoric paradise—and a marketing gold mine—are dashed when a test-tube T-Rex rampages through the park.

British actor and director Richard Attenborough plays the role of the park founder, a fascinating cross between Walt Disney and Marlon Perkins. In one poignant scene a consultant chastises Attenborough's character for misusing genetic power: "Your scientists were so preoccupied with whether or not they *could,* they didn't stop to think if they *should.*" This film exposes the shipwrecked notion that science can safely navigate uncharted waters without a moral rudder.

While *Jurassic Park* was breaking box-office records on one side of the Atlantic, Attenborough was breaking ground on another anachronistic endeavor in Britain. But this one was different. There were no eye-popping special effects, no heart-pounding prehistoric predators—just the portrait of a man whose kind is on the verge of extinction, a man who once said, "Speaking not only for myself but for all Old Western Men who you meet, I would say, use your specimens while you can. There are not going to be many more dinosaurs."[4] This specimen was, of course, popular author and Christian apologist C. S. Lewis.

Attenborough's remake of *Shadowlands* offered a rare glimpse at a true classicist, and it did so by providing a refreshing counterpoint to Hollywood's incessant fascination with the profane. The film displaced lust with geriatric romance, gore with the piercing problem of evil, and blasphemous expletives with a script leavened with spirituality. It was a surprising box-office success.

The movie's appeal left many thirsting to learn more about Lewis. Publishers responded by flooding the market with a new wave of critiques, articles and books. The tourism industry also profited. An increased flow of enthusiasts journeyed to landmark sites on the Lewis register, such as the Marion E. Wade Center at Wheaton College—the American mecca of Lewisiana. Founded by Lewis scholar and Wheaton professor Clyde Kilby, the Wade Center is home to the hand-carved wardrobe that inspired the Narnia tales, Lewis's writing desk, a healthy portion of his personal library and a wealth of research material. At the zenith of the *Shadowlands* craze, the volume of visitors to the Wade Center nearly doubled.[5]

Today an increasing number of technotourists are accessing Lewis on the information superhighway. Nearly a dozen cyberspace stations are dedicated to the Oxford don.[6] "Into the Wardrobe," perhaps the most popular web page on the Lewis circuit, welcomes more than eight thousand visitors each month. Other sites offer biographical background, insights into Lewis's group of Oxford colleagues known as the Inklings, interactive fantasy games, a detailed tour of Narnia and lively chats with those of like mind. Lewisians from London to Los Angeles religiously discuss his musings on a wide variety of topics. It is not uncommon to find one of Lewis's stepsons, Douglas Gresham, feeding the faithful tantalizing tidbits of trivia.

Bruce Edwards, an English professor at Bowling Green State University, uses his web page to promote scholarly interest in Lewis. In addition to snippets about upcoming seminars and workshops, he posts essays, critiques and articles of interest to the Lewis community. In one such offering, entitled "Lewis Redux: A Postmodern Dialogue," Edwards creatively imagines what it would be like to hang ten with Lewis "the web surfer." This fictitious conversation ebbs and flows over the paradoxes and profundities of postmodern life, transporting Lewis out of his silent planet and into the vast galaxies of interactive cyberspace. During one stretch of the dialogue, Edwards informs Lewis of his continued appeal: "Well, Jack...I suppose you've noticed you're still very popular—Catholics and Protestants alike read you, but especially those ultra-conservative fundevangelicals ... why they hardly read any other Christian writers."[7]

Though such a claim is surely hyperbolic, a 1993 *Christianity Today* readers poll shows it is not too far off the mark. When subscribers were asked which book (other than the Bible) had influenced their spiritual lives the most, Lewis's *Mere Christianity* received more than twice as many votes as any other work, dwarfing timeless giants such as *The Cost of Discipleship*, *My Utmost for His Highest* and *Pilgrim's Progress*. In the "all-time favorite novel" category, three of Lewis's fantasies (the Chronicles of Narnia, *Perelandra* and *Till We Have Faces*) turned up among the top twelve.[8]

This insatiable appetite for Lewis's work is hardly new. During the past four decades, interest in his writing has never seriously waned. Since his death, the public has feasted on a steady diet of biographies, anthologies and scholarship. Conferences are held in his honor. Societies perpetuate his legacy. His original works continue to line bookstore shelves.

Indeed, one is hard-pressed to refute the staggering and arguably unparalleled impact of C. S. Lewis on the contemporary evangelical psyche. As we enter a new millennium it would appear Lewis could not have been more mistaken. Far from extinct, this dinosaur has safely weathered the icy age of modernity.

Missionary to the Intellectuals

In 1947 a portrait of C. S. Lewis graced the cover of *Time* magazine. The accompanying article highlighted the astounding apologetic impact the Oxford don was having through his popular Christian books. Fourteen years later, not long before Lewis's death, *Time* turned the spotlight on a new advocate for the old faith. The American periodical featured a "missionary to the intellectuals," an eccentric, goateed, knicker-clad evangelist who was welcoming beatniks, existentialists and other spiritual seekers to his chalet in the Swiss Alps. His name was Francis Schaeffer.

Schaeffer's L'Abri community combined hospitality with honest intellectual inquiry. By the warmth of a crackling fire, Schaeffer chiseled away at the foundations of Enlightenment rationalism one moment and fanned the flame of classic Christianity the next. He treated each pilgrim with respect and dignity, listening patiently to stories of struggle, confusion and heartache. Often with tears streaming down his face, Schaeffer compassionately exposed the futility of any lifestyle or worldview that shrouded the Christian vision of reality.

Countless wayward lives found meaning and purpose through the trek to L'Abri, but it was Schaeffer's prolific writing that most profoundly influenced a generation of believers. Between 1968 and 1980, he was a powerful voice in the evangelical world, with a string of best-selling books on subjects ranging from apologetics to spiritual formation to contemporary culture. College students were the first to encounter his works, but by the end of the seventies Schaeffer had carved a broad swath through much of conservative Protestantism with his impassioned defense of the unborn and aged.

During the early eighties Schaeffer battled cancer, speaking widely, but contributing little to his expansive body of work. When he died in 1984, many wondered if Schaeffer's movement could maintain momentum without its influential leader. J. I. Packer pondered Schaeffer's place in history in a fitting foreword to *Reflections on Francis Schaeffer:*

> What long-term significance has Schaeffer for the Christian cause? Neither this foreword nor the book that it introduces can answer that question; it is far too soon to tell. . . . Perhaps the clique for whom "Schaeffer says" has long been the last word in human wisdom will disperse; or perhaps its members will now labor to build the prophet's tomb, embalming into hallowed irrelevance thoughts that were once responses to the desperation of our time. We wait to see. The law of human fame will no doubt treat Schaeffer as it has treated others, eclipsing him temporarily now that he is dead and only allowing us to see his real stature ten or twenty years down the road.[9]

More than a decade has passed since Packer posed this question, and it would appear Schaeffer's posterity is beginning to become clear. Signs of vitality, creativity and even unparalleled growth within the institutions that bear his mark all testify to continuing influence and relevance.

The most obvious testament to Schaeffer's lasting legacy is the ongoing impact of L'Abri. This movement, which started with one chalet in the mid-fifties, has burgeoned to ten sites in eight countries (Australia, England, India, Korea, the Netherlands, Sweden, Switzerland and the United States). Dick Keyes, long-time director of the Southborough L'Abri (near Boston), reports that many branches are packed to capacity with total enrollment at an all-time high.[10] In addition, many who are unable to visit an actual L'Abri branch are seeking stimulation through seminars and weekend conferences. One recent conference, held on the Asbury Theological Seminary campus, welcomed more than four hundred participants from thirty-six states. Many others were turned away due to space limitations.

While leaders of L'Abri continue to revere the ministry of Francis Schaeffer and use many of his works and tapes in their teaching, Schaeffer has not been enshrined or divinized. Keyes and other members of this movement still find great value in much of Schaeffer's thought, noting his prophetic tendencies to anticipate the flow of culture, but L'Abri leaders are best seen as following Schaeffer's example and reinterpreting his thought for a new day, rather than parroting his arguments.

Another sign of vitality is the Francis Schaeffer Institute at Covenant

Theological Seminary. Since the institute opened in 1989, the seminary has experienced sharp growth. In 1991 enrollment was tenuously dangling at one hundred and seventy students, but by the mid-nineties the student count had risen to more than five hundred. According to James Albritton, a former administrator at the institute, a new generation of Schaeffer enthusiasts appears to be emerging. Young people are discovering a message that is as relevant today as it was two or three decades ago. The challenge to develop an integrated view of the world from a thoroughly Christian perspective is a breath of fresh air to an age tainted by the pollution of pluralism.[11]

A third sign of enduring influence is the current level of interest in Schaeffer's writing. Lane Dennis, publisher of Crossway Books, reports sales of *How Should We Then Live?* increased fifty-five percent during a recent four-year stretch—an unusual trend for a work that has been on the market for two decades.[12] Another glance at the *Christianity Today* 1993 readers poll reveals Schaeffer's classic *The God Who Is There* tied for seventh in the "most influential book" category, just one spot behind Calvin's landmark *Institutes*. Schaeffer was the only other writer of apologetics to join Lewis on this prestigious list.

These pieces of converging evidence—the vitality of L'Abri, the success of the Schaeffer Institute and the considerable ongoing interest in and the enduring influence of Schaeffer's writings—support the claim that the legacy of this unique evangelist to the intellectuals is secure.

The C. S. Lewis of My Generation

It is not uncommon to find the names of C. S. Lewis and Francis Schaeffer popping up together these days. More and more historians, philosophers and cultural analysts are recognizing the powerful influence of this apologetic pair upon the development of twentieth-century evangelicalism.

Consider the recent *Christianity Today* cover story on Francis Schaeffer, written by historian Michael Hamilton. In this extensive feature, Hamilton highlights Schaeffer's influence upon a "wildly diverse" cross-section of Christian leaders, including musician Larry Norman, Moral Majority founder Jerry Falwell, 1996 vice-presidential nominee Jack Kemp and theologian Clark Pinnock. Hamilton suggests, "Perhaps no intellectual save C. S. Lewis affected the thinking of evangelicals more profoundly."[13]

Jeff Jordan, a philosophy professor at the University of Delaware, also draws a connection between Schaeffer and Lewis. In an essay in *God and the Philosophers*, a volume that features the spiritual autobiographies of leading theistic philosophers, Jordan shares how he came across one of Schaeffer's books during his college years. Like many during the sixties and seventies he found the content revolutionary. Instead of retreating from the world, Schaeffer's readers were challenged to engage all facets of culture with biblical truth: "Schaeffer was, I think, the C. S. Lewis of my generation. In the next year or so, I read nearly every book written by Schaeffer. . . . [H]e had a powerful effect on many people of my generation, opening our eyes to the rich interplay possible between Christian faith and the great ideas of philosophy."[14]

Jordan is not alone. In fact, half of the contributors to *God and the Philosophers*, including one of the authors of this book, referenced Lewis, Schaeffer or both as influential factors in their development as Christian philosophers.[15] Not the least of these is Thomas Morris, editor of the volume and author of *Francis Schaeffer's Apologetics*. Morris speaks for many when he credits an awakening toward Christian philosophy to the work of popular apologists like Lewis and Schaeffer.[16]

Some of today's brightest Christian leaders, not only in philosophy but across a wide variety of disciplines, originally began to sense the intellectual potency of historic, orthodox Christianity through books like *Miracles, Mere Christianity, Escape from Reason* and *The God Who Is There*. A generation ago the "chronological snobbery" of Enlightenment rationalism dominated the canons of scholarship in the hallowed halls of most institutions of higher learning. With this ideology ensconced in the leading chairs of academia, classic Christian theism appeared to be on its last leg. But the past thirty years have seen a remarkable turnaround in many academic circles. Today many prominent philosophers of religion are staunch proponents of paleo-orthodoxy.[17] Lewis and Schaeffer met a need when there were few believers venturing into the deep and murky waters of philosophical inquiry.[18] They encouraged subsequent generations to reconcile faith with reason and consequently inspired many budding scholars to detail what was already being accomplished in broad strokes.

But as we have noted, many beyond the realm of the academy have been influenced deeply by Lewis and Schaeffer as well. In the fortieth anniversary issue of *Christianity Today*, John Stackhouse, a professor at the University of Manitoba, provides an overview of the books that have shaped the broader evangelical community during the past four decades. Stackhouse pays homage to a diverse spectrum of authors, ranging from Hal Lindsey to Carl Henry and James Dobson to John Stott, but concludes with this highly influential apologetic pair:

> Many, *many* evangelicals—including some of the most prominent evangelical intellectual leaders—were first inspired to serious Christian thought about culture by Schaeffer's pioneering books *Escape from Reason* and *The God Who Is There* (1968). It is perhaps fair to say, however, that

one author's books indisputably affected American evangelicals during this period more than did Francis Schaeffer's.... And that author was neither American nor quintessentially evangelical. I mean, of course, C. S. Lewis.[19] While Hamilton, Jordan, Morris and Stackhouse all speak from within evangelicalism, Richard John Neuhaus, a keen cultural analyst, offers a perspective from a different tradition. Yet this prominent Roman Catholic theologian arrives at the same conclusion:

> But we can say, truly, that some of our best friends were formed in crucial ways by Francis Schaeffer and his L'Abri community in Switzerland. For many Evangelicals, Schaeffer, an astonishing autodidact, made accessible a large part of the history of Western thought construed according to his distinctive Christian vision. In the evangelical community, his influence was possibly only second, albeit a very distant second, to that of C. S. Lewis.[20]

The evidence is impressive. The sentiments of *Christianity Today* readers, historians, philosophers, cultural analysts and evangelical leaders all seem to point to one thing: a compelling case can be made to declare C. S. Lewis and Francis Schaeffer the most influential apologists of the twentieth century.

The Emergence of Postmodernity

Of course, influence does not necessarily entail expertise. At least this has been the opinion in some evangelical academic circles, where distancing oneself from popular apologists like Lewis and Schaeffer is almost a rite of passage.[21] According to typical critiques, Lewis and Schaeffer frequently fall into the inherent trap of popular apologetics by presenting the false dilemma, failing to exhaust logical options and boiling complex philosophical issues down to simplistic solutions. The critiques also take issue with the triumphalistic tone that often accompanies these "underdeveloped" arguments. Critics frequently point to Lewis's famous "trilemma" and Schaeffer's controversial account of the development of Western civilization as prime examples of inordinate rhetoric and shoddy scholarship.

The situation is further exacerbated when book jackets, press releases and promotional advertisements elevate the philosophical prowess of these writers to grandiose heights. Consider a recent ad for Frank Schaeffer's book *Dancing Alone*. This sensationalistic ad pits the younger Schaeffer against his father and his teachings. At first, there appears to be nothing misleading about this—after all, Francis most likely would have been at odds with Frank's recent conversion to Eastern Orthodoxy. The problem arises, however, when the elder Schaeffer is unequivocally described as "the Greatest Evangelical Philosopher of our century." This is not an isolated incident. Two decades earlier, a philosophy text was released with heavyweights like Aquinas, Descartes,

Kant, Hume and Wittgenstein listed on the cover. The final name in this illustrious list was none other than Francis Schaeffer. Similar implicit and explicit claims are made for Lewis, whose academic discipline was not philosophy (though he did teach this subject for a brief period at the beginning of his academic career) but medieval and Renaissance literature. One can understand how such propaganda can become disconcerting to professional philosophers who take the rigor of their discipline seriously. Thomas Morris succinctly summarizes the concern of some scholars:

> Having worked hard at philosophy for years, having come to understand the difficulty of ever proving anything by pure reason alone, and having reconciled themselves to living with the uncertainties of this world, they are more than a little irritated to see their students and the general reading public idolizing some good writer as a great philosopher who has proved this, that, and everything else of real philosophical significance, when it is clear to a trained eye that no such results have been attained at all.[22]

For some scholars, however, the biggest problem is not the questionable persuasion of these popular apologists, but rather the insistence of so many of their followers to serve up the same old apologetic recipes to an age that is no longer dining at the table of modernity. Our world is changing. The once unshakable confidence in the Enlightenment project, which promised us unfettered freedom and humanistic happiness, has fractured like the Liberty Bell.

The tenets of modernity—autonomous self-sufficiency, the supremacy of reason, the inalienable right of freedom and the certainty of inevitable progress—have given way to the denial of absolutes, a celebration of connectedness, a renewed quest for spirituality and a threatening nihilism.[23] The West is no longer defined by any particular metanarrative (e.g., Christianity or naturalism); in fact, all previous paradigms are viewed as epistemologically tainted social constructions and oppressive, marginalizing maneuvers designed to stifle diversity of thought and expression.[24] Since objective reality and absolute truth have no ontological status, all viewpoints are equally valid. In such a context, pluralism sits on the cultural throne with tolerance as the undisputed law of the land.

Of course, postmodernity can hardly be nailed down with pat descriptions and neat definitions. In order to define something, one must have a clear idea about its shape, size and texture. This we do not have. We are living in an emerging age of transition that is mutating into a final form we cannot yet identify. The one thing we do know is that contemporary culture is so multidimensional and diverse that it might be ill-advised to even attempt to erect a single canvas over the whole bizarre circus. William Abraham offers a view of the big top:

I perceive the modern world as thoroughly fragmented and chaotic. In fact, to speak of a single modern world is an oxymoron. . . . If we look at our culture as a whole, we are confronted by a *discord* of voices, of worldviews, of moral traditions, of life-styles, and of inner informal logics which cannot be flattened out into a comprehensive theoretic analysis— whether intellectual, economic, or sociological.[25]

Within the evangelical community there is little consensus about how to go about responding to the emerging contours of postmodernity. Volumes like *Christian Apologetics in the Postmodern World* and *The Challenge of Postmodernism: An Evangelical Engagement* illustrate the diversity of opinion that exists.[26] Some Christian scholars find the postmodern critique both poignant and liberating. This perspective welcomes the break with an epistemology they claim owes more to Enlightenment empiricism than to the apostolic tradition. Many of these scholars believe Christianity's worth is best expressed through faithful example rather than cognitive argumentation.

Other scholars believe classical apologetics is still viable in our day. Though they may appreciate some of the insights from Rorty, Fish, Derrida and the other postmodernists, there is a strong aversion to severing ties with the correspondence theory of truth. According to this school of thought, one cannot escape the self-evident principles God has built into the universe, including the laws of logic. What the world needs is not freedom to think and act however it likes, but rather the freedom to think and act as it ought. Only then will postmodern people see "the way, the truth and the life" and experience the unity and diversity they so desperately desire.

Is, then, the ongoing fascination with Lewis and Schaeffer a help or a hindrance to the contemporary apologetic task? Are those who continue to appreciate the works of these men hopelessly clinging to the past? Does the shift from Enlightenment rationalism to postmodern uncertainty force us to jettison all ties with previous argumentation and methodology, or does this strange new world call for merely a tune-up? This study seeks to offer some answers.

A Microcosm of Evangelicalism

But before we can focus on the future, we must take a good, hard look at the past. A proper comparative analysis of these two men must be set against the backdrop of their native, twentieth-century context. Who were they? What influences helped shape their thinking? What apologetic approach did each utilize? What arguments did they employ to advance and defend the faith? How did their theologies inform their apologetic systems?

A detailed look at these apologists reveals intriguing consonance and contrast. Each man is remembered for his insatiable search for truth, fascination with the classics, large lay followings, ministry in war-torn Europe and personal encounters with the ravages of cancer. But distinct differences exist as well. Schaeffer was an ordained Presbyterian minister, Lewis an Anglican layman; Schaeffer was a self-confessed teetotaling fundamentalist, Lewis a beer-drinking, pipe-smoking critic of puritanical rigidity; Schaeffer was a blue-collar frontline evangelist, Lewis a white-collar Oxford don. In chapter one we will look at some of these similarities and differences in a brief biographical overview.

In chapters two through five we will consider the theological commitments of these men. If we are to appreciate Lewis and Schaeffer as apologists, we must first understand the doctrines they defended and the beliefs that informed their apologetic sensitivities. Both men were in the business of communicating the essence of the faith, what Lewis called "mere Christianity." But defining what is central to the faith is a task that has challenged the church for centuries. Though these apologists held a great deal in common, some key theological distinctions exist. In fact, a comparison of Schaeffer's Calvinism and Lewis's Anglican Arminianism provides a fascinating microcosm of evangelicalism as a whole, revealing some of the significant tensions that continue to undermine unity within the contemporary church and hamper the ongoing apologetic/evangelistic task.

One key distinction can be found in the arena of biblical authority and divine inspiration. Undoubtedly, the question of authority and textual integrity is an important consideration for the apologist. Chapter five will address this issue. Though both writers were firm defenders of objective, absolute truth, fundamental differences arise when their views on inspiration, hermeneutics and higher criticism are explored. Schaeffer, who saw acceptance of strict inerrancy as the litmus test for evangelicals, would certainly have challenged Lewis's comfortable application of literary criticism to the biblical text. Lewis had no problem categorizing many miracles of the Old Testament as mythology and even suggested the possibility of finding errors in the gospel accounts. This chapter should begin to shed light on some important epistemological distinctions.

While chapters one through five are designed to reveal the worldview of each man, the second half of the book will focus on the ways in which these apologists went about defending their views to the world. In other words, apologetics, properly speaking. In chapter six we will explore the differences between three different schools of apologetic approach: presuppositionalism, evidentialism and verificationism. We will evaluate the methodology of Lewis and Schaeffer to determine which school best characterizes their respective strategies.

The next three chapters will be devoted to apologetic arguments. William

Lane Craig divides the field of apologetics into two categories: offensive and defensive apologetics. According to Craig, "Offensive apologetics seeks to present a positive case for Christian truth claims. Defensive apologetics seeks to nullify objections to those claims."[27] Chapters seven and eight follow Craig's helpful categorical distinctions.

In chapter seven, we will consider the primary offensive arguments employed by these apologists: Lewis's moral argument, the "Trilemma," the argument from rationality, the argument from desire and the argument from agape, as well as Schaeffer's metaphysical, moral and epistemological arguments. In chapter eight, we will explore the defensive responses Lewis and Schaeffer developed to combat attacks upon Christian theism. Much of the chapter will be spent on the most powerful logical and existential challenge to the Christian faith, namely, the problem of evil. In light of the disturbing violence, racism, abortion and family disintegration of our day, the problem of evil continues to be exceptionally acute. An intellectually credible and existentially sensitive Christian response is an important part of contemporary apologetics.

After sketching out the offensive and defensive arguments marshaled by these men, we will offer a critical analysis in chapter nine. We will determine the major points of contrast and contact between these two apologists and consider the strengths and weaknesses in their respective systems. Special attention will be devoted to the relationship between the apologetic arguments and the theological resources available to each man.

In the final chapter we will summarize and synthesize what has been developed in the first nine chapters. We will seek to determine what Lewis and Schaeffer can offer our pluralistic, therapeutic, consumeristic, visually oriented age. Without question, Christians must offer a significant degree of ingenuity, creativity, sensitivity and versatility if we are to be heard above the cacophony of voices in today's chaotic marketplace of ideas.

C. S. Lewis once wrote, "The standard of permanent Christianity must be kept clear in our minds and it is against that standard that we must test all contemporary thought. In fact, we must at all costs *not* move with the times."[28] As Christians we have every reason in the world to enter the twenty-first century with confidence and eager anticipation. We have at our disposal the greatest intellectual tradition the Western world has ever known. Indeed, the standard of permanent Christianity has weathered two millennia of epistemological fads and fetishes. All that is necessary to meet the needs and desires of our postmodern world can be excavated from the ancient riches of paleo-orthodoxy. And it is our contention that the most influential apologists of our time can be valuable resources in retelling the old, old story to a brand-new age.

In the Trinity Term of 1929 I gave in, and admitted that God was God, and knelt and prayed; perhaps, that night, the most dejected and reluctant convert in all England. I did not then see what is now the most shining and obvious thing; the Divine humility which will accept a convert even on such terms.[1]

C. S. Lewis

I faced a spiritual crisis. . . . I walked, prayed, and thought through what the Scriptures taught, as well as reviewing my own reasons for being a Christian. . . . Gradually I saw that the problem was that with all the teaching I had received after I was a Christian, I had heard little about what the Bible says about the meaning of the finished work of Christ for our present lives. Gradually the sun came out and the song came.[2]

Francis Schaeffer

It fascinates me to consider that as Fran was born, C. S. Lewis was a boy of thirteen in his miserable boarding school.[3]

Edith Schaeffer

1

The Biographical Foundation

The Path to Apologetic Prominence

Clive Staples Lewis (1898-1963)

Every generation has its defining moments. In the 1990s it was the O. J. Simpson verdict. In the 1980s it was the Challenger disaster. In the 1970s it was the Watergate hearings. And in the 1960s it was the assassination of President Kennedy.

November 22, 1963, was a day of international mourning. Condolences from around the world flooded the White House. A Muslim telegraph read, "How sorrowful bad." In Israel, David Ben-Gurion could only wonder aloud, "Why, why?" In Berlin, twenty-five thousand students participated in a torchlight march. In London, Big Ben tolled every minute for an hour—an honor generally reserved for royalty.[4]

While the death of President Kennedy shrouded Downing Street and the rest of the world that day, acclaimed author and popular BBC wartime broadcaster Clive Staples Lewis slipped silently into eternity at his nearby Oxford home.

The loss of the American leader totally overshadowed the passing of Lewis. Few newspapers reported his death and only a handful of friends attended his funeral. Hardly a fitting tribute for one of the century's most powerful and articulate representatives of the Christian faith, but just the way Lewis would have wanted it.

Unlike Kennedy, Lewis was never quite comfortable in the limelight, preferring the charms of a good book and the conversation of a few close friends to the glitz and glamour of public life. He died one week prior to his sixty-fourth birthday, and if he had lived to see it, he undoubtedly would have celebrated it like most of the previous sixty-three—quietly, with a handful of confidants.

Lewis and Kennedy did have a couple of things in common, however. Both traced their heritage to Ireland, and both preferred to be called Jack.

Pangs of Joy

As a small child, young Clive announced he would no longer answer to his given name. Instead he would go by "Jacksie," in memory of the family dog, one of Belfast's first automobile casualties. The nickname stuck, although his older brother Warren (a.k.a. Warnie) continued to call his sibling "piggiebottom," a moniker foisted on the pair by their amiable nursemaid.[5]

Jack and Warnie were inseparable in the early days, creating fantastic worlds of make-believe. Though their tastes differed, both boys tapped into their imaginative powers to spin tales of far-off lands. Warnie staked claim to India, while Jack, three years the younger, spent his time toiling in the fields and forests of "Animal-Land."[6] From the beginning, the younger Lewis had a special place in his heart for the natural world.

Sickness, along with the damp Belfast weather, often forced Jack to appreciate nature from afar. A view of the mystical Castlereagh Hills from the nursery window captured his fancy and evoked a powerful longing that was difficult to define. Inside the house, nothing provided visual stimulation. His father was a successful lawyer and his mother possessed a keen mathematical mind, but neither excelled in the realm of interior decorating.[7]

One day Warnie brought a fresh taste of nature into the sterile confines of their home. It was a small toy garden made out of moss and encased in a biscuit tin. This rudimentary botanical paradise gained an everlasting foothold in Jack's memory. The "cool, dewy, fresh, exuberant" characteristics of Warnie's garden evoked the same kind of longing that the distant hills had stirred.[8] For the rest of his life, the sights and scents of nature possessed the power to instantaneously transport Lewis back to this mossy paradise. He would later recognize this mysterious experience in the writings of Traherne, Coleridge and Wordsworth, an experience these authors called *Sehnsucht* or "Joy."[9] But it was not joy in the typical sense. Words like *pleasure, fulfillment* and *happiness* do not capture its essence. In fact, Joy in the Romantic sense is quite the opposite: it is the absence of fulfillment, a deep-seated longing, an awareness of one's lack, the realization of incompleteness. At times it manifests itself as a tantalizing, fleeting flood of euphoria. At other times it comes as a hollow, painful pang of loss. In either case, Joy is characterized by its elusive, unpredictable, consistently inconsistent nature. It never surfaces on command, and often when one least expects it.

The rest of Lewis's boyhood is largely a tale of meeting Joy in a variety of venues. Sometimes it rushed over him on the cool, colorful autumn afternoons of County Down; other times it gripped him through the creative forms of nursery tales, Celtic and Norse mythology, or Wagner's riveting *Ride of the Valkyries*. Lewis longed for such moments. All of life paled next to the thrall of this mystical experience.

These romantic moments were offset by a surprisingly sour outlook on life. Lewis's pessimism was largely due to an inherited genetic flaw, a jointless thumb. This abnormal digit excluded Lewis from the typical boyhood pastimes like working a wrench or swinging a bat. Not that he longed for grease under his nails or dirt on his trousers, for engines and athletics were two things for which Lewis lacked both proclivity and interest. What he did long for, however, was the ability to bring his dreams to life. He wanted to build cardboard castles and animals in dashing coats of armor—three-dimensional expressions of his imagination. Yet his attempts at construction yielded nothing but frustration. Unable to build his imaginary world by hand, Lewis settled for the next best thing—constructing it with words.[10]

Of course, literary excellence is hardly guaranteed by physical ineptitude alone. Fortunately for Lewis, he possessed three other resources that nurtured his aspirations: a precocious mind, a house full of books and a great deal of tranquillity. Lewis paints a vivid picture of his early years:

> I am a product of long corridors, empty sunlit rooms, upstairs indoor silences, attics explored in solitude, distant noises of gurgling cisterns and pipes, and the noise of wind under the tiles. Also, of endless books. . . . In seemingly endless rainy afternoons I took volume after volume from the shelves.[11]

While other boys were climbing trees and chasing balls, Lewis was steeping himself in the works of Twain, Nesbitt, Tenniel and Potter.[12] Reading fed his desire to create. By this time "Animal-Land" was becoming a full-scale country with appropriate geographical and historical detail.

But at the age of nine Jack's imaginative world was shattered by a harsh dose of reality. His mother was diagnosed with cancer. When he learned of his mother's illness, the young boy fought off his doubts and gathered all the faith he could muster in hopes of a healing. But the healing never came. What did come was a renewed pessimism that haunted him well into adulthood.

Doing Time

Just weeks following his mother's funeral, Jack was shipped off to the first of many boarding schools. He likened his stay at his initial school, Wynyard, to a stint in a concentration camp. At Wynyard, students toiled under an oppressive, deranged schoolmaster who dished out regular beatings for mathematical miscues. After two years of misery, Jack entered a school named Campbell, where he encountered the beauty of poetry, the charm of nursery tales and the enchantment of fantasy. Unfortunately, his pleasant respite at Campbell lasted only a year. The next stop was Cherbourg House, where the mystique of the occult and sensuality spun a web of beguilement around the awakening adolescent. After two years at Cherbourg, Lewis enrolled at Malvern, a university prep school. At Malvern he evolved into a self-confessed "prig," shunning the superficial social structure of public school life.[13]

A few adolescent experiences are worth highlighting. The first came at Wynyard. While Lewis was counting the days to his "release," he started to attend church regularly. For the first time Lewis heard the doctrines of the faith proclaimed by people who clearly believed them. This powerful display of authentic Christianity animated his nominal beliefs. The doctrine of hell was especially gripping. Like the New England parishioners who sensed the heat of hellfire during the oratory of Jonathan Edwards, Lewis began to fear for his soul. The result was a desire to practice the spiritual disciplines. In addition to regular church attendance, Lewis started to pray, read the Bible and obey his conscience.

The resolution, however, did not last. The seed was choked out by the time he left his third boarding school. It was here, at Cherbourg, that the flames of passion overwhelmed the fear of hellfire. A dancing mistress and a matron who dabbled in the occult opened the door to a world of forbidden pleasures. But it was more than passion that drove Lewis from the faith. Three other factors contributed to his slide.

First, at Wynyard Lewis had developed a rather ascetical approach to the Christian faith. He regularly recited his prayers at night but believed none of his offerings were satisfactory without an accompanying "realization."[14] Hour after hour he would lie awake in bed, trying to conjure up the appropriate images and concentration that would qualify for an acceptable prayer. To his dismay, Lewis experienced endless nights of sleepless frustration, believing his repetitious utterings were falling on deaf ears. The seeds of uncertainty were sown.

Second, Lewis began to read the classics and was accordingly confronted with a host of conflicting religious and philosophical persuasions. Many modern commentators were dismissing all pagan religious sensibilities out of hand. Lewis began to consider the sheer odds of the Christian faith's being true. If all other religious systems are nonsense, why should Christianity be viewed differently? With little intellectual grounding in the faith, Lewis could not answer this question.[15] The weeds sprung up.

Third, the problem of evil continued to torment Lewis. The cumulative effect of his physical ineptitude, his mother's death, his father's pessimistic disposition and the reading of science fiction continued to feed his sour view of life. Lewis could not reconcile the aesthetic beauty of the natural world with all its apparent flaws.[16] The weeds of atheism finally choked out the vitality of his faith.

The Great Knock

Lewis was at last released from the predominantly negative experience of boarding schools altogether. He convinced his father to send him to a private tutor, W. T. Kirkpatrick, whom they affectionately referred to as "the Great Knock."[17] Lewis's father had cut his teeth on the teaching of Kirkpatrick and was confident Kirkpatrick would prepare Jack for a shot at Oxford. (Lewis would one day hail Kirkpatrick as a key factor in his intellectual development.) But at first the relentless pressure to continually clarify, refine and sharpen his logical faculties was a rather intimidating experience for a boy who had spent most of his childhood toiling in the garden of his imagination.

That is not to say Lewis was a flabby thinker—far from it. But he had never encountered anyone like Kirkpatrick. No statement was off limits. Around the Great Knock even casual comments about weather and scenery were roped into the ring of dialectical debate.

One catches a glimpse of Kirkpatrick in *The Lion, the Witch and the Wardrobe* in the person of Digory Kirke, the kindly professor who invites the Pevensie children to stay with him during the war.[18] In an early scene, Lucy tries to convey her first Narnian adventure to her siblings, but no one will believe her. In frustration, the children appeal to the professor to bring little Lucy back to her senses. After probing the children in the finest Socratic sense, the professor promptly proceeds to lay out what he believes to be the only conceivable options:

"Logic!" said the Professor half to himself. "Why don't they teach logic at these schools? There are only three possibilities. Either your sister is telling lies, or she is mad, or she is telling the truth. You know she doesn't tell lies and it is obvious that she is not mad. For the moment then and unless any further evidence turns up, we must assume that she is telling the truth."[19]

There is one major difference, however, between Kirkpatrick and the professor. As a relentless rationalist and staunch atheist, Kirkpatrick had no time for the nonsensory and supernatural. One gets the impression that if the Pevensie children had confronted the real Kirkpatrick, they would have received an altogether different response—possibly a lecture on Hume and the a priori improbability of miracles.

The teaching of Kirkpatrick heightened the internal tension Lewis was already sensing between the concrete and the mystical, the reason and the imagination, the analytical and the intuitive. Lewis summarized his plight accordingly: "Nearly all that I loved I believed to be imaginary; nearly all that I believed to be real I thought grim and meaningless."[20]

Kirkpatrick labored to reinforce his pupil's commitment to naturalistic realism, the view that ultimate reality is discovered by the senses. However, the imagination refused to surrender. In the spring of 1916, while waiting for a train, Lewis purchased a copy of George MacDonald's *Phantastes*. Lewis was once again swept up in the thralls of Joy. But this experience was different. It possessed more depth, and a quality that seemed to bring some semblance of continuity to his woefully divided existence. All previous encounters with Joy had left the tangible world in a tarnished heap, but this experience did just the opposite. The mystical was somehow transported into the realm of reality.

> But now I saw the bright shadow coming out of the book into the real world and resting there, transforming all common things and yet itself unchanged. Or, more accurately, I saw the common things drawn into the bright shadow. . . . That night my imagination was, in a certain sense, baptized; the rest of me, not unnaturally, took longer. I had not the faintest notion what I had let myself in for by buying *Phantastes*.[21]

Though it would take many more years for Lewis to recover his Christian faith, the encounter with *Phantastes* served as a turning point. Lewis became an avid reader of MacDonald and would eventually edit an anthology of his works. It is hard to overstate the debt he owed MacDonald. According to Lewis, every book he would ever publish included at least one quotation from this Scottish Romantic.

The Great War
The years with Kirkpatrick proved invaluable. Lewis excelled on his entrance exams and was admitted to Oxford's University College in 1917. The days of bouncing around from one school to another were a thing of the past. With the exception of two years of service during World War I, Lewis wound up spending the rest of his life in Oxford.[22]

Indeed, the hallowed halls of academia suited Lewis like a well-worn pair of shoes. It is hard to imagine what other direction his life might have taken if he had failed to realize his scholastic aspirations.[23] His whole life had prepared him for a career of reading, writing, reflecting, tutoring, lecturing and debating.

Oxford had a profound impact on the intellectual and spiritual trajectory of Lewis's life. He found the intellectual stimulation invigorating and with little prompting climbed into the ring of debate, where he proceeded to defend his views with admirable tenacity. One of his favorite sparring partners was Owen Barfield, who had arrived at Oxford the same time as Lewis. Barfield, who was to become an exceptional lawyer, proved a formidable opponent, rivaling earlier bouts with the Great Knock. These countless battles with Barfield eventually became known as "the Great War."[24] Years of intense debate sharpened the thinking of both men, but it was Barfield who eventually placed Lewis's realism on the ropes.

Though Lewis could not accept Barfield's worldview, he did come to recognize two weaknesses in his own. First, Barfield helped Lewis see the arrogance of his own "chronological snobbery," the belief that new systems of thought are inherently better than those of bygone days.[25] Like his contemporaries, Lewis had the tendency to use the term *medieval* in a pejorative sense. The exposure of this bias helped him gain a renewed appreciation for classical thinking. Second, Barfield showed Lewis that his view had no resources for making sense of reason and knowledge. If reason is purely subjective, then the means by which one comes to such a conclusion is invalid.[26] Realism gave way to idealism, the belief that ultimate reality is mental. Barfield had convinced Lewis of the existence of the Absolute, but it would take additional persuasion before he would embrace theism.

Some of that persuasion came through the pages of his favorite authors. The works of MacDonald, Chesterton, Johnson, Spenser, Milton, Plato and Virgil had sustained Lewis with a depth that other authors lacked. The one thing that tied them all together was a religious view of the world. At the same time, Lewis came to realize that authors who were promoting his own worldview seemed superficial. Before long, Lewis sensed hot breath on the back of his neck: "The fox had been dislodged from the Hegelian Wood and was now running in the open. . . . And nearly everyone was now (one way or another) in the pack; Plato, Dante, MacDonald, Herbert, Barfield, Tolkien, Dyson, Joy itself."[27]

Lewis realized the bankruptcy of the nontheistic vision of reality. Like it or not, he could no longer cling to his idealism. From his earliest days as a boy in County Down, he valued his autonomy above all—the freedom to do what he wanted, when he wanted. He resented authority figures interfering in his affairs. And now the ultimate authority figure, the cosmic cop, had cornered him into a decision. In 1929 Lewis finally gave in "and admitted that God was God, and knelt and prayed; perhaps, that night, the most dejected and reluctant convert in all England."[28]

The Prodigal Returns

Lewis was a convert to theism, but the prodigal was still some distance from the doorstep. In fact, it took two more years before Lewis returned to Christianity. He remembers getting into the sidecar of his brother's motor-cycle an unbeliever and, after a short ride, getting out a Christian.[29] There was no sudden bolt of lightening, no Damascus Road experience, just the clear conviction that Jesus Christ was indeed who he claimed to be—the Son of God and the only path to salvation.

The final hurdle was perhaps the most challenging for Lewis. As stated earlier, one of the factors that contributed to his adolescent apostasy was his inability to reconcile the truth of Christianity with the falsehood of every other religion and philosophy. With the help of colleagues J. R. R. Tolkien and Hugo Dyson a few nights prior to his conversion, Lewis came to see the overarching hand of God in not only the history of Christianity but other belief systems as well. The myth of dying and rising corn gods in pagan religions did not nullify the claim that Jesus Christ died and rose again. On the contrary, these pagan myths unwittingly worked to reinforce the truth of the Christian account. According to Tolkien and Dyson, a loving God has been working diligently to prepare each and every culture for the gospel of his son. In so doing, mythical stories have been given to anticipate or preconfigure a factual, historical outworking. Christianity is not only the fulfillment of Judaism, it is also the fulfillment of all other religious and philosophical systems.[30]

This new angle of vision on the problem of exclusivity made sense to Lewis. Christianity is indeed true, but that does not mean all other world-views are entirely false. All God's creation has been given some measure of insight, however limited or opaque, for the purpose of pointing to the fullest expression of divinity in the person of Jesus Christ.

As Lewis realized how Christianity and other belief systems could harmoniously dovetail at certain points, the lifelong tension between reason and imagination began to subside as well. Under the Christian rubric, both hemispheres of the brain could harmoniously coexist. And most important, Lewis came to realize that Joy is not an end unto itself but merely a pointer to guide us further up and further in. Lewis was eager to communicate this epiphany to any who would listen.

A Jack of All Trades

What followed was a prolific writing career. Barfield has pointed out that there were really three different C. S. Lewises: the one who wrote scholarly works of literary criticism, the one who wrote fantasies and novels, and the one who wrote theological and apologetic treatises in defense of historic, orthodox Christianity.[31] Part of what accounts for Lewis's widespread popularity is this amazing literary range. Many appreciate his work in one genre without realizing his proficiency elsewhere. Such range surely brings new meaning to the old phrase "a jack of all trades."

The diversity of the Lewis corpus, however, is bound by two unifying threads: a thoroughly Christian vision of reality and a sincere desire for the reader to adopt the same vantage point. Lewis admits without hesitation that most of his books, whether overtly apologetic or not, have a decidedly evangelistic thrust to them. Lyle Dorsett has aptly tabbed Lewis a "literary evangelist."[32]

Today more than forty million copies of his books are in print.[33] Yet one could never have predicted this remarkable popularity at the outset of his literary career. Prior to his conversion Lewis published two books of poetry, *Spirits in Bondage* (1919) and *Dymer* (1926). Neither sold well, nor did they receive favorable reviews. His third work did not fare much better. Just two years following his conversion, Lewis published an allegorical apologetic for Christianity, reason and imagination—*The Pilgrim's Regress*, in the tradition of Bunyan's famous work. Many considered his not-so-subtle attacks on modern thinking distasteful. Though *The Pilgrim's Regress* is largely a lively and witty piece of writing, a more spiritually seasoned Lewis would one day recognize the "needless obscurity and occasionally uncharitable temper" of his first Christian work.[34]

In 1936 Lewis made his mark as a literary scholar with *The Allegory of Love*. This original piece of scholarship explored the concept of romantic love and allegory during the Middle Ages. It met with rave reviews and is considered by many one of the century's best works of literary criticism. Nearly twenty-five years later, Lewis would probe this relational subject on a more popular level in *The Four Loves* (1960).

By the end of the thirties, Lewis turned to fiction and the first of many attempts at "smuggling" the gospel into unsuspecting minds through imaginative forms of literature.[35] Having been weaned on the science fiction of H. G. Wells, Lewis set out to produce an alternative vision of the cosmos. Instead of sinister extraterrestrials and an overarching evolutionary framework, *Out of the Silent Planet* (1938), *Perelandra* (1942) and *That Hideous Strength* (1945) paint a colorful and concrete picture of other worlds enchanted by a rich variety of rational, moral and aesthetically sensitive creatures. Lewis's space trilogy stands in sharp contrast to works like *War of the Worlds* that caricature aliens as evil beings. In the Lewisian galaxy, Earth is the domain of the demonic, and an unbridled imperialism is the greatest threat to the ultimate survival of the universe.[36]

As Lewis's imagination was busy smuggling theology through the back door, his reason was relentlessly pounding on the front door through overtly philosophical works such as *The Problem of Pain* (1940), *The Abolition of Man* (1943) and *Miracles* (1947). *The Problem of Pain* was Lewis's first attempt at addressing a serious philosophical and theological issue head-on. The question of evil, suffering and injustice had plagued Lewis since his childhood. In this lucid work, Lewis sought to square an all-powerful, all-loving God with the undeniable horror of our world.[37]

Such horror was especially poignant during the early forties. The German war machine was advancing with frightening efficiency. It was against this backdrop that Lewis bolstered the morale of millions through his talks on BBC radio. Countless Brits found hope and meaning in Lewis's winsome, colorful and inspiring vision of the historic Christian faith. These talks would eventually be released in print as *Mere Christianity* (1952).

The forties proved to be an exceptionally prolific period for Lewis. He could hardly crank out the books quickly enough for an audience that reveled in his invigorating wit, rigor and style. While *The Abolition of Man* and *Miracles* built a credible case for objective values and the supernatural, *The Screwtape Letters* (1942) and *The Great Divorce* (1945) animated the invisible world with palpable plausibility. This one-two punch of reason and imagination, credibility and plausibility, was never more evident than during the forties.

By the end of the decade Lewis had begun to focus most of his energy in the realm of the imagination, feeling less competent to engage the emerging logical positivism that was gripping England's intellectual elite. Many trace this shift in emphasis to a famous 1948 debate with professional philosopher Elizabeth Anscombe, who deftly challenged the chief argument Lewis had marshaled against naturalism in *Miracles*. Opinions range widely on the effect of Anscombe's critique. Some suggest Lewis was devastated and publicly humiliated at the hands of a highly trained philosopher, while others seem to imply that the experience hardly fazed him. While the personal effect of the debate may be disputed, there is no question that Lewis took the critique seriously. In fact, Anscombe's insights led Lewis to rework a key chapter in the revised version of *Miracles*.[38]

The final full decade of Lewis's life produced his most famous work, the seven-volume Chronicles of Narnia. Lewis never lost the itch for developing imaginary countries and talking animals. His boyhood fixation reached mature expression in characters like Aslan, Reepicheep and Bree. As was his custom, Lewis introduced a first draft to his author colleagues. He received a mixed response. Tolkien, who spent years laboring over the development of his imaginary world for the Lord of the Rings trilogy, objected to Lewis's less painstaking creation and suspect mixture of mythological characters.[39] Despite Tolkien's dissatisfaction with Narnia, millions of children and adults have been captivated by the Chronicles' vivid imagery and profound theological symbolism.

A Prophet for Our Age

The fifties proved to be another exceptionally productive decade for Lewis. In addition to the Narnia tales, he rounded out his varied body of work with an autobiography, *Surprised by Joy* (1955), a classical myth, *Till We Have Faces* (1956), and a book on biblical interpretation, *Reflections on the Psalms* (1958).

But the fifties were also a decade of flux. First, Lewis's professional life was unsettled when Cambridge offered him a full professorship. Lewis, who had spent thirty years as an Oxford tutor and fellow, filled the newly formed chair of Medieval and Renaissance English Literature, a position he held until the year of his death.

Second, Lewis's predictable personal life was turned upside down. What started as a friendly exchange of letters led to a deep friendship and eventually to marriage. His well-documented union with Helen Joy Davidman brought new heights of ecstasy, as well as unparalleled depths of despair. The final years were spent on an emotional roller coaster as Joy got cancer, experienced a full remission and eventually succumbed to the disease in 1961, after just a few fleeting years of wedded bliss.

The death of Joy plunged Lewis into a dark night of the soul. *A Grief Observed* (1961), which was originally published under a pseudonym, is a journal of Lewis's struggle to come to terms with his wife's demise. Lewis's faith, though shaken, emerged unshattered.[40] This work serves as a fitting existential complement to his earlier philosophical treatment of evil in *The Problem of Pain*.

Just two short years after the loss of his wife, about an hour before Kennedy's death, Lewis passed away quietly at "the Kilns," his home near Oxford. Lewis was not the only prominent figure to have his death lost in the shuffle that day. Kennedy's demise also obscured the passing of prominent philosopher Aldous Huxley. In *Between Heaven and Hell*, Peter Kreeft uses this uncanny coincidence to conduct a fascinating purgatorial confrontation between these three men, each representing a different worldview: Christian theism (Lewis), modern humanism (Kennedy) and Eastern pantheism (Huxley).

Though Kennedy undoubtedly remains the most recognizable figure of the bunch in the collective public consciousness, Kreeft believes the other two men are in a league by themselves when it comes to anticipating the future. In another book, *C. S. Lewis for the Third Millennium*, Kreeft writes, "I believe the two most prophetic books of our century are Aldous Huxley's *Brave New World* and C. S. Lewis's *The Abolition of Man*. If you want to see the third millennium, read these two books."[41]

Lewis's thoughts have far outlived his earthly existence. In fact, secondary sources on his life and thought now dwarf his own voluminous contribution. In a very real sense Lewis has not only anticipated the future, he has helped shape it.

Francis August Schaeffer (1912-1984)

A primary theme woven throughout *The Tapestry*, Edith Schaeffer's account of life with her husband, is the conviction that people and their decisions matter. Every choice we make is like a ripple on the sea, affecting not only ourselves and those close to us but, in some instances, even people on the other side of the world or in a subsequent age. We live in a web of interconnectedness.

In the early pages of her book, Edith contextualizes Francis's life against the broader global backdrop. At the time of Schaeffer's birth, Jean-Paul Sartre was seven, Salvador Dali eight, and Pablo Picasso had already painted his groundbreaking *Demoiselles d'Avignon*. In addition, and what is most interesting for our purpose, Edith writes, "It fascinates me to consider that as Fran was born, C. S. Lewis was a boy of thirteen in his miserable boarding school."[42]

Sure enough, Lewis was off at boarding school awakening to the occult as Schaeffer was awakening in the hands of a drunken doctor. While his mother labored, his father coaxed a physician away from his bottle long enough to facilitate their son's arrival. The delivery came off without a hitch, but the lingering effects of alcohol kept the doctor from recording the birth the following day. Thirty-five years later, as Francis was applying for a passport, it became clear that he had never received a birth certificate. Fortunately his mother was still alive and could vouch that Francis August Schaeffer had indeed entered the world on January 30, 1912.[43]

The focal point of young Francis's world was a modest home in Germantown, Pennsylvania. In contrast to Lewis, Schaeffer grew up in an environment where the physical was nurtured and the intellectual ignored. The Schaeffers took great pride in working with their hands, and Francis spent countless hours assisting his father with all sorts of manual tasks. Climbing ladders, sawing wood, repairing pipes and adjusting wires became second nature. He seemed destined to follow in his father's footsteps and earn a living by the sweat of his brow.

It was only natural that Francis would focus his schoolwork on refining his manual dexterity. At an early age, however, signs of exceptional intellectual acuity emerged. A letter indicated that Francis's cognitive aptitude scores ranked him the second smartest pupil to pass through the doors of his elementary school in twenty years.[44] Most parents would have rejoiced, but not Francis's. They chose to hide this news from their son, apparently fearing it would send him down the wrong track toward an ivory-tower world of irrelevant book knowledge. Instead, the Schaeffers continued to nudge Francis toward a technical vocation, one that would prepare him for a practical trade and an honest day's work.

Ovid and Moses

By high school, Schaeffer's vocational future was set. Classes in woodworking and electrical wiring reinforced the practical skills his father was teaching him at home. But a young tradesman can never be too careful: the siren song of cultural delights can arise in the most unlikely places. Such a temptation came for Schaeffer while passing a display at an electrical show. The sound of Tchaikovsky's "1812 Overture" pulsated through the air, gripping Schaeffer the way Wagner's *Ride of the Valkyries* must have gripped a young C. S. Lewis. Schaeffer's love for classical music was born.

His next encounter with culture was even more unlikely. The Schaeffers were not a religious family, but they did attend a liberal Presbyterian church. A Sunday-school teacher at his church asked Francis if he would be willing to tutor a Russian count in English. Francis agreed and attempted to procure an appropriate text from a nearby bookstore. The attendant at the shop, however, gave Francis the wrong book. Instead of an English text, he received a book of Greek philosophy.[45] This error proved to be serendipitous. Francis was fascinated with the content and began to ponder the big questions of life.

Though underdeveloped, Schaeffer's mind was active and keenly analytical. He began to critique the hollow, liberal gospel flowing from the pulpit at his church on the one hand and the metaphysical musings of the Greek philosophers on the other. He decided to abandon Christianity altogether. But in a commitment to intellectual honesty, he would not do so until he had read the Bible.

So at the age of seventeen Schaeffer embarked on his quest for truth. During a six-month period he read the Bible, interchanged with Ovid, comparing and contrasting the two pieces of literature. It did not take long before Francis realized his Greek philosophy was asking the right questions but providing no plausible answers. The Bible, on the other hand, was loaded with answers. And most of these answers could be found right at the beginning, in the book of Genesis. It told him how we got here, why we are here and where we are going. It made sense of the baffling good and evil in the world. And it provided a basis for meaning in all realms of life. Schaeffer's lifelong commitment to the self-authenticating power of Scripture and its inerrant message is rooted in his own experience, as affirmed by Edith:

> If you want to know why Fran has such a high regard for the Bible and feels it is adequate in answering the questions of life, the answer is right here. As a seventeen-year-old boy with a thirst for the answers to life's questions, he began to discover for himself the existence of adequate and complete answers right in the Bible.[46]

Schaeffer turned his life over to Christ, and the universe was suddenly charged with meaning. In addition to reading Scripture, Francis began to nurture his fledgling spiritual life through prayer. Since the gospel preached in his church was totally foreign to what he had embraced in the pages of Scripture, Schaeffer felt like he was the only Bible-believing Christian in the world. Then one day, as he was walking down the street, he heard the sounds of an impassioned evangelist wafting through the air. He followed the noise to a meeting where hundreds had gathered under a tent to hear the proclamation of historic, biblical Christianity. Schaeffer was overjoyed to find he was not alone after all. There were others who believed as he did. At the time Schaeffer did not realize the big role this little street, Ashmead Place, would play in his life story. But before long, he would find himself returning to Ashmead to court his future wife.[47]

Heads It Is

As Schaeffer's faith began to take root, he sensed a tug to shift his career focus to a life of full-time ministry. His parents steadfastly insisted that he stay the course and pursue a career in electrical engineering. His father could not bear the thought of Francis's becoming a preacher. As far as he was concerned, preachers were freeloaders.

In an effort to please his parents, Francis attended a nearby vocational school for a semester, studying electrical engineering. But the call to ministry continued to dominate his thoughts. Against his parents' wishes, he finally decided to follow God's leading and enrolled at Hampden-Sydney College in Virginia.

On the morning he was to depart, he rose early to bid his father farewell. What ensued was a pivotal confrontation. His father expressed extreme disapproval, insisting that Francis reconsider. Out of parental respect, the younger Schaeffer went to the basement to pray about the matter one final time. Francis sought the Lord feverishly, setting out a fleece the only way he knew how. He pulled a coin from his pocket and, in essence, prayed, "Lord, if you want me to go, make it be heads." The coin tumbled through the air and landed heads up. He repeated the process, "Lord, if you want me to go, make it tails." This time, it landed tails. Just to make sure, Francis offered a third petition: "Lord, if you want me to go, make it heads again." Heads it was. To his father's chagrin, Francis headed off to Hampden-Sydney, believing God's hand was upon his future. Schaeffer would one day point to this pivotal moment as a key link in the chain leading to his father's salvation. From that moment on, his parents could not question their son's resolve and tenacious commitment to the Christian faith.[48]

At Hampden-Sydney, Schaeffer was like a fish out of water. Most of the boys were free-spirited southern aristocrats. This straight-laced Yankee was surrounded by roughnecks who shot out the lights in the dormitory hallways and bullied the pint-sized Schaeffer as often as possible. But Francis refused to be intimidated. He held dormitory Bible studies and ministered to his classmates in word and deed. One of the most powerful expressions of Christlikeness came each Saturday night. While most residents of the dorm were out drinking and carousing, Schaeffer stayed up studying. Week after week they returned in a drunken stupor and relied on Francis to guide them through the darkened hallways to their respective beds. This expression of kindness had only one hitch: Francis insisted they get up and go to church with him the following morning.[49]

On Sunday mornings he would go off to worship, and in the afternoons he would venture through cornfields to a small African-American church, where he taught Sunday school to children. His years at this church laid the foundation for what would one day become an international children's ministry.

He returned home as often as he could, visiting his parents and friends at the Presbyterian church. This church was so unorthodox that on one particular evening a Unitarian minister was speaking to the youth. The title of his talk was "How I know that Jesus is *not* the Son of God, and how I know the Bible is *not* the Word of God."[50] The minister spread his beliefs before these impressionable minds until Schaeffer could take it no longer. He stood and voiced his objection with the boldness of Luther, but unfortunately, he had no treatise to offer in return. At this juncture, his gusto clearly outweighed his knowledge. All Schaeffer could do was appeal to the authority of his college Bible teachers, who insisted there were good and sufficient reasons for affirming orthodox Christianity.

As Francis was speaking, a young woman on the other side of the room took notice. She asked a friend who he was. The friend told her he was Francis

Schaeffer and his parents had mistreated him because he wanted to be a minister. As soon as Schaeffer sat down, this young woman popped up and began to declare some of the good and sufficient reasons to which Schaeffer had only alluded. Francis was flabbergasted. He leaned over to a friend and asked who this woman was. His friend said her name was Edith Seville and she had just recently moved in from Toronto. Francis had found a soul mate.[51]

Edith was the daughter of missionaries. Born in China, she learned from an early age the power of prayer and dedicated discipleship. She also understood the importance of a reasoned faith. As Edith's family settled into their new surroundings on Ashmead Place, professors from nearby Westminster Theological Seminary began to frequent their home. Dinner at the Seville table would often be seasoned with lively conversation about Reformed theology and radical liberalism. With pen in hand, young Edith would frantically record all the choice nuggets of insight she could gather. It would not be a stretch to suggest that Edith was more theologically astute than Francis at the beginning of their relationship. In fact, she was the one who introduced Francis to the writings of J. Gresham Machen, a man who was to have a profound effect on both their lives.

The Separated Movement

After a three-year courtship, Francis and Edith married. Schaeffer graduated from Hampden-Sydney magna cum laude and enrolled at Westminster Theological Seminary in the fall of 1935, not knowing the turmoil to come. He enjoyed his classes with professors such as Machen, Cornelius Van Til and Allan MacRae, but was disturbed by a growing controversy within his denomination. It soon became clear that the Presbyterian Church was losing its battle with modernism as liberal bureaucrats seized an ever-increasing degree of ecclesiastical and institutional control.

The point of no return came when Machen was defrocked for establishing an independent missions board. Schaeffer would come to see the expulsion of Machen as one of the key events of the century. The Christian movement had been infected by a serious strain of modernity and the disease was quickly spreading throughout the entire organism. It was the contention of many, including Schaeffer, that the only way to salvage the body was to quarantine the uninfected. A formal separation ensued.

Machen led the way in forming the Presbyterian Church in America.[52] But a further split came shortly thereafter, as the separated believers quarreled among themselves over peripheral matters like eschatology and personal ethics. Disagreement on these and other issues led to the formation of Faith

Theological Seminary and the Bible Presbyterian Church. Schaeffer left Westminster and joined professors like James O. Buswell Jr., Carl McIntire and Harold Laird in establishing the new institution. In 1938, Schaeffer walked the platform as a member of Faith's first graduating class.[53]

Schaeffer was the first newly ordained pastor in the Bible Presbyterian Church and spent the next decade shepherding flocks in Pennsylvania and Missouri. The bulk of his ministry with Edith was centered on working-class people and children. Schaeffer's blue-collar background provided an immediate point of contact and credibility with many of his parishioners. During visitation, Francis displayed a great deal of creativity. In order to break the ice he would often bring along some kind of manual project as a sign of solidarity. It is easy to imagine Francis and a farmer conversing over a pile of sawdust or a row of radishes. Schaeffer's upbringing provided a profound appreciation for the dignity of all people, despite their class or status in life. This conviction permeated all aspects of his ministry and would one day inspire a book of sermons entitled *No Little People.*

During these early years, the Schaeffers also focused their energy on nurturing children and youth. Hot dog roasts, vacation Bible school and summer retreats attracted children by the car loads. There was plenty of fun and games, but it was also a time of serious spiritual instruction. Without question, Francis and Edith both displayed a special gift for children's work. This gift was cultivated during their time in St. Louis, as the Schaeffers nurtured a fledgling ministry named Children for Christ into an international organization.

On the surface one might suggest little continuity between these years and Schaeffer's future ministry to the educated world, but nothing could be further from the truth. A closer look reveals Schaeffer honing his pastoral skills, learning to listen and touch each person at the point of need. A closer look reveals Edith and Francis living by faith and maximizing their resources through creativity and hard work. A closer look reveals an ever-increasing life of prayer and consecration. In short, a closer look reveals the groundwork being laid for the community of L'Abri. Consider this excerpt from one of Schaeffer's Children for Christ director's reports:

> Children for Christ is one of the greatest living demonstrations of what can be done by the power of the Holy Spirit without great fanfare. It has gone from its beginning in St. Louis to national and international size so that at the present time twenty foreign countries, thirty-five states, and the District of Columbia have works in them. God has given an international work to us with very little human pressure. And all that time there was only one half salary being paid to a half-time secretary.[54]

The Spiritual Crisis

In 1947 Schaeffer toured Europe for three months, assessing the status of the European church for the Independent Board for Presbyterian Foreign Missions and the American Council of Churches. During this time he cultivated his aesthetic sensitivities, visiting museums through France and Italy as he had opportunity. The beauty on the gallery walls served as a poignant contrast to the pain and suffering that permeated postwar Europe.

The following year, Francis and Edith packed up their limited belongings and children (by this time they had three daughters: Priscilla, Susan and Deborah; their fourth child, Franky, came along in 1952) and moved to Switzerland to serve as missionaries. The next few years were absorbed with Children for Christ responsibilities and administrative tasks associated with the formation of the International Council of Christian Churches.[55]

The war in Europe was over, but the battle continued to rage within the separated movement back in America. Schaeffer became increasingly distressed over the attitudes of many within the movement. He was fully committed to the "purity of the visible church" but was thoroughly disheartened by the movement's uncharitable spirit and its total incongruity with the gospel of grace.

This huge gap between belief and practice began to rip at the fabric of his faith. During the winter of 1951, Schaeffer was plunged into a full-blown spiritual crisis. He felt he had no choice but to reassess his Christianity, to go all the way back to his agnosticism and systematically review his foundational beliefs. Day after day, Schaeffer wandered through the mountains and paced back and forth in his hayloft, pondering, praying and searching the Scriptures.[56]

The dark night of the soul gradually gave way to the dawning of a new light.[57] Schaeffer's orthodoxy was vindicated. He believed more than ever in the existence of God, the truth of the Christian message and the reliability of Scripture. But his searching led to a new revelation as well. Christianity was not just about justification, it was also a matter of sanctification—living a life that truly reflected the character of Christ and glory of God in a moment-by-moment existence. Schaeffer came to realize the necessity of holding God's holiness and love in continual balance. He saw that an overemphasis on righteousness can lead to spiritual pride and bitterness, while an overemphasis on love can lead to toleration of heretical views.

Schaeffer emerged from this experience with a renewed appreciation for the truth of historic Christianity, a deeper understanding of Christ's sanctifying power and a new trajectory for ministry. During the course of the next three years, Schaeffer talked frequently about this experience. He returned to

America on furlough in 1953 and spoke 346 times in 515 days.[58] The content of these talks would later be developed into a book entitled *True Spirituality*.

L'Abri and the Rise to Apologetic Prominence

By the mid-fifties, the Schaeffers were becoming increasingly open to a new work. What kind of work they did not yet know, but they prayed diligently for God's direction. Then one weekend their oldest daughter, Priscilla, invited some friends over. These friends were struggling with some big questions, so Priscilla asked her father to speak with them. Francis helped them work through some of their problems and explained how historic Christianity makes sense of life and offers concrete solutions. The friends left encouraged, and word spread that Priscilla's father had a special knack for communicating the ancient faith in understandable terms.[59] More young people showed up and additional conversations ensued. Before long the Schaeffers were welcoming a steady stream of visitors to their chalet for discussions, counseling and prayer. L'Abri was born and a new ministry was launched.

The Schaeffers never envisioned such a ministry. They certainly had no idea that it would become their focus for thirty years and attract thousands of travelers and students from all corners of the globe. L'Abri merely grew out of a sincere longing to be used by God to meet the needs of modern people. As Schaeffer explains,

> Edith and I committed ourselves to God with one aim. It was not an evangelistic work we wished to start nor a young people's work nor a work for intellectuals nor an outreach to drug people. It was simply that we offered ourselves to God and asked him if he would use us to demonstrate that he exists in our generation. That's all L'Abri is; that's the way it began.[60]

The Schaeffers' approach to this new ministry reflected what they had learned with Children for Christ. Prayer, hard work and a passion for the lost undergirded their efforts. Time and again, God blessed the commitment to make L'Abri a ministry of faith. The Schaeffers refused to broadcast their financial needs, instead entrusting their requests to God through fervent prayer. Day after day, prayers were answered, needs were met, and before long Switzerland became known for more than bank accounts and snowcapped mountains.

With a steady flow of ministry opportunities coming through the door each week, many might have been tempted to settle into a reclusive pattern. Not Schaeffer. He wanted to take on the road the material that was emerging from his conversations with an eclectic collection of visitors and the fruit of what was now extensive cross-disciplinary reading. These were some of the hardest years for the Schaeffers' marriage, and initially Edith was reluctant for Francis to be gone for extended periods of time. Both Schaeffers were intense by nature, and their relationship was at times stormy. This was exacerbated, moreover, by Francis's struggle to control his occasionally volatile temper.[61]

Francis's natural intensity easily merged with his growing passion to share his message with a wider audience. Edith recalls many nights after discussions at L'Abri when he would come up to their bedroom and pound the wall until his fist turned red, saying, "Oh, Edith, I'm sure I have true answers. . . . I know they can help people. . . . But no one is ever going to hear . . . except a handful. . . . What are we doing? What am I doing?"[62] Eventually Edith relented, and over the years Francis would speak at many of the world's leading institutions of higher learning, including Oxford, Cambridge, Harvard and MIT.

In these talks Schaeffer typically traced the devolution of Western culture across a variety of disciplines. He critiqued the work of philosophers like Søren Kierkegaard, artists like Vincent Van Gogh, poets like Dylan Thomas and musicians like John Cage. He talked about "the line of despair," "the upper story" and "the leap of faith." He offered a cohesive understanding of Western decay and proposed historic Christianity as the only solution to society's epistemological and moral void. Many left the lectures inspired but spinning, undoubtedly sharing the sentiments Cal Thomas would one day offer upon hearing Schaeffer for the first time: "After listening for three hours to this funny-looking little fellow dressed in knickers, with a slender goatee dangling from the end of his chin, I hadn't the foggiest notion of what he was talking about, but I knew he had said something significant."[63]

Schaeffer's message gained greater clarity when it was translated into print. The content of these talks became the basis for his first books, *Escape from Reason* and *The God Who Is There* (1968). *He Is There and He Is Not Silent* followed four years later. This apologetic trilogy was to serve as the hub of his entire corpus and the proper entry point into his thinking.

During the seventies, Schaeffer published a prolific amount of work on a broad range of subjects, including biblical authority (*Genesis in Space and Time*, 1972), sanctification (*True Spirituality*, 1971), ecology (*Pollution and the Death of Man*, 1970), ecclesiology (*The Church Before the Watching World*, 1971) and the sanctity of life (*Whatever Happened to the Human Race?* 1979). Though some criticized Schaeffer for shifting his focus from the gospel to social and political issues, he insisted all his works formed a unified whole. According to Schaeffer, each book, along with the monographs that Edith had produced about L'Abri and art, sought to promote a holistic, cohesive vision of reality and a commitment to placing all aspects of life under the banner of Christ's Lordship.[64]

By the mid-to-late seventies Schaeffer turned to a new medium to communicate his old message. In conjunction with his son, Franky, he produced a pair of films: *How Should We Then Live?* and *Whatever Happened to the Human Race?* which served as companions to books that were being marketed under the same titles. Cross-country tours and extensive promotion effectively moved Schaeffer's thinking into the churches and homes of mainstream evangelicals.

This first production, *How Should We Then Live?* offered a Christian commentary on the erosion of the Western world and an alternative to films like Jacob Bronowski's *The Ascent of Man* and Kenneth Clark's *Civilization.* The Schaeffers collaborated with C. Everett Koop on the second film, which provided a moving look at the rapid devaluation of human life. For many years the issue of human rights had vexed the Schaeffers, especially Edith, who was confronted with the horrors of infanticide as a young girl in China. Her frequent walks through the city of Wenchow were often haunted by the heartbreaking whimpers of newborn baby girls who had been discarded beyond the city wall.[65] These memories and Francis's keen sensitivity to cultural trends motivated the Schaeffers to sound a clarion call to the church to stand for human life. According to Richard John Neuhaus, no one was more influential in rallying Protestants to the prolife cause than Francis Schaeffer.[66]

In addition to fighting social ills during the final years of his life, Schaeffer attempted to stem the tide of liberal biblical scholarship. He wrote and spoke out frequently against those who, in his view, were undermining the authority of Scripture. In 1977 he was a key impetus behind the formation of the International Council on Biblical Inerrancy and helped draft the subsequent Chicago Statement. In 1984 *The Great Evangelical Disaster* was published in book and film form just weeks prior to his death. In his final book we find Schaeffer boldly confronting what he believed to be heresy, as he had done his entire life. But unlike his earlier years of participation in the separated movement, he longed to do it with love and grace. In an appendix entitled *The Mark of the Christian,* Schaeffer offers a final expression of what it means to live a balanced Christian life.[67] As he had so often preached since his spiritual crisis in the early fifties, Schaeffer underscored the importance of speaking the truth in love. His ultimate apologetic was not rational argumentation, it was the expression of authentic Christian community, grounded in a firm commitment to historic, biblical orthodoxy.

On his deathbed, exhausted from a lifetime of rigorous ministry and a six-year battle with cancer, Schaeffer offered this final prayer: "Dear Father God, I have finished my work. Please take me home. I am tired."[68] Hours later, Schaeffer's valiant battle against cancer was over. The conservative Christian world had lost one of its most tenacious and impassioned representatives.

Vernon C. Grounds, who had been one of Schaeffer's classmates at fledgling Faith Seminary so many years before, offered a fitting farewell that concluded on a prophetic note:

> It is difficult for a contemporary to pronounce definitive judgment on the achievement of his peers. Time performs a winnowing process in which once-towering heroes sink into oblivion, and those who were little applauded while living gain in stature and significance. My own surmise, however, is that, while many evangelical current luminaries will fade into obscure references in church history, Francis Schaeffer will be recognized as a key figure in twentieth-century evangelicalism.[69]

As we close the book on the twentieth century, Grounds's conjecture appears to be sound. Schaeffer spoke historic Christianity into the modern world with character and conviction, and in so doing offered his generation a compelling view of the God who is there.

The Points of Contrast: Worlds Apart

So where are the points of biographical contrast and contact between C. S. Lewis and Francis Schaeffer? We will start by exploring key differences. Some of the most obvious can be seen with a sociological lens. First, the career paths that both men had mapped out for them early in their lives ran in different directions. Physically inept, Lewis seemed destined for the white-collar world of academia from the start. Schaeffer, on the other hand, knew nothing but manual labor growing up, as his father diligently prepared him for a blue-collar livelihood. It was only during his teenage years, subsequent to his conversion, that Schaeffer began to cultivate his latent intellectual and aesthetic sensibilities and pursue a new career objective. Schaeffer's blue-collar background certainly came in handy during his pastoral years, providing a critical point of contact with many everyday people. Physical work was also an important component of the entire L'Abri experience, as students, visitors and staff all helped keep this self-sustaining community functioning.

Second, their ministries unfolded in two very different worlds. Lewis spent his entire adult life teaching and writing among the world's intellectual elite. He disliked traveling immensely and consequently had limited contact with those outside his relatively homogenous ethnic and social circle. That is not to say, however, that Lewis lived a provincial life. Though he did not enjoy physical travel, he was a frequent flyer in the vivid world of his mind. His reading and writing transported him back to the days of Homer, Plato,

Augustine and Shakespeare one moment and out into the vast galaxies of interplanetary exploration the next. Lewis soared across an eclectic collection of ages, cultures, disciplines and worlds—all without leaving the comfort of the Kilns.

Schaeffer, by contrast, spent the bulk of his ministry in the trenches, day after day talking with laborers, existentialists, beatniks and travelers from all parts of the globe and all walks of life. It would be a caricature to suggest that Schaeffer gained all his knowledge from informal conversations, however. He graduated with honors from both Hampden-Sydney and Faith Seminary, and continued his education as a voracious reader until the day of his death. Though Lewis's Oxford pedigree undoubtedly dwarfs Schaeffer in the minds of many, one should remember that in the realm of theology it was Lewis, not Schaeffer, who received no formal training.

A third point of contrast emerges when comparing their literary careers. From the earliest days, Lewis longed for literary achievement. The structure of his entire life, from childhood through adolescence and into adulthood, prepared him for his subsequent success as an author. His prodigious output of scholarly, imaginative and overtly theological and philosophical offerings is a rare expression of literary diversity and a testament to a lifetime of diligent stylistic development. Schaeffer, on the other hand, never aspired to publish. In fact, his first title did not hit the bookstores until he was fifty-six. In a 1979 *Christianity Today* interview, Schaeffer told Philip Yancey that he never intended to write; his passion was talking with people. After each lecture it was Schaeffer's pattern to discuss follow-up questions into the early hours of the morning.[70]

Schaeffer might not have envisioned bookstores lining their shelves with his titles, but others did—namely, InterVarsity Press. According to a short history located in IVP's *Author Handbook,* the publishing of *The God Who Is There* and *Escape from Reason* "put IVP on the map as a noteworthy publisher." The enormous success of these first two titles paved the way for a consistent flow of books and booklets during the seventies.

While a few of his works were written with a print medium initially in mind, the bulk of his books emerged from transcribed lectures and L'Abri talks. This translation from the spoken to written word explains, at least in part, why Schaeffer's composition is occasionally cumbersome. Content and pathos carry Schaeffer's writing, not style. Edith and son Frank are the stylists of the family.

When it comes to style and composition, however, few can match Lewis. His clarity, vivid imagery and frequent analogies make him a joy to read. Many who would never subscribe to the substance of his works can still appreciate his style. Philosopher Peter van Inwagen is a case in point. He was initially attracted to Lewis not because of what he had to say but because of how he went about saying it. But in van Inwagen's case, it was not long before he grew to appreciate the content of the message as well.[71] One should not underestimate the power of style in apologetics, especially in our day. Lewis is an excellent example of how style and substance can work hand in glove to achieve maximum impact.

The fourth and final point of contrast deals with family life. Lewis spent most of his existence as a confirmed bachelor, while Schaeffer's ministry grew out of his long-time union with Edith and commitment to his four children. For the Schaeffers, Christian community starts in the family and works its way out into the larger ecclesiastical and societal structures. Their commitment to home and family life is best expressed in Edith's book *What Is a Family?*

Though Lewis was unmarried most of his life, he did have a family of sorts, sharing the Kilns for many years with his brother and the mother and sister of a friend who was killed during World War I. Though much has been made of this unusual living arrangement, there is no compelling evidence to suggest it was anything more than a platonic, gracious gesture. Lewis's generosity was further exhibited during World War II, as a number of children found shelter and safety at the Kilns during the German air raids on London. These experiences helped Lewis develop a knack for communicating to the common, everyday person.[72]

Points of Contact: Cognition, Creativity, Community and Compassion

Arguably the most important area of common ground that can be gleaned from the lives of these two prominent apologists is an insatiable quest for truth. Lewis encountered a wide variety of philosophical schemes in his pilgrimage back to Christianity, while Schaeffer rejected liberal theology on the one hand and Greek philosophy on the other. Both men, therefore, came to believe that historic, orthodox Christianity ought to be embraced, not because of its pragmatic or utilitarian value but because of its truth claims. This honest intellectual search for the truth during the formative years of their lives provides a powerful existential backbone to each man's apologetic message.

The second point of consonance can be seen in a shared sensitivity to aesthetics, creativity and beauty. An appreciation for the natural world welled up within Lewis at a tender age and found expression through the imaginative forms of poetry, allegory and myth. Though culturally impoverished as a child, Schaeffer developed his latent appreciation for beauty as an adult. Over time and through important relationships with people like Dutch art critic Hans Rookmaaker, Schaeffer acquired a refined taste for painting, sculpture, poetry and classical music.

A third parallel can be placed under the rubric of community. Neither man worked in isolation. Schaeffer, whose L'Abri Fellowship has become for many a paradigmatic example of what Christian community ought to be, surrounded himself with a circle of capable thinkers in a variety of disciplines. Dialogue on subjects ranging from logical positivism to impressionism to musique concrète dominated the daily discussions at L'Abri. Schaeffer batted ideas back and forth constantly with men like Rookmaaker, to the extent that it eventually became impossible to determine the origin of every thought. These opportunities for interchange helped shape the emerging message that would one day work its way into books like *The God Who Is There* and *Whatever Happened to the Human Race?* Though Schaeffer was a prolific reader and a capable thinker, one cannot help but wonder if these books would have materialized outside a fertile environment like L'Abri.

Lewis was also surrounded by a circle of scholars, a group known as the Inklings. This gathering of Oxford intellectuals assembled weekly to critique one another's work and engage in lively conversation. Long bouts of intellectual jousting would often follow the reading of a paper in process or a chapter under construction. Lewis reveled in these evenings of inspiration and refinement and frequently voiced his sincere indebtedness to colleagues like J. R. R. Tolkien, Charles Williams and Owen Barfield.

For Lewis and Schaeffer the concept of Christian community was not limited to a select inner circle, however. Both men interacted with an international following, carrying on an extensive ministry of correspondence. The fourth point of contact, then, is a common commitment to pastoral apologetics. No less than five volumes of Lewis's correspondence have been published. A reading of his letters reveals opinions and advice on a broad spectrum of speculative and practical matters. As a layman, Lewis frequently qualified his comments by underscoring his sense of inadequacy to offer specific pastoral direction. Nevertheless, he spent hours each week responding to piles of letters with provocative and characteristically insightful advice.

With a decade of parish experience, Schaeffer assumed his pastoral role at L'Abri with ease. One of his greatest strengths was an ability to listen with empathy. His eyes were often moist with compassion as wayward teenagers unloaded their pain and confusion. Schaeffer was fond of saying, "If I only have one hour to spend with someone, I will spend the first fifty-five minutes listening, and the final five providing an answer." His love and concern for people of all stripes is what many L'Abri workers remember most about the founder of their movement. Like Lewis, Schaeffer was a faithful letter writer. A sampling of his correspondence can be found in *Letters of Francis A. Schaeffer*. This volume reveals a deeply pious man and compassionate shepherd, who was skilled at providing practical spiritual advice.

The empathy of these men undoubtedly grew out of their own intellectual and personal struggles. This leads to our fifth and final point of common ground—an existential encounter with the evil of cancer. Lewis stared into the dark face of cancer at the age of nine, as the disease eroded his mother's life and his own sense of security. His subsequent adolescent apostasy came in large part to a mounting pessimism that had been fueled by his mother's early demise. Later in life, he also watched cancer snatch his father and his wife, Joy, well before her prime.

Though Schaeffer did not contract cancer until his late sixties, he lived with the disease for six years. During the final phase of his life, he remained productive and positive. Like Lewis, Schaeffer prayed for a healing, but it did not come; unlike Lewis, Schaeffer never became embittered. Instead, he seemed to focus primarily on the good that was coming out of an inherently evil situation. Rather than spending his time questioning his plight, Schaeffer capitalized on numerous opportunities to share the gospel with the influential medical personnel at the prestigious Mayo Clinic. As a result, many were touched by the gospel and a L'Abri branch was started nearby.

We will explore the problem of evil in greater detail in chapters eight and nine; for now it is sufficient to note the shared existential encounter with evil and its effect on their lives.

The Foundation Is Laid

A single chapter cannot begin to do justice to the depth and breadth of one man's life, let alone two, especially when the men under consideration are as prolific and multidimensional as C. S. Lewis and Francis Schaeffer. The preceding pages do not offer an exhaustive biographical exposition, but rather a general introduction to the lives and times of these men. This modest orientation will prove helpful as this analysis unfolds.

As we have seen, a fascinating symmetry of consonance and contrast is starting to emerge. While these two men grew up in very different worlds and with very different aspirations, their lives converged around a common commitment to truth, aesthetics, community and compassion. These biographical contours offer a context out of which we can begin to operate. The foundation is in place; it is to the task of framing that we must now turn.

The world does not consist of 100 per cent Christians and 100 per cent non-Christians. There are people (a great many of them) who are slowly ceasing to be Christians but still call themselves by that name: some of them are clergymen. There are other people who are slowly becoming Christians though they do not yet call themselves so.[1]

C. S. LEWIS

After becoming Christians by accepting Christ, we learn that God the Father has chosen us. The Christian could be lost again only if the first person of the Trinity, the Father, failed.[2]

FRANCIS SCHAEFFER

They, whom God hath accepted in His Beloved, effectually called, and sanctified by His Spirit, can neither totally nor finally fall away from the state of grace, but shall certainly persevere therein to the end, and be eternally saved. This perseverance of the saints depends not upon their own free will, but upon the immutability of the decree of election.[3]

THE WESTMINSTER CONFESSION

2

The Nature of Salvation
Envisioning the Highway to Heaven

*I*MAGINE YOU ARE OUT FOR AN EVENING WALK. AS YOU ARE STROLL-
ing down the street, you notice a portly, middle-aged man, with a billowing
pipe clenched between his teeth, inviting you into his stately home for a spot
of tea. You accept. As you reach the front door, the host politely introduces
himself with a distinct Ulster accent. His name is Lewis. Suddenly you realize
he is not the owner of this majestic manor but rather a servant, a butler of
sorts. Once inside, you marvel at the ornate foyer. You feel at home.

He escorts you down the long, impressive hallway, lined with venerable,
priceless objects. He describes each one. You never imagined such tradition,
such grandeur. A sparkling chandelier floods the hall with brilliant streams
of light. The great creeds of the church hang alongside portraits of the saints:
the Apostles, Athanasius, Augustine, Anselm, Abelard, Aquinas . . . You
return to the foyer, where an open Bible rests next to the guestbook of life.
You sign in and are told to stay as long as you like.

After a while you inquire about the tea. "Ah, yes," replies Lewis, and adds
with a gesture, "Just find your way into one of these adjoining rooms." Only
then do you notice the countless doors lining the grand hallway. Lewis assures
you that tea will be waiting, a fire will be burning and others of like mind will
be chatting. But you are puzzled. There are so many rooms. You turn for some
advice, but by now Lewis has returned to the front door, where he is guiding
another soul across the threshold.

When you finally retrieve his attention, Lewis explains his role is to lead people into the common hall of faith. He cannot tell you which room to live in, but he does offer one piece of advice: Choose the door you think correct, not the one most pleasing to the eye.

At the top of the hour, Lewis retires for the evening. He is replaced by another able servant, a diminutive, knicker-clad gentleman by the name of Schaeffer. You notice Schaeffer fulfills his duties with similar vim and vigor, inviting people into the home and escorting them down the grand hall of faith. The majestic tour begins the same, but before long you notice some subtle shifts. A few portraits have been moved. The color scheme seems different. Maybe it is the lighting—you are not quite sure. Following the tour you sign the guestbook. The eternal security system activates. Leaving is no longer an option.

As Christian apologists, C. S. Lewis and Francis Schaeffer were in the business of ushering converts into the common hall of faith, the corridor through which all true believers must pass. Though inhabitants of the Anglican and Presbyterian wings, respectively, both men launched their apologetic campaigns on behalf of the entire house. In *Mere Christianity* Lewis wrote, "Ever since I became a Christian I have thought that the best, perhaps the only, service I could do for my unbelieving neighbours was to explain and defend the belief that has been common to nearly all Christians at all times."[4] Schaeffer emphatically shared these sentiments, to the point of enduring criticism from some Calvinistic colleagues who accused him of sacrificing his Reformed distinctives for a more ecumenical message.

But despite substantial core agreement, Lewis and Schaeffer held some distinctly different views on how the common corridor should be adorned. This is hardly surprising, for the issue of deciding which doctrines have a claim to the hallway and which should be relegated to the confines of the closet is a matter of longstanding dispute. Indeed, conflict over interior design has torn at the fabric of the church for nearly two millennia. Lewis was fully aware of the challenge of finding a common core agreement: "One of the things Christians are disagreed about is the importance of their disagreements. When two Christians of two different denominations start arguing, it is usually not long before one asks whether such-and-such a point 'really matters' and the other replies: 'Matter? Why, it's absolutely essential.'"[5]

Schaeffer held an unwavering conviction about what "really matters." He confidently arranged the hallway according to *The Fundamentals*, a series of paperback volumes designed to defend the heart of historic, orthodox Christianity against the growing tide of liberalism at the beginning of the twentieth century. According to Schaeffer, influential men like B. B. Warfield, James Orr, W. H. Griffith Thomas and G. Campbell Morgan were not squabbling over secondary issues, they were fighting for the "heart of the Christian faith—the authority of the Bible, the deity of Christ, the meaning of salvation."[6] These men believed five essential truths constitute the nonnegotiable content of the faith: (1) the inspiration and inerrancy of the Bible, (2) the deity of Christ and the virgin birth, (3) the substitutionary atonement of Christ's death, (4) the literal resurrection of Christ from the dead, and (5) the literal return of Christ.[7] Schaeffer affirmed *The Fundamentals* as an accurate expression of what all orthodox Christians have believed in every denomination, in every age.

Lewis, on the other hand, offered his vision of the common Christian corridor in *Mere Christianity*. A close reading reveals tight agreement with Schaeffer on three key doctrines—the deity of Christ and virgin birth, the literal resurrection of Christ from the dead, and the literal return of Christ—but clear divergence on inerrancy and the substitutionary view of the atonement as proper furnishings for the hallway. While Lewis affirmed the *inspiration* of Scripture and the *efficacy* of the atonement, he emphatically rejected as essential the inclusion of theories about how the Bible is inspired or how the atonement restores fallen creatures. He believed such theories should not be confused with Christianity itself; they are simply attempts at explaining how it works.[8] This is a significant bone of contention, for Schaeffer did not consider inerrancy and the substitutionary view of the atonement theories at all, but rather essential foundational dogma upon which the authority of the Bible and the meaning of salvation rest.

In the next four chapters we will focus our discussion on these two subjects of central dispute: the meaning of salvation and biblical authority. These disputes are especially relevant to our study, for few subjects are more integral to the apologetic task. But these disputes are noteworthy on one other count as well: they represent points of deep division within evangelicalism at large. As we shall see, a discussion of soteriology and biblical authority reveals not only dissonance between Lewis and Schaeffer, but tension within the entire Christian home, a tension some Christians would prefer to overlook. But as Schaeffer pointed out in his final book, *The Great Evangelical Disaster*, there is no virtue in ignoring conflict when the heart of the faith is at stake: "Evangelicalism is divided, deeply divided. And it will not be helpful or truthful for anyone to deny this. It is something that will not simply go away, and it cannot be swept under the rug."[9]

Our discussion of theology will require airing out some old issues and overturning some dusty rugs. But such a housecleaning is essential if we are to evaluate the apologetic thinking of these men properly. As Clark Pinnock has aptly stated, "theological judgments precede apologetics and affect its agenda."[10] In other words, apologetic motivation, methodology and argumentation are an extension of one's theology. In the next four chapters we will construct the theological framework out of which these apologists operated. Only then will we properly appreciate the apologetics of these men, as well as the ongoing family friction in the common Christian corridor.

Envisioning the Highway to Heaven

Both C. S. Lewis and Francis Schaeffer placed evangelism at the heart of their ministries. Lewis was a connoisseur of literature, savoring a good book the way others appreciate fine cuisine. But this cultured academician would have traded a lifetime of literary feasts for "the salvation of a single soul."[11] He believed the task of evangelism is the "real business of life" and the only way humans can bring glory to God.[12] This conviction led Lewis to conjoin his great passion for literature with evangelism.

Schaeffer was equally forthright about his calling. Unlike the popular public perception, he did not view himself as a "missionary to the intellectuals" or a sophisticated scholastic apologist but rather as an "old-time evangelist," whose primary concern was presenting the message of reconciliation to an estranged world. Whenever a visitor would pray the sinner's prayer at L'Abri, Schaeffer would crank up the volume on his record player, throw open the windows of the chalet, and fill the surrounding Alpine countryside with a vibrant rendition of the "Hallelujah Chorus."[13]

Despite their common passion for the salvation of souls, Schaeffer and Lewis held distinctly different soteriological perspectives. As already noted, Schaeffer insisted upon placing the substitutionary understanding of the atonement in the hallway, while Lewis rejected any particular view of the atonement as essential. But the divergence does not stop there, for when Lewis does offer his theory of the atonement, his picture is a radical alternative to the legal imagery of the penal substitutionary model.

A detailed discussion of the atonement naturally leads to foundational soteriological questions that cannot be ignored. Is salvation primarily a matter of forgiveness or transformation? Can one fall away from grace, or is the certainty of heaven sealed at conversion? Has God determined the eternal destiny of each person, or are humans free to accept or reject salvation? Ultimately one's vision of God's character and human significance hinges on the answers to such questions. We will consider these key soteriological issues in some detail, beginning with Francis Schaeffer and the centrality of the substitutionary atonement.

Schaeffer's Understanding of the Centrality of the Substitutionary Atonement

Francis Schaeffer believed salvation entails three distinct aspects, each corresponding to a different dimension of time. For the Christian, *justification* is an act that takes place in the past, *sanctification* a continuing process in the present and *glorification* the actual culmination of salvation when we reach heaven in the future. These three aspects of salvation should be seen as a unified whole, flowing like a stream "from justification through sanctification and to glorification."[14] Schaeffer believed salvation is rooted in two space-time historical acts: first, the substitutionary atonement of Jesus Christ on the cross of Calvary, and second, the precise moment the individual makes a conscious decision to accept Christ as Savior.[15] It is in this definite moment of decision that the sinner is justified.

Justification. According to Schaeffer, the sole basis for salvation is the substitutionary atonement of Christ. But one is not saved until the finished work of Christ is personally appropriated through the instrument of faith. Schaeffer insists salvation is obtained by faith in Christ, plus nothing. Faith includes both the active acceptance of God's promises and the passive open-handed reception of the free gift of salvation "without trying to add humanistic religious or moral good works to it."[16]

Faith in Christ and his finished atoning work results in the justification of the sinner, a "declaration on God's part that we are just in His sight."[17] God considers the justified sinner righteous not on the basis of good works or an infused righteousness but because Christ's obedience is imputed to the sinner's account. This obedience includes both Christ's perfect fulfillment of the law and his perfect substitutionary death on our behalf. Once God declares the Christian justified, the believer is pardoned and the guilt of sin is removed. Schaeffer insists that Christ paid the price not only for past sin but for present and future sin as well. Consequently, "justification must be understood as absolutely irrevocable."[18] In other words, once believers are saved, they are always saved. Justification is a one-time act that nails down the believer's salvation with certainty. Schaeffer insists that once we have been justified, "it is as though [we] had never sinned."[19]

Schaeffer illustrates the nature of imputation with a simple picture from his own life. He recalls a time when one of his young daughters entered a local Swiss market over a series of days and purchased a number of items on credit. The storekeeper finally reported this suspicious behavior to the Schaeffers. After confronting the child with her guilt, Edith called the storekeeper back and instructed him to charge the items to her account. In so doing she erased the debt and settled the score. Schaeffer envisions the substitutionary atonement in this way. Since the child cannot pay the debt, the parent pays it instead.[20] This is what our heavenly Father has done for us. "God charges the punishment due to the guilt of our sin to the account of Christ."[21]

This model also can be pictured with courtroom imagery. All humans stand condemned before the bar of God's righteous judgment, guilty of breaking the divine holy law. But instead of getting what we deserve, Christ died on the cross in our place to pay the full penalty for our sin. If we will appropriate Christ's substitutionary sacrifice by faith, then we are pardoned, forgiven and justified by God. Righteousness is imputed to our account, and God from that moment forward considers us blameless. We will never again be tried for any sin, past, present or future. Both scenarios paint a forensic picture, with the focus on setting the legal record straight.

It is worth noting that Schaeffer is open to exploring other facets of the atonement, but he is unwavering about where the accent must be placed: "The strongest emphasis ought to be . . . on the substitutionary and propitiatory death of Christ, for without this we have nothing."[22] He believes the Bible is crystal clear in stating God could not have forgiven us any other way. It was necessary for Jesus to pay "the price for the guilt of our sin."[23] In short, Schaeffer believes the substitutionary atonement is the only path to divine satisfaction, forgiveness and, consequently, salvation.

Sanctification. According to Schaeffer, the act of justification wipes away the guilt of sin, but the process of sanctification deals with the power of sin.[24] Not only are we pardoned and forgiven at justification, but we are also adopted into the family of God and empowered to live a life of obedience. While justification and the new birth are once-for-all past acts in the Christian's life that can never be repeated, sanctification is a moment-by-moment process, whereby the believer progressively grows in Christlikeness. Although our salvation is sure, God's character demands holiness. Therefore Christians should strive for ever-increasing consecration and faithfulness, not out of obligation but out of sincere love for God and a desire to bring glory to his name.[25] We do not earn our salvation by good works or obedience to the law, but we do show forth our gratitude after becoming Christians by a lifestyle of conformity to the character of God. Of course, holy living cannot be achieved in one's own strength. The means and basis for sanctification are the same as justification: faith in Christ and his atoning work. But this is not a one-time crisis experience like justification, but rather a moment-by-moment reliance upon Christ and his finished work.[26]

But God is not concerned only about righteousness; he wants to cultivate a loving relationship with his creatures as well. At the moment of conversion the believer enters into a relationship with the three persons of the Godhead.

Though there is a legal side to salvation, as we have seen in justification, there is also a relational side. This relationship with the Trinity is cultivated through ongoing interaction with the Father, Son and Holy Spirit. God is not only our Judge and King of the universe; he is also our loving heavenly Father. The Son is not only the advocate interceding on our behalf; he is also our brother and bridegroom. The Holy Spirit is not just some distant, nebulous entity; he is our Comforter who regenerates, indwells and empowers us for a life of ever-increasing holiness and intimacy. As our relationship with God deepens, the fruit of love and righteousness springs up in our life.[27]

As noted, this strong accent on holiness and experiential reality was not always part of Schaeffer's teaching; it grew out of his spiritual crisis in the 1950s. When sharing this experience, he challenged his Calvinistic brethren to reconsider sanctification, a doctrine at times deemphasized within the Reformed tradition. He called believers to recognize the present reality of the finished work of Christ and to consciously act on it.[28]

This new emphasis led some to wonder whether Schaeffer had shifted his doctrinal allegiance. Schaeffer took great pains to put such fears to rest, repeatedly explaining what he did *not* mean by sanctification. He did not endorse a second work of grace, nor did he support the notion of sinless perfection. When speaking of sanctification, Schaeffer simply meant the present aspect of salvation, the Christian's ongoing, moment-by-moment reliance on and relationship with each person of the Godhead. This entails ever-deepening intimacy and substantial progress in the realm of moral development, but never total perfection in this life.[29]

Glorification. Though God demands perfection, Schaeffer believed Christians would only reach such a state when salvation culminates at glorification. Schaeffer affirmed two distinct moments of glorification. The first comes at death. He believed only two states of existence are possible for the believer: life in this world and afterlife with Christ. Obviously, this rules out any form of purgatory.[30] Presumably, death is accompanied by a unilateral and instantaneous work of grace that transforms the justified believer into a state of entire sanctification, thus eliminating any need for further purgation or purification. God no longer just considers the Christian righteous, the glorified person has been completely transformed into a holy, perfected being. The second moment of glorification, according to Schaeffer, comes at the final resurrection when the believer's body and soul are reunited. The glorified believer is then caught up in eternal worship of and fellowship with the holy Trinity—the very purpose for which humans were originally created.[31]

It should now be apparent why the legal view of the atonement is so critical to Schaeffer's soteriology. Even though Schaeffer places a heavy emphasis on sanctification and the relational aspect of salvation, he clearly gives justification the logical priority. For until a sinner is justified, a relationship with the infinite-personal God is out of the question. With Schaeffer's position in clear view, the soteriological distinctions between these apologists should naturally emerge from an overview of Lewis's perspective.

Lewis and the Transformational Vision of Salvation

In the preface to *Mere Christianity* Lewis writes of two theological objections to his broadcast talks. A Roman Catholic clergyman thought he "had gone rather too far about the comparative unimportance of theories in explanation of the Atonement" and a Methodist minister thought there was not enough said about faith.[32] In a personal letter Lewis specified the objection of the Methodist, who complained that Lewis had entirely omitted any discussion of justification by faith.[33]

Here is a glaring point of contrast. While Schaeffer places the logical soteriological priority on justification, Lewis does not even mention justification by faith in his discussion of salvation.

This omission of the term *justification* might be explained in two ways. First, Lewis worked diligently at translating Christian terminology into the vernacular of the unchurched, so he seldom used terms like *justification, sanctification* and *glorification.* This, however, cannot fully explain the omission, for though Lewis avoided such terms, he did not avoid the treatment of these subjects. He simply discussed these doctrines in words and images that were more accessible to his audience. But when it comes to "justification by faith," Lewis avoids not only the actual phrase but the commonly understood content behind the phrase as well.

This leads us to a second and more telling reason for Lewis's apparent aversion to this characteristically Protestant doctrine.[34] He simply does not envision the atoning work of Christ as a legal act. For Lewis the atonement is not fundamentally a matter of pardon, imputation and forgiveness, but rather the actual transformation of fallen beings into Christlike creatures. In Lewis's view, God does not want to simply impute righteousness to our account and consider us just, he wants to impart righteousness and transform us into fully justified persons. In *The Problem of Pain* Lewis makes it clear that salvation is not primarily a matter of having our sins wiped away but rather overcoming the chief sin of self-will or pride.[35] Salvation is nothing other than complete renunciation of pride in every part of one's life. Such a renunciation will naturally lead to perfected humility, the one character quality necessary for heaven.

It may be that salvation consists not in the cancelling of these eternal moments [of sin], but in the perfected humility that bears the shame forever, rejoicing in the occasion which it furnished to God's compassion and glad that it should be common knowledge to the universe. Perhaps in that eternal moment St. Peter—he will forgive me if I am wrong—forever denies his Master. If so, it would indeed be true that the joys of Heaven are, for most of us in our present condition, "an acquired taste"—and certain ways of life may render the taste impossible of acquisition.[36]

Lewis does not believe we are primarily in need of having our sins blotted out so that it is "as though [we] had never sinned," as Schaeffer suggests, but rather we are in need of becoming the kind of creatures capable of joyfully bearing with perfect humility the eternal knowledge of our sinful choices. Only then will we be the kind of creatures who are capable of enjoying heaven.

Instead of envisioning heaven as some kind of ethereal Disneyworld where anyone who has been pardoned can partake with pleasure, Lewis believes the joys of the celestial city can only be appreciated by those who are properly purified and prepared. But how do we become fit for heaven? Lewis believes the atonement is the key.

According to Lewis, humans are in a serious hole, a moral quagmire, if you will.[37] In fact, our plight is so serious that mere improvement will not solve the problem; a complete overhaul is needed. In other words, humans must undergo radical moral transformation. This type of transformation takes time and often can be painful. In *Mere Christianity* Lewis summarizes the full intention of Christ to carry out a relentless campaign of progressive moral transformation in the lives of his followers:

"Make no mistake," He says, "if you let me, I will make you perfect. The moment you put yourself in My hands, that is what you are in for. Nothing less, or other, than that. You have free will, and if you choose, you can push Me away. But if you do not push Me away, understand that I am going to see this job through. Whatever suffering it may cost you in your earthly life, whatever inconceivable purification it may cost you after death, whatever it costs Me, I will never rest, nor let you rest, until you are literally perfect."[38]

Some have read passages like this and have accused Lewis of advocating a works-righteousness soteriology.[39] But this charge simply will not stick. This passage makes it clear that Lewis believes salvation can come only by placing oneself in the hands of Christ. It is God who works in us to conform us to the image of his Son; we do not do this in our own strength. What we must do is place our ongoing faith in the divine doctor, who will finish the job if we trust his prescription for purification. For Lewis, faith clearly entails trust, and if we really trust someone, we will do what that person says.[40]

It should be evident that Lewis does not think we can earn salvation by our own self-will or mammoth efforts. We cannot earn God's favor, nor can we heal ourselves. On the contrary, Lewis is suggesting exactly the opposite. The key to salvation is a willingness to surrender, repent, even die to all that is contrary to the character of Christ.

We are rebels, so the starting point is putting down our weapons. But this is only the beginning. We must, with God's assistance, crawl out of enemy territory and back to the divine encampment. Along the way there may be landmines, barbed wire and artillery shells. We might even lose our lives en route. No matter. The process will continue in the next world. One way or another, in this life or the next, the commander promises to get us home if we will follow his orders.[41]

In other words, this concept of repentance is much more than simply eating humble pie. It involves the actual undoing of all the self-centered character traits that have embedded themselves in the sinner's heart. Repentance is not a prerequisite before God is willing to take us back, as if he could take us back without it if he wanted to, but rather a description of what "going back to God is like."[42] And if a person dies before this transformational process is complete, purification will continue beyond the grave. In *Letters to Malcolm* Lewis writes: "Our souls *demand* Purgatory, don't they? Would it not break the heart if God said to us, 'It is true, my son, that your breath smells and your rags drip with mud and slime, but we are charitable here and no one will upbraid you with these things, nor draw away from you. Enter into the joy'?"[43] Lewis does not believe God will unilaterally transform us into perfect beings at the point of death, but rather insists that we must freely cooperate in this process of character development until we are fully purified, transformed, perfect. Only then will we see the gates of splendor. Only then will we be the type of creatures who can truly enjoy and appreciate heaven.

But there is a hitch. Fallen humans are incapable of this type of perfect repentance and submission. They are full of pride, the very antithesis of humility. Lewis points out a curious irony at this juncture: "Only a bad person needs to repent: only a good person can repent perfectly."[44] Since all humans are bad, they cannot repent. God alone is good, but he is in no need of repentance. In fact, God is not capable of repentance, surrender and death in his eternal state, because he is immutable. These concepts are all foreign to him. Here is where Lewis sees the Incarnation as the ideal solution. God becomes human to become the perfect penitent. By accepting human nature, Christ is able to repent, surrender and die in perfect humility on our behalf—something God in his divine nature cannot do. This is what the atonement is all about.[45] Christ does not live a perfect life and die on the cross merely so we can be pardoned and considered righteous. Nor does Christ live a perfect life and die on the cross simply to show us how we should do it, as a works-righteousness model or the moral influence theory suggests. Instead, Christ lives a perfect life and dies on the cross so that he might do the same through us, if we will let him. This entails an active, ongoing faith. The atonement is not primarily an act of legal punishment, it is an act of enablement. The atonement enables God to perfectly repent on our behalf. He, in turn, then enables us to overcome prideful self-will through a process of repentance, submission and death, which culminates in a perfected humility, the one character quality necessary for eternal life.

This vision of salvation as a transformational process that requires true human cooperation is a recurrent theme in Lewisian literature. He makes it clear that the only thing that can hinder our character formation and ultimate salvation is an unwilling attitude. But Lewis understands that although salvation is primarily a process, there are times when definite moments of decision and surrender are required.

This is graphically illustrated in a memorable scene from *The Great Divorce*, in which Lewis describes a ghost who shrinks back from the life of heaven because of the interference of a little red lizard on his shoulder. The lizard (which represents lust) whispers discouraging words in his ear, telling him that he cannot possibly be happy or go on living without him. An angel offers to silence the lizard. Initially, the ghost agrees, until he learns that the angel means to kill it. Then the ghost retreats: "Honestly, I don't think there's the slightest necessity for that. I'm sure I shall be able to keep it in order now. I think the gradual process would be far better than killing it."[46]

The angel assures him, however, that the gradual process will be of no use in this case. He puts the issue to him as follows: "I cannot kill it against your will. It is impossible. Have I your permission?"[47] Eventually, after a dramatic struggle, the ghost agrees to allow the angel to kill it. When he does, a remarkable thing happens. The lizard is transformed into a shining stallion, which the ghost, likewise transformed into a substantial person of radiant beauty, rides off into the glory of heaven.

Lewis offers the following lesson: "Nothing, not even the best and noblest, can go on as it now is. Nothing, not even what is the lowest and most bestial, will not be raised again if it submits to death. . . . Lust is a poor, weak, whimpering whispering thing compared with that richness and energy of desire which will arise when lust has been killed."[48] This underscores the crucial point that true character formation represents our ultimate satisfaction and fulfillment, just as sin represents our ultimate destruction and misery, despite its seductive promises. If we are to enjoy heaven, complete moral transformation is a nonnegotiable prerequisite.

Summarizing the Soteriological Distinctions

A summary should help crystallize the areas of soteriological consonance and contrast between these two apologists. We start with the area of common ground. First, both men believed that humanity's problem is primarily moral. Humans are separated from God by sin. Second, both men believed humans cannot work their way back to God or earn their salvation in any manner. Third, both men believed God's solution to humanity's dilemma is the atonement. Fourth, both men believed personal faith is necessary for salvation.

Despite substantial agreement, these apologists articulated two very different visions of how the atonement reconciles sinful humanity with a holy God. Schaeffer viewed the atonement primarily as a legal act of substitutionary *punishment*, while Lewis saw it primarily as an act of divine *enablement*.[49] Consequently, Schaeffer emphasized justification, pardon, imputed righteousness and unilateral transformation at death. By contrast, Lewis highlighted repentance, regeneration, imparted righteousness and cooperative transformation, even after death. These soteriological distinctions emerge with clarity when comparing Schaeffer's *Basic Bible Studies* and Lewis's *Mere Christianity*. Schaeffer emphasizes the central soteriological importance of justification by faith but hardly mentions the concept of repentance. By contrast, Lewis emphasizes the central soteriological importance of repentance but entirely omits any discussion of justification by faith. This is a stark contrast, to be sure, but possibly the most significant point of divergence can be seen in how these men address the subject of eternal security.

As noted, Schaeffer believed the certainty of heaven is secured at conversion. Though he emphasized the moment-by-moment, progressive dimension of salvation, Schaeffer did not believe one's eternal destiny in any way hinges on sanctification. It is the act of justification that seals one's salvation. As a committed Calvinist, Schaeffer ultimately grounded the perseverance of the saints in God's immutable decree of unconditional election. In *Basic Bible Studies* Schaeffer writes, "After becoming Christians by accepting Christ, we learn that God the Father has chosen us. The Christian could be lost again only if the first person of the Trinity, the Father, failed."[50]

Lewis, by contrast, believed humans must freely cooperate with God's grace from conversion to glorification. Since Lewis saw salvation primarily as a process, he consequently understood the issue of eternal security in a much different light than Schaeffer, who believed one is either a Christian or one is not. In Lewis's view, "The world does not consist of 100 per cent Christians and 100 per cent non-Christians. There are people (a great many of them) who are slowly ceasing to be Christians but still call themselves by that name: some of them are clergymen. There are other people who are slowly becoming Christians though they do not yet call themselves so."[51] For Lewis, the choice is not once-for-all, but the moment-by-moment decision of availing oneself in faith to the scalpel of the master physician, until that final moment when the surgery is over and the believer arises from the gurney a fully transformed creature, truly fit for eternal health, happiness and glory.

Discussion of eternal security ultimately leads to the thorny fundamental issue of human freedom, divine election and predestination. Has God determined who will be saved, or do humans have the live option of either accepting or rejecting God's offer of salvation? Many contemporary evangelicals in our day have adopted the assumption that this question cannot be adequately answered, therefore it should not be addressed. It is an impenetrable mystery, a paradox. Any attempt to harmonize human freedom and predestination is a rationalistic maneuver motivated by an inability to live with one's own finitude. Contrary to this perspective, great strides have been made in recent years in contemporary philosophy of religion to bring greater clarity to the puzzling issue of free will and determinism. Indeed, this is one of the most hotly debated and carefully scrutinized topics in contemporary philosophy. One reason for the intensity of interest and passion is that the stakes are high. One's perspective on this matter has significant implications not only for soteriology but for many facets of life, including how one views the nature of God's goodness and justice as well as human dignity and responsibility.

In addition, the perspective one adopts must be self-consistent. Lewis and Schaeffer both understood that the great mysteries of the faith could never be fully probed by finite persons, yet at the same time they believed the Christian vision of reality must be a self-consistent, unified whole. The law of noncontradiction, or "antithesis" as Schaeffer put it, is the foundational principle of reality and undergirds any type of knowledge or communication. Therefore, holding beliefs that are ultimately self-contradictory was anathema to both Lewis and Schaeffer.

It should now be clear what is at stake with the issue of human freedom and predestination—nothing less than God's character, human significance and a noncontradictory vision of reality. These are central issues, to be sure, and an appeal to mystery on such vital matters should be avoided until the subject has been properly probed.

I think we must take a leaf out of the scientist's book. They are quite familiar with the fact that for example, Light has to be regarded both as a wave in the ether and as a stream of particles. No-one can make these two views consistent. Of course reality must be self-consistent; but till (if ever) we can see the consistency it is better to hold two inconsistent views than to ignore one side of the evidence. The real inter-relation between God's omnipotence and Man's freedom is something we can't find out.[1]

C. S. Lewis

In terms of what I call "the theology of the Fall," the really vital factor is that there is *no prior conditioning*. What we have is the unit of personality making an absolutely unconditioned choice, *in the thought-world.* Thus there is a *true first cause* [emphasis ours]. The whole of Christian theology and every Christian answer falls to the ground if we allow a previous deterministic conditioning to enter in at this point. There is a unit of personality which makes a true choice in the thought-world, which in turn becomes a true first cause of an external result.[2]

Francis Schaeffer

God from all eternity, did, by the most wise and holy counsel of His own will, freely, and unchangeably ordain whatsoever comes to pass: yet so, as thereby neither is God the author of sin, nor is violence offered to the will of the creatures; nor is the liberty or contingency of second causes taken away, but rather established.[3]

The Westminster Confession

3
....

God's Sovereignty and Human Significance

Predestination, Divine Election and the Power to Choose Freely

*F*RANCIS AND EDITH SCHAEFFER STRUGGLED WITH TWO KEY IS-
sues during their short time at Westminster Theological Seminary. The first
was how to take a stand for righteousness and scriptural truth without slipping
into bitterness and strife. This, of course, came to a head fifteen years later,
when Francis underwent a spiritual crisis. Out of that crisis Schaeffer adopted
a newfound commitment to holding holiness and love in continual balance.

The second issue the Schaeffers confronted at Westminster was a deterministic outlook on life. The paramount emphasis on God's providential
control not only was taught in the classroom but worked its way into the arena
of everyday life. On one particular evening, for instance, Edith was repri-
manded by a faculty member's wife for offering a prayer for material need.
The older woman told her that she ought not be praying for details of daily
life because God has already determined these things. Instead prayers should
be limited to general spiritual blessings.

Edith was stunned. While growing up in China, she had seen her family's
specific, material needs met time and again in response to detailed prayer. She
had always envisioned a God who cares about the minutiae of life and covets
our requests about such matters. Edith found this form of theological
determinism unsettling.[4]

The relationship between God's sovereignty and human significance
would become a key subject for the Schaeffers. In fact, one cannot properly
understand their ministry apart from understanding their position on this

issue, for the issue of determinism and free will has implications for not only the subject of divine election but for nearly all aspects of life.

Consider some of the most basic choices that nearly every person is confronted with each day. The clothes one wears, the food one selects, the TV programs one watches are all a matter of personal choice. Most people intuitively operate under the assumption that a real live option exists: either the black jacket or blue blazer; either Apple Jacks or bran flakes; either *Monday Night Football* or *The Movie of the Week*. There is no necessity in the matter; one is free to choose any number of ways when faced with such situations.

Yet there are other considerations in life that seem to undermine this intuition. One obvious challenge to legitimate human freedom comes from the consideration of causality. In particular, there is the intuitively simple and appealing principle of universal causality, which states that every event has a cause and thereby stands in a causal chain with an exceptionally long history. According to this view, all events are deterministically linked together; everything is interlocking. We notice this clockwork principle operating in the natural world all around us. Some have even suggested that science, if it knew all the laws of nature at any given moment, could flawlessly predict the future, down to the smallest detail.[5]

Therefore it would appear that two seemingly contradictory propositions are operating in our daily lives. On the one hand, we share a strong intuitive belief that true choice is within our power; on the other hand, we recognize causation in the natural world and our place in that nexus.

Three paradigms have been used to explicate the relationship between determinism and free will: *hard determinism, libertarian freedom* and *soft determinism* or *compatibilism*.[6] If we are to understand the subtleties and implications of this complex issue we must first familiarize ourselves with these three paradigms. After a brief overview, we will then evaluate the perspectives Schaeffer and Lewis held on the subject of predestination, divine election and human freedom.

What Is Freedom?
Since two of the three paradigms are forms of determinism, we must first get a firm handle on this important concept. The governing assumption of determinism is that science demands universal causality. All of reality, including the motions of humanity, is bound up in a nonnegotiable causal chain. Determinism, therefore, can be defined "as the view that for every event which happens, there are previous events and circumstances which are its sufficient conditions or causes, so that, given those previous events and circumstances,

it is impossible that the event should not occur."[7] With this definition clearly in view, we are now in position to detail each paradigm.

Hard determinism. This model suggests that freedom and moral responsibility are incompatible with determinism. Since everything, down to the smallest details of life, is necessitated, determined, unavoidable, humans can hardly be held accountable for their actions. The hard determinist recognizes the intuitive sense of freedom but insists that it is an illusion. The sheer impossibility of freedom can be seen in how the hard determinist defines a free action. According to this position, a true free choice cannot have a cause. Since every thought, movement and event is a result of causation, freedom is excluded. Under this model, humans and their actions are explained mechanistically like the rest of the physical universe. We are physical objects and our actions are subject to natural laws, the same sort of laws that govern the movement of the planets and the rise and fall of the tides.

This paradigm can hardly be attractive to the Christian. The Christian system claims that humanity is made in the image of God and therefore possesses rationality, aesthetic sensitivities and moral motions. Hard determinism provides no basis for rationality, the appreciation of beauty and moral accountability. Such a view clearly undermines human dignity and responsibility, as well as the concept of divine justice.

Libertarian freedom. While recognizing the deterministic nature of much of reality, this second model seeks to take the intuitive sense of freedom and moral responsibility seriously. This position does not ignore the reality of the natural law of causation in the physical world but insists that it does not account for all events, particularly the actions of humans and other agents. Libertarianism therefore can be defined "as the view that some human actions are chosen and performed by the agent without there being any sufficient condition or cause of the action prior to the action itself."[8] Free agents perform actions for reasons, and it is these that explain why the agent acts one way rather than another. Reasons explain actions but do not cause or determine them.[9]

The libertarian readily admits that some events in life might be necessitated but rejects the claim that every decision is the result of a prior sufficient condition or cause. An example should bring this position into sharper focus. Let us return to the opening vignette in chapter two. According to our story, Lewis offers a cup of tea and you accept. The offer is certainly a condition of your accepting it, and Lewis's polite overture is considered a factor in that acceptance. Indeed, other reasons and factors certainly might have contributed to your affirmative response as well, including the degree of your thirst, a weakness for caffeine or curiosity about the inside of the manor. All these factors might have played a role in the decision, but according to the libertarian, none are considered a *sufficient* cause, for ultimately you decided which factors to attend to and you actually could have rejected Lewis's offer. Instead of pursuing a hot beverage with a new acquaintance, you could have politely refused (or rudely refused for that matter) and opted to continue your evening walk. There were reasons for doing as you did, though these did not cause your decision. The decision to enter the house and drink tea was not a matter of necessity—neither Lewis's offer nor any other factor determined your will. The ability to resist the overture was a live option.

The libertarian, then, acknowledges the principle of causation in the physical world at large but believes human actions should be explained in terms of inner states, motives or reasons. Actions are free precisely because it is the individual who deliberates and decides what weight to give these factors. So a free act in this paradigm cannot be reduced to anything beyond the choice of the agent. In other words, outside factors might contribute to the decision, but ultimately it is up to the person to make a true choice between two or more live options.

Soft determinism (compatibilism). The third and final paradigm we will explore is offered as a way of bridging the gap. This model affirms a completely deterministic outlook on reality but does not suggest that moral responsibility and freedom are incompatible with it. This position "holds that there is no logical inconsistency between free will and determinism, and that it is possible that human beings are free and responsible for their actions even though these actions are causally determined."[10]

At first blush, this definition appears suspect. The logical incongruity that exists between complete determinism and libertarian freedom is obvious. For if everything is determined, then choosing otherwise is an impossibility. These are mutually exclusive propositions and, according to the law of noncontradiction, cannot coexist. The only way to harmonize these two propositions is to modify at least one proposition to relieve the tension. This is precisely what the soft determinist does. While maintaining the same definition of determinism as the hard determinist, the soft determinist chooses to redefine the notion of a free action. Although the word *soft* might seem semantically misleading, implying limited or partial determinism, the soft determinist is just as committed as the hard determinist to a complete notion of determinism. The basic difference between these two paradigms is how freedom is defined.

Indeed, the key distinction between all three models comes at this point. Each position defines freedom differently. The hard determinist states that a free act cannot have a cause, the libertarian states that a free act is one in which the agent has the ability to choose between two or more live options, but the soft determinist states that a free act is merely a matter of doing what one wants or wills to do, even though one has been caused to do so. In other words, a free act consists in consonance between the agent's choice and the agent's inner state.

Let us return to our vignette to illustrate this model. Lewis invites you in for a cup of tea. You accept, because you enjoy tea and believe it will be a pleasant experience. According to the soft determinist, this is a free act, because you choose what you want. You were not forced against your will. But at the same time the principle of universal causality is operative. Your will or desire is the proximate or immediate cause, but it can be traced through a complex web of connections to prior causes and eventually back to its ultimate antecedent. Thus your choice was determined.

This chain would include the numerous factors that brought you to the point and place in time that made an offer of tea physically possible, as well as the sufficient conditions and causes that through the years had shaped your desires and convictions about tea, Irishmen and butlers. Given the positive response, these past experiences must have been favorable, at least for the most part. So the soft determinist argues that such a response is a free act because the immediate cause flows from the inner state of the person and that person makes the choice willingly. Those who adhere to the soft determinist model insist that the principle of universal causality is honored and humans do indeed possess freedom, although not libertarian freedom. According to the soft determinist, this paradigm maintains all the advantages of determinism, without forfeiting important concepts like moral responsibility.

We can now summarize these three models accordingly. The *hard determinist* believes all reality is interlocked in a causal chain and there is no such thing as freedom because a true free act has no cause. The *libertarian* believes much of reality is part of a causal chain, but some human actions are the result of a real, legitimate first-cause choice between two or more live options. The *soft determinist* believes all reality is interlocked in a causal chain, but humans are free, even though they are determined, because their choices are executed willingly.[11]

Schaeffer: The Perfectly Balanced Mobile

We have already ruled out hard determinism as a serious option for the Christian. With this in mind, we will evaluate Schaeffer and Lewis in light of the two remaining models: libertarian freedom and soft determinism. We will consider Schaeffer's perspective first.

Schaeffer clearly saw himself standing in the stream of Reformed Christianity. He attended a Presbyterian college (Hampden-Sydney) and two Presbyterian seminaries (Westminster and Faith) and was an ordained Presbyterian minister for almost fifty years. As a committed Presbyterian, Schaeffer accepted the Westminster Confession of Faith as a binding creedal statement and accurate expression of scriptural teaching. In 1942 Schaeffer read a paper entitled "Our System of Doctrine" at the General Synod of the Bible Presbyterian Church and in so doing left little question about his commitment to the work of the Westminster divines: "We are a doctrinal church. Not just mildly so but with emphasis. . . . We have established our Church upon the System of Doctrine of the Westminster Confession of Faith and Catechisms as that which is Biblical, and this System is doctrinally definite and solid."[12] This strong commitment to the Westminster Confession would one day lead Schaeffer to offer a detailed chapter-by-chapter exposition of the entire statement.

One of the lectures from that expositional series is entitled "God's Sovereignty and Man's Significance."[13] In this nearly three-hour lecture we find the clearest expression of Schaeffer's belief on the subject of predestination and human freedom. Schaeffer emphasizes three key points: God's total sovereignty, the significance of history and humanity, and the delicate balance of these important truths. In the next few pages we will focus primarily on this lecture, but we will also consider a variety of other sources, including another lecture and his published works, to arrive at a fuller picture of his thinking on this subject.

God's total sovereignty. In *No Little People* Schaeffer points out, "I am a Presbyterian, so I will emphasize above all the doctrine of predestination."[14] True to this statement, Schaeffer begins his lecture "God's Sovereignty and Man's Significance" by underscoring the importance of God's total providential control over all reality. The foundational tenet to Schaeffer's understanding of providence is the conviction that "there is no chance back of God."[15] In other words, God governs the universe with total control, leaving no room for chance or true contingency. Everything that happens is part of an all-inclusive divine plan. He is emphatic about this point, insisting that "if there is such a thing as luck, Christianity is wrong."[16] Schaeffer believes prayer, prophecy and the promise that "in all things God works for the good of those who love him" (Rom 8:28) would be meaningless if chance is admitted. In reality, though it appears that much of life is a result of random chance, everything—acts of nature, the direction of the nations, the acts of persons and the salvation of individuals—is under the control of God.[17]

When Schaeffer says that the salvation of individuals is under the total providential control of God, he is concurring with the doctrine of unconditional election as the Westminster Confession defines it: "By the decree of God, for the manifestation of His glory, some men and angels are predestined unto everlasting life; and others foreordained to everlasting death."[18] God predestines some to heaven and others to hell, not on the basis of foreseeing their future free acts but on the basis of the divine plan, which is constructed according to "the unsearchable counsel of His own will, whereby He extendeth or withholdeth mercy, as he pleaseth."[19] Presumably, in keeping with the Westminster Confession, Schaeffer believes the only proper account of God's sovereignty entails total, unconditional predestination of every detail of life, including the eternal destiny of human souls.

Significantly, Schaeffer carefully avoided words like *election* and *predestination,* choosing more general terms instead. This was a common maneuver for Schaeffer. According to James Hurley, Schaeffer carefully crafted his language, especially when unbelievers were present, so his message might receive a proper hearing.

He [Schaeffer] indicated that if he spoke of Calvinism, or of the sovereignty of God, or of predestination, many understood him to be speaking of a harsh fatalism and would not listen to anything more that he might have to say. He chose instead to avoid catchwords and to speak of the sure hand of God, of God's faithfulness to his own, of his rule over history, or of his calling of his sheep. He felt that by using such terms he could "get behind the screen" and be heard. Eventually, if someone asked whether he was in fact speaking of predestination, Schaeffer would readily acknowledge the term.[20]

Schaeffer illustrated the purpose of this strategy with a story. Imagine a man walking down the street and arriving at a temple with the words "Whosoever will may come" written above the doorway. The man walks through the door but upon reaching the sanctuary begins to question whether he really belongs. He is then taken down to the basement, where he is shown the foundation stones. His fears are put to rest by the comforting words inscribed on one of the stones: "Chosen before the foundation of the world." His election is sure.

According to Schaeffer, this story illustrates the Reformed belief that salvation is grounded in God's immutable election, but it is senseless to try to bring people into the faith through the foundation stones when God has provided a door. In other words, Schaeffer did not believe the doctrine of unconditional election was something to be used in evangelism but should be reserved for the purpose of assuring believers once they have entered the fold.[21]

The significance of history and humanity. Though Schaeffer affirmed total, unconditional predestination, he was equally emphatic that Christianity is not a deterministic or fatalistic system. God is a nondetermined Being who created freely, so humans, created in the image of God, are also nondetermined and capable of free choice.[22] Consequently, history and humanity are not caught in the wheels of determinism. This point of emphasis is an important thread that can be traced through the entire Schaeffer corpus. In fact, contrary to his Presbyterian priorities, Schaeffer consistently emphasizes the significance of human freedom in his books, while hardly ever mentioning the doctrine of predestination in any discernible manner.[23] When it comes to human freedom, Schaeffer speaks freely and forcefully in order to challenge the ever-increasing mechanistic mindset of the twentieth century.

Schaeffer's view of freedom is clear, direct and unfettered by the ambiguity that tends to obfuscate his discussion of predestination. He states that a human choice flows from "the whole personality" and is "a *true* and *sufficient* cause."[24] We are not determined by chemical factors, psychological factors or sociological factors. In *The God Who Is There*, Schaeffer leaves little question about his view of freedom: "If this is the case [determinism being true], then man is not the tremendous thing the Bible says he is, made in the image of God as a personality who can make a free first choice."[25] In *True Spirituality* Schaeffer delivers an even stronger statement in favor of human freedom:

> In terms of what I call "the theology of the Fall," the really vital factor is that there is *no prior conditioning*. What we have is the unit of personality making an absolutely unconditioned choice, *in the thought-world.* Thus there is a *true first cause* [emphasis ours]. The whole of Christian theology and every Christian answer falls to the ground if we allow a previous deterministic conditioning to enter in at this point. There is a unit of personality which makes a true choice in the thought-world, which in turn becomes a true first cause of an external result.[26]

This is a crystal-clear expression of libertarian freedom, the belief that humans are in and of themselves a sufficient first cause for many of their choices.[27]

The perfectly balanced mobile. Schaeffer is affirming the doctrine of total, unconditional predestination as well as a libertarian notion of freedom. But how can humans possess the power to choose between different options if God has predestined everything that is going to happen, including the eternal destiny of each soul? Schaeffer does not answer this question. Indeed, he sees it as futile and possibly even irreverent to try. According to Schaeffer, Scripture clearly teaches both doctrines: humans live "above the level of consciousness" as free beings who make significant choices, while "below the level of consciousness" the Holy Spirit is carrying out the sovereign will of the Father.[28] The biblical authors do not try to harmonize the mysterious doctrines of free will and predestination but simply present them in parallel fashion. In other words, we do not find a biblical explanation for how God could predestine everything and humans could make first-cause choices, but both must be true because both are clearly taught in Scripture. Since the Bible does not try to work it out, we should leave the issue unresolved.

In an attempt to validate this principle of balance or parallelism, Schaeffer suggests a pair of models. He sees the predestination-freedom issue as a "perfectly balanced mobile,"[29] with God's total control on one side and humanity's true freedom and significance on the other. He also likens Scripture's treatment of the subject to a Ping-Pong ball bouncing back and forth in perfect rhythm.[30] Schaeffer offers a strong rhetorical flourish near the end of his lecture:

> The conclusion shouldn't be doctrinal death on either side. The conclusion should be adoration, that was Paul's conclusion.... "O the depth of the riches both of the wisdom and knowledge of God! How unsearchable are his judgments, and his ways past finding out! For who hath known the mind of the Lord? or who hath been his counsellor? Or who hath first given to him, and it shall be recompensed unto him again? For of him, and through him, and to him, are all things: to whom be glory for ever. Amen." That should be the reaction.... Why? For one basic reason ... Because of who God is. He is infinite, we are finite. And because He is infinite and we are finite we are not going to be able to search out all His ways. Because He is infinite and we are finite we can never exhaust Him. Never exhaust Him. So in order to state the truth of His person, the truth of what He is, the only way to state it to finite men is the way the Bible states it: this side, then that side. There is no other way to say it. To begin to tone it down on either thing is to destroy the marvel of the Bible ... it is to destroy the understanding of the total infinity of God. Our God is so infinite that He can make history with significance, man with significance, and yet retain His total infinity. This is our God.[31]

We can now summarize Schaeffer's position accordingly: Along with the Westminster divines, he believes God has unconditionally predestined everything that comes to pass. But at the same time, Schaeffer believes humans are a true and sufficient first cause for their actions. Since God is nondetermined and creates freely, humans likewise are nondetermined and free. We must hold these two truths—God's total, unconditional predestination and first-cause human freedom—in constant tension. Scripture does not resolve the matter, but rather affirms both with balanced parallelism. We must, therefore, do the same. Instead of trying to harmonize the two, which will surely lead to either diminishing divine sovereignty or undermining human significance, we should bow before God in awe, reverence and unbridled worship.

Lewis: The Eternal Now

In *Surprised by Joy* C. S. Lewis recalls his first metaphysical argument. While off at boarding school, he and his comrades vigorously debated whether "the future was like a line you can't see or like a line that is not yet drawn."[32] Over time Lewis came to forget which side he defended but was quite certain he had entered the fray with gusto and conviction. Many years later a seasoned Lewis would return to this metaphysical topic in an effort to sort out the interrelationship between human freedom, foreknowledge, predestination and election. In the next few pages we will consider his thoughts on these subjects by surveying a variety of material, ranging from his overtly apologetic writing and imaginative literature to some of his personal correspondence.

Human freedom. As we have already seen, one of the most prominent themes in the entire Lewisian corpus is a deep commitment to significant human freedom, particularly as it relates to the process of character development. Indeed, one cannot properly appreciate Lewisian theology without understanding his perspective on the nature of free will.

In *Mere Christianity* Lewis outlines the relationship between freedom and character development in a section entitled "Nice People or New Men." In this chapter Lewis introduces his readers to two fictitious characters, Christian Miss Bates and unbelieving Dick Firkin.[33] The interesting thing about this pair is that Miss Bates, though a woman of faith, possesses a venomous tongue, while Mr. Firkin, though an unregenerate soul, possesses a pleasant, congenial personality. In fact, if one were to ask a stranger to select which of the two seemed most Christlike, chances are Mr. Firkin would get the nod, but according to Lewis we are not in proper position to make such a judgment. We should not compare one person to another, but rather ask what Miss Bates would be like if she were not a believer and what Mr. Firkin would be like if he were.

Lewis recognizes that many human infirmities (as well as many apparent virtues) are a result of natural causes and environmental factors that are outside the control of each individual. We cannot pick our parents, our gene pool, the zip code into which we are born. For better or for worse, these and other factors have helped shape our temperament, personality and perceptual framework. But according to Lewis, physiological and environmental factors have very little, if anything, to do with the essence of a person's character. God sees the hand each person has been dealt and realizes how the deck is stacked. He knows that Miss Bates's disposition might have been quite different if she had not been saddled with a low IQ or a poor set of nerves. He also knows that Mr. Firkin's pleasant demeanor might suddenly disappear should his perfect digestion be disrupted.[34] God will rectify these inequities in due time, but for now they are a disturbing and sometimes misleading part of life.

Character development, on the other hand, is a matter of volitional choice. Humans have the capacity to choose whether or not they are going to become the kind of creatures God desires. Of course they cannot do this on their own. Cooperation with God's grace is essential. But Lewis stresses that God cannot do it alone either. He needs humans to freely cooperate in the process of their own character formation. There is a live option either to accept God's plan of character formation or to refuse it, for a truly free act entails the power to do otherwise. Humans must, therefore, possess a will that is unconditioned, unprogrammed and undetermined to any particular end.

> What [God] is watching and waiting for is something that is not easy even for God, because, from the nature of the case, even He cannot produce it by a mere act of power. He is waiting and watching for it both in Miss Bates and in Dick Firkin. It is something they can freely give Him or freely refuse to Him. Will they, or will they not, turn to Him and thus fulfill the only purpose for which they were created? Their free will is trembling inside them like the needle of a compass. But this is a needle that can choose. It can point to its true North; but it need not. Will the needle swing round, and settle, and point to God?[35]

This passage offers a clear view of how Lewis envisions the nature of human freedom. The first line suggests that there are things that even God cannot do, namely, determine his creatures to freely choose him. This view cuts against the grain of soft determinism, for the claim that God has the power to bring about his will without overriding human freedom is precisely what compatibilism affirms. This type of freedom, however, is not at all what Lewis has in mind. According to Lewis, the needle of the compass can either point to the North or point to the South—it is not determined. Miss Bates and Mr. Firkin have it within their power to truly cooperate with God's purpose for their lives, or they can truly choose to refuse his overtures. In other words, like Schaeffer, Lewis is affirming libertarian freedom. It is worth noting that in *Mere Christianity,* a book dedicated to the common core beliefs of all Christians, Lewis includes a vision of human liberty that entails the power of contrary choice.

Divine foreknowledge, predestination and providence. Lewis realized there are potential logical threats to significant human freedom. One such threat would appear to be the doctrine of complete foreknowledge, the belief that God knows in advance and with certainty all that will come to pass.[36] It is argued that if God, whose knowledge is by definition perfect, knows with certainty that a future event will take place, then one cannot possibly stop that event from unfolding. If God knows with certainty today that you will eat a peanut-butter sandwich tomorrow, it is hard to see how you could choose not to eat that sandwich. To suggest that you can eat something other than a peanut-butter sandwich when God knows with certainty that you will eat a peanut-butter sandwich is to challenge the impeccable nature of God's knowledge. On the other hand, to suggest that you could not choose other than a peanut-butter sandwich tomorrow because God already knows that you will eat a peanut-butter sandwich appears to challenge the notion of libertarian freedom, the power of contrary choice. Lewis clearly felt the force of this dilemma and turned to an ancient maneuver to relieve the tension between God's knowledge and human freedom.

Lewis deals with this subject in a number of places, including *Mere Christianity* and *Letters to Malcolm*. He even uses a demon to help enlighten his readers. In *The Screwtape Letters* Uncle Screwtape addresses this issue in a diabolical letter to his upstart apprentice and nephew, Wormwood. He begins by laying out the logical problem as it relates to the subject of prayer.

> If you tried to explain to [the human] that men's prayers today are one of the innumerable coordinates with which the Enemy [God] harmonises the weather of tomorrow, he would reply that then the Enemy always knew men were going to make those prayers and, if so, they did not pray freely but were predestined to do so.[37]

Screwtape seems to suggest that divine foreknowledge is evidence that a certain event must have been necessitated and therefore was not free.[38] And if an event is necessary, it must, of course, come to pass precisely that way. But according to Screwtape, the whole discussion is a nonissue, because the problem of foreknowledge and predestination is simply one of perception. Humans view all reality through a temporal grid and assume God must share their mode of perception. But God is not bound by temporality. He exists outside space and time, viewing the past, present and future simultaneously. With God there is no such thing as "pre" or "post," for all is eternally present from his vantage point. Screwtape concludes, "For the Enemy does not *foresee* the humans making their free contributions in a future, but *sees* them doing so in His unbounded Now. And obviously to watch a man doing something is not to make him do it."[39] Lewis apparently believes if we can eliminate all prefixes that mislead us into thinking God possesses prior knowledge, the logical problem is resolved.[40]

Lewis did not believe in *fore*knowledge or *pre*destination, properly speaking, but he did have a robust appreciation for God's providence. In an appendix to *Miracles*, entitled "On Special Providences," Lewis makes it clear that all that comes to pass is God's will, and at creation "God determined the whole history of Nature" in one single creative act.[41] But contrary to the teaching of the Westminster Confession and traditional Calvinism, Lewis believes God determined all that will happen by taking into account the petitions and free choices of His creatures. He does not determine what choices humans will make but rather sees the choices they will make in each situation and dovetails these choices and the events of the natural world into one cohesive, harmonious unit. This creative act, of course, does not take place in time but in the Eternal Now. Lewis likens God's creativity to that of an author or filmmaker who weighs innumerable variables in the process of formulating a desired plot or screenplay. Of course this analogy is imperfect, since God has in mind the ultimate good of his creatures, not simply entertainment. The divine screenplay is also infinitely more complex, for God must take into account true free choices instead of merely determining the choices of his characters. Lewis believes every free choice, as well as the whole history of the material world, is woven into the great screenplay of life in a single timeless act.[42]

Divine election and free will. Lewis seemed quite certain that his view of the Eternal Now eliminated any logical tension between divine omniscience and human freedom, but he simply did not know what to do with the doctrine of divine election. For an appeal to the Eternal Now cannot resolve the tension between divine election and human freedom, because this issue has nothing to do with God's mode of perception but is rather a matter of God's determining will. It does not matter if God is inside or outside time; if he has determined one to a particular end, there is no possibility of doing otherwise.

The doctrine of divine election posed a significant logical challenge to Lewis, since he was committed to a libertarian form of freedom. But despite a commitment to the power of contrary choice, Lewis could not dismiss the ambiguity he found in Scripture and in his own personal conversion surrounding the issue of free will and determinism.

Lewis thought the Bible was especially enigmatic on this subject. Jesus speaks of separating the sheep and the goats on the basis of their works with no reference to predestination or even faith. Paul, on the other hand, emphasizes the doctrine of predestination and the role of faith, while repudiating any type of works-righteousness approach to salvation. Lewis confesses that he does not know how to reconcile these passages but is certain that the proper understanding of election will not rule out true human agency. Instead of dismissing either side of the evidence, we should hold the two in tension until further enlightenment arrives, which presumably will not be in this life.[43] Lewis believes the mysterious relationship between human agency and divine election is best summarized in a puzzling passage from the second chapter of Philippians, which Lewis discusses in this way:

> "Work out your own salvation in fear and trembling"—pure Pelagianism. But why? "For it is God who worketh in you"—pure Augustinianism. It is presumably only our presuppositions that make this appear nonsensical. We profanely assume that divine and human action exclude one another like the actions of two fellow-creatures so that "God did this" and "I did this" cannot both be true of the same act except in the sense that each contributed a share. In the end we must admit a two-way traffic at the junction.[44]

Experience seems just as mysterious to Lewis. An event leading up to his own conversion is a good example. Lewis was riding a bus and began to sense the overtures of God. It was as if he were wearing some type of restrictive garment and God wanted to set him free. He believes he was given "what now appears a moment of wholly free choice. . . . I could open the door or keep it shut; I could unbuckle the armor or keep it on. . . . I chose to open, to unbuckle, to loosen the rein."[45] Then Lewis suddenly shifts gears and offers a different perspective:

> I say, "I chose," yet it did not really seem possible to do the opposite. . . . You could argue that I was not a free agent, but I am more inclined to think that this came nearer to being a perfectly free act than most that I have ever done. Necessity may not be the opposite of freedom, and perhaps a man is most free when, instead of producing motives, he could only say, "I am what I do."[46]

This is another example of two-way traffic at the junction. Lewis recognizes both divine and human agency in the process of salvation but does not think we can ever determine the precise interrelationship between the two. After all, divine-human interaction is not like two humans cooperating, for God is both outside and inside us. In fact, God is the source of all we are and all we have, including our freedom. Such a web of interconnectedness seems too complex to ever unravel. Lewis believes "we can't find a consistent formula"[47] and offers an analogous situation from the realm of science:

> I think we must take a leaf out of the scientist's book. They are quite familiar with the fact that for example, Light has to be regarded both as a wave in the ether and as a stream of particles. No-one can make these two views consistent. Of course reality must be self-consistent; but till (if ever) we can see the consistency it is better to hold two inconsistent views than to ignore one side of the evidence. The real inter-relation between God's omnipotence and Man's freedom is something we can't find out.[48]

Since we do not have the necessary faculties or proper perspective to resolve this mystery, Lewis believes the whole discussion of free will and predestination is "really a meaningless question" and "that in *any concrete case* the question never arises as a practical one."[49] With intellectual resolution out of reach, Lewis offers a pragmatic suggestion for dealing with the issue in everyday life: "I find the best plan is to take the Calvinist view of my own virtues and other people's vices; and the other view of my own vices and other people's virtues."[50]

We can now summarize Lewis's position accordingly: God has given humans the power of contrary choice or libertarian freedom. Humans must freely cooperate with the activity of God in their lives if they are to become what they were intended to be. But there are two apparent threats to libertarian freedom: foreknowledge and predestination. Lewis believes that foreknowledge is evidence that a particular choice or event has been predetermined. But Lewis believes this is really just a problem of perspective. We mistakenly assume God shares our temporal mode of perception and existence. On the contrary, God lives in the Eternal Now, outside time and space, where he perceives all reality simultaneously. Once we realize God exists outside time, the tension disappears. To watch someone engage in an activity is not to make that person do it.

Lewis does not believe in *fore*knowledge or *pre*destination, properly speaking, though he does believe everything happens according to God's will and plan. But contrary to the teaching of the Westminster Confession, it is a plan that takes true human choices into account. In other words, God knows what humans will choose and these free, libertarian choices help determine the ultimate plan that is devised. Lewis is certain that Scripture and experience support the reality of both human agency and divine causation, but it is impossible to discern the precise interrelationship between these two in any given situation. This is a mystery only God can unravel. We must hold free will and determinism in tension until resolution arrives, but Lewis is sure of one thing: however divine causation is to be ultimately understood, it will not exclude true freedom. Since a harmonious rational solution appears to be out of reach, Lewis offers a pragmatic proposal: attribute your own virtues and other people's vices to divine causation and your own vices and other people's virtues to human agency.

The Mystery Button

We have now completed our soteriological overview of Schaeffer and Lewis, and our survey suggests a significant degree of contrast and consonance. While Schaeffer affirmed the penal substitutionary view of the atonement, with a logical emphasis upon justification and pardon, Lewis affirmed a transformational view of the atonement, with an emphasis on enablement and human cooperation from beginning to end. Schaeffer grounded salvation ultimately in God's eternal decree of unconditional election, but he nevertheless believed humans make significant, first-cause choices. How these two apparently incongruent assertions are harmonized is a mystery to Schaeffer. Similarly, Lewis affirms libertarian freedom but holds a significantly different view of God's providence. In contrast to traditional Reformed teaching, Lewis believes God plans all that will happen by taking into account true human choices, but the precise interrelationship between these choices and divine causation is unknowable from a limited human perspective. Though this baffling mystery cannot be resolved in this life, Lewis is certain that the proper understanding of divine causation will not rule out true human agency.

As we noted earlier, with so much at stake, including God's character, human significance and a self-consistent worldview, an appeal to mystery should be reserved until the matter has been properly probed. It will take another chapter to decide whether or not Schaeffer and Lewis have pressed the mystery button prematurely.

If you choose to say "God can give a creature free will and at the same time withhold free will from it," you have not succeeded in saying *anything* about God: meaningless combinations of words do not suddenly acquire meaning simply because we prefix to them the two other words "God can." . . . Nonsense remains nonsense even when we talk it about God.[1]

C. S. Lewis

I want to suggest that scientific proof, philosophical proof and religious proof follow the same rules. . . . After the question has been defined, in each case proof consists of two steps: (A) The theory must be noncontradictory and must give an answer to the phenomenon in question. (B) We must be able to live consistently with our theory. . . . Christianity, which begins with the existence of the infinite-personal God, man's creation in His image and a space-time Fall, does offer a nonself-contradictory answer which explains the phenomena and which can be lived with, both in life and in scholarly pursuits.[2]

Francis Schaeffer

If no real contradiction from a human level is meaningful and God would not reveal nonsense, then the primary purpose for attempting to determine whether certain Biblical statements are self-contradictory . . . should be to attempt to identify the truth. . . . If two seeming truths are really incompatible, then reinterpretation or suspension of judgment is necessary.[3]

David Basinger

4
....

Evaluating the
Mystery Maneuver
The Necessity of "True" Truth

*I*N 1992 FRANK SCHAEFFER WROTE A FASCINATING NOVEL ABOUT AN
American missionary family and their annual journey from the snowcapped
Swiss Alps to the picturesque shores of an Italian beach resort. The parallels
between the characters in Frank's story and his own personal upbringing are
striking: the parents are zealous Presbyterian missionaries sent from St. Louis
to Switzerland after the war for the purpose of evangelizing Roman Catholics.
In addition to such remarkable factual correspondence, similarities in personality and temperament surface. These similarities have led some to suggest
that *Portofino* is a thinly veiled, far-from-fictitious, autobiographical account
of Frank's life with his parents, Francis and Edith Schaeffer. Though the
parallels are amazingly accurate in many sections, one finds, in at least one
chapter, a portrait of a clan that appears to be quite different from the real-life
Swiss family Schaeffer.

The story is told from the perspective of Calvin, a mischievous ten-year-
old boy. On the final night of their vacation, Calvin's sisters are bemoaning
the poor weather of the final day. The mother quickly offers a chastisement
for not giving thanks in all things, but the father seizes the moment to
expound on the sovereignty of God.

One of the daughters, Rachel, reformulates her father's abstract teaching
into a concrete speculation: "You mean if I had gone out to the point, I might
have had a cramp or something and drowned, and God knew it so He made
it rain to save me?" While the parents offer Rachel praise for her spiritual

discernment, Janet, the other sister, softly suggests an even more horrific alternative: "Or might have been raped." This comment sparks a series of angry exchanges and prompts Calvin to exploit the moment by asking, "Mommy, what's 'rape'?"[4]

After his inquiry is ignored for the third time, Calvin offers the reader his perspective on the unfolding events:

Then Janet made a big mistake, or rather God did because He's sovereign. Dad had said many times how the great Reformation hero, Calvin, showed us we are in a state of Total Depravity and so is our free will so we really can't even think with our fallen minds or choose to do good things because we are so depraved. So God made her say, "I only asked!" Then God made Dad throw down his napkin and say, "That's it!"[5]

After Janet is sent to her room, Calvin begins an experiment with a saltshaker to see if he can confound God's knowledge and plan by shaking the granules in unpredictable ways. Eventually the salt fills his hair. The father's wrath suddenly shifts from the daughters to his only son. When asked why he has dumped the shaker of salt on his head, Calvin exclaims, "God made me do it."[6]

While Calvin is sitting in his room awaiting his corporal punishment for blasphemy, he begins to ponder his father's Reformed teaching on predestination and free will. He wonders why his father would punish him if God has determined all things and humans cannot really choose otherwise. Calvin remembers his father saying that free will really just means that we are "free to recognize God's plan."[7] Little Calvin is confounded.

In the end, Calvin is given a stay of execution on the condition that he will never again attribute his sin to divine causation. He exchanges hugs and kisses with his father and begins to reflect on his love for his dad. The warmth of the moment, however, is suddenly cooled by a nagging thought: "I wondered if God had known he would change his mind and not spank me and if this was part of the plan."[8]

This humorous vignette illustrates how easily our implicit convictions about God's sovereignty and human freedom can slip into everyday life. The relationship between predestination and personal accountability even has practical implications for a ten-year-old child who senses the injustice of being punished for something he really could not have avoided.

According to Frank Schaeffer, his father would have rejected the type of "theological correctness" the parents of this story demand of their children. During his vacations to Italy, as Frank remembers, his father talked much more about Italian art than about John Calvin.[9] But the theological correctness of this fictitious father is not the only thing Francis Schaeffer would have resisted in this story. He also would have resisted the view of freedom these parents appear to hold. As mentioned in the previous chapter, Schaeffer affirmed libertarian freedom and believed humans are capable of significant, first-cause choices. The Schaeffers often found themselves at odds with many Reformed colleagues, whose systems deemphasized or seemed to undermine the significance of human choice. As time passed, Schaeffer became more and more disillusioned with any formal theological system that claimed to capture the mysterious nature of predestination, divine election and human freedom. Some issues are just too complex and elusive to put under a microscope. Schaeffer saw this unresolvable matter as a grand opportunity to accept one's own finite limitations and worship God with deep reverence and humility. In short, he pressed the mystery button.

In this chapter we will evaluate the views of both Schaeffer and Lewis on predestination, divine election and free will, including their respective appeals to mystery. First, however, we must draw an important distinction. Few would squabble with Schaeffer over the call to humility in the face of lofty subject matter. There is an immense chasm that separates the finite from the Infinite, the contingent from the Necessary, the creature from the Creator. Who can fully explicate the doctrines of the Trinity and Incarnation? Who can drain the mind of God? Without question, reverence, humility and a healthy sense of proportion should undergird any theological undertaking. But let us be clear about the issue at stake. A desire to adjudicate the relationship between predestination, divine election and human freedom is hardly an irreverent attempt to exhaust the depths of divine knowledge. Surely the matter is not about resolving the issue in its entirety but rather a question of discerning whether or not we are on the right track. And we need not have the finish line in clear view to know we are in the correct lane.

Schaeffer was certainly familiar with this critical distinction. He frequently discussed the difference between "true truth" and "exhaustive truth" and was convinced that God has provided understandable, though inexhaustive, noncontradictory propositions in Scripture.[10] In other words, humans are capable of seeing the truth accurately, but not completely. We must keep this important distinction in mind as we probe the positions of Schaeffer and Lewis in this chapter. To think clearly and deeply about the things of God is hardly a futile or irreverent task but rather an attempt to take the great commandment seriously. With this said, we must now carefully slice through the tangled thicket of confusion that often shrouds the sensitive and sacred issue of mystery.

Demystifying Mystery

Appeals to mystery, antinomy and paradox are quite common in Christian circles, but what is much less common is a precise understanding about the meaning of such terms. These concepts are often used interchangeably in a rather haphazard and indiscriminate manner whenever two apparently contradictory propositions are encountered. David Basinger, however, helps us cut through a significant degree of the confusion with a series of important distinctions.[11]

Basinger divides apparent contradictions into four categories. The first type of apparent contradiction can be called a *Verbal Puzzle.* Here the confusion dissolves with little effort by simply defining the decisive concepts. A good example is the biblical principle that "one must die in order to live." Once we realize this statement is not suggesting a physical demise but rather a death to the flesh and self-centered autonomy, the tension disappears.

The second type of apparent contradiction is properly considered a *Mystery.* A Mystery is a proposition or theory that is suprarational but does not contain any self-contradictory assertions. In other words, we are just missing some of the data or lacking the rational penetration to fully explore the matter; the data in question has not been decisively shown to be self-contradictory. This is the category of true but inexhaustive truth. Examples of Mystery include the Christian doctrines of the Trinity and Incarnation, doctrines beyond the ability of finite humans to grasp in their entirety, but nevertheless fully self-consistent concepts.[12]

The third type of apparent contradiction that Basinger discusses is what we will call *Temporary Agnosticism.* This includes propositions that not only are apparently self-contradictory but are in fact decisively incompatible. Lewis's analogy of light is a good example. In the early twentieth century, scientists were baffled by the fact that light appeared to behave like a particle in some settings and a wave under other conditions. Theoretical scientists were completely aware that light could not ultimately be both essentially a particle and essentially a wave, because particles and waves, as these concepts were at that time understood, contained mutually exclusive properties. For about twenty-five years, the problem of "wave-particle duality," as it was referred to, baffled the scientific community. The only honest thing to do was to hold these two incompatible theories in tension until more data surfaced. Then around the middle of the century the revolutionary discovery of quantum electrodynamics (QED) resolved the logical problem. QED provided a new set of axioms, which enabled scientists to understand that light is essentially made up of particles but that all elementary particles are capable of "wavelike" behavior. By showing in a logically consistent manner how light was capable of behaving like a wave on some occasions and a particle on others, this breakthrough produced one self-consistent paradigm that satisfactorily resolved the confounding puzzle of "wave-particle duality."[13]

This example from the realm of science is an excellent illustration of how the tenacity of holding two incompatible theories temporarily in tension can lead to a fully self-consistent solution. The key point to underscore here, however, is that the temporary agnostic does not for one moment believe two decisively self-contradictory concepts can both be ultimately true in their current incompatible form but rather holds the two in tension until it becomes clear how one's view of the phenomena must be adjusted. In this instance QED opened the door to a deeper understanding of particle dynamics, thus resolving the previous logical tension and moving the issue of light from the category of Temporary Agnosticism into the fully self-consistent category of Mystery (true but inexhaustive truth).

This leads us to the fourth and final category: *Paradox.* According to Basinger's definition, a Paradox is nothing short of a flat-out self-contradiction—a statement on par with the concept of a square-circle. There is a fine but critical distinction here between the position of Temporary Agnosticism and that of Paradox. Both the temporary agnostic and the proponent of Paradox hold two incompatible propositions in tension, but there is diametrical opposition in how that tension is viewed. Whereas the temporary agnostic acknowledges that two incompatible propositions cannot both be ultimately true without some eventual adjustment to one or both propositions, the adherent of Paradox states that the incompatible propositions are in fact both ultimately true in their current form—it is simply impossible to see how this is so.

There is a world of difference between these two claims. If we return to the subject of the nature of light, the distinction crystallizes. Prior to the advent of QED, the temporary agnostic saw no good reason to dismiss either side of the evidence. There were good reasons to support the belief that either light is essentially a wave or light is essentially a particle (or light is some combination of the two, but of course this would have required a reformulation of the concepts involved), but light could not be at the same time both essentially a wave and essentially a particle, as these terms were understood, because the essential characteristics of a wave and a particle contain mutually exclusive properties. If one were to have applied the paradoxical perspective to this case, however, the suggestion would have been that light is both essentially a wave and essentially a particle at the same time, even though these phenomena contain mutually exclusive properties. We are just not able to see how these two propositions in their current incompatible form are indeed ultimately compatible. In other words, the temporary agnostic honors the law of noncontradiction by presenting the logical dilemma in either-or terms while diligently gathering more information to bring relief to the obvious tension. The adherent of Paradox, on the other hand, undermines the law of noncontradiction by presenting the proposition in both-and terms and shuts the door on any further dialogue or research.

We see that the first two types of apparent contradictions, Verbal Puzzles and Mysteries, surface as fully self-consistent propositions after the proper probing and reflection. There is no logical problem here. The other two categories, Temporary Agnosticism and Paradox, however, contain incompatible propositions, and nothing can harmonize these propositions as they exist in their current form. But the temporary agnostic has no logical problem, because the two propositions are held in tension only temporarily while a harmonious resolution is pursued through ongoing research and dialogue. The only position that presents a logical problem is Paradox. As we have seen, the proponent of Paradox affirms two self-contradictory propositions and pronounces them both ultimately true in their current form. Such a position undermines the law of noncontradiction and reduces the assertion in question to a nonsensical statement on par with the concept of a square-circle.

We are now in position to evaluate the commitments of Schaeffer and Lewis on this subject. In the remainder of this chapter we will recap the positions of these men, identify the problems that surface in their formulations and consider some proposed solutions. Finally, we will suggest some apologetic considerations in light of our soteriological study. We start with Schaeffer.

Schaeffer: Perfect Balance or Self-Contradiction?

As we have seen, Schaeffer was deeply committed to both a libertarian notion of freedom and a total, unconditional form of predestination. He believed that both doctrines are ultimately true but humans are incapable of harmonizing these two positions with their finite minds. Schaeffer offered a pair of models, the perfectly balanced mobile and the picture of a Ping-Pong ball bouncing back and forth in perfect rhythm, as a way of bringing some measure of plausibility to his proposal. In the end, however, there is no satisfying cerebral solution. The proper response to this mystery should not be intellectual frustration or artificial harmonizations but rather an attitude of humility, reverence and worship.

At first glance it would appear Schaeffer has successfully safeguarded the necessary attributes of both God and humanity. His position affirms a complete notion of divine providential control but protects God's justice and goodness by attributing libertarian, first-cause freedom to humans. In so doing, humans are not only accountable creatures but capable of rational thought, meaningful communication, aesthetic appreciation and moral judgments. On the basis of biblical authority, Schaeffer affirms both doctrines and pronounces the whole matter irreconcilable by finite rationality.

A closer look at Schaeffer's position, however, reveals two points of tension in his thought. The first is a glaring inconsistency with the inner logic of his own Reformed tradition. Though Schaeffer affirmed the teaching of the Westminster Confession in the arena of total, unconditional predestination, he parts company with the divines over the nature of human freedom. Schaeffer does not acknowledge this point and would certainly have resisted such a suggestion, yet a brief analysis should sufficiently substantiate this claim.[14]

The third chapter of the Westminster Confession, entitled "Of God's Eternal Decrees," makes the position of the Westminster framers quite clear. The first article reads:

> God from all eternity, did, by the most wise and holy counsel of His own will, freely, and unchangeably ordain whatsoever comes to pass: yet so, as thereby neither is God the author of sin, nor is violence offered to the will of the creatures; nor is the liberty or contingency of *second causes* taken away, but rather established.[15] (emphasis ours)

Two important points are revealed in this statement. First, God is the cause of all that transpires. Before the beginning of time, God predestined "whatsoever comes to pass," the full gamut of reality from start to finish. His sovereignty requires complete determinism of all events.[16] But the second point is of equal importance, for the Westminster divines realized the need to protect God's innocence. Though God ultimately determines every action, he must not be held accountable for sin. The only way the Creator can escape culpability is by holding the proximate or second causes accountable for wrongdoing, and the only way second causes can be considered morally responsible is if their choices are freely executed. It should be clear where this is leading. The only model that affirms both a complete notion of determinism and human freedom is the paradigm of soft determinism.

As we have already noted, however, Schaeffer clearly affirms a libertarian notion of freedom and, in so doing, parts company with not only the Westminster Confession but with the logical position of traditional Calvinism on this pivotal point. The paradigm of soft determinism is clearly discernable in the teaching of Reformed patriarchs like John Calvin and Jonathan Edwards, whose positions require some form of compatibilism to hold together total, unconditional predestination, divine justice and human accountability.[17] In his *Institutes* Calvin writes, "Man falls according as God's providence ordains, but he falls by his own fault."[18]

Schaeffer is certainly not alone in resisting this compatibilistic view of human freedom. Many contemporary theistic philosophers have suggested that soft determinism simply does not account for a legitimate notion of freedom.[19] They insist that for an act to be free it must be more than just a willing choice, there must also be the real live possibility of doing otherwise. How we choose must be genuinely up to us. According to William Abraham, "Everything hangs at this point on its account of human freedom. Without this, God becomes accountable for all moral evil, and he seems unjust for punishing the reprobate."[20]

Though the proximate cause of free actions for the theological soft determinist is internal, the antecedents of those actions are ultimately controlled from without, by God. Wishes, desires and intentions are internal but are traced back to the ultimate antecedent, namely, God, the ordainer of all things. God's role in this model would seem to be similar to that of the hypnotist who can prompt certain desires and responses, which in turn lead to a prescribed action.[21] The will is manipulated and there is no real possibility of choosing otherwise.

The soft determinist might disagree at this juncture, suggesting that a person could choose otherwise in any given situation, if that person had willed or wanted to. But this is the point: the only way the person could have willed or wanted anything differently is if the previous causes and conditions also had been different. And these previous causes and conditions could only have been different if the events and circumstances prior to them had been different. It should be apparent where this line of reasoning is leading us: through a determined web of nonnegotiable causal connections that ultimately leads back to its divine antecedent. In short, according to the soft deterministic model, the only way one could have chosen otherwise is if God had determined one to choose otherwise. Thus soft determinism does not offer a sufficient expression of freedom, that is, the ability to choose between two or more live options. It is mere illusion—there really is no alternative to what God has willed.

The position of the Westminster Confession, which requires compatibilism, intends to safeguard divine glory. But, ironically, this position actually undercuts it. If humans are held accountable for their second-cause sinful actions, then does it not stand to reason that humans also should be given credit for their second-cause good deeds? The sword cuts both ways. The reprobate do the evil they desire, but they cannot do otherwise; the elect do the good they desire, but they cannot do otherwise. Either all second-cause deeds are the responsibility of humans or none of them are. If all decisions and actions are a result of God's choice, then the reprobate can stand before God and be completely justified in saying they could not have avoided acting as they did considering the desires, beliefs and convictions God allotted them. But if humans are responsible for their second-cause actions, then the elect will be equally justified in taking pride in their decision to choose Christ and pursue good deeds. Either God is unjust for punishing those who could not have done otherwise, or he has provided an opportunity for humans to boast in their own salvation. Neither is a biblical option.

One of the problems with theological compatibilism is that adherents are often misled by the surface grammar of the language when it comes to the issue of human freedom in salvation. While God is the primary agent in salvation, he is not the only agent. To ensure freedom, humans are agents too. Does such a view allow for pride? No more so than for the alcoholic who willingly goes to a rehabilitation clinic for assistance in overcoming his addiction. The alcoholic cannot shake the bondage of the drug on his own, but he would not have been in position to break the chains of the addiction if he had not availed himself of the assistance the clinic provides.[22] In a similar sense, there is a dual agency at work in the mysterious process of salvation. God is the initiator, filling his world with prevenient and saving grace. He tenaciously seeks the lost, wooing them, convicting them and drawing them to himself. Yet sinners can be saved only if they freely cooperate with the grace that is offered.

Presumably, the compatibilism of traditional Calvinism was the type of "theological determinism" Schaeffer repudiated at Westminster Seminary. The extent to which Schaeffer realized the problems with this paradigm is uncertain, but even a cursory reading of his corpus reveals a consistent, careful resistance to many forms of determinism. Though Schaeffer never overtly rejected the teaching of the Westminster Confession on this issue, it is clear that the divines would never have attributed first-cause freedom to humans, something Schaeffer emphatically insists on. Schaeffer is so emphatic that he rests the integrity of the entire gospel upon this issue: "The whole of Christian theology and every Christian answer falls to the ground if we allow a previous deterministic conditioning to enter in at this point. There is a unit of personality which makes a true choice in the thought-world, which in turn becomes a true first cause of an external result."[23] Schaeffer appears to have a clear understanding that first-cause or libertarian freedom is the only type of freedom that can account for God's justice and the significance of humanity and history.

Though Schaeffer never acknowledged this key point of departure from traditional Reformed theology, some staunch Calvinists noticed the tension in Schaeffer's thought. R. K. McGregor Wright, author of *No Place for Sovereignty: What's Wrong with Freewill Theism?* recalls a time when he confronted Schaeffer with this inconsistency. Wright asked Schaeffer why, as a confessing Calvinist, he would teach "a version of 'free will' that looked much like Arminianism." Schaeffer said he wanted students to clearly understand that Christianity is different from "the 'determinism' emphasized in the psychology and sociology courses on the secular campus."[24]

This response, however, did not satisfy Wright, who believed Schaeffer's view of freedom could not harmonize with a Reformed understanding of sovereignty. When he pursued this further with Schaeffer, Wright was told that he did not understand the concept of human "autonomy" and that he should reread *The God Who Is There* and *Escape from Reason.* According to Wright, however, the problem was not a matter of defining Schaeffer's notion of autonomy but rather a matter of Schaeffer's unwillingness "to challenge people to be consistent Calvinists by speaking against the free-will theory."[25]

The comments of Cornelius Van Til, one of Schaeffer's (and Wright's) most influential instructors at Westminster, appear to corroborate Wright's sentiments. In a personal letter to Schaeffer, Van Til questions his former student's commitment to consistent Calvinism:

> According to your own stated conviction man is "wonderful" primarily because he is created in the image of God. He is wonderful even after he has sinned. The fall has not reduced him to "junk." Man can "impregnate history." . . . But surely this is true because, in the last analysis, God's plan directs history. Man's freedom, his ability to "influence significant history" . . . is a freedom and ability that works *within* the plan of God. When you say that man is not caught in the *wheels of determinism* you do not mean for one moment to deny that God has determined whatsoever comes to pass in history, including the thoughts and acts of man, do you?[26]

Like a bloodhound hot on the trail of its prey, Van Til, like Wright, sniffs out a view of freedom that is inconsistent with Reformed theology. Indeed, the internal logic of Calvinism demands some form of soft determinism if its account of God's sovereignty and human freedom is to be coherent.[27] Schaeffer presumably was unwilling to live with the inherent problems of five-point Calvinism and consequently opted for first-cause freedom, a maneuver that put him not only at odds with classic Reformed theology but also at odds with his own passionate commitment to the law of noncontradiction.

This brings us to a second and more serious point of tension. Simply put, Schaeffer's view of predestination and human freedom is logically incoherent. To suggest that God is the first cause of everything that comes to pass (total, unconditional predestination) and humans are the first cause of many of their choices (libertarian freedom) is nothing short of a flat-out contradiction, a nonsensical statement. It is a logical impossibility. Schaeffer clearly sensed the tension in his position and recognized the inability of finite rationality to harmonize it. He insisted on holding these self-contradictory propositions in perfect tension, cautioned strongly against tinkering with either doctrine, and believed that these incompatible assertions are both ultimately true in their current form—we just cannot see their compatibility. What we find with Schaeffer then is an appeal to the category of Mystery (true but inexhaustive truth) when in fact he is affirming a Paradox (flat-out contradiction).

One might argue, however, that we have pegged Schaeffer incorrectly, and he really belongs in the category of Temporary Agnosticism instead of Paradox. But this is clearly not the case, because, as we have seen, the temporary agnostic realizes that the two incompatible propositions, temporarily held in tension, cannot both be ultimately true in their current incompatible form and ongoing research and dialogue should be pursued to relieve the logical problem. Schaeffer, to the contrary, insists the Bible teaches both doctrines and they are both essentially, though inexhaustively, true in their current form, but our finite minds cannot relieve the tension. Therefore we should stop seeking a resolution and simply worship God in humility. There is a clear distinction here, and it should now be obvious that Schaeffer is properly placed in Basinger's category of Paradox.

To illustrate further the logical problem of Schaeffer's position, let us briefly consider another soteriological issue: the debate between eternal hell and universal salvation. Some have suggested that there is clear biblical support for both the belief that some people will spend eternity in hell and the belief that all humans will spend eternity in heaven. Walter Hollenweger is one well-known theologian who has recognized this tension and struggled with the balance of evidence.

> What do we do with this diversity of opinions on heaven and hell in the New Testament? We could of course—as has often been done—ignore those lines of interpretation which do not suit our thinking. Or we could also try to harmonize them, a process which does considerable violence to the texts. Barth, Brunner and Althaus leave the case open and state the seemingly contradictory theses together: If we take the Bible seriously we cannot deny Heaven and Hell. And: If we take the Bible seriously we cannot deny universalism. . . . A logical contradiction is no proof against the biblical statements on Hell and Heaven or Universalism.[28]

It is not entirely clear whether Hollenweger is affirming the position of

Paradox or Temporary Agnosticism in this passage, but it does seem clear that he is suggesting we not try to harmonize these disparate citations but fall into rank behind these Continental theologians in affirming two self-contradictory propositions. Most evangelicals, including Schaeffer, would hardly find such a suggestion satisfying. To suggest that all humans will spend eternity in heaven and that some humans will spend eternity in hell is nothing short of a flat-out contradiction, a nonsensical assertion. But Schaeffer's position is no less problematic. To put it in the form Hollenweger has outlined, Schaeffer is essentially saying, "If we take the Bible seriously, we cannot deny that God has determined who will accept salvation and who will not. And if we take the Bible seriously we cannot deny that humans can choose whether or not to accept salvation." Such a proposition cannot exist in both-and terms, for there is no possible way a person could ever choose to accept salvation if God has determined that person to spend eternity in hell. This is every bit as irrational and dissatisfying as the suggestion that some humans will be eternally damned and all humans will be eternally saved.

There might be some who still do not see the problem with such an appeal. It might be argued that the adherent of Paradox is simply acknowledging the unbounded nature of God's knowledge and power. His rational discernment is not only "higher," but "other." Therefore, God's categories of logic are in some way different than ours, and God alone is capable of seeing how two decisively self-contradictory assertions are in fact somehow compatible. Indeed, this would appear to be one way of interpreting Schaeffer's stirring conclusion to his lecture entitled *God's Sovereignty and Man's Significance:* "Our God is so infinite that He can make history with significance, man with significance, and yet retain His total infinity. This is our God."[29] In light of the way Schaeffer defines these concepts, it certainly seems he is insisting that God's power is not even constrained by the human categories of logic. But if this is the position Schaeffer is taking here, it is inconsistent with one of the foundational premises of his entire apologetic, namely, the necessity of the law of noncontradiction.

In *The God Who Is There* Schaeffer outlines the necessary criteria for a viable theory on any subject: "(A) The theory must be noncontradictory and must give an answer to the phenomenon in question. (B) We must be able to live consistently with our theory."[30] Schaeffer believed the first criterion, the law of noncontradiction, is the basis for all knowledge and communication. He consistently affirmed the belief that God has given us true but inexhaustive truth. In other words, God's knowledge does not contradict our knowledge; it is higher but not other. We bear the divine image, even after the Fall, and share God's categories of thought. These categories form the rational framework for interpreting reality and set the parameters for intelligible communication. Without common categories of logic, we would have no way of distinguishing fact from falsehood, which would lead to all sorts of conflicting, self-contradictory truth claims. And we would also have no way of knowing whether or not our communication with other humans and with God is accurate and meaningful. In short, without the law of noncontradiction, humans have a full-scale epistemological crisis.

This leads us to the crux of Schaeffer's problem. His view of predestination, divine election and human freedom does not meet his own criteria for a viable theory. He is affirming self-contradictory statements as ultimately true propositions and, consequently, undermines his staunch commitment to the law of noncontradiction. Schaeffer is therefore guilty of harboring an incoherent worldview: a dualistic, divided field of knowledge—the very charge he so often leveled against the inconsistent beatniks, existentialists, pantheists and naturalists he continually confronted. On this critical issue, however, it is Schaeffer himself who constructed a split-story abode.

We will discuss the unified field of knowledge in greater detail in chapter seven, but for now we must offer a brief preview to illustrate the severity of Schaeffer's problem. If Schaeffer insisted on anything, it was a unified field of knowledge. Since Jesus Christ is Lord over all reality, there should be no duality in life. There can be no artificial dichotomy between the natural and supernatural, the secular and the sacred, science and religion, reason and faith. But Schaeffer was convinced that twentieth-century humanity could not arrive at a unified vision of reality because its basic presupposition (naturalistic determinism) excluded the possibility of true, first-cause freedom, a prerequisite for all that is meaningful in life: love, relationships, significance, morality and the like. But modern people cannot live with the implications that they are machines, so they have built an artificial second story where meaning can reside, completely cut off from the lower story world of naturalistic determinism. Ultimately, however, such a dualistic existence is unlivable, because God has made humans to exist as integrated beings. According to Schaeffer, this autonomous basis for reality, in this case naturalistic determinism, eventually destroys all the components of the upper story.

The lesson is: Whenever you make such a dualism and begin to set up one autonomous section below, the result is that the lower consumes the upper. This has happened time after time in the last few hundred years. If you try artificially to keep the two areas separate and keep the autonomous in one area only, soon the autonomous will embrace the other.[31]

In *Escape from Reason,* Schaeffer offers a picture of twentieth-century dualism:

NATURE—PHYSICS, SOCIAL SCIENCES AND PSYCHOLOGY—
DETERMINISM

The above chart illustrates this dualistic, divided field of knowledge with all-encompassing, naturalistic determinism forming the foundation of the home.[32] Everything is caught in the wheels of a clockwork universe. But since humans cannot live like machines, an artificial room is constructed to house all that is meaningful upstairs. But, ultimately, the intuitive need for unified cohabitation erodes the flimsy second-story floor, collapsing all meaning and purpose into the relentless jaws of complete determinism.

By now it should be apparent that Schaeffer is unknowingly tossing stones at his own glass house, for he too has constructed a two-story home. The only difference is that in Schaeffer's house, God has moved from the upper story to the lower story, and now stands behind nature as the ultimate determinator of reality. Schaeffer valiantly tries to keep the two incompatible compartments of libertarian freedom (and all that comes with it, namely, love, rationality, significance and morals) and total, unconditional predestination separate under the guise of "balance," but this arrangement is destined for the same sort of fate as the dualistic proposals he rejects. No type of complete determinism, naturalistic or theistic, can make provision for true, significant first-cause freedom. And no type of flimsy, artificial dualism can keep complete determinism from devouring all meaning and significance in life. We can illustrate Schaeffer's split-story structure accordingly:

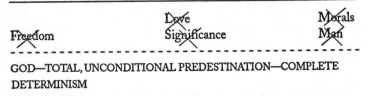

GOD—TOTAL, UNCONDITIONAL PREDESTINATION—COMPLETE
DETERMINISM

This dualistic perspective not only discredits Schaeffer's claim to a unified field of knowledge but undermines his primary apologetic strategy as well. His apologetic methodology is designed to force unbelievers to the logical point of tension or inconsistency in their thinking. Once this point of tension is encountered, Schaeffer "takes the roof off" the person's house, exposing a two-story interior. With the self-contradictory claims identified and confronted, Schaeffer is in position to present the good news of historic, orthodox Christianity as the only fully self-consistent alternative. There is only one problem: Schaeffer's vision of Christianity is not self-consistent either. While forcing others to discard their worldview at the point of tension, Schaeffer tenaciously clings to an artificial two-story paradigm predicated upon Paradox. Once the non-Christian discovers the appeal to Paradox on the part of Schaeffer, what criterion can keep the unbeliever from executing a similar maneuver? Schaeffer's primary apologetic approach is to expose the unbeliever's inconsistencies, but if Paradox is good for the goose, why not the gander? This dualistic doctrinal position presents a formidable challenge to Schaeffer's apologetic methodology.

Schaeffer's Options
Schaeffer's position in its current form presents a serious problem. If safeguarding the law of noncontradiction is a nonnegotiable necessity, as we believe it is, Schaeffer has no alternative but to reevaluate his perspective. There are three potential maneuvers that could relieve the tension and eliminate the logical problem.

The first option is to maintain a dual commitment to total, unconditional predestination and libertarian freedom but exchange the incoherent paradoxical perspective for the weaker position of Temporary Agnosticism. This maneuver would allow Schaeffer to hold both propositions in tension until a harmonious scriptural solution surfaces. Such a shift, however, would require the admission that the paradoxical perspective is self-contradictory and would ultimately require him to revise either his understanding of divine sovereignty or his understanding of human freedom. Though Temporary Agnosticism is a coherent option, it seems Schaeffer is generally dissatisfied with the wait-and-see approach: "No one can live with this answer for it simply is not possible to hold one's breath and wait until some solution is found in the future."[33] In short, this maneuver would reclaim Schaeffer's first criterion for a viable theory (the law of noncontradiction) but sacrifice the second (the ability to live consistently with one's hypothesis).

If Schaeffer would not shift to Temporary Agnosticism, only two options remain: either he could modify his view of freedom or he could modify his view of predestination. We have already detailed the logical problems with the traditional Reformed perspective, so exchanging libertarianism for some kind of compatibilistic freedom would not lead Schaeffer out of the jaws of theological determinism. This only leaves one option: rethinking the doctrine of total, unconditional predestination. Since Schaeffer was committed to a notion of total predestination, he might have found some sort of Molinist perspective plausible.

Molinism refers to the belief system of medieval theologian Luis de Molina. The key idea in Molinism is the notion of "middle knowledge," God's awareness of what all possible persons would freely do in all possible circumstances and scenarios. Molina's view was that God providentially ordered the world in light of his knowledge of the free choices humans would make in every possible situation. There is "no chance back of God" because God chooses which scenarios to actualize, yet humans truly influence history and make true, first-cause choices. Such a perspective would allow a substantial view of providence (though not unconditional predestination) and libertarian freedom to harmoniously coexist. What Schaeffer would sacrifice with such a maneuver would be the heart of the Reformed perspective, since the doctrine of middle knowledge was repudiated by the Council of Dort.[34] Calvinism insists that God knows the future because he has determined it, and is not based on the foreknowledge of any future free choice. Molinism turns the tables, insisting that God perceives the precise choice every person would freely make in every situation, then he simply actualizes the world he chooses, making use of his middle knowledge in this process. A middle knowledge maneuver would indeed sever Schaeffer's claim to traditional Calvinism, but his staunch commitment to libertarian freedom has already left him out of sync with the inner logic of the Reformed perspective. This option would simply resolve Schaeffer's most disconcerting problem—his violation of the law of noncontradiction.

Lewis: The Problematic Pragmatic Proposal

Schaeffer and Lewis held similar views on freedom, but they articulated significantly different perspectives on foreknowledge, predestination and providence. In fact, Lewis believed discussion of foreknowledge and predestination is really misleading, for God exists outside time in the Eternal Now. There is no such thing as "fore" or "pre" with God; he sees all reality in one simultaneous moment. But despite this dismissal of foreknowledge and predestination, properly speaking, Lewis does affirm a robust notion of providence. Everything unfolds according to a divine plan, but this plan is based, at least in part, on human free choice. The precise interrelationship between these choices and divine causation is unknowable from our limited human perspective. Though this baffling mystery cannot be resolved in this life, Lewis is certain that the proper understanding of divine election will not rule out the significance of human choice. With a cognitive solution out of reach, Lewis offers a pragmatic course of action: We should attribute our own virtues and other people's vices to divine agency and our own vices and other people's virtues to human freedom. Lewis apparently believes this approach leads to a proper sense of charity and humility.

Lewis is generally a clear and helpful interpreter, but some of his comments on this subject reveal uncharacteristic confusion and ambiguity. Consider first the matter of foreknowledge. Lewis held the questionable belief that knowledge of the future excludes the power of contrary choice. But this assertion is simply misleading, as the following illustration should sufficiently show. Imagine a time machine that allows travel between the present and the future. One day you hop aboard and fast-forward twenty-four hours into the future, where you observe your best friend eating a bowl of soup for dinner. As he is wiping his bowl clean, you return to the previous day with this knowledge intact. You know for certain your friend will eat a bowl of soup for dinner tomorrow, but does this knowledge in any way affect your friend's choice of cuisine? It is hard to see how. Your friend will indeed eat that bowl of soup, but your knowledge of that future free choice has no bearing on the matter. You simply observed the execution of the choice; your knowledge did not determine the choice, nor is it evidence that the choice has been determined. Contrary to what Lewis suggests, it is hardly clear that foreknowledge is evidence that an action has been predestined or determined.

This first error leads to a second area of confusion. Because he believed prior knowledge is evidence of determinism, Lewis invoked the Eternal Now perspective to preserve human liberty. But this maneuver does not relieve the tension, because the real challenge Lewis senses is not the existence of divine foreknowledge but rather the existence of divine certainty concerning particular events that are to us still future. The problem is not the advance knowledge of your friend's culinary choice but rather the certain knowledge of that choice. And if certain knowledge is the problem, then shifting God's perspective from "prior" to "present" does not resolve the issue. If foreknowledge is a problem for freedom, so is eternal knowledge; if eternal knowledge is not a problem, neither is foreknowledge. In either case, what God knows with certainty will surely happen. But as we have already seen from the time machine illustration, this is really a moot point. Certain knowledge, either from a prior or present perspective, does not mean the action has been predestined or determined. So we see that Lewis appears to have made much ado about nothing.

Another area of confusion swirls around the issue of freedom. In most instances Lewis possesses clear libertarian leanings. This is especially evident when he discusses his view of the atonement and the need for human cooperation in the process of salvation. Lewis is quite certain that humans possess the power of contrary choice, the option to either cooperate with God's grace or refuse it. But his account of an event leading up to his own conversion, is much more ambiguous. In this account Lewis appears to slip between libertarian freedom one moment and some type of compatibilism the next. During a bus ride, Lewis sensed two live options before him, what he called "a moment of wholly free choice. . . . I could open the door or keep it shut."[35] Either he could accept the overture of God or he could reject it. Both options seemed viable, and he chose to cooperate with God. But suddenly Lewis shifts gears and offers what appears to be a completely different angle of vision:

> I say, "I chose," yet it did not really seem possible to do the opposite. . . . You could argue that I was not a free agent, but I am more inclined to think that this came nearer to being a perfectly free act than most that I have ever done. Necessity may not be the opposite of freedom, and perhaps a man is most free when, instead of producing motives, he could only say, "I am what I do."[36]

Now this statement certainly has a compatibilistic ring to it. Lewis makes it clear that he made a choice, but it did not seem as if he could have done otherwise. In addition, he suggests the possibility that freedom and determinism might not be mutually exclusive propositions after all. It would appear that Lewis has placed two very different views of freedom side by side in this account. How are we to explain this apparent contradiction? How could Lewis, a ruthlessly logical thinker, affirm the power of contrary choice and also say "it did not really seem possible to do the opposite"?

The answer to this puzzling question might be found in an interview conducted by Sherwood Wirt just months before Lewis's death. In this interview Wirt asks Lewis about his conversion and whether or not he made a decision for Christ at that time. Lewis refers back to his enigmatic comments in *Surprised by Joy:* "Well, I would say that the most deeply compelled action is also the freest action. By that I mean, no part of you is outside the action."[37] This is an important point of clarification, for Lewis is not saying that determinism and freedom are compatible but that a true free choice is a holistic act, one that involves the entire person—mind, will and emotions. The freest act is the one in which there is no internal tension, each faculty is on board, harmoniously pulling in the same direction. And if all your faculties are properly aligned, so that no part of your being is "outside the action," then certainly you will execute that choice, at least so far as it is up to you. Such a scenario could easily be viewed as the freest possible act because there is no resistance or internal struggle. This suggestion resonates with Schaeffer's belief that a true free choice is not caused by any particular outside force or internal faculty but rather "involves the whole personality."[38]

But in what sense is such an action compelled? After all, one certainly can be fully committed to a decision without a sense of compulsion. What was Lewis suggesting? It could be that Lewis was saying that a holistic action, one that receives the full endorsement of the entire person, is compelled in the sense that one would not do otherwise. Why would you? If your mind, will and emotions are the faculties involved in arriving at a decision and these faculties are in complete agreement, then surely you would make that choice. But it does not follow from the assertion that one *would not* do otherwise that one *could not* have done otherwise. For you ultimately had the power to choose which thoughts, emotions and impulses to attend to in the process of coming to internal consensus on the issue at hand. This might be the point of confusion for Lewis. If one could not have done otherwise, then we have a determined act. But if one possesses the power to do otherwise but simply would not, given the internal consensus on the matter, then this is not paradoxical or deterministic at all. If this is the point Lewis intended when he said, "The most deeply compelled action is also the freest action," then it would appear that he has confused the concept of a compelled choice, one that could not have been otherwise, with a decisive choice, one that simply would not have been otherwise given the settled state of your decision-making faculties.

It is also quite possible that a passionate aversion to the unhealthy practice of obsessive introspection influenced Lewis's perspective. Consider again the language used in this account: "Necessity may not be the opposite of freedom, and perhaps a man is most free when, instead of *producing motives*, he could only say, 'I am what I do' " (emphasis ours).[39] Lewis clearly despised the modern Freudian practice of combing the deep recesses of one's psyche in a constant quest for motivating factors and influences. He recognized this destructive tendency in his own life prior to conversion and later criticized the widespread overpsychologization of the modern world.[40] He also fought against this tendency as a literary critic, encouraging students and colleagues to let the text speak for itself instead of engaging in an incessant search for literary influences and psychological motivations. Lewis called this practice the "Personal Heresy."[41]

We certainly resonate with Lewis's objection to obsessive introspection. Such an activity is surely misguided and counterproductive. But there is no parallel between fussy self-reflection and the freedom-determinism discussion. For the latter is not primarily a matter of discerning what particular motives, reasons or outside forces influenced someone in a given situation.

Nor is it a matter of knowing the precise interrelationship between divine causation and human agency. Rather, the freedom-determinism discussion is a foundational philosophical and theological issue that holds implications for how we understand God's character, in particular his love for all persons and his genuine desire to save everyone. We would suggest that one can discuss the issue of freedom and determinism without succumbing to unhealthy introspection. Indeed, one can affirm the power of contrary choice, a strong notion of God's enabling grace, and the importance of a holistic, integrated response, while repudiating self-saturation and an excessive quest for motivating factors and influences.

However we explain Lewis's enigmatic autobiographical comments, there appears to be ample evidence to rule out a commitment to compatibilism and unconditional divine election. Consider the following four points.

First, even a deterministic reading of Lewis's account does not eliminate the power of contrary choice on the whole. Determinism of a particular choice, by definition, rules out the possibility of choosing otherwise in that particular context, but it is quite possible that God could determine some choices without determining all. But, one might say, if God determines who will be converted is this not an affirmation of the Reformed doctrine of unconditional election? The answer to this question is no. For, unlike the Calvinist, Lewis does not believe salvation is secured at conversion but rather requires ongoing human cooperation and complete transformation before heaven is certain. According to Lewis, true believers can fall from grace if they choose to stop cooperating with God's transformational plan. Even if Lewis did hold open the possibility that God determines the conversion of some, this does not entail the belief that God has elected those people to final salvation. A thorough process of definite libertarian human cooperation and complete transformation is required after conversion for one's election to be sure.

Second, it is hard to make sense of Lewis's Eternal Now maneuver from a compatibilistic perspective. The whole purpose of the maneuver is prompted by the belief that the existence of foreknowledge is evidence that contrary choice is not possible. But the compatibilist does not believe contrary choice is essential for one to be free. So Lewis's appeal to the Eternal Now perspective reveals clear libertarian intuitions. Along the same lines, Lewis believed there are some things that even God cannot do, namely, determine his creatures to freely choose him. This perspective undermines the core compatibilistic belief that complete determinism and human freedom are fully consistent concepts.

Third, we must consider the context and tone of the comments in question. When Lewis discusses freedom and determinism in a formal, theological context, his views reveal a clear endorsement of libertarian freedom. In fact, much of his corpus is bound by this theme. In contrast, his view of freedom begins to blur when he discusses this subject in personal, informal letters and in an autobiographical account. In these subjective moments it is worth noting the qualified way in which he presents his cautious comments and feelings. Consider again this passage from *Surprised by Joy:* "It did not really *seem* possible to do the opposite. . . . Necessity *may not* be the opposite of freedom" (emphasis ours).[42] One would be ill-advised to draw any hard and fast conclusions from such subjective and tentative evidence.

Fourth, Lewis believes that God has a total providential plan, but this plan is based, at least in part, on nondetermined human choices. This, of course, is contrary to the traditional Reformed belief that God's plan does not in any way depend upon the activity of humans. These four points make it sufficiently clear that Lewis did not endorse compatibilism and unconditional divine election.

Though Lewis did not affirm compatibilism, he ultimately found himself with the same problems. For his inability to resolve the freedom-determinism issue led to the problematic pragmatic proposal of attributing one's virtues and other people's vices to God and one's vices and other people's virtues to human agency. Such a position is problematic because it undercuts God's glory and blamelessness and places Lewis in the same boat as the compatibilist by making God the author of sin and humans responsible for their good deeds. In addition, this maneuver cuts against the grain of Lewis's consistent aversion to pragmatism over truth. Apparently in this situation Lewis thought truth could not be had, so pragmatism was the best available option.

The Nonsense of Theological Nonsense

So what form of mystery is Lewis affirming? We should first note that Lewis does not have the same logical problem as Schaeffer. Lewis was quite certain that two self-contradictory statements do not magically become true because one attributes them to divine revelation.

If you choose to say, "God can give a creature free will and at the same time withhold free will from it," you have not succeeded in saying *anything* about God: meaningless combinations of words do not suddenly acquire meaning simply because we prefix to them the two other words "God can." . . . Nonsense remains nonsense even when we talk it about God.[43]

Lewis would never have accepted Schaeffer's paradoxical proposal that total, unconditional predestination and libertarian freedom are both ultimately true. But that is not to say Lewis was unwilling to live with tension. He believed we could possess intellectual clarity on the essentials of the faith, but when it comes to the peripheral matters, we must be willing to live with some measure of cognitive dissonance. As a result, he tended to let each biblical passage or personal experience speak for itself. If the evidence did not harmonize easily, he simply left it unresolved, adopting a temporary agnostic perspective on the matter. He preferred temporary intellectual tension to forced harmonizations. In other words, Lewis often employed the prototypical Anglican via media approach to controversial issues, which highlights the points of common ground and deemphasizes areas of dispute.

But it would not be altogether accurate to label Lewis a thoroughgoing temporary agnostic on this issue. He does appear to opt for Temporary Agnosticism when discussing the subject in the realm of the subjective, informal and particular. But when he discusses the matter in the realm of the objective, analytical and general, his views are more accurately placed in the category of Mystery. Consider *Miracles*, Lewis's most carefully reasoned work. The thesis of this book largely hinges upon a commitment to indeterminacy. Lewis believes that if our thought processes are determined, we have no basis for rationality. So if we are to take our reason seriously, we must assume that humans are nondetermined creatures.[44] This point is particularly significant when we recall that a free action is one that is explained in terms of *reasons*, which, as we previously noted, are distinct from *causes*. Lewis then concludes this book with an appendix in which he offers his vision of how total providence and a libertarian form of freedom harmoniously coexist. So in Lewis's most rigorous work, we find a consistent view of freedom and predestination and a proper appeal to the category of Mystery.

How do we account for this slippage between Temporary Agnosticism and Mystery? The answer might be very simple. When Lewis discusses this subject in the more rigorous philosophical realm he offers a vision of freedom and predestination that is self-consistent and coherent. But when he attempts to translate this subject into the domain of the colloquial and concrete, his clarity clouds. One can certainly understand why, for how could we ever solve this issue in the realm of the particular? We cannot know the precise interrelationship between divine and human causation, nor can we trace a specific action to any particular motive or cause. How could we? Lewis is correct in saying that such a pursuit is pointless.

But does this invalidate the discussion altogether? Surely not. Lewis has simply taken this discussion into a realm where it does not belong. We do not need to know these specifics in order to get to the heart of the matter. The freedom-predestination issue is not about fussy introspection, it is about God's goodness and his desire to save all people. The freedom-predestination issue is not about the precise nature of dual agency, it is about God's justice and an equal opportunity for everyone. The freedom-predestination issue is not about self-autonomy and sinful rationalism, it is about God's revealed truth and a coherent vision of reality. In short, the freedom-predestination issue is about God's character, human significance and a self-consistent worldview. Lewis could have saved himself and his readers a good deal of confusion and problematic advice if he had consistently allowed these important scriptural truths to guide his biblical, theological and experiential reflections.

The Apologetic Considerations

In the last three chapters we have detailed the soteriological systems of Schaeffer and Lewis, identifying some important points of common ground and divergence. So what bearing does all this material have on the apologetic task? We conclude our soteriological study with five apologetic considerations.

1. *Compatibilism undermines God's justice, glory and goodness.* Our critique of soft determinism or compatibilism reveals a paradigm riddled with problematic implications. First, this position undermines God's justice, for all actions and thoughts are ultimately traced back to God's determining will. One does not really have the live option of doing other than what God has determined. Second, this position undermines God's glory, because it holds humans accountable for their second-cause sins. But if humans are held accountable for their second-cause sins, should not the elect be given the credit for their second-cause good deeds? Either God is unjust for punishing those who could not have done otherwise or he has provided a way for humans to boast in their good deeds. Third, this position cannot account for God's goodness, because if God can determine free human choices why has he not determined everyone to freely choose him? If humans need not possess the power of contrary choice in order to be truly free, then what could possibly keep a perfectly loving and entirely good God from predestining all humans to freely choose his offer of salvation? We have yet to hear a plausible response to this critical question. The bottom line is this: libertarianism is the only model of freedom that does justice to both God's character and human significance.

2. *Our soteriology should reflect a libertarian notion of freedom.* If libertarianism is truly necessary to give a satisfying account of God's character and human significance, then our soteriology must reflect a consistent commitment to this view of freedom. It is our contention that Lewis's transformational model does a better job than Schaeffer's legal model in this regard. Three points can be made here. First, a libertarian view of salvation means humans, with the assistance of the Holy Spirit, can either receive God's gift of salvation or reject

it. Unconditional election and libertarian freedom are simply incompatible. Second, a libertarian view of freedom means ongoing, dynamic faith is necessary for salvation, in contrast to a one-time act of faith. If salvation is sealed at conversion, then one's freedom in the most important area of life, one's eternal destiny, has been eliminated. Third, a libertarian view of freedom suggests the concept of true dual agency from beginning to end in the transformation process. And, as Lewis has stated, this will necessarily entail further purification beyond the grave for those who die before the process is complete.

For most Protestant evangelicals, this last suggestion is hard to stomach. This doctrine conjures up visions of unscriptural Middle Age fundraising techniques. Not only that, but from the perspective of the legal model such a doctrine is totally unnecessary. For if God imputes righteousness, forgives past, present and future sins, and promises unilateral transformation at death, then why in the world would we need a doctrine of purgatory? But from the perspective of the transformational model, Lewis's suggestion of postmortem purification is a logical entailment. If salvation is primarily about transformation, and transformation requires human cooperation from beginning to end, then it stands to reason that those who die before the process of purification is complete will have an opportunity for further transformation beyond the grave. In short, Lewis did not endorse the concept of indulgences or other abuses traditionally associated with this doctrine; he simply carried his transformational soteriology to its logical end.

So the question of purgatory cannot be answered on pure exegetical grounds alone. One must push the biblical data to its logical conclusion. If one is convinced that libertarian freedom and Lewis's transformational model make best sense of the biblical data, then a place of purification would appear to be the logical implication. But a place of purification will make no sense if one holds the belief that God unilaterally effects transformation at the point of death, for no further purification would be necessary.

3. We must follow "true" truth wherever it leads. If we are to hold other faith systems to the criterion of logical self-consistency, Christians must with all integrity hold themselves to that very same standard. But this does not always happen, as we have seen with Schaeffer's paradoxical position. If we believe God is a God of logic, order and truth, then we must possess a self-consistent system that embodies true but inexhaustive truth. This means Christians must be willing to think more rigorously about the issue of mystery. If a legitimate point of tension is encountered, we must either follow Lewis into the temporary agnostic camp or rethink our doctrinal position. Paradox will not do. In light of the exhibited need to preserve libertarian freedom, we would encourage readers to explore alternative formulations of divine omniscience and omnipotence that do justice to both the biblical data and the character of God before casting the issue of free will and determinism into the sea of irresolvability.[45]

4. *Theological forthrightness is an apologetic necessity.* There is something dubious about only using unconditional election as a means of assurance and intentionally shrouding this doctrine from the view of unbelievers. This was a problem for Schaeffer. If God has really unconditionally elected some to salvation and passed over the rest, we need not be ashamed of his methodology but should fully own up to this doctrine and the implications that flow from it. Would Schaeffer not insist on forthrightness from his dialogical partners in other faith systems? Surely he would. Again, we must hold ourselves to the same standard. As Christians we should pave the way in the pursuit of truth wherever this may lead. All truth is God's truth, and we should be ashamed of none of it. We would suggest that the very instinct that kept Schaeffer from sharing his belief in unconditional election with unbelievers is an intuitive signal or warning that this doctrine is suspect. If we cannot share our full system with honesty and integrity, then something is amiss.

Along these same lines, we must question the practice of dichotomizing systematic and pastoral theology. Schaeffer held the contradictory concepts of total, unconditional predestination and libertarian freedom in tension, but in a pastoral setting his strategy shifted. Instead of "perfect balance," Schaeffer chose to emphasize the more comforting doctrine while ignoring the problematic implications of his other beliefs.[46] Similarly, Lewis appears to justify his pragmatic proposal under the banner of pastoral or devotional advice. There are times when it is pastorally appropriate to emphasize a particular doctrine, but never in such a way that would misrepresent the total picture of what we truly believe. Likewise, it is inappropriate to offer pastoral advice with implications that cannot stand up to biblical and theological scrutiny. If Jesus Christ is Lord over all reality then there should be consistency between one's pastoral and systematic theology. Schaeffer certainly resonated with this point, insisting that "answers are necessary . . . if I am going to maintain my intellectual integrity, and if I am to keep united my personal, devotional and intellectual life."[47]

We would suggest one way of testing the integrity of one's theology is asking whether its implications can be honestly endorsed when the rubber meets the road. When a child has been murdered, does our view of sovereignty allow us to say with complete integrity and theological consistency that God did not will that child's death? When a loved one is rejecting the faith, can we say with complete integrity and theological consistency that God truly desires the salvation of this person and is doing everything he can to draw this person into the fold? Or is there a hitch in our spirit when a tragic death occurs or a nonbeliever rejects the faith? If we truly believe God has determined all that comes to pass, including brutality toward children and the unconditional damnation of the nonelect, then we must be willing to live with these implications in the real world. If we cannot apply our systematic theology in concrete situations, then something is terribly wrong with our doctrinal position.

5. Apologetics is a systematic enterprise. There is a strong connection between the apologetic task and systematic theology. Some people appear to treat apologetics like a basketball game or soccer match: Whoever accumulates the most points wins. It is simply a matter of sheer quantity. But we would suggest that apologetics is more like assembling a complex jigsaw puzzle. The goal here is to bring a jumbled, confusing array of pieces together into a coherent, ordered vision of reality. In this context, you might say the one with the fewest pieces left over wins.[48] We are not called to simply accumulate vast quantities of disconnected empirical evidence, but rather we are to show how that evidence fits together to form a rational, existentially satisfying picture of reality. It is the task of systematic theology and apologetics to fit these pieces together so the coherence and beauty of the Christian proposal can emerge with clarity to those who are confused by the confounding puzzle of life. If this is true, then our soteriological vision must be coherent, comprehensive and compelling.

The Sharpest Clash Is Yet to Come

Schaeffer understood the need for a coherent, comprehensive and compelling vision. In *The God Who Is There* he suggests that we are in need of a unified view of reality, but it would appear that all we have are disconnected fragments. Reality is like a book, but we only have a small, mutilated portion of the text, about "one inch of printed matter on each page."[49] This is enough to know there is some sort of author but not enough to understand the story. If only we could find the missing sections, we could piece together the fragments into a coherent message.

This is how Schaeffer envisioned the relationship between natural and special revelation. Humans have part of the answer because they are created in the image of God and live in God's universe. But this is not enough information to make sense of reality, because we live in an abnormal, fallen world. We need the generous revelation of Scripture to fill in the gaps and interpret the anomalies of life. When we piece the fragments of natural and special revelation together, a coherent, comprehensive and compelling vision of reality emerges.

But according to Schaeffer this clarity has been clouded in many Christian circles. The twentieth century has produced a new wave of biblical critics who have sliced and reshaped the text so that it no longer coheres with the fragments of natural revelation. A unified vision of reality and the story of God's solution to humanity's plight have given way to a disjointed, dichotomized juxtaposition of faith and special revelation on one side and verifiable facts and natural revelation on the other. That is why Schaeffer insisted on inerrancy. It was his contention that a unified vision of reality could only be protected by a dogged commitment to this doctrine. To Schaeffer, anyone who denies the inerrant quality of Scripture is destined for a divided field of knowledge and a truncated worldview.

Our soteriological study has unearthed some key rifts between Schaeffer and Lewis—the nature of the atonement, eternal security, unconditional election, purgatory and the appeal to Paradox—but the most pointed difference is arguably yet to come. For there is no question that Schaeffer was uncomfortable with some of Lewis's comments on this controversial subject of biblical inspiration. No one knows this better than longtime InterVarsity Press editor James Sire.

Sire recalls the time when he accompanied Schaeffer to the 1973 Christian Booksellers Association Convention in Cincinnati. One evening the pair sauntered down to the edge of the Ohio River, where barges and steamboats were gliding up and down. An off-night for the Reds left typically raucous Riverfront Stadium looming silently over the banks of the river. As the two turned to head back toward the hotel, Schaeffer was in a characteristically dour, reflective mood. Melancholy by nature, he did not often smile or engage in lighthearted, robust laughter. He was a powerful communicator, engaging the mind, will and emotions, but rarely the funny bone.

Sire knew Schaeffer did not like Lewis's stance on biblical inspiration. His mythological interpretation of the creation account, his questioning of the space-time factuality of some Old Testament miracles and his concession to the possibility of reporting errors in the Gospels presented a challenge to the doctrine of biblical inerrancy. Schaeffer was particularly critical of *Reflections on the Psalms* yet refused to publicly challenge this relatively obscure work, fearing it would draw attention to Lewis's deficient view of Scripture and detract from the predominantly positive apologetic influence of his other writings.

During a lull in the conversation, Sire painted an intriguing scenario. He said he would have enjoyed locking Schaeffer and Lewis in a room and climbing up above to eavesdrop. An unusually rich smile spread across Schaeffer's time-worn face. Envisioning the scene in his mind, he turned to

Sire and said, "Oh, if we could have talked, I'm sure he would have come around."[50]

It is our suspicion that Sire is not the only person who would have been fascinated to watch the most influential apologists of our time discuss this important topic. Though we do not necessarily share Schaeffer's certainty regarding the outcome, we suspect such an encounter might have packed Riverfront Stadium that night. Who knows what might have happened? Such a discussion might have offered some hope of spanning the great divide that separates not only Schaeffer and Lewis but much of the evangelical world. The next chapter is a modest attempt to bring Sire's intriguing wish to life.

But it must be the Bible as the Word of God in *everything it teaches*—in matters of salvation, but just as much where it speaks of history and science and morality. If it is compromised in any of these areas, as is unhappily happening today among many who call themselves evangelicals, we destroy the power of the Word of God and put ourselves in the hands of the enemy.[1]

FRANCIS SCHAEFFER

That the over-all operation of Scripture is to convey God's Word to the reader (he also needs inspiration) who reads in the right spirit, I fully believe. That it *also* gives true answers to all the questions (often religiously irrelevant) which he might ask, I don't. The very *kind* of truth we are often demanding was, in my opinion, not even envisaged by the ancients.[2]

C. S. LEWIS

We deny that it is proper to evaluate Scripture according to standards of truth and error that are alien to its usage or purpose. We further deny that inerrancy is negated by Biblical phenomena such as a lack of modern technical precision, irregularities of grammar or spelling, observational descriptions of nature, the reporting of falsehoods, the use of hyperbole and round numbers, the topical arrangement of material, variant selections of material in parallel accounts, or the use of free citations.[3]

THE CHICAGO STATEMENT ON BIBLICAL INERRANCY

5

....

Biblical Authority and Divine Inspiration
The Great Evangelical Divide

*I*N HIS FINAL BOOK, *THE GREAT EVANGELICAL DISASTER,* FRANCIS
Schaeffer describes a vivid scene in the Swiss Alps. Not far from his chalet a
high ridge of rock towers over the surrounding terrain. Frequent snowfalls
cap this ridge with a seamless blanket of fresh powder. Yet this placid unity
is a mere illusion, for when the temperatures rise the true contour of the ridge
divides the melting snow into opposite valleys.

This particular ridge sends part of the moisture into the Rhine River and
eventually the icy waters of the North Sea. The rest of the snow flows into
Lake Geneva and finally the warm waters of the Mediterranean. The frozen
flakes that once settled side by side atop the ridge ultimately end up time
zones apart, in polarized climates.[4]

This natural phenomenon illustrates the decisive nature of a watershed, a
great divide. In the concluding years of his life, Schaeffer believed evangelicalism was precariously straddling a watershed of critical importance: the
issue of biblical authority.

> Within evangelicalism there are a growing number who are modifying
> their views on the inerrancy of the Bible so that the full authority of
> Scripture is completely undercut.... Like the snow lying side-by-side on
> the ridge, the new views on biblical authority often seem at first glance
> not to be very far from what evangelicals, until very recently, have always
> believed. But also, like the snow lying side-by-side on the ridge, the new
> views when followed consistently end up a thousand miles apart.[5]

Schaeffer sketches a gripping portrait of the evangelical dilemma. Yet an increasing number of scholars are questioning its accuracy. Is inerrancy really the watershed issue for the evangelical movement? Can the precise location of the ridge be identified? Are those who hold a differing view of inspiration necessarily destined for the frigid fate of the North Sea? One must certainly wonder if Schaeffer's watershed would have sent C. S. Lewis slip-sliding down the opposite slope.

While Schaeffer devotes a great deal of time and energy to the subject of biblical authority and inspiration,[6] Lewis offers limited commentary.[7] The inerrancy controversy of which Schaeffer speaks reached its pinnacle the decade following Lewis's death and was largely concentrated within North American evangelicalism. Given the somewhat provincial nature of this debate, it is hardly surprising to find Lewis rarely addressing the matter. Inerrancy simply was not a burning issue for him. For Schaeffer, however, this issue was hardly provincial or peripheral. From his early battles with the liberal element in his denomination to his involvement with the International Council on Biblical Inerrancy near the end of his life, Schaeffer consistently demanded that this doctrine must be tenaciously safeguarded if a slide into liberalism is to be averted.[8]

In the following pages we will compare and contrast our apologists' views on the important subject of biblical authority and divine inspiration. We begin with Schaeffer's case for inerrancy, a doctrine many evangelical scholars consider fundamentally flawed and exegetically suspect. But before we evaluate the cogency of Schaeffer's position, we must first identify the issue at stake.

The Epistemological Necessity: Schaeffer's Case for Inerrancy
Francis Schaeffer was deeply entrenched in the culture war of his day. During the 1970s and 1980s he played an instrumental role in enlisting hundreds of thousands of Christians in the prolife movement. He wrote and lectured passionately about the disintegrating moral fiber of Western culture and inspired a generation of believers to stand for biblical values on all fronts. But as much as he opposed abortion, euthanasia and all other forms of autonomous amorality, he believed ethical tensions were merely symptomatic of a much deeper problem. According to Schaeffer, the fundamental problem facing our decadent society at the end of the twentieth century is a nagging lack of certainty: "Epistemology is the central problem of our generation; indeed, the so-called 'generation gap,' is really an epistemological gap, simply because the modern generation looks at knowledge in a way radically different from previous ones."[9]

This crisis in epistemology is linked to the widespread rejection of absolutes. For Schaeffer, absolutes can only find their proper grounding in an inerrant Bible. Without a strong doctrine of inspiration, humanity seems destined to drown in a sea of subjectivism, drenched by the depths of doubt.

For Schaeffer, then, inerrancy is not just another inventory item in the sprawling evangelical storehouse of beliefs. To consider it as such is to misconstrue its role. Rather it is the one doctrine that supports all else, the foundation of the entire structure. Without the strength of inerrancy, the key doctrines of the faith—the Trinity, Incarnation, atonement and resurrection—are all susceptible to the shifting sands of subjectivism. Any other foundation inevitably transforms the Christian domicile into a hopelessly unstable house of cards.

We are now in position to consider the converging pieces of evidence that undergird Schaeffer's case for inerrancy: the argument from human communication, the Bible's self-attestation and the historic stance of the church.

The argument from human communication. In an appendix to *He Is There and He Is Not Silent,* Schaeffer argues that the battle over inerrancy and propositional revelation is primarily a conflict at the presuppositional level.[10] If one holds naturalistic assumptions—an impersonal beginning in a closed system of cause and effect—the very suggestion of verbalized communication between an uncreated, personal God and a created, personal being is not merely unlikely, it is sheer nonsense. Such a scenario is an a priori impossibility within a naturalistic framework. If one holds Christian assumptions, however—a personal beginning in a limited system of cause and effect open to supernatural influence—the proposition of verbalized communication between the infinite-personal Creator of the universe is not only possible but indeed quite plausible.

According to Schaeffer, most people who challenge inerrancy, including some within the Christian fold, are guided by naturalistic assumptions. He believes most critics have not rejected inerrancy "because of the consideration of detailed problems objectively approached, but because they have accepted, either in analyzed fashion or blindly, the other set of presuppositions."[11]

We might construe this argument for inerrancy as a track and field event. Imagine Schaeffer as a hurdler. He glances down the asphalt lane and identifies three distinct barriers separating him from the finish line. But strangely enough these hurdles are staggered in height, becoming progressively less challenging as the race proceeds. Schaeffer walks down the track to gain a closer look at these peculiar constructions. Upon careful scrutiny the first two hurdles, Christian presuppositions and propositional revelation, are clearly the most formidable. Once these are cleared, the diminutive hurdle of inspiration is all that separates Schaeffer from the prize of inerrancy.

But that first hurdle is exceptionally high. Schaeffer offers a curious appeal. Instead of clearing the highest hurdle at the beginning of the race, he wonders if it would be possible to place it at the end. If he can move the presuppositional hurdle to the rear, Schaeffer appears to believe that it, too, will somehow conform to the staggered form and diminish in size. His opponent agrees to move the presuppositional hurdle to the rear for the sake of starting the race.

For Schaeffer's argument to work the skeptic must momentarily suspend his naturalistic assumptions. This approach allows Schaeffer the luxury of laying out his hypothesis without first proving his foundational beliefs. Presumably, Schaeffer believes the validity of his Christian presuppositions will come into focus once the cumulative force of the theory has been properly detailed. Or, to stick with our metaphor, Schaeffer appears to believe the accrued momentum of the sprint will successfully propel him over this final and decisive hurdle.

Given the temporary assumption of Christian presuppositions, Schaeffer builds his case for propositional revelation upon the traditional view of an Anselmian conception of God[12] and a human race created in the image of God with the ability to communicate. The argument progresses as follows. If God is infinite, he is powerful enough to communicate to finite humanity. Though finitude will never fully comprehend the infinite, accurate communication is nevertheless possible. The ongoing successful transfer of information between impaired, limited beings is a confirmation of this truth. If finite human beings can exchange accurate information, surely they are capable of receiving some measure of accurate information from an infinite being. But according to traditional Christian claims, God is not only infinite, and therefore capable of communication, but also personal, and therefore motivated to connect with his creation. This combination of ability and desire is a potent epistemological guarantee. Buttressed by uncompromising love and veracity, the impeccable delivery of the divine message is all but assured, as is the successful negotiation of the hurdle of propositional revelation. Schaeffer concludes the only way to rule out the possibility of limited but accurate propositional revelation is to cling to naturalistic presuppositions. If one is open to the possibility of supernatural interjection, then the idea of communication between the infinite and the finite is a viable option.

Once God's ability and desire are established, we must consider the means by which this type of communication might be accomplished. Though God could have delivered a detailed telegram to the summit of Mount Sinai, he appears to have taken a different course of action. According to orthodox Christianity, God has not only chosen to disclose himself *to* humanity but *through* humanity. Schaeffer finds the whole matter of inspiration a mere molehill once the mountain of propositional revelation has been successfully scaled.

> If the uncreated Personal wished to give these communications through individual created personalities in such a way that they would write (in their own individual style, etc.) the exact things the uncreated Personal wanted them to write in the areas of religious truths and things of the cosmos and history—then by this time it is impossible to make an absolute and say that he could not or would not.[13]

Once the hurdles of propositional revelation and inspiration have been mastered, Schaeffer believes the race is won. He is quite baffled by anyone who imagines a perfect God offering anything less than an inerrant message. A divine communiqué that commingles religious truth with historical, scientific and cosmological falsehood seems implausible. "How strange that if the non-created Personal is not a liar or capricious, that he should give 'religious truth' in a book in which the whole structural framework, implicitly and explicitly, is historic, and yet that history be false or confused."[14] Schaeffer offers similar sentiments in *No Final Conflict:* "What sense does it make for a God to give us true religious truths and at the same time place them in a book that is wrong when it touches history and the cosmos?"[15] Schaeffer apparently believes inerrancy is a virtual entailment of the traditional Christian position.

With the hurdles of propositional revelation and inspiration behind him, the presuppositional hurdle, which once loomed large, is now quite manageable for Schaeffer. Through a balance of deductive and inductive appeals to Scripture and empirical evidence, he asks which set of presuppositions, theistic or naturalistic, offers a better explanation of the baffling phenomenon of human communication.

> By this stage, two things should be obvious: first, that from the presupposition that all things started from mass or energy, the idea of revelation or infallibility is unthinkable; and second, that from the presupposition of a personal beginning, these ideas are not unthinkable or nonsense at all. The reasonableness of the matter rests totally on which way one begins. . . . If one does begin with a nonpersonal everything [naturalistic assumptions], there is a question that now really shouts: Is not man-to-man communication equally nonsense? With this presupposition no one has discovered a way to find meaning either in man's speaking to man or in man's hearing, except through an act of faith against his whole basic presuppositional structure. Worse yet, for those who hold this other presupposition, the little men (I and the others) are not content to think that they do not speak meaningfully; and furthermore everything in experience convinces us that the others hear truly, though not exhaustively.[16]

Schaeffer believes there are really only two reasonable sets of presuppositions available. Compared to the presuppositional challenge facing the naturalist, a hurdle in need of a pole vault, Schaeffer encourages the skeptic to avail himself of the explanatory power and internal cohesion of the Christian position. "Well now, in the light of this total confusion to which the other presupposition (the impersonal plus time plus chance) leads us, the presupposition of a personal beginning is worth another very careful look."[17]

Schaeffer is saying that the phenomenon of communication makes sense only from the perspective of Christian presuppositions. Naturalists have two options. Either they can continue to doggedly cling to their set of presuppositions in the face of the evidence, or they can follow the facts and shift their paradigm in favor of the Christian alternative. Once one accepts the Christian alternative, inerrancy is part of the package deal. Schaeffer finds it highly implausible that an all-powerful, all-loving, entirely truthful God would deliver a message laced with falsehood.

The Bible's self-attestation. A critical piece of evidence in Schaeffer's cumulative case for inerrancy is the Bible's own testimony. While the words *inerrancy* and *infallibility* do not actually appear in Scripture, Schaeffer is convinced the whole canon, from Genesis to Revelation, testifies to the irrefutable nature of the doctrine. According to Schaeffer, the key to unlocking the issue of inspiration is found in the first book of the Bible. A commitment to interpreting all fifty chapters of Genesis as space-time history is pivotal. Inerrancy stands or falls with the opening pages of Scripture. In *No Final Conflict* Schaeffer offers two complementary streams of evidence. The internal evidence focuses on the literary thread that unifies the first book of the Pentateuch, while the external evidence reveals how Jesus, Paul and other biblical figures treat the Genesis accounts.

Schaeffer's argument for internal unity rests upon the assumption that the second half of Genesis is commonly interpreted as space-time history. In other words, Abraham, Isaac and Jacob are seen as real people who lived at a specific time in a particular location. With the commonly accepted historicity of these patriarchs in place, Schaeffer appeals to the literary continuity between the first eleven chapters of Genesis and the balance of the book.

Schaeffer offers two strands of evidence for internal continuity. The first deals with the genealogies. The author uses the same terminology and literary structure throughout the entire book of Genesis when origins are detailed. From 5:1, "This is the book of the generations of Adam," to 37:2, "These are the generations of Jacob," we find the same consistent treatment throughout. Schaeffer cites the literary principle of parallelism, suggesting parallel literary treatment requires parallel interpretation. If Jacob is viewed as a historical figure, Adam should be treated likewise.

The other strand of evidence Schaeffer offers for internal continuity is what he considers a rather unique literary pattern. The author deals with the inessential matters tersely, then proceeds to develop the more important material. Schaeffer writes, "We can consider, as an example, those places where an unimportant son is dealt with quickly and then an important son is dealt with in detail. And the subsequent movement of biblical history flows on from the important son."[18] On the basis of these literary threads, Schaeffer believes the entire book is properly understood as a seamless whole. Either it is all historical fact, or entirely fiction.

Schaeffer then turns to the external evidence to confirm his belief that Genesis is indeed a space-time account throughout. According to Schaeffer, a careful study of the New Testament reveals a uniform treatment of the first half of Genesis as history. From Luke's genealogy to the numerous Pauline passages that parallel Adam and Christ, Schaeffer believes the evidence to be undeniable. In light of this data, Schaeffer finds the alternatives to a literal interpretation highly problematic. If one denies the space-time authenticity of the Genesis accounts, one must attribute uniform error to the New Testament authors. Such a maneuver undermines the credibility of the authors, and, consequently, the veracity of the entire New Testament. An equally troubling entailment for those who interpret Genesis figuratively is the undeniable parallelism in Paul's treatise on the first and second Adams. Apparently Schaeffer believes the figurative interpretation of Adam opens the door to a figurative interpretation of Jesus. Therefore, the integrity of Scripture and the historicity of Jesus are inextricably bound up with a space-time interpretation of the entire book of Genesis.

The historic stance of the church. Ironically, much of the debate within evangelicalism has swirled at this point. Conservative evangelicals have traditionally greeted appeals to tradition with grave skepticism but in the arena of inspiration such appeals are common. Apparently, Schaeffer hopes to simply corroborate the previous arguments already outlined. He clearly traces his understanding of this doctrine back through Machen, the Princeton theologians, the Reformers, Augustine and ultimately to the Apostles but offers surprisingly little verification that this view of inerrancy has received uniform acceptance. Schaeffer believes the Roman Catholic Church and the Reformers were in essential harmony on this point. Though other problems plagued the church universal, all was well on the inerrancy front.

Schaeffer seems to believe the historical commitment of the church is so well established that a substantiation of this claim is superfluous. He does not cite historical sources, nor does he deal with the apparent anomalies that surface in the writings of Luther, Calvin and Charles Hodge. Rather, he points to Enlightenment rationalism as the pied piper that has led the church away from the historic, homogenous, orthodox understanding of inerrancy. This is precisely what is claimed in the first argument we considered. A shift away from inerrancy is primarily the result of adopting the wrong set of presuppositions. Naturalistic assumptions are the legacy of the Enlighten-ment. Though tradition does not carry the same weight as Scripture's self-at-testation, Schaeffer sees the unwavering continuity between Jesus, the Apostles and two thousand years of church history as a powerful testament to the truth of this doctrine.

The Merits of Critical Rationalism

How should we characterize Schaeffer's tripartite argument for inerrancy? This argument is not cleanly circumscribed, but he appears to be buttressing an a priori hypothesis with confirming pieces of evidence. In other words, Schaeffer incorporates both deductive and inductive streams of thought. A mild circularity seems to emerge, where intuitive expectations and empirical evidence mutually reinforce one another to mold the emerging trajectory of the proposed hypothesis. This type of mutual confirmation makes it difficult to establish which piece of evidence commands epistemic primacy.

William Abraham is one philosopher who has defended the merits of this type of reasoning. He offers an illustration for what he calls *soft rationalism* (or *critical rationalism*). Abraham envisions a man named Smith arriving at his home and finding a large boulder blocking his front door. No immediate explanation for this puzzling occurrence springs to mind. Naturalistic expla-nations (e.g., wind, rockslide) are incapable of accounting for this phenome-non. Then he recalls a conversation he had earlier in the day, in which a friend told him that a mutual acquaintance, a champion weightlifter named Adams, was planning to pull a prank on Smith. Since he had not seen Adams around recently, Smith doubted the plausibility of this threat. Yet the foreboding formation blocking his entrance sheds new light on the matter. The previously dismissed story now appears quite plausible, since placing a large boulder in front of Smith's door is not only something a champion weightlifter *could* do but something he *would* do given certain intents and purposes.[19]

Abraham suggests mutual confirmation of blocked entry and the rumor of a prank work together to synthesize a reasonable hypothesis for the phenomenon. If challenged to give up the belief that Adams placed the object in front of his door, Smith can appeal to the rumor of the prank. Likewise, if challenged to give up the belief that Adams spoke with his friend about the prank, he can appeal to the boulder in front of his door. Abraham is untroubled by the mild circularity of the argument, citing the undeniable nature of mutual supporting pieces of evidence. What ultimately matters is the theory's overall coherence and power to explain the phenomenon in question.[20]

It appears Schaeffer is offering a similar type of hypothesis. The Bible describes the character and intentions of a infinite-personal Creator and claims to be his inerrant, propositional revelation to humanity. An independent appeal to revelation is inconclusive, but when this claim is coupled with two thousand years of church history and the observation of humanity's ability to successfully communicate, the hypothesis gains steam and offers considerable explanatory power. This cumulative case argument for inerrancy is properly considered the cornerstone of Schaeffer's entire epistemology.

Lewis: A Wolf in Sheep's Clothing?

Now that we have identified Schaeffer's position on biblical authority and inspiration, we turn our attention to Lewis. It is not clear which would have troubled Schaeffer more, Lewis's provocative reflections on the subject of biblical authority and inspiration or the relegation of the issue of inerrancy to the periphery. While Schaeffer builds his entire epistemology around an inerrant Bible, Lewis rarely probed the matter. When he did discuss the subject, his thoughts were often partially developed and qualified. This was a typical pattern for Lewis. He forcefully defended the essentials of orthodoxy, while offering only tentative opinions on matters he considered marginal in nature. Undoubtedly, one of the most striking contrasts between Schaeffer and Lewis is the differing weight they assign this issue.

Since Lewis did not offer a detailed, systematic treatment of biblical authority and inspiration, we must rely on an inductive sweep through a variety of material, ranging from his thoughts on literary and biblical criticism to some of his personal correspondence. Though his exact position is not easily identified, one thing is clear: He resists the extremes. This should come as no surprise. Lewis has a love-hate relationship with the fringes of Christendom. He has a knack for captivating readers one moment and confounding them the next. His musings on mythology, purgatory and world religions trouble many conservatives, while his dogged defense of objective truth, the divinity of Christ and the miraculous exasperate many self-avowed liberals. He charms and alienates the extreme opposite elements of his audience with equal ease.

An essay entitled "Modern Theology and Biblical Criticism" is a case in point. Speaking to clergy-in-training, Lewis presents himself as a learned lamb "telling shepherds what only a sheep can tell them."[21] The bulk of his bleating is riddled with affronts to modern theologians and biblical scholars cut from Bultmannian cloth. But just when the conservative is about to offer his final "Amen," Lewis rotates his guns 180 degrees: "You must not, however, paint the picture too black. We are not fundamentalists. We think that different elements in this sort of theology have different degrees of strength. The nearer it sticks to mere textual criticism, of the old sort, Lachmann's sort, the more we are disposed to believe in it."[22] Lewis expresses similar sentiments in *Reflections on the Psalms:* "I have been suspected of being what is called a Fundamentalist. That is because I never regard any narrative as unhistorical simply on the ground that it includes the miraculous. . . . I have to decide on quite other grounds (if I decide at all) whether a given narrative is historical or not."[23]

Unfortunately, conservative evangelicals have too often used carefully selected sections of Lewis's thought to buttress their own cause, while ignoring that which would appear to undercut it. This type of Lewisian proof-texting is illustrated in the writing of Harold Lindsell, a key popularizer of the inerrancy debate during the seventies. In his influential book *The Bible in the Balance,* Lindsell eagerly cites a barrage of anti-Bultmannian attacks from "Modern Theology and Biblical Criticism" but ignores Lewis's critique of fundamentalism, the very position Lindsell seeks to advance.[24] Uninformed readers are naturally left with the impression that this patron saint of evangelicalism is firmly positioned in Lindsell's camp. Yet in writing the foreword to a volume entitled *The Best of C. S. Lewis,* published prior to *The Bible in the Balance,* Lindsell is clearly aware of Lewis's provocative views on biblical inspiration. His discomfort prompts a word of caution. "Lewis is not infallible. I do not agree with him at every point, but I respect his opinions and humility. If he were alive today he would probably admit to having changed some of his ideas for he was willing to learn—a fitting attribute for one whose works make it clear that he was an able scholar and a true Christian gentleman."[25] Lindsell has since confirmed that he had inerrancy in view when writing this paragraph.[26]

These examples illustrate exactly what we must not do with Lewis. First, we must not extract sections of Lewis's thoughts for partisan purposes while ignoring clear statements to the contrary. Second, we must be careful when speculating about what Lewis might have done if he were still alive. After all, Lewis is "dead and can't blow the gaff."[27] When speculation becomes necessary, it must be supported by good and sufficient evidence. And all the evidence in this case points to Lewis's rejecting not only liberalism but fundamentalism as well. Lindsell offers no warrant for making Lewis an "honorary inerrantist."[28] He attributes teachability, academic integrity and

Christian commitment to Lewis and seems to believe the additional component of time would naturally have led the Cambridge scholar to the truth of
inerrancy. Lindsell appears to join Schaeffer in the confident assertion that
sooner or later Lewis "would have come around."

In our investigation we must continually resist the impulse to stuff Lewis
into a prepackaged system—liberal, conservative or otherwise. He defies this
type of uncritical, superficial categorization. Lewis believes an honest, forthright, inductive approach to the textual data is the only way to uncover the
meaning of a given passage. Unearthing Lewis's views on Scripture will
require the same type of open inquiry.

The Holistic Reception

In the next few pages we will consider Lewis's thoughts on biblical authority,
revelation and inspiration. After determining his views on each of these
matters, we will attempt to locate Lewis on Schaeffer's Alpine ridge.

Biblical authority. In the eighth chapter of *The Problem of Pain*, Lewis deals
with possibly the thorniest of all Christian claims, the doctrine of eternal
damnation. This is the one doctrine Lewis would love to scratch from his list
of beliefs. But to do so would be to ignore the weight of the evidence: "It has
the full support of Scripture and, specially, of Our Lord's own words; it has
always been held by Christendom; and it has the support of reason."[29] This
sentence is revealing, for it shows Lewis, a self-confessed nonfundamentalist,
sitting at the table of scriptural authority, even when the chair is uncomfortable and the cuisine unappealing. Lewis swallows hard and digests a doctrine
that clearly causes a great deal of heartburn. This immediately separates him
from many contemporary biblical scholars who simply fashion a hermeneutic
that ensures a reading yielding precisely what they had hoped and expected.

This reference also offers a glimpse inside Lewis's epistemology. This list,
though far from exhaustive, clearly shows a commitment to reason and
tradition. Though taking a backseat to Scripture, both play an indispensable
role in the exegetical and hermeneutical process.[30] Lewis found the doctrine
of hell buttressed by reason and tradition, yet not all scriptural data can claim
such support. In such cases, when tradition is split and reason lags, Lewis
tenaciously sides with Scripture. His take on the freedom-predestination
issue, as we noted in the previous chapter, illustrates this well. Lewis was
incurably logical. He did not revel in mystery. Yet he preferred to live with
some measure of tension rather than offer easy answers in the face of the facts.
He would have preferred resolution to the freedom-predestination issue but
was unable to find such. He felt bound by Scripture to hold apparently
contradictory passages in tension until enlightenment arrives. Lewis was

firmly committed to the concept of biblical tenacity.

> If we are free to delete all inconvenient data we shall certainly have no theological difficulties; but for the same reason no solutions and no progress. The very writers of the detective stories, not to mention the scientists, know better. The troublesome fact, the apparent absurdity which can't be fitted in to any synthesis we have yet made, is precisely the one we must not ignore. Ten to one, it's in that cover the fox is lurking. There is always hope if we keep an unsolved problem fairly in view; there's none if we pretend it's not there.[31]

The question on the table at the moment is not whether the freedom-predestination debate can be resolved but whether Lewis was willing to sit under the authority of Scripture, even at the expense of intellectual resolution. This he certainly was willing to do. He had full confidence in the internal consistency of Scripture, believing that all apparent difficulties would eventually evaporate if we continue to seek the truth with patient tenacity.[32]

It should be clear that Lewis honored biblical authority. He sacrifices emotional comfort in the case of the doctrine of hell and intellectual comfort in the case of freedom and predestination. On both counts, he subordinates his own natural longings to the authority of Scripture. But how did he ground the Bible's authority? How do we recognize the Bible's claim on our life when there are so many competing claims? Lewis realizes everyone accepts authority on a regular basis, often without realizing it. In fact, we could not survive without accepting the assertions of others. We hardly have the time, expertise or requisite power to verify every proposition that comes our way. Therefore, we must place faith in a wide variety of authorities. The question is not whether we will accept authority but which authority we will accept.[33]

While it appears Lewis simply assumes the authority of Scripture, a closer look reveals three undergirding pillars of support: the Bible's self-attestation, the tradition of the church and, possibly the most important consideration for Lewis, the Bible's marks of authenticity. Lewis recognizes as highly significant the phrase "Thus saith the Lord" woven throughout the fabric of the canonical writings. He calls the Bible a "remorselessly and continuously sacred" book.[34] Likewise, church history reveals a consistent commitment to the authority of Scripture.[35] But mere claims can be hollow without corroborating support.

The support in this case is surprising. Lewis takes some of the most troubling charges against biblical reliability and turns them on their head. Skeptics claim the Bible is riddled with inconsistencies and self-refuting statements. But for Lewis anomalies are not necessarily incriminating; they might merely be a clear sign of authorial integrity. In Mark 13:30 Jesus apparently predicts his eschatalogical return will take place during the generation of his listeners. The failure to make good on this assertion appears to refute his own claim to divinity. Lewis undoubtedly feels stumped by these words, calling it the most embarrassing passage in all of Scripture. Yet instead of losing faith, Lewis finds surprising consolation: "This passage (Mark 13:30-32) and the cry 'Why hast thou forsaken me?' (Mark 15:34) together make up the strongest proof that the New Testament is historically reliable. The evangelists have the first great characteristic of honest witnesses: they mention facts which are, at first sight, damaging to their main contention."[36]

Why would the biblical authors, and subsequent scribes, leave these passages in the text? According to Lewis, there is only one answer: they are the words of Jesus. This, of course, undermines the contention of many modern biblical scholars who accuse the early church of inserting their own theology into the mouth of Jesus. Such apparently embarrassing statements would never have been fabricated. It is here, nestled within an enigma, that Lewis hears the ring of truth most clearly. As with the freedom-predestination issue, Lewis chooses to hold these difficult passages in tension with Christ's claim to divinity until proper illumination comes.

Revelation. If creatures are going to communicate with the Creator, one thing is clear: the Creator must take the first step. Lewis writes, "If Shakespeare and Hamlet could ever meet, it must be Shakespeare's doing. Hamlet could initiate nothing."[37] Lewis has a generous view of revelation. Intimations of the truth exist in all religions, cultures and historical periods. God's providential care and self-revelation are expressed through a wide variety of mutually supporting means, including the idea of the holy, the natural law, the nation of Israel, good dreams, natural desires, intuition, experience, the Incarnation, the miracles and teachings of Christ, edifying literature and the Holy Scriptures. Lewis sees a strong continuity between each type of revelation. Since ultimate reality is self-consistent, revelation must exhibit a basic unifying quality as well.

Everyone has access to some form of revelation, but the amount and degree of clarity vary from religion to religion, culture to culture, age to age. Lewis accounts for this phenomenon, in part, by viewing divine disclosure as a graded and progressive process.[38] Lewis suggests a pattern of revelation that begins with a feeling of awe or dread, an awareness of the Numinous. The next stage of spiritual development is the recognition of the natural law, the moral code that is built into the universe. The third stage is the ability to connect the Numinous with the natural law, to recognize one's obligation to more than a mysterious law—to a lawgiver. Spiritual enlightenment culminates when one recognizes that the "aweful haunter of nature and the giver of the moral law" has broken into human history. In other words, the Incarnation represents God's fullest, clearest form of revelation.[39]

This notion of progressive revelation is also seen in the "good dreams" or mythology that God has given to all humanity. Lewis is not surprised by similar mythological stories in different cultures and time periods. It ought to be so. The near east creation stories anticipate the Genesis account.[40] The monotheistic writings of Egyptian Pharaoh Akhenaten anticipate the poetry of the Psalter.[41] The rising and dying corn kings anticipate the actual death and resurrection of Christ.[42] Like a seed that grows as it is watered and nourished over time, mythology blossoms and develops into maturity as it passes from one generation and culture to the next. Lewis believes this is all done under the guidance and providential care of the Creator.

This principle of progressive revelation extends to the pages of Scripture. Just as pagan revelation is a partial foretaste of Judaism, so the Old Testament is an inchoate preview of the Christian faith. Lewis believes some of the Old Testament accounts are mythology chosen by God as vehicles of the earliest sacred truths.[43] Likewise, God has progressively revealed himself in space-time history. Fully developed myth and fully developed history find their perfect marriage in the Incarnation. It is here that revelation finally crystal-lizes. The lens of the Incarnation brings all mythology and history into proper focus.[44]

God reveals himself not only through a variety of mutually reinforcing means but in a progressive manner. Instead of concentrating on the differ-ences between religions, cultures and historical periods, Lewis identifies essential continuity between them. Overlap testifies to God's generous, albeit disproportionate, distribution of truth throughout the world. Revelation comes to people in varying degrees of opacity, condensing and focusing over time until the clearest, fullest presentation of divine revelation breaks forth in the Incarnation.

Inspiration. In 1959 Lewis penned a letter to Wheaton College professor Clyde Kilby, expressing tentative thoughts concerning the subject of inspira-tion. In this letter Lewis identifies six factors that ought to be considered in developing a sound theory of inspiration: (1) Paul's distinction between his own words and the words of the Lord, (2) the apparent inconsistencies between Matthew's and Luke's genealogies and the accounts of Judas's demise, (3) Luke's rather normal method of research, (4) the "universally admitted unhistoricity (I do not say, of course, falsity)" of portions of Scrip-ture, including the parables and possibly Jonah and Job, (5) the suggestion that all true and edifying writing is in some sense inspired and (6) the paradoxical nature of John 11:49-52, in which inspiration operates "in a wicked man without his knowing it, and he can then utter the untruth he intends . . . as well as the truth he does not intend."[45]

Lewis believes points two and four rule out the view that all scriptural passages must be historical to be true. The remainder of the statements reveal the multifaceted nature of inspiration, which apparently varies in mode and degree. The statistical accounts of many Old Testament armies, which lack modern precision, should not be considered exact just because the resurrection record is historically accurate. Consequently, Lewis rules out the view that the Bible is uniformly inerrant throughout.

It is important to understand Lewis correctly at this point. He is not challenging the doctrine of inerrancy here. Interpreting these Old Testament accounts as in some sense inerrant remains a viable option. Rather, Lewis is debunking the notion that inerrancy can be flattened out into a one-dimensional, homogenous phenomenon that operates with mechanical predictability throughout the canon.

That the over-all operation of Scripture is to convey God's Word to the reader (he also needs inspiration) who reads it in the right spirit, I fully believe. That it *also* gives true answers to all the questions (often religiously irrelevant) which he might ask, I don't. The very *kind* of truth we are often demanding was, in my opinion, not even envisaged by the ancients.[46]

This paragraph offers a number of hints to Lewis's position. First, Lewis suggests the purpose of Scripture. It is to carry God's Word. Lewis does not see Scripture as God's Word proper but rather as a vehicle that has been chosen and elevated above itself for this calling.[47] Its purpose is to guide us to the reality behind the printed page. In an apparent effort to guard against bibliolatry Lewis writes, "It is Christ Himself, not the Bible, who is the true word of God. The Bible, read in the right spirit and with the guidance of good teachers, will bring us to Him."[48]

Second, Lewis believes that the process of inspiration is too often limited to just the author of the communiqué. He takes a more holistic position, insisting on inspiration for not only the sender of the message but also the receiver. Inspiration is the process whereby God superintends the totality of his message, from conception to reception. Lewis's view of varied degrees of inspiration parallels his understanding of graded revelation. Since revelation is progressively unveiled, it stands to reason that the clarity of inspiration will correspond to God's progressive plan. In other words, the degree of inspiration imparted to the psalmist in 1000 B.C. would correspond directly to the amount and clarity of revelation God chose to disclose during that time period, not necessarily to the degree of inspiration a Gospel writer might receive.

It would be misleading to suggest Lewis saw inspiration as a unilateral activity. Humans have a legitimate role to play in the process too. Though God may sometimes appear to override individual freedom, inspiration generally requires cooperation. Lewis wants us to see the need for heart purity in the inspiration process, a clear channel through which God's message can be sent and received. Dissonance and ambiguity can often be attributed to the frailty of the human condition or outright sin. "The human qualities of the raw materials show through," Lewis explains. "Naïvety, error, contradiction, even (as in the cursing Psalms) wickedness are not removed."[49] In order to get to the pure Word of God, we must approach the text holistically. It requires "a response from the whole man"[50]—a discerning mind, a baptized imagination, a pliable will and a pure heart.

As we have already seen, Lewis notices the ambiguities in Scripture and refuses to offer superficial harmonization. He believes such unresolved tension forces us to search the text and ourselves. It forces us to pull from all our God-given resources and maximize our God-inspired faculties in a quest to mine the deep and rich mysteries of the universe. Knowledge apart from the proper degree of sanctification can be dangerous. Lewis suggests God may have chosen to reveal himself in this manner to keep us from approaching the Bible in a rationalistic, one-dimensional fashion. Revelation is not given to satisfy our curiosity but to help us become the kind of creatures God desires.[51] The polarized responses to the parables of Jesus illustrate this well. Insight is largely dependent on one's heart and desire for the truth.

Third, Lewis does not believe the Bible should be judged by our modern standards but according to the intents and purposes of the original authors. He was all too familiar with contemporary literary critics bringing their own modern assumptions to the text. In *An Experiment in Criticism* Lewis draws an important distinction between "using" and "receiving" the text.[52] If we are to understand an ancient text, or any text for that matter, we must get out of the way. We must toss all our culturally and historically conditioned biases aside and "receive" the text in the manner in which the author intended.[53] When we approach the biblical text, we must read it in light of its own cultural, historical and literary context. Since modern scientific and historical precision were foreign to the ancient writers, we must not hold them to such standards.

The total result is not "the Word of God" in the sense that every passage, in itself, gives impeccable science or history. It carries the Word of God; and we (under grace, with attention to tradition and to interpreters wiser than ourselves, and with the use of such intelligence and learning as we may have) *receive* that word from it not by *using* it as an encyclopedia or an encyclical but by steeping ourselves in its tone and temper and so learning its overall message.[54] (emphasis ours)

Lewis says we might have expected a systematic, unambiguous presentation of doctrine, "something we could have tabulated and memorised and relied on like the multiplication table,"[55] but an honest inquiry reveals something quite different. Our expectations must conform to the data an honest exegetical analysis yields.

A brief summary at this point should crystallize Lewis's overall view. We have seen a staunch, tenacious commitment to the authority of the Bible, even at the expense of emotional and intellectual comfort. Lewis recognizes the claim of Scripture upon his life and grounds its reliability in its marks of authenticity. God reveals himself progressively through a wide variety of means. All revelation points toward the Incarnational event, the fullest expression of divine disclosure. This notion of progressive revelation explains both the continuity and differences that exist between not only Christianity and Judaism but Christianity and all religions.

Like revelation, inspiration is multifaceted and graded. God superintends not only how much revelation will be disseminated but also the degree of inspiration that is imparted. But in most instances a human response on the part of the sender and receiver of the message is required. This process requires a holistic response—a pure heart, a baptized imagination, a pliable will and a keen intellect. Varying degrees of opacity spur us on to deeper commitment and inquiry. Lewis believes apparent contradictions serve an important purpose, forcing us to seek the divine with our whole being. The sanctification process reveals a direct correlation between obedience and insight.

Finally, Lewis insists that the only way to avoid eisegesis is to receive the text in its proper historical, cultural and literary context. Imposing modern scientific standards on antiquity clouds and distorts the intended message. Reading the text in its native literary genre is an indispensible hermeneutical principle.

Evaluating the Ridge

We now turn to the task of locating Lewis on Schaeffer's ridge. This comes rather easily. Though Schaeffer and Lewis share much in common—the primacy of Scripture in matters of faith and doctrine, the Bible's internal coherence and supernatural presuppositions—the points of contention are significant. Lewis takes a mythological interpretation of the creation account and many Old Testament miracles, questions the historical, cosmological and scientific precision of some of the biblical data, and does not view Scripture as the Word of God per se but rather as the vehicle that carries the Word.

From Schaeffer's vantage point, these cardinal sins undoubtedly would have sent Lewis sliding down the slippery northern slope and into the frigid waters of neo-orthodoxy.

In *The Great Evangelical Disaster* we get a taste of what Schaeffer might have said to Lewis. Schaeffer offers a note about the doctrinal position of contemporary evangelical theologian Thomas Oden, whose shift from liberalism to classic Christianity is well documented. While applauding this courageous maneuver, Schaeffer believes Oden falls short of a full confession of historic orthodoxy:

> This has led [Oden] toward what is essentially a neo-orthodox position, but one that tries at the same time to take the full range of historic Christianity seriously. Since, however, he does not accept the full authority and inerrancy of the Bible he is still left with a serious problem—namely, upon what will he finally base his faith? Without the objective truth of the Bible as his foundation, Oden is still left without any way to appropriate with confidence the truth of the Scriptures. . . . He is left without any final authority and caught in the same basic problem that he started with.[56]

Neo-orthodoxy does not solve the epistemological dilemma for Schaeffer. It forces the reader to subjectively sift through the scriptural data to divide truth from error, placing the reader as the judge of Scripture. Schaeffer acknowledges Oden's serious, though insufficient, attempt to embrace historic, orthodox Christianity. Lewis and Oden would appear to be in the same boat. Both affirm historic orthodoxy, including the great ecumenical councils and creeds, but refuse to view Scripture as the final word on matters outside the realm of faith and practice.

So it seems that Schaeffer and Lewis would have found themselves on opposite sides of the Great Evangelical Divide. But what about the ridge itself? How sturdy is this construction? Can it withstand serious scrutiny? It is our contention that Schaeffer's ridge of inerrancy is suspect on at least three counts.

First, the biblical data does not appear to mesh with Schaeffer's a priori assumptions. As we have seen, Schaeffer believed inerrancy is largely a result of holding the correct set of presuppositions. He thought that it would be out of character for an all-loving, all-powerful God to send his creatures a communiqué that mingles pure religious truth with cosmological, historical and scientific error. If God is really the perfect Being that Christianity has traditionally insisted on, then the Bible, his message to humankind, must be impeccable on all fronts.

Lewis would not necessarily disagree with these a priori expectations. We might have anticipated an all-powerful, all-loving Being to deliver "something we could have tabulated and memorised and relied on like the multiplication table," but an honest evaluation of the available data just does not support such expectations.[57] Lewis believes it is dangerous to place too much stock in our a priori assumptions:

> One can respect, and at moments envy, both the Fundamentalist's view of the Bible and the Roman Catholic's view of the Church. But there is one argument which we should beware of using . . . God must have done what is best, this is best, therefore God has done this. For we are mortals and do not know what is best for us, and it is dangerous to prescribe what God must have done—especially when we cannot, for the life of us, see that He has after all done it.[58]

Lewis believes it is a perilous proposition to predetermine what God must have done on the basis of what we think best and then interpret the evidence in light of our a priori assumptions. Schaeffer appears to be vulnerable to this charge. Let us consider the formal structure of Schaeffer's argument as suggested by Lewis: (1) God is perfect, so he must have done what is best; (2) inerrancy is best; (3) therefore God has provided an inerrant Bible.

Lewis and Schaeffer would have agreed on premise number one. Both men believed that God not only is capable of doing what is best but also is willing to do what is best. But that is where the agreement ends, for premise number two is the one Lewis questions. He believes it is a vast leap for fallible humans to predetermine what divine course of action is best, especially when such assumptions simply do not align with the biblical evidence. This approach tends to conform the data to one's expectations, inevitably leading to foolproof hermeneutical constructions. William Abraham has identified this very tendency in the Princeton theologians, the tradition in which Schaeffer firmly stands:

> Warfield and the whole tradition he elaborates approached the issue of inspiration deductively. That is, they began with very firm convictions about the meaning of inspiration and from this they deduced by normal rules of inference what this entailed for the content and character of the Bible. From within this framework they then attempted to accommodate the results of direct, inductive study of the Bible as best they could. Where there was a strain between these two elements, that is between the deductions as to what Scripture must be like if it is truly inspired and between what Scripture seems to be like when it is studied like other literature, the former was given logical priority. The deductions ruled.[59]

So what do we do when the evidence does not cohere with our expectations? Three options appear to emerge. First, we can tenaciously insist upon interpreting all the biblical data through the guiding grid of our a priori assumptions. Second, we can discard the original theory as essentially flawed and seek an entirely new hypothesis. Or third, we can allow a new theory to grow out of the dynamic interaction between our a priori assumptions and an inductive study of text.[60] Schaeffer appears to opt for the first, while Lewis chooses the third.

According to Lewis, it would be nice to have an inerrant Bible or an infallible pope to solve all our epistemological problems, but an open investigation of the biblical data suggests God must have chosen to pursue a different course of action. But why would an all-perfect, all-loving God not provide the type of communiqué Schaeffer has suggested? Lewis appears to think such a message might have merely engaged the mind, not "the whole man." This line of reasoning is reminiscent of a fascinating statement from Pascal's *Pensees:* "God wishes to move the will rather than the mind. Perfect clarity would help the mind and harm the will. Humble their pride."[61] Lewis and Pascal seem to be on to the same insight. God is not primarily interested in satisfying our intellectual curiosity. His primary concern is transforming his beings into holy creatures. For all we know, the ambiguity that exists in the Bible and in the world at large might be necessary to elicit the holistic response God requires. As we respond to God's revelation with all our being, ever-increasing insight and psychological certitude will follow.

The second reason to doubt Schaeffer's ridge of inerrancy is that the biblical data does not appear to mesh with Schaeffer's modern assumptions. For all his commendable effort in defending Christianity against the damaging effects of modernity, Schaeffer himself occasionally appears to fall prey to the Enlightenment mindset. Alister McGrath notes the dependence of the Princeton school on extrabiblical assumptions and identifies this hermeneutical tradition as largely a North American phenomenon.

> One of the things that we notice about North American evangelicalism from our European perspective is that it's been very heavily influenced by a series of extrabiblical presuppositions. As far as I can see, they are presuppositions deriving from the Enlightenment. This goes back to the old Princeton school in America. . . . So you're left with this remarkable situation in which Scripture is actually being defended on the basis of Enlightenment ideas and values. Certainly in Europe we've never wanted to do that.[62]

What are these Enlightenment assumptions? According to Kent Hill, one such assumption is an inordinate emphasis on empiricism: "Ironically, despite Schaeffer's distaste for the Enlightenment and his fear of accommodation to the spirit of the age, his fundamentalist preoccupation with inerrancy seems remarkably in step with modern demands that only verifiable truth be accepted."[63] Schaeffer wrote extensively about the modern tendency to dichotomize faith and reason. In an effort to reunite these divided fields of knowledge, Schaeffer emphasized the importance of safeguarding the historical texture of Scripture, particularly the first eleven chapters of Genesis. By insisting on the space-time factuality of the biblical record, Schaeffer hoped to keep holy writ in the realm of the verifiable. To sever Scripture from the empirical realm would mean a mystical leap into the upper story of nebulous faith. Hill finds this insistence on verification a misguided notion, since even the discovery of the skeletal remains of Adam and Eve could not verify the *theological* claims of Scripture.[64]

Another Enlightenment assumption that Schaeffer appears to embrace is the tendency to define the concept of truth in terms of modern scientific precision. He writes, "What sense does it make for a God to give us true religious truths and at the same time place them in a book that is wrong when it touches history and the cosmos?"[65] Many evangelical biblical scholars would take issue with the way Schaeffer has couched this dilemma. Does rejection of the Bible as a scientifically precise textbook entail a belief that the Bible is in error? Surely not. What many scholars insist on is the importance of evaluating the biblical data in light of the original intent of the biblical authors and accepted standards of precision in that particular culture and time period. This requires careful historical, cultural and literary study.

The so-called third quest for the historical Jesus has made some helpful contributions in this regard. For example, consider the recent progress that has been made in determining the literary genre of the Gospels. Thanks in large part to the research of Richard Burridge, the author of *What Are the Gospels? A Comparison with Graeco-Roman Biography,* many scholars are now accepting the theory that the Gospels are best understood as ancient biographies and should be interpreted with this genre in mind.[66]

Ancient and modern biographies are quite different. Modern biographies generally chronicle a person's life in great detail, from womb to tomb. As the subject's life is chronologically presented, modern biographers will often probe the critical persons, events and circumstances that affected the psychological and emotional state of the subject at various points of development. Ancient biographies were much more general. While concerned about presenting a true, accurate and gripping portrait of the subject, ancient biographers felt a great deal more freedom. It was common and quite acceptable to insert thematic material within a broad chronological outline without providing detailed precision on every point. What mattered was the significance of an event, not strict chronology or precise accuracy. A close look at the

Gospels reveals a great deal of common ground with ancient biographies. When one realizes broad chronology, limited precision and the insertion of thematic material were par for the course in ancient biographies, questions surrounding the timing of the temple cleansing and the number of Petrine denials become much less problematic.

So is the text wrong if it does not meet our modern expectations? Certainly not. We must evaluate the biblical writers in light of the standards and expectations of their culture and age if we are to understand the intended message and arrive at a meaningful doctrine of inerrancy. This appears to be the sort of point Lewis was making when he wrote, "The very kind of truth we are often demanding was, in my opinion, not even envisaged by the ancients."

Unfortunately, Schaeffer at times appears to place the finest modern mesh over the text, viewing these works of antiquity through a grid of scientific precision that would have been largely alien to the biblical authors and unexpected by the initial recipients of that culture and age. Schaeffer's tendency to undervalue the historical, cultural and literary context of the text is noted by Jack Rogers:

> Schaeffer's lack of understanding of culture and his antithetical method-
> ology lead him to violate the most basic rule of biblical interpretation: a
> passage must be understood in its context. There are absolutes in the Bible:
> love your neighbor; Christ is the only way to salvation; don't lust. There
> are also things which are relative: the kind of garment a priest must wear;
> whether to eat meat or not; and whether a man should have long hair.
> (Schaeffer seemingly interprets Paul's apparently absolute proscription
> against men wearing long hair as applying only to that time and culture.)[67]

While Schaeffer appears to violate this key hermeneutical principle at times, Lewis consistently interpreted literature in light of its original setting. As a literary scholar and student of history, Lewis was especially adept at spotting eisegetical tendencies, a propensity he certainly recognized in fundamentalism.

The third reason to doubt Schaeffer's ridge of inerrancy is that the biblical data does not appear to mesh with Schaeffer's implicit deterministic assumptions. In chapter three we identified a clear commitment to libertarian freedom in Schaeffer's teaching. But when it comes to the issue of inerrancy, it appears Schaeffer might have shifted to an implicit reliance on a compatibilistic notion of human freedom.

> If the uncreated Personal wished to give these communications through
> individual created personalities in such a way that they would write (in
> their own individual style, etc.) the exact things the uncreated Personal

wanted them to write in the areas of religious truths and things of the cosmos and history—then by this time it is impossible to make an absolute and say that he could not or would not.[68]
Two points can be made here. First, Schaeffer insists that the Bible contains exactly what God desires, down to the very words. Second, Schaeffer appears to be suggesting that God can precisely control what his human agents write without overriding their freedom.[69] This statement certainly has a compatibilistic ring to it. If compatibilism is what Schaeffer has in mind, then this maneuver, as we noted in the last chapter, is problematic. The most decisive problem is its inability to explain why, if God can accomplish precisely what he wants through humans without overriding their freedom (in this case determine the exact wording of the biblical writers), he does not determine everyone to always freely choose what is right. This point will be pursued in greater detail in chapter nine; for now it is sufficient to note what might be an implicit reliance on a problematic compatibilistic paradigm.

This insistence on God's selecting exactly what the authors wrote also appears to be remarkably congruent with the modern insistence on precision. Ironically, this insistence on precision seems to undermine the very certainty Schaeffer hopes to protect. He affirms the Chicago Statement's assertion that inerrancy should be applied only to the original autographs. Schaeffer even concedes scribal errors.[70] Yet if the original, inerrant writings are nowhere to be found, how does this affirmation provide modern humanity the epistemic certainty Schaeffer insists on? Why would God carefully craft every word in the original text but not ensure the same degree of precision in the scribal process?

The slippery-slope argument requires one hundred percent accuracy. It is all or nothing. Remove one piece from the construction, and the whole structure is liable to collapse. Using Schaeffer's logic, we would expect a perfect God to ensure not only the accuracy of the original text but also the subsequent transmission with the same degree of care and precision. If God communicated the exact things he wants through the pen of a human author without overriding human freedom, why did he not do the same with the scribes during the transmission process? The epistemic certainty Schaeffer desires requires not only the successful transmission of the perfect text to subsequent generations but also a guaranteed means of arbitrating each passage of Scripture. But we all know that consensus on every passage of Scripture, even among conservative Christians, is illusory. The truth of Scripture does not embed itself in our minds without some mediating process.

An inductive study of the biblical data leads us to the conclusion that God was apparently less concerned with the exact wording of Scripture and more concerned with the essential reliability of his overall message. The ambiguity that arises out of the data points to the possibility that God did not determine precisely what the authors would say but rather ensured that his essential message was communicated while allowing the authors legitimate libertarian freedom in crafting that message. The same is true in the transmission process. God has ensured the successful transmission of the essential components of Scripture. If this is true, it is important to acknowledge the integral role humans have played in the process of shaping and transmitting the canonical writings. This does not diminish the role of God but rather heightens his creativity, since he dynamically engages creatures with true libertarian freedom, rather than determining their precise move at each turn. It also reinforces the dignity of humanity by the way God has chosen to allow his creatures to play an authentic role in delivering his message to the world.

We have now seen that Schaeffer's theory of inerrancy appears to be constructed upon unstable a priori, modern and deterministic assumptions. If our critique is sound, then Schaeffer's ridge is fundamentally flawed and unnecessarily narrow. So is there any hope of bridging the great chasm that separates Schaeffer and Lewis, or are these two men at an impasse? Despite significant points of contention, it appears that the Chicago Statement on Biblical Inerrancy, a document fully endorsed by Schaeffer, constructs a much broader ridge—one that accommodates not only Schaeffer's sentiments but much of Lewis's perspective as well. This generous latitude is represented in the following passage:

> We deny that it is proper to evaluate Scripture according to standards of truth and error that are alien to its usage or purpose. We further deny that inerrancy is negated by Biblical phenomena such as a lack of modern technical precision, irregularities of grammar or spelling, observational descriptions of nature, the reporting of falsehoods, the use of hyperbole and round numbers, the topical arrangement of material, variant selections of material in parallel accounts, or the use of free citations.[71]

This passage seems to acknowledge the critical point that Scripture must be read in its native literary, historical and cultural context and must be evaluated in light of the intents and purposes of the original authors. Furthermore, if the books of the Bible were originally written for a premodern audience, then these works should not be viewed through an Enlightenment-tainted lens. This statement just might eliminate the primary concern that Lewis had with the fundamentalist interpretation of Scripture—the tendency to ignore historical, cultural and literary hermeneutical considerations. If this is true, then it would appear that the ridge of the Chicago Statement just might be broad enough to rescue Lewis from the frigid fate of the icy North Sea.[72]

The Apologetic Considerations

In this chapter we have detailed the positions of Schaeffer and Lewis on biblical authority and divine inspiration, identifying some key points of common ground and tension along the way. We must now determine what bearing this material has on the apologetic task. We conclude this chapter with five apologetic considerations.

1. The historical nature of the Christian faith must be defended. We must always remember that Christianity is a historical religion, not simply a set of philosophical propositions or an ethical system. To ignore the historical texture of the faith is to drift dangerously toward gnosticism. The Bible is a record of God's intervention into human history and dynamic interaction with his people. Schaeffer's general insistence upon guarding the historicity of Scripture is commendable and on the right trajectory. Though Schaeffer might at times place too high a premium on verification, there is no question that key Christian doctrines stand or fall as space-time occurrences. If the Son of God did not enter the world as a little baby in Bethlehem, live a sinless life in Jewish flesh, die a cruel death on Calvary and leave an empty tomb on Easter morning, then the whole Christian faith falls to the ground.

2. Though historicity is critical for certain core Christian doctrines, it is not at all clear that this extends to a literal reading of the opening chapters of Genesis. The relationship between science and Christianity remains one of the truly central apologetic issues of our time. The long shadows of the Galileo incident and the Scopes monkey trial will likely extend well into the twenty-first century. It is strategically unwise to pit Christianity against the claims of science unless this is required by the essential claims of orthodoxy. This is not to say Christians should accept uncritically all the latest pronouncements of science or let go unchallenged the naturalism that is often taken as integral to science itself.[73] But it is to say that Christians have a variety of creation models that do justice to the core orthodox beliefs of the faith. Naturalists, by contrast, basically have only one option, namely, some version of naturalistic evolution. The Christian, ironically, has more freedom to follow the scientific evidence wherever it leads and to adopt whichever model seems best supported as research and discovery go forward.

It is interesting to note that Schaeffer dedicates a whole chapter in *No Final Conflict* to such freedoms and even leaves the door open a crack to the possibility of theistic evolution, the position Lewis endorsed.[74] Schaeffer does not discuss Lewis's theory of how humanity evolved (see chapter 5 of *The Problem of Pain*), but he does interact with Lewis's suggestion that the rebellion of Satan fractured the natural world and introduced death and destruction prior to the creation of humans. Schaeffer tells us that "if Lewis' position is the case, then man was put in a prepared garden in a spoiled universe and the statement 'have dominion' (Gen 1:28) takes on added depth. The phrase 'and ye shall die' also appears in a different light because it would mean that death already existed."[75] Though Schaeffer finds Lewis's hypothesis lacking biblical support, he nevertheless presents it as a possibility.

3. It is important to maintain that God can and has successfully communicated with us. This claim is at the heart of any substantive account of revelation. If what God revealed is not accessible and the essential message is not identifiable, then the claim that God has revealed himself must be forfeited. It is an eminently plausible notion that a personal God would reveal himself in this fashion and it is a crucial claim of distinctively Christian apologetics that the living God has done so through the events and words recorded in Scripture. The nonnegotiable nature of such distinct and identifiable communication is the essentially correct insight of those who insist on inerrancy.

4. Our approach to Scripture must reflect a sensitivity to the cultures and historical periods in which it was written. This is essential to the hermeneutical task and is essential if we are to allow Scripture to speak to us on its own terms. Moreover, the fact that Scripture can speak to us is a powerful instance of crosscultural communication, an important apologetic consideration that takes on increasing significance in light of the recent emphasis on multiculturalism. Of course, much that flies under the banner of multiculturalism and global awareness is a thinly veiled advocacy of moral and epistemological relativism. The task of the apologist is to avoid contemporary relativism as much as modern canons of scientific and historical precision in the hermeneutical process. This can be achieved by a reading of Scripture that is culturally sensitive as well as theologically and historically informed.

5. We would suggest that it is preferable to argue for historical reliability than for inerrancy in the apologetic arena. To insist on inerrancy in the early stages of discussion will likely lead down trails that will distract from the more central claims of the faith that are the proper concerns of apologetics. To make these claims hinge on inerrancy is to make these claims unnecessarily controversial at the outset. This is not to say that one may not argue for a carefully defined inerrancy later on as the best way to construe the authority of Scripture, once the faith has been accepted. But at this stage of the conversation, it is a misguided focus of energy. This is the approach that the prince of the Princeton theologians, B. B. Warfield, adopted. And as we shall see in the next chapter, it was also the strategy of Francis Schaeffer.

Let us suppose we possess parts of a novel or a symphony. Someone now brings us a newly discovered piece of manuscript and says, "This is the missing part of the work. This is the chapter on which the whole plot of the novel really turned. This is the main theme of the symphony." Our business would be to see whether the new passage, if admitted to the central place which the discoverer claimed for it, did actually illuminate all the parts we had already seen and "pull them together."[1]

C. S. LEWIS

What we should notice is the method. It is rather like trying to find the right key to fit a particular lock. We try the first key and then the next and the next until finally, if we are fortunate, one of them fits. The same principle applies, so Christians maintain, when we consider the big questions. Here are the phenomena. What key unlocks their meaning? What explanation is correct?[2]

FRANCIS SCHAEFFER

In answer to the historical query of why [Christianity] was accepted, and is accepted, I answer for millions of others in my reply; because it fits the lock; because it is like life. It is one among many stories; only it happens to be a true story. It is one among many philosophies; only it happens to be the truth.[3]

G. K. CHESTERTON

6

....

Strategic Apologetics
Delivering the Faith

*I*N 1958 FRANCIS SCHAEFFER MADE THE FIRST OF MANY VISITS TO Cambridge University to speak with students about the credibility of the Christian faith. During one of these visits a handful of students attempted to arrange a face-to-face meeting between Schaeffer and C. S. Lewis, but to no avail. According to Edith, their time in England was always too brief, and a rigorous schedule could not accommodate such an encounter.[4]

One can only imagine what such a meeting might have been like: perhaps a friendly conversation over a cup of steaming hot tea in Lewis's study. The discussion might have spanned a wide array of topics: the health of Joy, the challenge of logical positivism, the dynamics of L'Abri. The conversation might even have touched upon the nature of contemporary apologetic strategy.

Though Schaeffer never enjoyed the privilege of afternoon tea with Lewis, he did experience a memorable moment involving tea on the Cambridge campus. One evening Schaeffer was conversing with a small group of students in a dorm room, when a young Hindu emphatically challenged the claims of Christianity. In response to this challenge, Schaeffer turned to the Indian student and said, "Am I not correct in saying that on the basis of your system, cruelty and noncruelty are ultimately equal, that there is no intrinsic difference between them?"

The student confirmed this to be true. His fellow students were shocked at such an admission. But one quick-thinking student, who was busy preparing the tea, seized the moment for an object lesson. He grabbed the pot of boiling water and held it ominously over the head of the Indian student. When the Hindu nervously asked what he was doing, the student simply replied, "There is no difference between cruelty and noncruelty."

Without responding, the young Hindu rose to his feet and "walked out into the night."[5]

Such a story is reminiscent of a comment once offered by the eleventh-century philosopher Avicenna: "Those who deny a first principle [e.g., the law of noncontradiction] should be beaten and burned until they admit that to be beaten is not the same as to not be beaten and to be burned is not the same as to not be burned."[6]

This encounter with the Hindu student is a graphic example of Schaeffer's passionate commitment to antithesis or the law of noncontradiction. It is also an existentially gripping illustration of his apologetic methodology in action, what Schaeffer called "taking the roof off." In this chapter we will explore this apologetic strategy and then go on to consider the distinctive manner in which Lewis went about presenting the claims of Christianity to an unbelieving world.

The Apologetic Options

Before we turn to the task of discerning the particular apologetic strategies of Schaeffer and Lewis, however, it will be worthwhile to acquaint ourselves with the methodologies generally employed by Christian apologists.[7] According to Gordon Lewis, three distinct methods have been commonly used in the pursuit of justifying one's rational assertions. The first is the inductive, empirical or evidential method, which "starts with an 'objective' mind observing specific phenomena and infers general conclusions with degrees of probability."[8] The evidentialist therefore works from particular data to a universal conclusion. This method has been employed by Christian apologists ranging from Thomas Aquinas to J. Oliver Buswell.

The second approach is often called the deductive or presuppositional method, which "starts with assumed premises (presuppositions) and reasons to conclusions with the possibility of syllogistic certainty if the premises are true."[9] The presuppositionalist, therefore, works from unchallengeable universal premises to account for the particular phenomena in question. In Christian apologetics, this school of thought is prominently associated with Cornelius Van Til.

The third approach is the abductive, scientific or verificational method, which starts "with tentative hypotheses from any type of experience (e.g., presupposition, observation, creative intuitions, imagination). Then the verificational method subjects these hypotheses to testing and confirmation or disconfirmation by the coherence of their account with the relevant lines of data."[10] The verificationist, therefore, compares various hypotheses with the particular data to see which theory makes best sense of the phenomena in question. This approach incorporates both inductive and deductive considerations. Like evidentialism, this method tests one's theory against the empirical data; like presuppositionalism, it starts with a definite premise. Yet, in contrast to presuppositionalism, this ultimate premise or hypothesis is open to verification and, consequently, the possibility of falsification. Christian philosophers ranging from Edward John Carnell to Richard Swinburne have employed some version of this approach. With these three distinct methodologies in clear view, we can now consider Schaeffer's apologetic strategy.

The Elusive Methodology of Francis Schaeffer

The question of apologetic methodology is probably the most disputed and controversial subject surrounding the life and ministry of Francis Schaeffer. He has been called a "presuppositionalist" by Thomas Morris,[11] a "compassionate presuppositionalist" by Jerram Barrs,[12] an "inconsistent presuppositionalist" by Kenneth Harper,[13] a "modified presuppositionalist" by Os Guinness,[14] an "inconsistent empiricist" by Robert L. Reymond[15] and a "verificationist" by Gordon R. Lewis,[16] Colin Brown[17] and Lane Dennis.[18] How could the ministry of one man yield such radically diverse interpretations? The answer to this question will emerge in the next several pages.

It is easy to see how a surface reading of his apologetic trilogy, *The God Who Is There, Escape from Reason* and *He Is There and He Is Not Silent*, could lead to befuddlement. Schaeffer never systematically spells out his methodology in any of these works and frequently discusses the need for both presuppositional apologetics and rational proof in communicating the historic faith to modern humanity. In addition, Schaeffer emphatically resisted those who attempted to pigeonhole his approach into one distinct camp. He once said, "I'm not an evidentialist or a presuppositionalist. You're trying to press me into the category of a theological apologist, which I'm really not. I'm not an academic, scholastic apologist. My interest is in evangelism."[19] He thought others might be called to such an undertaking, but he sensed a call to frontline evangelism. Though Schaeffer's approach is not easily discerned, four distinct themes emerge from his writings. For Schaeffer, contemporary apologetics must be presuppositional, rational, relational and plausible.

Apologetics Must Be Presuppositional

The naive notion of pure empiricism and complete objectivity has come under intense scrutiny in recent years, thanks in large part to the groundbreaking work of scholars like Michael Polanyi and Thomas Kuhn. According to these men, the scientist, philosopher, historian and construction worker all view data through some sort of lens or noetic framework. One's perspective or worldview might be formal or informal, explicit or implicit, conscious or subconscious, but there is no question that everyone views reality through a grid of guiding assumptions.

Schaeffer was an influential popularizer of this valuable insight, loading his books and lectures with commentary on presuppositional apologetics and worldview thinking.[20] He consistently encouraged his readers to view all God's creation from a thoroughly biblical angle of vision and pointed out that every person, either consciously or subconsciously, filters the world through a system or set of presuppositions.[21] Since there is no such thing as complete objectivity, Schaeffer thought it was imperative that Christians consider presuppositions when doing apologetics.

Schaeffer opens his most important apologetic treatise, *The God Who Is There*, with an apology for presuppositional apologetics. One of the key premises presented in this work is the belief that until around 1890 in Europe and 1935 in the United States, nearly everyone in the Western world was operating with the same basic set of presuppositions, namely, a commitment to the concept of absolutes. Even though people did not necessarily agree on the content of those absolute standards, they did agree that if one thing is true, the opposite is false; if one thing is right, the opposite is wrong. In other words, everyone affirmed the classical laws of logic, particularly, the law of noncontradiction or antithesis.[22] In such an environment the use of classical apologetics was effective because there was a common commitment to the self-evident canons of classical logic, a prerequisite for getting any evidential argument off the ground.

Then a significant shift took place. The twentieth century ushered in a relativistic mindset that undermined the concept of antithesis and drove a massive epistemological wedge between the orthodox Christian and many nonbelievers. The shared allegiance to absolute truth, objective morality and the law of antithesis became a thing of the past. This was a tragic occurrence. But, according to Schaeffer, the greatest tragedy was the failure of Christian leaders to anticipate the shift and train believers to communicate in a new way. This negligence left most Christians speaking as if nonbelievers were still committed to absolutes and antithesis. In other words, believers continued to employ the methodology of classical apologetics, with little or no consideration of the nonbeliever's new presuppositions. Schaeffer put it this way:

The really foolish thing is that even now . . . many Christians still do not know what is happening. And this is because they are still not being taught the importance of thinking in terms of presuppositions. . . . The use of classical apologetics before this shift took place was effective only because non-Christians were functioning, on the surface, on the same presuppositions, even if they had an inadequate base for them. In classical apologetics though, presuppositions were rarely analyzed, discussed or taken into account.[23]

Schaeffer believes that starting with a classical, evidential approach in the contemporary climate is generally a tactical error; it is "fighting the battle on the wrong ground"[24] and tantamount to "beating the air."[25] We must first attack the various paradigms of relativism and naturalism if the classical arguments for Christian theism are to have any leverage.

Apologetics Must Be Rational

Some might suggest that we have already introduced ample evidence to place Schaeffer in the presuppositional camp. His repeated emphasis upon presuppositions and suspicion of pure induction seem clear enough. But it would be misleading to label Schaeffer a thoroughgoing presuppositionalist. For as we saw in the previous chapter, Schaeffer believed the claims of Christianity, particularly the content of Scripture, should be subject to the same type of empirical inquiry as all other types of phenomena. Scientific, historical and religious claims all play by the same rules. For a theory in any of these disciplines to be viable it must be self-consistent, comprehensive and livable.

Schaeffer insisted that religious truth be held to the same standard as scientific truth in light of the modern tendency to relegate religion to the realm of the unverifiable. Under such a proposal there simply is no way to adjudicate competing religious truth claims. All are equally viable with no consideration of whether or not they are objectively true. But Christianity is grounded in the claim that it is a true, historical, space-time religion and therefore open to verification and falsification. Schaeffer writes, "Christianity is realistic because it says that if there is no truth, there is also no hope; and there can be no truth if there is no adequate base. It is prepared to face the consequences of being proved false and say with Paul: if you find the body of Christ, the discussion is finished; let us eat and drink for tomorrow we die."[26]

One could hardly overemphasize Schaeffer's commitment to the concept of objective, absolute truth. According to Os Guinness, who lived in the Schaeffers' chalet for five years, Schaeffer laughed about a variety of things, but he never joked about the subject of truth. Like Nietzsche, he believed "all truth is bloody truth to me."[27] And for Schaeffer, truth can be found only through rational testing of the phenomenon in question. It cannot be found by a mystical semantic leap or blind faith in the realm of religion any more than it can in the realm of science.

How do we square all this talk about verification with Schaeffer's commitment to presuppositional apologetics? On the one hand, he claims that the shift to relativism necessitates a presuppositional approach; on the other hand, he insists upon rational proof and empirical evidence for what we believe. So which is it: deduction or induction? Or is Schaeffer simply affirming two mutually exclusive propositions as he did with the freedom-determinism issue? To answer these questions, we turn to one of Schaeffer's most influential seminary professors, "the father of presuppositionalism," Cornelius Van Til.

Van Til was adamant about how Christian apologetics ought to be done and was not shy about criticizing those who operated outside his prescribed plan. He was particularly critical of classical evidentialism and believed the inductive, empirical approach to be not merely outdated but thoroughly unbiblical. Van Til underscored the profound noetic effects of total depravity and believed that in principle there is no common ground between the unregenerate sinner and the grace-enabled believer. Non-Christians hold a set of presuppositions about the nature of humanity and the world that rule out the God of the Bible right from the start. So no amount of evidence can ever convince such a person that Christianity is true, because the base-line assumptions of the nonbeliever eliminate the possibility of Christian claims on a priori grounds. Consequently, Van Til believed all competing paradigms must be discarded and Christian presuppositions adopted before the truth can be seen. In short, Van Til argued for a purely deductive apologetic approach.

As one might imagine, Van Til was bothered by Schaeffer's books and the confusing array of references to presuppositions and verification. It was bad enough that his former pupil had strayed from the purity of presuppositionalism, but to make matters worse an ever-growing readership was now beginning to interpret the presuppositional school of thought through Schaeffer's cloudy lens. In light of this disturbing development, Van Til decided to challenge Schaeffer through a series of personal letters. But instead of clarifying his position, Schaeffer simply refused to respond. There appear to be three reasons for his reluctance to engage Van Til.

First, as noted, Schaeffer was not a scholastic apologist. He felt that some might be called to this task, but he was consumed with the day-to-day conversion of souls. With evangelistic fruit hanging on the tree, he simply could not justify the energy to engage in an academic debate.

Second, Schaeffer sincerely respected Van Til and believed he was using a great deal of his mentor's thinking and teaching. This admiration was clearly displayed in one of Schaeffer's many return visits to Westminster. On this particular occasion, the president of the seminary sat the two down in his office and tried to mediate a resolution to the apparent rift. Van Til, eager to draw Schaeffer into a verbal clash, raised point after point, only to find Schaeffer agreeing with each statement. Finally, Van Til spent fifteen uninterrupted minutes laying out his apologetic methodology with great flair. When Van Til finished, Schaeffer respectfully responded, "That is the most beautiful statement on apologetics I've ever heard. I wish there had been a tape recorder here. I would make it required listening for all L'Abri workers."[28]

Third, Schaeffer knew how ugly academic debates could become, especially debates involving Van Til. In 1948 Van Til and J. Oliver Buswell engaged in an ongoing, heated exchange over apologetic methodology in a denominational periodical entitled *The Bible Today*. Week after week the battle raged between Van Til's presuppositionalism and Buswell's evidentialism. Eventually an annoyed reader crafted the following tongue-in-cheek poem with the hope of putting the dispute to rest:

I do not like your Presuppositionalism controversy; it is getting acrimonious, and doesn't show much grace, common or special. But I know you both could sing . . .
Scotch is Scotch,
And Dutch is Dutch,
But Calvin was French, you see,
And died at the age of fifty-five,
Not older than "B" or "Van T."
He wrote in the language of 1509
He wrote not English nor Dutch,
He wrote in the words he understood
And has been translated much.
And the mind of the Scotch interprets Scotch,
And the mind of the Dutch sees Dutch;
But God's great grace is working on
And souls respond to His touch.
And when the glorious crowning day
The Scotch and the Dutch shall meet,
They both will say "It is all of grace;
We have reached the Mercy seat."
But Buswell still will drive his "Bus"
And Van Til his "Van" will drive,

But whether thru tunnel or over bridge,

By *grace* they will both arrive.[29]

Schaeffer presumably agreed with the sentiments expressed in this poem, but he had his own plan for getting the evidential "Bus" and the presuppositional "Van" onto the same apologetic highway. In a short *Bible Today* article, Schaeffer highlighted the points of common ground between these Reformed apologists: the shared belief in the divine call in the act of salvation, the impossibility of reasoning someone into heaven, the necessity of talking and preaching to nonbelievers, the bankruptcy of all non-Christian worldviews, and the joint conviction that Christianity is the correct worldview and it could only hypothetically be wrong for the sake of discussion.[30] He then proceeded to sketch out a third way, a mediating methodology that takes into account the best insights of the other two schools of thought.

This article is fascinating on two counts. First, it shows Schaeffer displaying a remarkably irenic spirit during a time when heated exchanges were commonplace among his Presbyterian brethren. Second, he proposes a via media that reveals his entire apologetic methodology in embryonic form twenty years before *The God Who Is There* was published.[31] In the end, however, Van Til was unpersuaded by Schaeffer's mediating proposal.

In light of Schaeffer's aversion to academic apologetics, his sincere respect for Van Til and much of his presuppositional methodology, and this failed attempt to adjudicate the issue decades before, it is not surprising to find Schaeffer refusing to respond to Van Til's correspondence. Frustrated that Schaeffer would not acknowledge the error of his ways, Van Til eventually went public with a forceful critique of Schaeffer's methodology that became part of the professor's curriculum at Westminster. Van Til goes to great lengths in this treatise to distance himself and the presuppositional school of thought from Schaeffer's apologetic method. Even a cursory glance at this critique should settle any question about whether Schaeffer was a thoroughgoing Van Tillian. Consider the following excerpt:

So far we have not seen Schaeffer present a challenge to 20th century man in terms of the only God *who is there*. His constant appeal to the Bible is calculated to make us think that he starts with the presupposition of the God of the Bible as the only ground for the possibility of significant predication. The reality so far, however, is that in terms of methodology he has not really gone beyond the natural theology of Thomas Aquinas and the evidential method of Bishop Butler. His "presupposition" is to all intents and purposes identical with modern man's idea of *hypothesis*.[32]

Van Til apparently believes Schaeffer's consistent references to Scripture are "calculated" to mislead us into thinking he is a true presuppositionalist. But

Van Til will not let such deception go unnoticed. He says that although Schaeffer uses the term *presupposition*, he fills it with different content. For Van Til, biblical presuppositions are not subject to verification or falsification but are fully self-authenticating. To attempt to verify biblical data is to place fallen human reason in judgment of God's Word. This will not do. Sinful humanity should not inductively test and weigh the claims of the Bible in the balance of corrupt human reason but rather bow in abject humility before the throne of grace.

Schaeffer's idea of presupposition, on the other hand, is more like the modern notion of hypothesis. Far from a set of beliefs that are exempt from a posteriori testing, Schaeffer's "presuppositions" must be subjected to the process of verification if we are to honestly discern their truth value. Consider this revealing passage from *Whatever Happened to the Human Race?*

> The biblical system does not have to be accepted blindly, any more than the scientific hypotheses have to be accepted blindly. What a scientist does is to examine certain phenomena in the world. He then casts about for an explanation that will make sense of these phenomena. This is the hypothesis. But the hypothesis has to be checked. So a careful checking operation is set up, designed to see if there is, in fact, a correspondence between what has been observed and what has been hypothesized. If it does correspond, a scientist accepts the explanation as correct; if it does not, he rejects it as false and looks for an alternative explanation. Depending on how substantially the statement has been "verified," it becomes accepted as a "law" within science. . . .
>
> What we should notice is the method. It is rather like trying to find the right key to fit a particular lock. We try the first key and then the next and the next until finally, if we are fortunate, one of them fits. The same principle applies, so Christians maintain, when we consider the big questions. Here are the phenomena. What key unlocks their meaning? What explanation is correct?[33]

It is highly unlikely that Schaeffer tried to deceive his readers into thinking he was a Van Tillian presuppositionalist. But the above passage does lend considerable credence to Van Til's charge that Schaeffer's notion of a presupposition is more like a hypothesis than an ultimate truth claim that is beyond verification. This is clearly where Schaeffer and Van Til part company. Schaeffer could not stomach any irrational form of mysticism, from the extreme existentialism of Sartre to the false piety of believers who champion the virtues of blind faith: "At first acquaintance this concept gives the feeling of spirituality. 'I do not ask for answers, I just believe.' This sounds spiritual, and it deceives many fine people."[34] Schaeffer rejected the insistence that the

Bible must be blindly accepted hook, line and sinker apart from any evidence. "The truth that we let in first is not a dogmatic statement of the truth of the Scriptures, but the truth of the external world and the truth of what man himself is."[35]

In other words, Schaeffer believed the proper starting point in apologetics is not an authoritarian insistence on the inerrancy of Scripture and the unverifiable truth of the Christian system but rather an appeal to the external world and internal states common to all humanity. In adopting this approach Schaeffer followed in the footsteps of B. B. Warfield, who embraced the full inerrancy of Scripture but did not demand acceptance of this doctrine before conversation could start. Rather, Warfield believed there were good and sufficient empirical reasons for accepting the historical reliability of the biblical account. Once the nonbeliever accepts this premise, a proper argument can be made for inerrancy. But the starting point should be with the historical reliability of the biblical documents, not some unverifiable, ultimate claim.[36]

It seems that Van Til has correctly identified what Schaeffer meant by the term *presupposition*, but is he correct in labeling Schaeffer an evidentialist? We think not. Van Til apparently took only two apologetic options seriously. So after showing Schaeffer's inconsistency with the presuppositionalist approach, he simply relegates his former student to the "other" camp. But this is misleading, for Schaeffer is no more a pure follower of Aquinas than he is of Van Til. It would appear that Van Til simply was unaware of other apologetic options, particularly the option of verificationism. In light of Schaeffer's understanding of presuppositions as hypotheses and the need to test hypotheses against the relevant lines of data, it would appear that Schaeffer is neither a presuppositionalist nor an evidentialist but is best considered a verificationist.[37]

Apologetics Must Be Relational
All this talk about presuppositions, hypotheses and the like has prompted some to characterize Schaeffer's methodology as unduly rigid, austere and mechanical. Thomas Morris, author of *Francis Schaeffer's Apologetics*, has suggested that "the reader is almost led to imagine men formulating syllogisms and proof lines over lunch."[38] Charges like this undoubtedly motivated Schaeffer to craft an appendix to the complete works edition of *The God Who Is There*. In this appendix Schaeffer goes to great lengths to clarify his belief that the approach he outlines should never be applied mechanically, for everyone is different and should be treated with respect and dignity. Nonbelievers are not projects, science experiments or scalps to be won. We should

not rain down indiscriminate apologetic aerial assaults from the heavens but rather step out of our comfort zones and into the daily rough-and-tumble lives of the people around us. In short, apologetics must be relational.

Though Schaeffer's writing can occasionally come across as Morris suggests, the overall thrust of his presentation is remarkably compassionate and rich with references to the infinite value and diversity of human life. He consistently reminds the reader that nonbelievers are human beings for whom Christ died. He feels the anguish of painters such as Picasso, musicians such as John Cage and poets such as Dylan Thomas. When discussing Thomas, Schaeffer pleads for compassion, insisting that "he is not an insect on the head of a pin, but shares the same flesh and blood as we do, a man in real despair."[39] Schaeffer continues his impassioned appeal by describing a bronze statue of Thomas, which resides in a London art gallery: "Anyone who looks at it without compassion is dead. There he faces you with a cigarette at the side of his mouth, the very cigarette hung in despair. It is not enough to take a man like this or any of the others and smash them as though we have no responsibility for them."[40] Nothing irked Schaeffer more than callous, cavalier Christians who coldly dismissed the bizarre, groping and painful expressions of contemporary culture. Schaeffer challenged this apathetic attitude with a fresh Kierkegaardian passion:

> Dare we laugh at such things? Dare we feel superior when we view their tortured expressions in their art? Christians should stop laughing and take such men seriously. Then we shall have the right to speak again to our generation. These men are dying while they live; yet where is our compassion for them? There is nothing more ugly than a Christian orthodoxy without understanding or without compassion.[41]

Schaeffer believed apologetics is a deeply engaging activity that requires a holistic approach. We must not simply try to argue people into the kingdom; we must empathize with their plight. We must understand where nonbelievers are coming from and what it is that is gnawing away at their humanity. This type of compassion is what motivated Schaeffer to translate the content of Christianity into words and images that make sense to contemporary people. This type of compassion is what motivated Schaeffer to gain knowledge across a wide variety of disciplines so he could converse on subjects ranging from philosophy to physics. This type of compassion is what motivated Schaeffer to tailor an apologetic strategy to each person he met instead of offering a canned systematic presentation or prepackaged methodology.

When it came to apologetic discourse, Schaeffer was extremely sensitive to the context of his dialogical partner. If the person was open to hearing the gospel, he would never begin by waxing eloquent about the "line of despair";

he simply explained the basic plan of salvation. If the person was closed to the gospel, he did not try to introduce the plan of salvation but rather looked for angles into that person's life, an entry point that could generate conversation on some level.

Schaeffer was particularly effective with nonbelievers who were closed. He thought many Christians give up too easily on nonbelievers, writing them off as "nonelect" if they resist a gospel presentation. But Schaeffer was convinced that many critics of Christianity are not rejecting the authentic, historic, orthodox view of the faith but rather a false impression. Therefore, he worked diligently to help people see the truth and beauty of the Christian vision in a way that was both credible and captivating to the contemporary mind.

When dealing with nonbelievers who were closed to a straightforward presentation of the gospel, Schaeffer often employed a fascinating strategy called "taking the roof off." As we saw in chapter four, this strategy is essentially a matter of helping non-Christians recognize the implications of their own bankrupt belief systems. Schaeffer was thoroughly convinced that Christianity is the only perspective that makes sense of the external world and the internal states common to humanity, or as he put it, "the universe and its form" and the "mannishness of man." According to Schaeffer, all non-Christian worldviews logically lead to irrationality, amorality and total meaninglessness. And if everything is meaningless, then suicide is the most logical option. The choice is between Christianity or nihilism. Ultimately, these are the only two rational options.

Schaeffer was certain that consistent nihilism is an oxymoron, an existential impossibility. A cartoon that appeared in *National Review* a few years ago illustrates this assertion. Two disheveled, long-haired, bearded men have bellied up to a bar. One is holding a bottle and poised to speak; the other is clutching a cigarette, undoubtedly anticipating another dose of despair, when his friend speaks up: "I don't know . . . it seems like nihilism just isn't enough any more." This is precisely what Schaeffer is telling us: Nihilism might seem noble and honest in theory, but it is an existential impossibility. People simply cannot live an irrational, amoral, meaningless life all the way across the board. Such a position cannot be sustained. It logically leads to suicide.

Fortunately, however, nonbelievers are rarely consistent, and since their lives do not consistently square with their professed worldviews, they must live in perpetual tension. On the one hand, they sense a tug to be consistent to their presuppositions; on the other hand, they must live existentially in the real world God has created. Therefore, they are constantly confronted with anomalies that do not fit their paradigms. According to Schaeffer, they have no basis for communication, but they continue to converse. They have no basis for rationality, but they continue to think. They have no basis for morality, but they continue to make ethical judgments. They have no basis for aesthetics, but they continue to appreciate beauty. Schaeffer does not say that these people are not experiencing these things; they are. He simply says that non-Christian systems cannot adequately account for the undeniable reality of these experiences.[42] So the non-Christian is caught between two worlds: the artificial world of his non-Christian system and the real world created by the infinite-personal God. Schaeffer believes this inconsistency, the ability of the non-Christian to experience and appreciate God's world, is a result of common grace.[43] Since humans are totally depraved, Schaeffer believes common grace is necessary if the regenerate and the unregenerate are to have any common ground. Therefore, the inconsistency of the non-Christian is at the same time both a curse and a blessing. It causes the nonbeliever unpleasant cognitive and existential discomfort, but it also allows a point of evangelistic contact, which can lead to the Christian solution.

Once we realize every nonbeliever is living in dissonance, the first step is to locate the specific point of tension or anomaly in that person's life—the inconsistency between what nonbelievers preach and what they actually practice. Schaeffer was a master at this, loading his books with illustrations along these lines. Consider his critique of John Cage. This modern musician's belief in the random, irrational nature of reality led to a style of music that was thoroughly chaotic and unpredictable. Cage was more than a musician, however; he was also a nationally recognized mycologist. Yet when it came to collecting mushrooms, Cage could not live consistently with his philosophy of blind, random chance, for such a method would not allow for rational discrimination between safe and poisonous fungi. Consequently, the only way Cage could continue to record his irrational music was by rationally avoiding deadly mushrooms. In other words, Cage could not live consistently with his system.[44]

Or consider the life of Bernard Berenson, an internationally recognized art critic who justified his open marriage on the grounds that humans are simply animals and should follow our base urges wherever they lead. But when it came to his true passion, Renaissance art, Berenson refused to live like an animal. In fact, he was appalled by modern art because he considered it "bestial."[45] Though Berenson lived like a beast when it came to his marriage, he simply could not live that way when it came to what he truly valued, which, unfortunately for Mrs. Berenson, was not fidelity in the bedroom but paint on a canvas.

So Schaeffer tells us that the point of contact with nonbelievers is the point of tension in their lives. This point of tension can take a variety of forms. For

Cage, it was mushrooms; for Berenson, Renaissance art. This is where we must concentrate our apologetic efforts. We must converse with people to learn where they are coming from and put our finger on what they value, the spot where they just cannot bear to live consistently with their worldviews. Once we have done this, we must then lovingly but firmly drive them to the painful, logical implications of their presuppositions and show them that their paradigms cannot account for what they value. This is taking the roof off.

Once the artificial roof is off and nonbelievers have confronted and experienced the cold, harsh futility of their respective systems, then Schaeffer says we must offer the fully self-consistent, comprehensive and livable Christian system as the only option that can account for what is valuable.[46] Edith once asked her husband if he was concerned that this approach of exposing people to the despairing implications of their belief systems could lead someone to suicide. Schaeffer was fully aware of this possibility and warned Christians not to push people beyond the point that is necessary. But he thought it was imperative that non-Christians come to terms with the total meaninglessness and despair of their worldviews.[47] Only then will the truly closed person open to the intellectual and existential potency of the Christian faith.

Apologetics Must Be Plausible

As we have seen, Schaeffer believed Christian truth claims ought to be rationally credible and open to verification. If these claims do not stand up to careful, honest, intellectual scrutiny, then they should be rejected. But our evaluation of Schaeffer's apologetic methodology would be woefully lacking if we did not consider one other criterion by which Christianity is to be judged—the criterion of plausibility.

According to Schaeffer, tight doctrinal formulations and compelling cognitive arguments are necessary but only part of the package. All the proofs in the world will ring hollow unless believers make the faith plausible by modeling authentic Christian community. Schaeffer was all too familiar with the tragedy of hollow orthodoxy. His ministry was formed in the crucible of the denominational wars of the thirties and forties. Defrockings, schisms and hubris were commonplace during this era, and the effects of internal strife and habitual infighting eventually took a toll on Schaeffer's spiritual life. This led to his spiritual crisis in the early fifties, an event that proved to be a pivotal experience. Schaeffer emerged from this "dark night of the soul" with a renewed hunger for moment-by-moment personal spirituality and the corporate demonstration of Christian love.

In *The Mark of the Christian* Schaeffer underscores the importance of authentic community by telling his readers that Christians must realize they are on trial. Consider the words of Jesus in John 13:34-35: "A new commandment I give you: Love one another. As I have loved you, so you must love one another. All men will know that you are my disciples if you love one another." Schaeffer believes Jesus gives the world the right to judge Christians. On what basis will Christians be judged? Not according to their truth claims or their theological consistency or their doctrinal formulations, but rather on the basis of love—their love for each other. And what type of love must it be? Not some halfhearted, superficial, syrupy form of love, but the same type of tough-fibered, sacrificial, costly love that Jesus himself displayed toward his disciples.[48]

But that is not all. Jesus has not only given the world the right to judge Christians on the basis of their love for one another, he also has given the world the right to judge the truth claims of the Christian faith on the basis of visible love between the brethren. John 17:20-21 records a portion of Jesus' high priestly prayer: "My prayer is not for them alone. I pray also for those who will believe in me through their message, that all of them may be one, Father, just as you are in me and I am in you. May they also be in us so that the world may believe that you have sent me." Schaeffer said he cringed every time he encountered this particularly sobering text. He considered it "the final apologetic."

In John 13 the point was that if an individual Christian does not show love toward other true Christians, the world has a right to judge that he is not a Christian. Here Jesus is stating something else which is much more cutting, much more profound: We cannot expect the world to believe that the Father sent the Son, that Jesus' claims are true, and that Christianity is true, unless the world sees some reality of the oneness of true Christians.[49]

Schaeffer is not suggesting that Christians must be perfect in their exhibition of corporate love and unity, but he does believe there must be a substantial difference between community in the world and community among believers. The proper type of community will entail a variety of things, including the consistent practice of repentance and forgiveness,[50] a commitment to graceful, humble and loving theological discussion,[51] tangible financial and material support,[52] and the inclusivity of all true believers. Schaeffer insists that Christianity is the only worldview that can provide a unified diversity. It cuts across all languages, nationalities, age groups, ethnicities, classes, cultures, worship forms and styles of attire.[53] Christianity does not insist that believers become homogenous replicas or cookie cutter clones. Rather, the Christian system allows for a beautiful array of diversity, all built around a common commitment to the core doctrines of the faith. This type of community continues to be one of the most captivating features of the L'Abri movement.

In summary, Schaeffer's apologetic approach displays remarkable balance and flexibility. He emphasizes the need to undermine non-Christian presuppositions, while insisting on a rational basis for faith. He rejects prepackaged plans and "can't-miss" universal arguments in favor of a person-relative apologetic. Ultimately he realizes cognitive proofs and truth claims will have little or no force if Christians do not model true community before the watching world. Interestingly, for Schaeffer, the great defender of antithesis, Christian apologetics boils down to a balanced series of both-ands.[54] It requires both presuppositional thinking and rational proof. It requires both orthodoxy and orthopraxis. It requires both credibility and plausibility. Quite simply, Christian apologetics requires both a sharp mind and a warm heart.

The Gospel According to St. Lewis

The battle over apologetic methodology, much like the battle over inerrancy, has been largely limited to Reformed circles, so it is hardly surprising to find C. S. Lewis rarely addressing this topic in an overt manner. We generally do not find Lewis writing about methodology or discussing strategy but simply doing what he does best, making a credible case for the Christian faith.

We get a sense of what Lewis might have said about the issue of methodology from one of his most reliable interpreters, Peter Kreeft. In their *Handbook of Christian Apologetics*, a four-hundred-page tome with frequent references to Lewis, Kreeft and Ronald Tacelli offer some intriguing comments about the place of methodology in the overall scheme of things.

An introduction to apologetics usually deals with methodology. We do not. We believe that nowadays second-order questions of method often distract attention from first-order questions of truth. Our intent is to get "back to basics." We have no particular methodological axe to grind. We try to use commonsense standards of rationality and universally agreed principles of logic in all our arguing. We collect and sharpen arguments like gem collectors collecting and polishing gems; readers can set them into various settings of their own.[55]

It seems likely that Lewis would have resonated with such a statement. As we shall see, the pursuit of truth is one of the enduring features of Lewis's life and apologetic ministry, and he firmly believed "commonsense standards of rationality and universally agreed principles of logic" are necessary to set any argument in motion. Lewis once said that self-evident truths like these are something "no good man has ever disputed."[56]

There are two preliminary comments worth making at this point. First, the fact that Lewis did not generally engage in methodological discussions does not mean he operated without any type of implicit method. Surely he did. It just means we will need to dig a little deeper to unearth this underlying approach. Second, we need not spend our time digging for Van Tillian affinities, for Schaeffer was not the only popular apologist roundly criticized by the patriarch of presuppositionalism.

Os Guinness recalls an encounter with Van Til that illustrates this claim. Guinness had just finished delivering a lecture at Westminster when an elderly gentleman accused him of making "a bad mistake." This elderly man turned out to be Van Til, who accused Guinness of making numerous references to C. S. Lewis during the course of the lecture. Van Til chided Guinness for his carelessness, then marched him off to his office, where he produced a stack of his own books about presuppositional apologetics and piled them into the reluctant arms of the visiting lecturer.[57]

Presumably one of those books was Van Til's apologetic treatise *The Defense of the Faith*. In this work Van Til leaves little doubt about his disdain for Lewisian methodology: "One can only rejoice in the fact that Lewis is heard the world around, but one can only grieve that he so largely follows the method of Thomas Aquinas in calling men back to the gospel. The 'gospel according to St. Lewis' is too much of a compromise with the ideas of natural man to constitute a clear challenge in our day."[58]

The balance of this chapter will be dedicated to discerning the apologetic strategy of "St. Lewis." In our effort to identify his method, we will consider four key facets of his apologetic: the centrality of truth, the need for fair argument, the comparison of worldviews and the art of persuasive communication.

Men, Rabbits and the Centrality of Truth

C. S. Lewis was drawn to the task of apologetics after an honest spiritual search led to the conviction that Christianity is not merely a source of comfort, or a mystical, subjective experience but is objectively true. This commitment to absolute, objective truth cuts against the grain of both modern liberal theology and much of contemporary evangelicalism. The former often de-mythologizes and relativizes the message, while much of the latter caters to the self-indulgent and self-absorbed consumption of our age.

More than a generation ago, Lewis found it difficult to keep his audience focused on the subject of objective truth. Modern people simply are not used to thinking about religion in objective terms. Religion is something personal, subjective and private, valued for its comfort and pragmatic power. But

something objectively true? This is largely a foreign concept to the twentieth-century mind. That is why Lewis worked so hard to keep his listeners
and readers centered on the issue of truth. He achieved this with provocative
and memorable lines such as the following: "Christianity is a statement, which
if false, is of no importance, and, if true, of infinite importance. The one thing
it cannot be is moderately important."[59] And "if you look for truth, you may
find comfort in the end; if you look for comfort you will not get either comfort
or truth."[60]

Lewis had little patience with those who embraced Christianity for its
pragmatic appeal, with little or no concern for its truth claims. He considered
such people morally corrupt. Why would Lewis make such an assumption?
Quite simply, Lewis was convinced it is self-evident that we ought to seek
truth simply for the sake of truth. One cannot prove that we ought to seek
truth any more than one can prove that two plus two equals four or that the
laws of logic are reliable. Either you see it or you do not, and the normal
person should be able to see it. Lewis believed the thing that often keeps a
sane person from seeing the truth is moral corruption, a desire to suppress
the truth.

In his memorable essay "Man or Rabbit?" Lewis makes it clear that people
who place pragmatism and comfort over the pursuit of truth are not only
dishonest, they are less than fully human. Part of our humanity is a desire to
seek the truth wherever it leads. If the truth leads to despair, then nihilists we
must be. Lewis put it this way: "If Christianity is untrue, no honest man will
want to believe it, however helpful it might be: if it is true, every honest man
will want to believe it, even if it gives him no help at all."[61]

One way Lewis kept his audience centered on the issue of objective truth
was by reminding them that he was not defending his own personal beliefs
but rather the historic, orthodox doctrines of the faith handed down by the
saints. These doctrines are embedded in the scriptural data and summarized
in the classic, ecumenical creeds. So personal, subjective opinion is simply
irrelevant. The defender of Christianity is no more at liberty to alter the
historic content of the faith than the scientist is to tamper with the content
of his test tubes.[62]

Lewis thought the scientist and apologist are not only tied to objective
data, but both are bound as well by the same means of adjudication. In an
essay entitled "Religion: Reality or Substitute?" Lewis uses a story from his
childhood to illustrate his belief that there are three ways to arrive at the truth
in any given situation. When he was a boy, he and his brother, Warnie, would
occasionally snatch cigarettes from their father. On occasion his father's
cigarette supply would run so low that they could not risk swiping cigarettes,

so they would pilfer cigars instead. The boys thought cigars a poor substitute for cigarettes, but it was better than nothing. As they grew older they eventually came to realize the folly of considering cigarettes a preferable indulgence to cigars.

According to Lewis, these "bad boys" could have corrected their mutual misconception in one of three ways. First, they could have simply asked an adult which indulgence was more urbane. In so doing they would have determined the truth through an appeal to *authority*. Second, they could have gone down to the store and noticed that cigars are the more expensive vice. In so doing they would have determined the truth by using their *reason*. Third, they could have simply waited until they developed an adult cultivation. In so doing they would have determined the truth by *experience*.[63] Lewis thought authority, reason and experience, in varying degrees, are the necessary ingredients to discern the truth in any situation, in any realm of life, whether you are a scientist, an apologist or even a juvenile delinquent.

This strong emphasis on reason and objective truth may seem to leave little room for faith. But as Lewis saw it, faith and reason harmonize quite well. Like Schaeffer, Lewis repudiated the assertion that religious truth can be obtained only through a blind, fideistic leap. This is not faith at all. Faith and reason are allies; they are not enemies divided by an infinite epistemological chasm.

Lewis distinguishes between three types of faith. The first is belief grounded in the facts. Through authority, reason or experience—or some combination of the three—we come to the conclusion that a particular assertion is true. The doctrines of Christianity, for instance, are founded on firm evidence. If the evidence is compelling, we will believe it. If it is not, then we should reject it. This is the first type of belief or faith. The second type of faith is a quality of trust and commitment. In the realm of Christianity, believers are called to place their faith or full trust in the person of Jesus Christ. Again this is not a blind faith, but is rather a faith founded on the established reliability of the person in question. It is a faith that moves the believer beyond intellectual assent to an existential, personal response. The third type of faith is what Lewis considers "obstinacy"[64] or tenacity in the face of emotions, moods or the imagination. After we come to believe the Christian doctrines, we are often assaulted by wishes and desires that make us think "it would be very convenient if Christianity were not true."[65] In these moments, it is not new evidence that has surfaced to question the validity of our belief, but rather it is often a desire to engage in some type of immoral behavior. We must confront new evidence squarely,[66] but if it is simply an impulse or improper desire, we must be willing to tell our moods "where they get off."[67] Lewis sums up his perspective with this choice statement:

> If we wish to be rational, not now and then, but constantly, we must pray
> for the gift of Faith, for the power to go on believing not in the teeth of
> reason but in the teeth of lust and terror and jealousy and boredom and
> indifference that which reason, authority, or experience, or all three, have
> once delivered to us for truth.[68]

In short, faith has three important aspects. It is belief based on facts, it is
existential trust and response, and it is tenacity in the face of misguided
emotions, moods or imagination. But faith is never an irrational, fideistic leap.

The Need to Debulverize

Lewis opens *Miracles* with a story about the only person he ever met who
claims to have seen a ghost. This person did not believe she had seen a specter
but rather "an illusion or a trick of the nerves."[69] Why was this person
unpersuaded? Quite simply, her worldview would not admit the possibility
of any supernatural activity, therefore she insisted upon a naturalistic explanation.

In the previous section we underscored the centrality of seeking the truth
through authority, reason and experience. Sometimes this is easier said than
done. It is not always a simple matter of laying out the evidence, swearing in
the appropriate authority and appealing to the cognitive faculties of the jury.
Sometimes the jury is hung—not because they did not all view the same
evidence, hear the same testimony and attentively follow the logic of the case.
Sometimes it is not the empirical data that splits the jury but rather the
assumptions that the jurors bring to the data. According to Lewis, "What we
learn from experience depends on the kind of philosophy we bring to
experience. It is therefore useless to appeal to experience before we have
settled, as well as we can, the philosophical question."[70] Lewis's point is similar
in spirit to Schaeffer's emphasis on presuppositions. Both were sharply aware
that our judgment on many matters, including matters of fact, will hinge on
our basic philosophical commitments.

The guiding assumptions in Lewis's day, at least among the educated, were
predominantly naturalistic. Consequently, supernaturalism was often not
only denied a fair hearing but denied any type of hearing at all. Such claims
were simply inadmissible. Instead of evaluating the truth claims of Christianity on objective, empirical grounds, many naturalists assumed its falsehood
and spent their time explaining why Christians believe what they do. Lewis
insisted that this type of bias is the foundation of twentieth-century thought.
It was so prevalent during Lewis's era that he invented a name for it. He called
it "Bulverism."[71] Debulverization, therefore, is often the first step toward

meaningful dialogue between the naturalist and the supernaturalist.

What exactly is Bulverism? Quite simply, it is assuming your opponent's thoughts are tainted but yours are not. Lewis seems to be suggesting that a tainted thought is one that has a dubious source. It is a thought that can be traced to an origin of Freudian wishful thinking or to some form of economic, sociological or cultural conditioning. Consequently, the person holding a tainted belief has been duped, either by himself or by some external conditioner.

Lewis thought two questions must be asked of the bulverizer: First, are all thoughts tainted? Second, does such taint invalidate the truth claim that is being made? If the bulverizer responds by saying all thought is tainted (and consequently invalid) then we are all in the same boat, bulverizers and bulverizees alike. All reason is shipwrecked. If the bulverizer responds by saying that such taint does not invalidate the truth claim then, again, everyone is in the same boat and the tide rises for all truth claims. According to Lewis, the only way forward for the bulverizer is to admit that some thoughts are tainted and some are not. But if this is true, then how are we to adjudicate?

Lewis said the only way to determine which thoughts are tainted and which are not is to start with an empirical investigation of the data. If a person's position is thereby shown to be wrong, then one possibility worth pursuing is that some dubious motivation precipitated the error. But we must first figure out if someone is in fact wrong before we explain why that person is wrong. The modern approach, however, assumes that all supernatural claims are tainted and therefore wrong, then distracts us from the facts by quickly suggesting how the supernaturalist "became so silly."[72]

Of course, Bulverism can go both ways. Both Christianity and naturalism are susceptible. Naturalists say the Christian cause is perpetuated by the comfortable class who wants to keep the masses in check. But Christians can equally say that naturalists dismiss the concept of an ultimate moral judge so they can indulge their lascivious urges. Two can play this game, and it settles nothing. The only way to get to the truth is to engage the issue on philosophical and historical turf. In other words, "you can only find out the rights and wrongs by reasoning—never by being rude about your opponent's psychology."[73]

Completing the Pattern

Once Bulverism is debunked, the way is cleared to investigate the relevant data. It then becomes a matter of putting biases aside and comparing competing hypotheses to see which one offers the most consistent and comprehensive vision of reality.[74] Lewis provides this example in *Miracles:* "I do not maintain that God's creation of Nature can be proved as rigorously as

God's existence, but it seems to me overwhelmingly probable, so probable that no one who approached the question with an open mind would very seriously entertain any other hypothesis."[75] We must ask which hypothesis makes best sense of the order in the world? Which hypothesis makes best sense of our moral intuitions? Which hypothesis makes best sense of our rational faculties? Which hypothesis makes best sense of our aesthetic longings? There is no question in Lewis's mind which hypothesis fits the facts: "My reason ... show[s] me the apparently insoluble difficulties of materialism and prov[es] that the hypothesis of a spiritual world covers far more of the facts with far fewer assumptions."[76]

This is precisely the approach Lewis pursued in his own spiritual quest, which led him to test one bankrupt philosophy after another until he finally concluded that the Christian notion of the Incarnation is the "one hypothesis which, if accepted, makes everything easy and coherent."[77] What does Lewis mean by easy and coherent? To illustrate this point, Lewis suggests the human search for the ultimate context of life is like possessing a portion of a novel or an incomplete symphony. We have part of the story or score, but we need the missing sections to understand the overall meaning of the narrative or to appreciate the full beauty of the composition.

> Let us suppose we possess parts of a novel or a symphony. Someone now brings us a newly discovered piece of manuscript and says, "This is the missing part of the work. This is the chapter on which the whole plot of the novel really turned. This is the main theme of the symphony." Our business would be to see whether the new passage, if admitted to the central place which the discoverer claimed for it, did actually illuminate all the parts we had already seen and "pull them together."[78]

One should note the striking similarity between this passage and Schaeffer's mutilated book analogy, an illustration we considered in chapter four. Both men are on to the same point. We have access to a portion of reality, but a gaping hole remains. Natural revelation (the universe and its form and the mannishness of man) reveals a pattern, but it is incomplete. Lewis and Schaeffer both insist that the Christian hypothesis fills the gaps and completes the pattern.

Lewis first felt the force of this truth while reading Chesterton's *Everlasting Man*. This book had a profound impact on his thinking, offering an epiphanic glimpse of "the whole Christian outline of history set out in a form that seemed to me to make sense."[79] Chesterton presented the case for Christianity in a way that allowed a comprehensive and compelling pattern to emerge. It illuminated what Lewis already knew to be true and pulled all the previously disjointed pieces into a harmonious vision of reality. It made sense of the world like no other system, religion or philosophy could.

Elsewhere we find Chesterton, arguably Lewis's most important apologetic influence, likening Christianity to the key that unlocks the door of ultimate reality: "In answer to the historical query of why [Christianity] was accepted, and is accepted, I answer for millions of others in my reply; because it fits the lock; because it is like life. It is one among many stories; only it happens to be a true story. It is one among many philosophies; only it happens to be the truth."[80] This imagery bears a striking resemblance to a passage from *Whatever Happened to the Human Race?* in which Schaeffer explains that the search for the meaning of life "is rather like trying to find the right key to fit a particular lock. We try the first key and then the next and the next until finally, if we are fortunate, one of them fits."[81]

So what we find here are strong similarities between Lewis and Schaeffer in the realm of methodology. Reality is like an incomplete manuscript or a locked door. What we must do is find the missing portion that completes the pattern or the key that turns the handle. Both men engaged in an existential search for truth that ultimately culminated in the conviction that the Christian hypothesis alone completes the pattern and unlocks the door to reality. This data leads us to conclude that Lewis is best situated alongside Schaeffer in the verificational camp of apologetics.

Watchful Dragons and the Art of Persuasion

In the opening pages of *The Elements of Style*, a classic guide to English prose, E. B. White offers a fitting tribute to his deceased coauthor, William Strunk: "Will felt that the reader was in serious trouble most of the time, a man floundering in a swamp, and that it was the duty of anyone attempting to write English to drain this swamp quickly and get his man up on dry ground, or at least throw him a rope."[82] Although originally written about another stylist, this passage is an equally apt description of C. S. Lewis. Lewis was a masterful writer, as his remarkably readable corpus reveals. Clarity of thought, choice metaphors and effective timing all work together to make him one of our century's most effective literary communicators.

But White's passage is not only an apt description of Lewis the writer; it is an equally apt description of Lewis the apologist. For as we have already seen, Lewis was not just a writer, he was a "literary evangelist," concerned with rescuing his readers from both needless obscurity and the swamp of sin. In both cases Lewis went to great lengths to get the drowning man onto dry ground. In this section we will consider some of his rescue techniques.

Like Schaeffer, Lewis realized there are a wide variety of opinions when it comes to Christian truth claims. Some people are open, others closed. Most are somewhere in between. Consequently, the apologist must allow the attitude of the nonbeliever to dictate the technique to be employed. If the man in the swamp wants to be saved, by all means, toss him a rope. If he refuses the rope, do not simply call the coroner—find a way to drain the swamp. In other words, there is more than one way to save a drowning man. Lewis understood this and used a beautiful balance of both direct and indirect techniques.

His direct method is easily discerned in works like *The Problem of Pain, Mere Christianity, The Abolition of Man* and *Miracles.* When reading these books, one can almost imagine Lewis sitting down with an unchurched neighbor, a questioning colleague, a searching acquaintance. With a cup of tea in hand and blazing fire in the background, Lewis spreads the Christian cards on the table in a logical, orderly, coherent fashion. There is no sleight of hand and nothing up his sleeve. He seems to be saying, "Come, let us reason together. Common sense and a little bit of logic will lead us to the truth."

In *Mere Christianity* Lewis makes it clear that he is "not asking anyone to accept Christianity if his best reasoning tells him that the weight of the evidence is against it."[83] Note that Lewis is not suggesting reasoning alone can lead us to the truth; it takes our *best* reasoning. Lewis believes his job is to barricade the doors of irrationality, cart in the evidence and lay out the logical options.

Of course, such a method will work only with those who are willing to look honestly at the evidence. This method also requires a willingness on the part of the apologist to convey the unchanging truth of orthodox Christianity in ways that make sense to contemporary people. In his essay "Christian Apologetics," Lewis affirms that we must learn the language of our audience: "Our business is to present that which is timeless (the same yesterday, today, and tomorrow) in the particular language of our own age."[84] Later in this essay he adds: "You must translate every bit of your Theology into the vernacular.... If you cannot translate your thoughts into uneducated language, then your thoughts were confused."[85] This was essential for Lewis the philologist. He believed our written and oral communication must be clear, simple and concrete. Nothing will turn an open seeker into a closed skeptic any faster than a good helping of lofty, abstract "Christianese."

Closed skepticism, however, does not necessarily mean a closed door. If the front door is locked, try the back. Or to stick with our earlier metaphor, if our man refuses the rope, drain the swamp. Lewis suggests at least two ways to go about employing this indirect method.

First, if we want to reach the masses, we must be willing to "attack the enemy's line of communication."[86] This means we must inject Christianity into all facets of life, including the books that largely shape our culture. Lewis knew that most nonbelievers do not read overtly Christian material, so he thought one of the best ways to reach nonbelievers is to address a subject they are interested in but to do it from a Christian perspective. Of course this does not mean we weave a proverb into every paragraph or cram the plan of salvation into the conclusion. Instead, our Christianity must be latent.

It is not the books written in direct defence of Materialism that make the modern man a materialist; it is the materialistic assumptions in all the other books. In the same way, it is not books on Christianity that will really trouble him. But he would be troubled if, whenever he wanted a cheap popular introduction to some science, the best work on the market was always by a Christian. The first step to the re-conversion of this country is a series, produced by Christians, which can beat the *Penguin* and the *Thinkers Library* on their own ground.[87]

These comments anticipate the concerns many evangelical scholars have recently expressed about the need to engage our culture on a serious intellectual level. Lewis knew the thinking of the masses is largely shaped by the cultural intelligentsia of the age. If Christianity is to be taken seriously again, thinking Christians must be willing to dedicate themselves to their respective disciplines with unrivaled rigor. When Christian doctors, Christian biologists, Christian astronomers, Christian artists and Christian philosophers are all producing significant scholarship in their respective fields, the world will take notice. Lewis is a testament to this method. Along with his prodigious popular religious output, he left a lasting imprint on his academic field.

Lewis effectively employed another indirect method of persuasion, what Os Guinness calls "subversion by surprise."[88] This method is essentially a matter of catching people with their guard down. The author or speaker builds up momentum in one direction, drawing the listener along, then suddenly turns the tables or pulls the rug out. At this moment the listener is most susceptible to seeing the truth. Guinness considers this the primary method utilized in Scripture and cites a number of different ways it can be employed.

On its most basic level, this method can be pursued through a line of questioning. In Genesis we find God "smoking out" Adam and Eve's culpability through calculated interrogation. We see the same sort of approach in the book of Job and in the ministry of Jesus. Schaeffer consistently used this method with great skill. As noted, the majority of his time with nonbelievers was spent asking questions in order to identify inconsistencies.

Lewis, on the other hand, generally employed a more sophisticated form of subversion, something comparable to what goes on in the Beatitudes, the parables of Jesus, drama and poetry. Each form is indirect, involving and imaginative. It draws the listener in and then turns the tables. In the Beatitudes, Jesus soundly submarines the expectations of his Jewish audience with a series of shocking statements: "Blessed are the poor in spirit," "Blessed are those who mourn," "Blessed are the meek." In a culture that valued the rich, the bold and the festive, these words were like a splash of icy-cold water in an unsuspecting face.

The parables are an even more effective form of subversion. The parable of the good Samaritan is a perfect example. One can almost picture the faces of the Jewish religious leaders listening to the story as first the priest and then the Levite encounter the injured traveler and pass by on the other side, followed by the "detestable" Samaritan, who sees the victim and supplies the compassionate assistance the religious men refused to offer. By the time the story is over, Jesus has his audience at an impasse. They cannot deny which man acted more like a neighbor to the injured traveler, but to go and follow the example of a Samaritan, as Jesus suggests, is an outrageous proposal to a culture that considered Samaritans no better than dogs. Jesus hooks them on the horns of a dilemma. They can either fall to their knees and repent or turn on their heels and walk away from the truth. In either case, the trap door has been pulled and the truth is apparent to all.

The use of story can be a powerful form of subversion, as Lewis found out in his own life by reading MacDonald's *Phantastes*. As recounted in chapter one, Lewis had been laboring under the atheistic tutelage of "the Great Knock" when he purchased a copy of this romantic fantasy. Within minutes, the teenager was enthralled; a new quality emerged from the pages and a bright shadow enveloped him. At the time he could not quite put his finger on this new quality, but eventually he came to recognize it as holiness.[89] Lewis admits, "I had not the faintest notion what I had let myself in for by buying *Phantastes*."[90] In other words, Lewis was *surprised* by Joy.

This subversive experience undoubtedly influenced Lewis's penchant for indirect evangelism. In a letter many years later, Lewis wrote that "any amount of theology can now be smuggled into people's minds under cover of romance without their knowing it."[91] Many people are simply turned off by traditional religious forms. Christianity seems obscure, irrelevant, distant, dead. But an imaginative presentation of this same content can wipe away the dust and allow the true essence of holiness to shine through. In an essay on fairy tales, Lewis explained it like this: "But supposing that by casting all these things into an imaginary world, stripping them of their stained-glass and Sunday school associations, one could make them for the first time appear in their real potency? Could one not thus steal past those watchful dragons?"[92] These comments resonate nicely with the sentiments of good friend and colleague

J. R. R. Tolkien, who once suggested that slipping into an imaginary world "shocks us more fully awake than we are for most of our lives."[93]

Lewis employed this indirect technique through a wide variety of creative genres. He used allegory in *The Pilgrim's Regress*, science fiction in his space trilogy, and different forms of fantasy in *The Screwtape Letters*, *The Great Divorce* and the Chronicles of Narnia. In each case we see Lewis telling a captivating story with varying degrees of subtlety. In each case the reader is engaged, encountering the reality of Christianity (whether realizing it or not) in a way that many would never consider if it were presented in a more direct form.

Lewis once received a letter from a woman who was afraid that her son loved Aslan more than Jesus. Lewis kindly replied by saying that such a scenario is impossible, "for the things he loves Aslan for doing or saying are simply the things Jesus really did and said."[94] So we see Lewis's imaginative works are especially effective either with those who have a skewed impression of Christianity, as in the case of this boy, or with those who are not inclined to come to faith through the left hemisphere of the brain. But once they have encountered the reality of Christian truth, once they have touched, tasted and gazed upon the beauty of the eternal, faith becomes a live possibility.

The highest form of imaginative literature for Lewis was myth. Actually Lewis did not consider myth a form of literature, properly speaking, but rather an eternal pattern or story often communicated through the vehicle of literature. In *An Experiment in Criticism* Lewis underscores his belief that myth is extraliterary and suggests the possibility of conveying its essence through other forms: "It is true that such a story can hardly reach us except in words. But this is logically accidental. If some perfected art of mime or silent film or serial pictures could make it clear with no words at all, it would still affect us in the same way."[95] In whatever way myth comes to us, Lewis believes it is always inevitable, fantastic, grave and awe-inspiring.[96]

One of the most powerful qualities of myth, according to Lewis, is its ability to unite our woefully divided existence. Lewis thought it was impossible to both analyze a subject and experience it at the same time.

> This is our dilemma—either to taste and not to know or to know and not to taste—or, more strictly, to lack one kind of knowledge because we are in an experience or to lack another kind because we are outside it. As thinkers we are cut off from what we think about; as those tasting, touching, willing, loving, hating, we do not clearly understand. The more lucidly we think, the more we are cut off: the more deeply we enter into reality, the less we can think.[97]

According to Lewis, if we begin to study the concept of pain, we are not experiencing our subject. We are on the outside looking in. But as soon as a toothache flares up, we are transported to the inside, only to find that we can no longer analyze. Either we can study our subject from the outside, or we can experience it from the inside; we cannot do both at the same time. How are we to unite these two? Lewis thought the reception of a "great myth" was the closest we can get "to experiencing as a concrete what can otherwise be understood only as an abstraction."[98] As we have already seen, the concept of myth played a major role in Lewis's conversion and in his understanding of the Incarnation. Yet Lewis wrote only one myth, *Till We Have Faces.* Many of his works do have a mythical quality, but they are not strictly mythopoeic.

Peter Schakel has alleged there is an inconsistency between Lewis's high view of myth and his utilitarian use of the imagination.[99] Schakel challenges the frequently held assumption that reason and imagination were harmoniously united by Lewis's conversion. Schakel believes Lewis consistently subordinated the imagination to reason throughout the thirties and forties, using the right hemisphere primarily as a servant to flesh out the cognitive, logical points he was trying to prove. Vivid, rich analogies and metaphors are woven throughout *Mere Christianity* and *Miracles,* but this imagery is used largely for the purpose of advancing rational arguments. Schakel suggests that these two faculties were not finally reconciled and synthesized until the final years of Lewis's life.

It is beyond the scope of our study to pursue this line in greater detail. We do, however, question one of Schakel's apparent assumptions, namely, the impropriety of elevating reason above the imagination. Schakel seems to suggest that such an arrangement is flawed and imbalanced. Any work not entirely synthesized is somehow less than it ought to be. But this assumption is highly questionable, for some projects inherently require disparity. If one is presenting a rational case for the Christian faith, it is not surprising to find reason taking center stage, with the imagination filling out the supporting cast with illustrative metaphors. Surely there is a place in apologetics for predominantly rational works, just as there is a place in apologetics for predominantly imaginative works. The work should not be evaluated in light of its rational and imaginative balance but rather in light of its inherent purpose.

With this in mind, we simply highlight Lewis's remarkable balance and dexterity in utilizing both direct and indirect appeals. Lewis's advice to a young writer seems to suggest the need for a healthy dose of both faculties, regardless of the chosen genre of literature.[100] He believes good writing should be clear and simple and should display a judicious sense of word selection. These features are primarily a function of reason. He also believes good writing will include concrete imagery and will not tell the reader how to feel but will move the reader to actually feel the intended emotion. These features are primarily a function of the imagination. Quite simply, it seems good writing is both rational and imaginative. Lewis's advice reveals a balanced integration.

Of course, in the end there is no guarantee that persuasive communication, whether it is rational or imaginative, direct or indirect, will slay or distract watchful dragons. If our man does not want to be saved, he will get his wish. He can refuse the rope. He can even sit and stew in the muddy mire of a liquidated lagoon. Yet there is one thing of which he must beware: a drained swamp may no longer pose a threat of drowning, but water or not, swamps are notorious for lurking reptiles. And in the swamp of sin, surrounded by his cold-blooded cousins, even the most faithful dragon has been known to turn on its master.

On to the Arguments

Our study of methodology has revealed significant affinity between Schaeffer and Lewis. Both men employed a verificational approach, though if we were to locate them on a scale we might place Schaeffer closer to the presuppositional end and Lewis more toward the evidentialist side. Yet their respective spiritual quests and subsequent apologetic writings point to firm verificationism.

We also have suggested a joint commitment to objective truth, faith founded on fact, presuppositional awareness and a balanced arsenal of direct and indirect appeals, including the method of "subversion by surprise." Subversion can come in both negative and positive forms. Schaeffer often pursued the negative angle, forcing people to the point of tension in their lives, while Lewis frequently took the positive route, portraying the beauty of the faith through imaginative literature. It is not surprising that Lewis pursued this avenue, since fantasy, especially MacDonald's *Phantastes*, played a key role in subverting his own unbelief.

Finally, unlike many Christians, Schaeffer and Lewis were undeterred by closed doors. If no one answered the front door, they went around back. If the back door was bolted, they looked for a window. If the windows were locked, they climbed up to the chimney. Once inside, Schaeffer and Lewis both believed in the power of evidence and persuasive argument under the guidance of the Holy Spirit. But which arguments are convincing? That is the question we must now explore.

Imagine that Hegel was sitting one day in the local tavern, surrounded by his friends, conversing on philosophical issues of the day. Suddenly he put down his mug of beer on the table and said, "I have a new idea. From now on let us think in this way: Instead of thinking in terms of cause and effect, what we really have is a thesis, and opposite it an antithesis, with the answer to their relationship not a horizontal movement of cause and effect, but a synthesis." When Hegel propounded this idea he changed the world.[1]

FRANCIS SCHAEFFER

You must make your choice. Either this man was, and is, the Son of God: or else a madman or something worse. You can shut Him up for a fool, you can spit at Him and kill Him as a demon; or you can fall at His feet and call Him Lord and God. But let us not come with any patronising nonsense about His being a great human teacher. He has not left that open to us. He did not intend to.[2]

C. S. LEWIS

Lewis' *De Descriptione Temporum*, which has some striking parallels with Francis Schaeffer's essay *Escape from Reason*, argues that the greatest challenge in the history of the West took place around the beginning of the nineteenth century and ushered in a characteristically modern mentality.[3]

COLIN DURIEZ

7

···

Offensive Apologetics
Advancing the Faith

Y OU LISTEN TO THIS BLOKE," SHOUTS THE BARTENDER, ADJUSTING the volume on the radio. "He's really worth listening to." In a matter of moments the pub full of soldiers heeds the command in fine military fashion. As the conversation slowly tapers off, a steady stream of crisp and carefully crafted words begins to flow from the big brown box fastened above the bar. "If no set of moral ideas were truer or better than any other," suggests the speaker in a congenial, conversational tone, "there would be no sense in preferring one civilized morality to savage morality, or Christian morality to Nazi morality. In fact, of course, we all do believe that some moralities are better than others."

A sea of heads bobs up and down in agreement. One soldier chimes in, "That's the bloody truth." More heads nod. Glasses tip.

The crackling words from the big brown box continue to slice through the smoky air: "Very well then. The moment you say that one set of moral ideas can be better than another, you are, in fact, measuring them by a standard, saying that one of them conforms to that standard more nearly than the other. But the standard that measures two things is something different from either."

By the end of the fifteen-minute talk, the room is silent, reflective. The speaker, BBC wartime broadcaster C. S. Lewis, has delivered his arrow with the skill of a trained marksman.[4]

This was a common scene during the forties in Britain: soldiers, families, friends and colleagues gathered around a radio to hear this "very ordinary layman" delivering an extraordinary defense of historic Christian orthodoxy. These fresh, erudite and accessible talks stripped away the popular misconception that Christianity can be embraced only by those who hold an ignorant, unreflective view of the world.

The forties proved to be the heyday for Lewis the apologist. He became well-known through the BBC talks, Royal Air Force addresses, Socratic Club debates and, of course, scores of essays and books focused on making the faith credible to a skeptical age. Lewis's most recognized apologetic work, *Mere Christianity*, did not appear until 1952, but it was simply a compilation of the content of Lewis's BBC radio talks, which had been published in the forties in three small books: *The Case for Christianity, Christian Behaviour* and *Beyond Personality*.

In this chapter we will explore Lewis's case for Christianity by focusing on five of his offensive arguments, three of which—the moral argument, the argument from desire and the Trilemma—were featured in the BBC talks, and, consequently, figure prominently in *Mere Christianity*. The other two arguments, the argument from rationality and the argument from agape, are the foundational pillars in *Miracles* and *The Four Loves*, respectively.

After summarizing Lewis's key offensive arguments, we will then turn our attention to the central arguments Schaeffer developed: the metaphysical, the moral and the epistemological. Though Schaeffer discusses each of these arguments widely throughout his corpus, they are most neatly arranged in the third book of his apologetic trilogy, *He Is There and He Is Not Silent*. After sketching out these arguments, we will then proceed to the next chapter, where we will consider the arguments these apologists marshaled in defense of the faith. We will conclude our apologetic study in chapter nine, where we will offer a comparative analysis of these offensive and defensive arguments and discuss the relationship between the content of these arguments and the theological commitments of our apologists. We begin with Lewis.

The Moral Argument

In "Christian Apologetics" Lewis points out that the twentieth-century context differs greatly from the apostolic age, a time when nearly everyone who heard the Christian message was already "haunted by a sense of guilt" and therefore understood their moral culpability.[5] In our day, however, Freudian psychology has gone a long way toward explaining away guilt feelings, training people to blame others for everything that goes wrong in life. Guilt is no longer seen as a built-in warning system, signaling real moral failure, but rather it is seen as a dysfunctional feeling that must be rationalized away and expunged at all costs. It was this type of prevailing mindset that led Lewis to search out ways to awaken a sense of moral guilt in his audience. For Lewis was fully convinced that Christianity does not begin to speak until people recognize their need for repentance.[6]

Lewis did not claim to have a sure-fire method for awakening a sensitivity to sin in someone's life, but he thought it imperative that the discussion be kept out of the general realm of social ills and public policy and brought "down to brass tacks—to the whole network of spite, greed, envy, unfairness, and conceit in the lives of 'ordinary decent people.'"[7] In other words, the discussion should be focused on the particular sins that beset the average person.

This is precisely where Lewis begins in the opening pages of *Mere Christianity*. He starts by describing people quarreling over a seat on the bus, a piece of fruit, the breaking of a promise, cutting in line. In each instance, there appears to be an implicit appeal to some sort of objective standard the other person is supposed to know. Indeed, the other person nearly always acknowledges the standard. Instead of thumbing their noses at the standard, they look for loopholes or excuses for why it does not apply to them at present. In other words, the daily actions and comments of people everywhere seem to underscore the reality of an ultimate standard of right and wrong that governs human behavior. Lewis calls this standard the Law of Human Nature, Moral Law or Rule of Decent Behavior.[8]

We may share a sense of fair play, decency and moral obligation, but this does not mean we always treat each other fairly, behave decently and act morally. In fact, humans are notorious for self-centered, base behavior. According to Lewis, we can hardly make it through a day without some impropriety, and whenever our hand is called, we produce a multitude of excuses. We blame our fatigue, our limited cash flow, our busy schedules. This need to produce excuses proves our obligation to the standard. Lewis believes acknowledging these two points, the reality of a universal moral standard and our inability to obey it, is "the foundation of all clear thinking about ourselves and the universe we live in."[9]

Some might readily agree that humans share this curious sense of moral obligation but claim that there must be other ways to account for this phenomenon without resorting to a mysterious Moral Law. For starters, how about herd instinct? Lewis admits that instincts—such as maternal love, the sexual urge, hunger cravings—are genuine.[10] In each case we feel a strong prompting to engage in a particular action. Are not our moral urges of the same kind? Lewis does not think so. Consider the moments when our instincts conflict. What happens when our instinct for self-survival collides with our instinct to save a drowning child? Which instinct should we obey?

If morality is simply a matter of instinct, it would seem we would follow the stronger impulse. But if this were true, our world would be woefully lacking in acts of nobility and heroism. Lifeguards, firefighters and police officers would surely tell us the instinct of self-preservation is typically stronger than the urge to risk their own lives. In such cases they must awaken the slumbering instinct if they are to do the right thing.

If our conflicting instincts cannot be adjudicated by instinct itself, then the ultimate judge must transcend instinct. The Moral Law holds the gavel. To put it another way, our instincts are like the keys on a piano and the Moral Law is like a sheet of music. The Moral Law determines which notes are necessary in each situation to produce the proper tune.[11] Just as no single note is always featured in a score of music, no single instinct is always superior in life. There are times to protect your children and times when such protection leads to discrimination.[12]

If this sense of moral obligation is not instinct, then what about social convention?[13] After all, is not morality inculcated by parents, teachers and other societal leaders? Lewis readily agrees that morality is taught, but this does not necessarily mean it is arbitrary or of human origin. Lewis identifies two classifications of instruction. The first is that which could have been otherwise: the clothes we wear, food we eat, rules of the road. These are clearly human inventions. The second category, however, is one of real truths.[14] Things such as the multiplication table, the laws of logic and primary colors are built into the reality of the world. Though we might need to learn them, they are hardly subject to human alteration.

Lewis is quite certain that morality belongs to this second group, and offers two reasons for placing it alongside these other immutable truths. First, Lewis believes there is a core set of beliefs that cuts across all cultures and down through time.[15] In an essay entitled "On Ethics," Lewis tells us that the Moral Law "is neither Christian nor Pagan, neither Eastern nor Western, neither ancient nor modern, but general."[16] Many moderns want to emphasize the ethical distinctions between people groups and historical ages, but according to Lewis these simply do not amount to real, sturdy points of disagreement. We might disagree about how many wives a man can have, but everyone agrees a man should not have any woman he wants.[17] We might disagree about when it is proper to kill, but everyone agrees killing for the sake of killing is always wrong. What about those who conducted witch trials and burned innocent people at the stake? Surely this is a significant moral distinction between our culture and an earlier superstitious age. According to Lewis, however, this is not a difference in value but one in fact.

But surely the reason we do not execute witches is that we do not believe there are such things. If we did—if we really thought that there were people going about who had sold themselves to the devil and received supernatural powers from him in return and were using these powers to kill their neighbours . . . surely we would all agree that if anyone deserved the death penalty, then these filthy quislings did.[18]

The second reason Lewis believes morality should be considered an immutable truism is because it would be impossible to consider one set of values better than another without a fixed standard by which both can be gauged. As we saw in this chapter's opening vignette, Lewis used the existentially poignant example of comparing British and Nazi values. Without an objective right and wrong, we could not consider Hitler's value judgments inferior, nor could we hold the Nazis accountable for their actions without an ultimate standard that is just as intuitively apparent to Germans as it is to Britons.[19]

We should point out that in our day even the most tolerant do not tolerate behavior like rape and racism. But if there is no ultimate standard, by what means can we determine that rape and racism are wrong? Because it hurts someone else. But why should we abstain from inflicting pain on others? Because it is damaging to society. But why should society be safeguarded? This line of reasoning inevitably leads back to some type of ultimate standard. The conclusion is unavoidable. We all believe in some kind of ultimate standard, whether we acknowledge it overtly or not. Those who insist otherwise simply propagate an unlivable system.

Lewis also recognized the need for an unbending standard if we are to experience moral progress. But such progress can only occur if people are willing to admit the possibility of a moral mistake. Yet this hardly seems possible if whatever we think is right is in fact right for us. In short, without the willingness to acknowledge moral mistakes, there is no way forward in the realm of ethics.[20]

If this curious universal phenomenon cannot be explained by herd instinct or social convention, then some would suggest that immoral behavior is nothing more than that which we consider personally inconvenient or a threat to corporate survival. But these are not satisfying suggestions. An informant from the enemy camp, though personally convenient, is still contemptible,[21] and grounding our moral motions in a corporate survival simply misses the mark, for such a proposal never tells us why society ought to survive in the first place.[22]

In light of these unsatisfactory alternative proposals, Lewis concludes the Moral Law must be real. It cannot be boiled down to herd instinct, social convention, personal preference or a corporate survival technique. In the end,

Lewis writes, "it begins to look as if we shall have to admit that there is more than one kind of reality; that, in this particular case, there is something above and beyond the ordinary facts of men's behaviour, and yet quite definitely real—a real law, which none of us made, but which we find pressing on us."[23]

Once Lewis believes he has successfully dismissed the most common objections to the Moral Law, he turns his attention to potential ways in which this law can be grounded. In other words, what is behind the law? What is its basis? What hypothesis makes best sense of this phenomenon? He offers two possibilities: the materialist view and the religious view.[24] The materialist view would necessarily ground the Moral Law in the factual, material world, since that is all there is, while the religious view would ground it in some kind of conscious mind. Lewis believes the Moral Law cannot be rooted in the factual laws of nature, for they only tell us what happens, not what ought to happen. In other words, gravity has a hold on us whether we like or not, but we can choose whether or not to obey the Moral Law. Consequently, Lewis believes the Moral Law must be grounded in a mind, for only a mind can tell us which way to choose.[25]

The Trilemma

By the time Lewis draws the opening section of *Mere Christianity* to a close, he concludes that a real law is pressing on us and that that law is most likely grounded in some kind of a mind. But as Lewis is quick to point out, we are still "not yet within a hundred miles of the God of Christianity."[26]

Lewis may not have been within a hundred miles of Christianity at the end of the opening section, but less than ten pages into section two he has blazed a feverish trail toward the cross, leaving atheism, liberal Christianity, pantheism and dualism in his smoldering tracks. Our task at present, however, is not to follow Lewis to the finish line but to stop a mile shy, for it is here that we find one of Lewis's most memorable arguments, commonly known as "the Trilemma," designed to defend the deity of Jesus.

This argument, which Lewis originally came upon while reading Chesterton's *The Everlasting Man*, is specifically marshaled to undercut the widely held belief that Jesus can be dismissed easily with the simple suggestion that he was just a good moral teacher but not God in human flesh. But as we shall see, there is just no easy, simple answer to the question "Who is Jesus?"

Lewis lays the groundwork for this argument by highlighting some of the stunning and peculiar claims of Jesus. Among other things, Jesus claimed to forgive sins, claimed to be an eternal and necessary being and claimed that one day he would return to judge the world.[27] In other words, we find Jesus consistently saying things that would have led his audience to believe he considered himself divine.

Such a claim is hardly peculiar, however. One need look no further than the latest issue of *Rolling Stone* or *Entertainment Weekly* to find such claims. Claims to divinity in our "enlightened" culture are as common as minivans in the Disney World parking lot. Of course, this is where proper historical and cultural contextualization comes in. When Jesus laid claim to divinity, he was not promoting some sort of New Age philosophy or Eastern mysticism. He was a thoroughgoing Jew living in Palestine, the bastion of monotheism. For the Jew there is simply no wider divide than the chasm that separates the Creator from his creatures. Consequently, there is no greater sin in Judaism than to claim divine status. Such a claim was sheer blasphemy, punishable by death. In fact, this is precisely why the Jews eventually handed Jesus over to be crucified. The religious leaders clearly understood Jesus to be claiming equality with God—not some sort of New Age mystical deity but Yahweh, the God of Abraham, Isaac and Jacob. This kind of claim, in this kind of context, was indeed shocking.

Let us consider one of the things that irked the Jewish leaders the most, a claim that has a tendency to slip past many modern people: Jesus' claim that he could forgive people's sins. This is hardly an odd claim when the one forgiving the sin is also the one who has been offended. But in the case of Jesus, we find him issuing pardons for sins that have been perpetrated against others, sins that seemingly have nothing to do with him. You steal from me and I forgive you. But what if you steal from me and a total stranger offers you forgiveness? We would consider this ludicrous. There are only two who can offer forgiveness, the one who has been personally offended and the one who is ultimately offended by all sin—God. As Lewis states, "In the mouth of any speaker who is not God, these words would imply what I can only regard as a silliness and conceit unrivaled by any other character in history."[28]

Lewis points out something curious at this juncture. We find Jesus claiming to be eternal, pardoning people's sins, insisting that everyone will one day stand under his judgment, but not even the harshest enemies of Christianity are willing to characterize his words and actions as silly and conceited. On the contrary, they find in the Gospels a quality of life and teaching beyond reproach. The words of Jesus ring true with a mixture of frank simplicity and unique profundity. People of all religions, philosophies and cultures marvel over his impeccable character and remarkable insight. In short, there is nearly universal agreement that these are the words of a great moral teacher, not the words of a silly, conceited man.

So what are we to do with this highly complex figure? On the one hand we find an exemplary life and a masterful teacher, but on the other hand we find these shocking claims to divinity. How do we make sense of all this?

Lewis believes there are only three options before us and none are simple.

First, we could say Jesus was a lunatic. But if we conclude that Jesus was crazy, how do we make sense of his profound teaching? Second, we could say Jesus was a liar, a man who intentionally duped his followers into thinking he was God incarnate, but how do we square such deceit with the universally recognized moral quality of his life? Third, we could say Jesus was who he claimed to be, namely, Lord of the universe. These are our only options: lunatic, liar or Lord.

This point might be further crystallized by viewing the argument from a slightly different angle. What is required to be a good moral teacher? A variety of characteristics come to mind: an ability to communicate, patience with pupils, impeccable ethics, clarity of thought. In short, a good moral teacher must possess both a sound mind and a sturdy character, for one could hardly be considered a good teacher without a sound mind, and one could hardly be considered moral without a sturdy character. But a merely human Jesus who said and did the sort of things reported in the Gospels could not have possessed both a sound mind and a sturdy character. Lunatics are hardly known for their sound minds, and liars are hardly known for their sturdy character. In either direction, a strictly human Jesus lacks a requisite attribute to be considered a good moral teacher.

Ultimately, none of our options are simple. In one of the most memorable quotations in all of apologetic lore, Lewis framed it like this:

> You must make your choice. Either this man was, and is, the Son of God: or else a madman or something worse. You can shut Him up for a fool, you can spit at Him and kill Him as a demon; or you can fall at His feet and call Him Lord and God. But let us not come with any patronising nonsense about His being a great human teacher. He has not left that open to us. He did not intend to.[29]

The Argument from Rationality

As mentioned previously, Lewis's most philosophically rigorous book is undoubtedly *Miracles*. Chapter three, in particular, is an impressive challenge to the coherence and credibility of naturalism. This was the issue Lewis thought needed to be settled before one could rightly consider the actual evidence for miracles. This argument has attracted attention from philosophers from the first time Lewis presented it. Most famously, as noted in chapter one, the argument was criticized by the Roman Catholic philosopher Elizabeth Anscombe (who later received a philosophy chair at Cambridge) in a confrontation at the Socratic Club in 1948. Lewis revised his argument in response to Anscombe's criticisms in the 1960 edition of *Miracles*.

Naturalism, of course, is the view that the natural world is all that exists. It is a closed, uncreated system, and there is nothing or no one outside it that can interfere in any way. Lewis's general strategy in attacking naturalism is to point out that if there is anything that exists that cannot in principle be explained in naturalistic terms, then naturalism "would be in ruins."[30]

Lewis believed that thought itself falls in this category. His initial line of approach is to point out how reliant we are on reasoning for our claims to knowledge. In fact, he claims all knowledge depends on the validity of reasoning. Perhaps he overstated the case here, or did not strictly mean that literally all knowledge depends on reasoning, including even basic sense beliefs and the like. But it is beyond serious dispute that much of what we claim to know depends on the validity of reasoning.

Naturalism appears to discredit all our thinking and reasoning. According to Lewis, "every event in Nature must be connected with previous events in the Cause and Effect relation. But our acts of thinking are events. Therefore the true answer to 'Why do you think this?' must begin with the Cause-Effect *because*."[31] Lewis distinguishes the Cause-Effect because from the Ground-Consequent because. The latter sense of because comes to the fore in reasoning. Lewis illustrates the difference with these two sentences: "He cried out *because* it hurt him" is an example of the Cause-Effect relation, while "It must have hurt him *because* he cried out" is an instance of the Ground-Consequent relation.[32] As Lewis observes, nothing discredits a belief more easily than explaining it causally: "You say that because (Cause and Effect) you are only a capitalist, or a hypochondriac, or a mere man, or only a woman."[33] Such a belief, it is suggested, would arise whether it had any rational grounds or not.

To preserve reason from the ravages of naturalism, then, it is necessary that we have genuine insight into the Ground-Consequent relation. "One thought can cause another not by *being*, but by being *seen to be*, a ground for it.... An act of knowing must be determined, in a sense, solely by what is known; we must know it to be thus solely because it *is* thus."[34] While the naturalist faces a perhaps insurmountable obstacle in light of this, the theist has a ready account of our ability to reason and know.

> For [the theist], reason—the reason of God—is older than Nature, and from it the orderliness of Nature, which alone enables us to know her, is derived. For him, the human mind in the act of knowing is illuminated by the Divine reason. It is set free, in the measure required, from the huge nexus of non-rational causation; free from this to be determined by the truth known. And the preliminary processes within Nature which led up to this liberation, if there were any, were designed to do so.[35]

Not only does Lewis expose naturalism's inability to offer a plausible account of rationality, but he shows how the Christian worldview possesses all the necessary resources to provide an intellectually satisfying explanation for the phenomenon of human consciousness and knowledge.

The Argument from Desire

While the first three arguments were predominantly designed to engage the mind, the final two appeals, the argument from desire and the argument from agape, seek to engage the heart. Desire is a frequent motif in Lewisian literature. From John's search for the enchanting island in *The Pilgrim's Regress* to Reepicheep's journey to the utter east in *The Voyage of the Dawn Treader* to Lewis's autobiographical odyssey in *Surprised by Joy*, we find his works consistently saturated with a sense of longing for that which will satisfy our deepest desires.

Lewis believes this romantic experience is not peculiar to him alone, or to a select group of aesthetically sensitive seekers, but extends to all humanity: "Most people, if they had really learned to look into their hearts, would know that they do want, and want acutely, something that cannot be had in this world."[36] Many things promise the settled satisfaction we all crave, but none can quite quench our thirst. We fall in love, embark on a distant journey, pursue an invigorating subject, but sooner or later we come to the realization that "no marriage, no travel, no learning, can really satisfy."[37] But this applies not only to those unions that end on the rocks, or vacations spoiled by rainy weather, or careers that tumble off the corporate ladder. Even the most beautiful marriage, fun-filled holiday or successful business career cannot flood the human heart with the satisfaction we so desperately desire.

According to Lewis, there are three ways we can respond to such disappointment. First, we can take the position that the problem is with the particular things themselves. So we try different sexual partners, new sites or alternative vocations, believing the object of our ultimate desire will appear over the crest of the next hill or around the following bend. Lewis characterizes this approach as the Fool's Way.[38] If we are honest, human experience speaks with a unified voice that slices across all ideologies—every hill and every bend leads to the same disappointing dead end. No matter how many intimate encounters, uncharted explorations or new careers we pursue, we never quite grasp our elusive, mysterious butterfly.

The second manner of dealing with our dissatisfaction is to proclaim that all such references to ultimate fulfillment are the idealism of starry-eyed youth. Those who have tasted the reality of life and have "come to their senses" chalk up these incessant wild-goose chases to naive, wishful thinking. People who adopt this attitude simply suppress their deepest desires and wrap themselves in a cocoon of day-to-day "common sense." Lewis considers this a reasonable approach, if, and only if, there is no such thing as eternal life. This is the Way of the Disillusioned "Sensible Man."[39]

Lewis, however, believes there is a better explanation for our emptiness—what he calls the Christian Way. According to Lewis, every natural desire can be traced to a corresponding satisfaction. Ducks long to swim; there are ponds. People are sexually aroused; there is intercourse. Stomachs growl; there is food. Since all humans desire deep, lasting, unshakable joy, there must be a corresponding satisfaction for this natural craving as well. But since our world cannot satisfy this longing, "the most probable explanation is that [we were] made for another world."[40]

Some have countered that a natural desire hardly proves this desire will be satisfied. Some ducklings are eaten on the way to the pond, some humans live a lifetime of sexual frustration, and some beings die of starvation. Lewis was certainly aware of this truth but thought this objection misses the point. Although a natural desire does not prove each creature will experience satisfaction, it does seem to show that at least some of their kind will reach the water, engage in sex and ingest a meal. Likewise, Christianity tells us that although it is possible that not every person will experience the eternal bliss of heaven, our desire for ultimate satisfaction and deep fulfillment suggests that some of our kind will.[41]

Lewis concludes that our most profound desires are designed to spur us on toward God, who alone can fully satisfy. Certainly Lewis is not the first Christian to talk of such longing. In St. Augustine's familiar words, "Our hearts are restless until we find our place in Thee." Pascal was on to the same insight when he spoke of the God-shaped vacuum that resides within each of us. But Lewis, perhaps as well as anyone to date, captures the essence of this bittersweet experience and masterfully expresses its beauty through a number of literary genres.

The Argument from Agape

Another distinct, existential appeal is Lewis's argument from agape. This argument is similar in spirit to the argument from desire in that it begins from a pervasive and profound human longing and then proceeds to show it can only be satisfied through a right relationship with God. In this case, the longing is as fundamental to human experience and aspiration as anything can be. It is the longing for love.

Lewis's argument here is not as overtly apologetic as the other arguments we are considering. It is developed throughout the pages of *The Four Loves* but comes to explicit expression only in the final pages of the book. The bulk of this work is given to describing and depicting human loves, including a chapter devoted to "Likings and Loves for the Sub-human." From there, Lewis proceeds to the four loves proper, beginning with the humbly adorned "affection," advancing to "friendship" and then to the nearly divine "eros." This progression illustrates one of the main themes of the book, that "the highest does not stand without the lowest."[42] Thus lower forms of love such as the love of nature or the love of one's country, or the modest affection one feels for an acquaintance, can be training for the higher forms of love.

The really crucial argument of the book, however, can be stated as something of an inversion of the former principle: The lower cannot finally stand without the highest. Lewis first advances this point in the introduction when he notes that John's saying, "God is love," has been balanced in his mind by the remark of M. Denis de Rougement that "love ceases to be a demon only when he ceases to be a god."[43] Lewis reiterates and develops this thought throughout the following chapters. None of the loves can sustain themselves by their own resources. They can remain themselves only if they are rightly related to Love himself. At the very end of the chapter on eros, for instance, Lewis writes: "He cannot of himself be what, nevertheless, he must be if he is to remain Eros. He needs help; therefore he needs to be ruled. The god dies or becomes a demon unless he obeys God."[44]

This claim is spelled out more fully in the final chapter on the fourth love, namely agape or charity. There Lewis illustrates how all the natural loves can be transformed once God is invited into the human heart. Each of them can "become modes of Charity while also remaining the natural loves they were."[45] Indeed, Lewis sees in this process an echo of the Incarnation. Just as God became human by taking humanity into himself, so "natural love is taken up into, made the tuned and obedient instrument of, Love Himself."[46] Any love which is thus transformed is prepared to enter the eternity of heavenly life. Any love that will not submit to this transformation will cease to be love and become a demon. Those are our final choices.

Significantly, Lewis makes these same points in another genre in *The Great Divorce*. A number of characters in that book exemplify the perversion and self-destruction of natural love that will not submit to transformation by Love. In an especially memorable scene, one of the ghosts from hell is a mother whose son is in heaven. She meets her brother who is also in heaven, but her only concern in the conversation is to see her son, Michael. She also has no interest in God, except as a means to see Michael. Her identity is so wrapped up in her mother love that she is prepared to pay any price to sustain it. She is convinced that she would be happy "even in that town" (hell) if only she could be reunited with her son.[47] As the conversation progresses, it becomes apparent how self-centered and self-deceived she is in all her protests about love.

The claim that natural love self-destructs in this manner cannot, of course, be demonstrated in rigorous, philosophical fashion. The best that can be done is to depict the psychological and emotional dynamics of corrupted love, which most persons have observed in their own lives or the lives of others. This Lewis did in a masterful way.

This sets the stage to show how the resources of agape, or charity, can preserve and perfect love. Again, this cannot be demonstrated from obvious and uncontroversial premises, but it can be shown to be an integral part of the Christian vision. Those who are moved by the Christian story of perfect love and its power to redeem all facets of our lives will be more drawn to believe it is true. For Christianity is above all an account of why love is eternal and will finally prevail. This is very good news to anyone who recognizes the value of love but senses its frailty and vulnerability in all human relationships.

Schaeffer: The Big Questions

In the beginning of *He Is There and He Is Not Silent*, Francis Schaeffer tells us there are three classes of philosophical problems that must be addressed if a worldview is to be considered sufficiently comprehensive. The first class of problems or questions revolves around the issue of existence. Why is there something, rather than nothing? Why is the universe filled with structure, order and complexity? Why are humans different from everything else? These kinds of questions all belong to the domain of metaphysics.[48]

The second class of problem we must face is what Schaeffer calls "man and the dilemma of man." The human plight consists of two parts. First, humans are uniquely personal, yet finite. In other words, humans possess personality—aspirations, moral motions, rationality, aesthetic sensitivities, feelings of love—which places them atop the ontological totem pole. But despite their ontological superiority, humans are incapable of harmonizing their environment, mastering their domain, endowing their lives with meaning and ultimately satisfying their aspirations. As Schaeffer phrased it, humans are an insufficient integration point for themselves. But finitude is not the only challenge for humanity. Our second dilemma can be seen in the curious mixture of good and evil that is threaded throughout the human race. How can we account for the profound compassion of a Mother Teresa on the one hand and the diabolical wickedness of a Hitler on the other? In fact, how can we account for the confounding blend of nobility and wretchedness in our own hearts? Every worldview must address this puzzling phenomenon. When we begin discussing why humans are noble yet cruel, we have moved from the realm of metaphysics into that of morality.[49]

The third and final class of problem deals with the issue of rationality and knowledge. Why are humans capable of rational discernment? How do we acquire and process knowledge? How can we be certain our beliefs are accurate? According to Schaeffer, this was the central issue of his era. He thought the "generation gap" was more appropriately considered an "epistemological gap." So the final problem to be addressed is the problem of knowledge or epistemology.[50]

Though there are a variety of ways we can respond to these metaphysical, moral and epistemological questions, Schaeffer believed that when all is said and done every answer can be grouped into one of two categories. The first category of answers suggests that there are no answers—life is thoroughly irrational, chaotic and ultimately absurd. Schaeffer believed this could be proposed as a theory, but it could never be sustained in practice. Even an eccentric filmmaker like Jean-Luc Godard, who was known for sending his actors out through windows instead of doors, would not ask them to walk through walls.[51] In other words, the world has undeniable form, order and structure, and this cries out for an explanation. Those who claim everything is absurd and chaotic inevitably do so selectively. For without some structure and order, all rationality and communication would come to a standstill. In light of the implausibility of this first class of answers, Schaeffer turns his attention in the balance of the book to considering the second category, namely, the suggestion that there are logical, rational answers to our metaphysical, moral and epistemological ponderings. We start with Schaeffer's treatment of the possible metaphysical solutions.

The Metaphysical Argument

The problem in the realm of metaphysics is twofold: First, a complex universe exists; second, humanity is unique. How do we account for these phenomena? Schaeffer believes there are only three basic responses: the world came from nothing, the world came from an impersonal source, or the world came from a personal beginning.

This first suggestion claims that everything flows from absolutely nothing. Schaeffer is careful to point out that adherents to this position cannot be allowed to smuggle anything into the equation, "no mass, no energy, no motion, no personality."[52] The effect cannot be part of the cause. In fact, this position claims that ultimately there is no cause. One of the hallmarks of Schaeffer's ministry was his ability to coin new expressions. Such is the case here. In an effort to roadblock those who would attempt to smuggle something into the causal component of the equation, Schaeffer proposed the phrase "nothing nothing."[53] To illustrate his point, he would often draw a circle on a blackboard, indicating that everything inside the circle represents all there is. He then would erase the chalky sphere, leaving nothing but empty black space. This is "nothing nothing." Schaeffer considered it inconceivable to suggest that the existence of this complex universe and the uniqueness of humanity could be traced back to absolutely nothing.

If the origin of the universe cannot be traced to "nothing," then "something" must be the basis of reality. According to Schaeffer, that something must be either impersonal or personal. The suggestion of an impersonal beginning to the universe is the position that pantheists and many modern scientists and liberal theologians have taken. Here it is quite proper to begin with the basic building blocks of mass, energy or motion, but Schaeffer says we must not allow anyone to smuggle the notion of personality into these elements. Everything is equally impersonal. Schaeffer was fond of calling pantheism "paneverythingism," since "theism" conveys personality.[54]

Some who hold to an impersonal beginning, however, are quite willing to toe the line at this point, for they do not believe human personality is real and distinct from everything else. Personality is simply an illusion or a complex of chemical or physical properties necessary for survival. But according to Schaeffer, those who hold this view must do so in the face of two challenges. First, most of humanity has viewed personality as something that is real and has believed that humans are intrinsically distinct from all that is nonhuman. Second, "no chemical determinist or psychological determinist is ever able to live as though he is the same as non-man."[55] In other words, human consensus and the existential impossibility of living consistently with this theory discredit such a proposal.

The person who thinks personality is real and distinct from everything else, but that it arose from an impersonal source, is faced with challenges as well. For this position cannot adequately explain the diversity it affirms. In other words, the great problem here is finding any meaning for the distinct particulars of existence. If the origin of the universe is impersonal, then everything is ultimately reduced to homogeneity or oneness. But how could the "impersonal plus time plus chance"—all the factors available to such a worldview—blindly cough up personality?[56] In other words, how could the water rise above its source? Schaeffer says this position might explain the unity of the universe, but it certainly cannot account for the vast diversity we see in the world, including the uniqueness of humanity.

If an impersonal beginning cannot account for our complex universe and distinct humanity, then we naturally must turn to the hypothesis of a personal beginning. This proposal quite simply suggests that everything has meaning because everything ultimately flows from personality. According to Schaeffer, a tragic sense of meaninglessness plagues modern humanity. People who have grounded their lives in the belief that everything sprang from nothing or from an impersonal source simply do not have any way of endowing their lives with purpose and significance. But the Christian vision, on the other hand, provides all the necessary resources to charge the human experience with hope, meaning and dynamic direction.

Schaeffer believes the infinite-personal, triune God alone can answer the great metaphysical questions that haunt the human race. God is infinite, and therefore big enough to provide an integration point for humanity. God is personal, which explains how humans could be different from the rest of the world. And God is triune, which explains the puzzle of unity and diversity. In other words, we find in the infinite-personal, triune God a self-sustaining, eternal community of perfect individuality, harmony, love, meaning, intelligence and power. This provides a metaphysical basis that accounts for the complexity of the universe and the personality of humanity. The Christian key fits the lock of reality. And we have this answer to our metaphysical musings because the God who is there has chosen to reveal the answer in verbal, propositional form to those who bear his image.[57]

The Moral Argument

As we have seen, Schaeffer believes that humans are faced with two basic dilemmas. First, humanity is personal yet finite. In other words, despite possessing remarkable qualities like rationality, aesthetic longings and moral motions, humans are incapable of endowing their lives with purpose and meaning. Humans are not intelligent enough, good enough or creative enough to solve all their problems, live ethically or satisfy their deepest cravings. Ironically, if these aspirations and desires are ultimately unfulfillable and meaningless, then humans, the ontologically superior beings on our planet, are to be pitied more than a blade of grass for possessing deep-seated longings that ultimately go unheard and unmet. As Schaeffer put it, "The green moss on the rock is higher than he, for it can be fulfilled in the universe which exists."[58]

The second dilemma we must face is the confounding mixture of good and evil woven throughout the fabric of the human race and embedded in our very own hearts. How can we account for this baffling array of nobility and perversity in our world? Schaeffer tells us these two problems strike at the heart of the human dilemma and lead us into the sphere of morality.

As in the realm of metaphysics, Schaeffer believes there are really only two legitimate classes of answers to the human dilemma: the world can be traced back either to the impersonal or to the personal. Schaeffer says humans have always understood the dilemmas of finitude and cruelty as two separate problems, but if we start with the suggestion of an impersonal beginning, whether it is framed by the naturalist, the pantheist or the modern liberal theologian, these two dilemmas inevitably collapse into one metaphysical problem. For if "everything is finally equal," as this view suggests, then there is no way to distinguish right from wrong, good from bad, nobility from cruelty.[59] There is no absolute standard. Schaeffer says it does not matter if it is the "modern scientist with his energy particles, or the paneverythingism of the East, or neo-orthodox theology.... The answer to morals eventually turns out to be the assertion that there are no morals (in however sophisticated a way this may be expressed)."[60] From this perspective, morality is simply reduced to different forms of sociological, statistical or situational relativism.[61]

As hard as some people try to explain away true morality, they cannot shake an existential "feeling of moral motions."[62] This is an inextricable part of the human condition. Schaeffer says people differ over particular norms, but "men have always felt that there is a difference between right and wrong."[63] Herein lies the human dilemma if we trace everything back to an impersonal beginning. In an ultimately impersonal universe, there is no such thing as true morality, yet humans cannot rid themselves of the nagging notion that some things are truly right and others are truly wrong. In other words, this position reduces humanity to a freak of nature. Personality in general and moral sensibilities in particular have been coughed up by chance, kicking us "out of line" with an intrinsically impersonal, amoral world.[64] In such a context, moral motions are entirely abnormal, thoroughly absurd and finally futile. According to Schaeffer, this is "the ultimate cosmic alienation, the dilemma of our generation."[65]

If the impersonal beginning cannot make sense of the human dilemma, what about the personal beginning? Schaeffer believes by starting with a personal origin we can keep the metaphysical and moral issues separate, because a personal beginning provides the possibility of an ultimate ethical standard. Within this classification we find two possible theories.

First, we can suggest that humans are intrinsically cruel. In other words, the evil we find in the world is according to God's design. Schaeffer, however, believes this suggestion is unsatisfactory on two counts: it portrays God as a demon, and it undermines any possible hope of qualitative human moral development.[66]

The second possible answer in the classification of a personal beginning, however, is more promising. In fact, Schaeffer believes it is "not simply the best answer—it is the only answer in morals."[67] Of course, this is Schaeffer's articulation of the orthodox Christian position. This view insists that human cruelty is not intrinsic but rather inconsistent with God's original intentions and therefore an abnormal feature of our current existence. Quite simply, God created us good, but we chose to go bad. Schaeffer believes this position possesses four attractive features. First, it offers a rational basis for current human cruelty without attributing evil to God. Second, there is hope for a solution to humanity's moral dilemma, because humans are not intrinsically evil. This solution is grounded in the atoning work of Christ. Third, since evil is foreign to God's purpose and plan, humans can challenge evil without challenging God. Fourth, this position provides an absolute moral standard, rooted in the character of a perfectly righteous supreme being.[68] And we can perceive this moral standard because God has chosen to disclose his character in the form of verbal, propositional revelation.

In conclusion, it seems Schaeffer's moral argument can be summed up by answering one simple question: Is the human dilemma a matter of chance or choice? If it is a matter of chance, then the impersonal has somehow coughed up the abnormal, unfulfillable human qualities of personality, in which case humanity is the supreme sucker of the universe. On the other hand, if the human dilemma is a matter of choice, then either the personal Creator chose to create humans evil, in which case God is a demon and qualitative moral development is impossible, or the personal Creator made humanity good, but humanity chose to go bad. So our dilemma is a product of blind chance, a product of God's choice or a product of human choice. Schaeffer tells us that the third and final option is the only rationally defensible and existentially satisfying explanation to the human dilemma of finitude and cruelty.

The Epistemological Argument

This final class of philosophical problems deals with the challenge of knowing. How do we acquire knowledge and how can we be certain our beliefs are accurate? According to Schaeffer, who anticipated the rampant relativism and paralyzing uncertainty of our postmodern age, epistemology is the central issue in the latter half of the twentieth century.

Schaeffer believed most non-Christian worldviews, though diverse in expression, are operating from the same basic presuppositional base, namely, a commitment to an impersonal, closed system of cause and effect. This nearly monolithic commitment to a naturalistic framework has played a major role in sending the Western world under the line of despair.[69]

As indicated in the previous chapter, Schaeffer believed this line of despair or epistemological shift can be located around the end of the nineteenth century in Europe and approximately 1935 (around the time J. Gresham

Machen was defrocked) in the United States. Prior to these dates, the majority of the West still clung to the hope of finding a rational, unified field of knowledge or one overarching paradigm that would make sense of all areas of life, from the universe and its form to the mannishness of man. This is no longer the case. We now live in a time of division, with the upstairs world of meaning completely severed from the downstairs world of rationality. Science and mathematics are rationally discerned in the lower story with no correlation to the upper story of love, aspirations, relationships, morality and the like. In other words, humanity is in a state of despair over the possibility of ever finding a rationally discerned, integrated view of reality.

This schizophrenic type of existence has spawned two basic non-Christian epistemological options in the latter half of the twentieth century: grave cynicism and "romantic" mysticism.[70] Grave cynicism is the natural result of believing one is trapped in a lower story, closed, impersonal universe where meaning and purpose have been squashed by the steamroller of determinism. Schaeffer tells us that those who live consistently with this paradigm eventually find themselves staring suicidal nihilism squarely in the face. Consider the eloquent yet chilling words of naturalist Bertrand Russell:

> That man is the product of causes which had no prevision of the end they were achieving; that his origin, his hopes, his fears, his loves and his beliefs, are but the outcome of accidental collocations of atoms; that no fire, no heroism, no intensity of thought and feeling, can preserve an individual life beyond the grave; that all the labors of the ages, all the devotion, all the inspiration, all the noonday brightness of human genius, are destined to extinction in the vast death of the solar system, and the whole temple of man's achievement must inevitably be buried beneath the debris of a universe in ruins . . . only within the scaffolding of these truths, only on the firm foundation of unyielding despair, can the soul's habitation henceforth be safely built.[71]

These are sobering words, to be sure. But who can bear to live as if human devotion, inspiration and genius are ultimately absurd? As we have already seen, Schaeffer believes the notion of consistent nihilism is an oxymoron, an existential impossibility. In fact, Russell himself was unwilling to live as if life is totally meaningless, as revealed by his frequent humanitarian efforts. So given a closed, impersonal universe, where can hope be found? According to Schaeffer, the only way to seek hope in a world where reason and meaning are separated into mutually exclusive, airtight compartments is to make an irrational, unwarranted leap of faith into the upper story.

What we find then are two basic options for the person who embraces impersonal presuppositions. Either one can rationally follow the inescapable logic of an all-inclusive determinism to a position of "unyielding despair," or one can ignore the logical implications of this position and opt for an irrational, optimistic leap into the realm of mystical meaning. The former option preserves intellectual integrity but leads to physical suicide,[72] while the latter preserves physical integrity but leads to intellectual suicide. Neither option, however, can offer a fully integrated, holistic solution. Physical death or intellectual death: these are the only two options available to our woefully divided world.

So what has brought us to such a disturbing scenario? What has sent us under this line of despair? Where did Western culture go astray? Most importantly, is there an epistemological alternative to these suicidal options? These are the big questions confronting our world, and Schaeffer sought to provide some answers.

Schaeffer devoted a great deal of time, energy and ink to these questions. Much of his strategy is aimed at discrediting current non-Christian epistemologies by unearthing their corrupt historical roots. Schaeffer's expedition begins with the ancient Greeks, blazes a trail through the Roman Empire, the medieval world, the Renaissance, the Enlightenment and the Romantic period, and culminates in the topsy-turvy twentieth century. He covers all this ground in approximately two hundred pages in *How Should We Then Live?*—his most comprehensive and mature treatment—and much of this territory in less than seventy pages in *Escape from Reason*.[73] His most focused epistemological discussion of this material, however, can be found in the final two chapters of *He Is There and He Is Not Silent*. There is no need to rehash the detail of his sweeping cross-disciplinary survey here, but a brief summary of the major contours will prove helpful.

Schaeffer thought Plato understood the basic problem, "that in the area of knowledge, as in the area of morals, there must be more than particulars if there is to be meaning."[74] In other words, we need universal categories and standards to make sense of and give meaning to all the diverse particulars in our world. The particulars of oaks, pines and redwoods are united under the universal category of trees. The particulars of Smokies, Rockies and Ozarks are united under the universal category of mountains. The particulars of collies, poodles and terriers are united under the universal category of dogs. The particulars of Germans, Americans and Koreans are united under the universal category of humans. Such classification increases our comprehension, unifies our knowledge and sets the necessary epistemological parameters to make sense of the world.

But it is not enough just to have a number of disconnected universals endowing their respective particulars with meaning. These universals also must be somehow related to one another. Therefore, a higher level of universal comes into play. So we find the universals of trees and mountains united under the overarching universal of inanimate objects. Likewise, the universals of dogs and humans are appropriately grouped together under the overarching universal of animate objects. The goal is to eventually find one universal umbrella under which all the vast levels of diverse particulars and universals can fit. According to Schaeffer, people might use different categories or standards, but everyone is in the process, despite the discipline or pursuit, of "constantly moving from particulars to universals."[75]

Schaeffer saw this movement from particulars to universals as not simply an abstract academic exercise but "the very substance of how we actually know, and how we know that we know."[76] In other words, the system that offers a self-consistent, comprehensive and livable solution to the puzzle of particulars and universals is entitled to epistemic certitude. If everything fits, the loose ends are tied and all the details are properly cataloged, then there simply is no epistemological problem. Of course, this is easier said than done. History is strewn with layers of ancient philosophies and religions buried beneath the pressure of this demand. Schaeffer contends that the infinite-personal, triune God of Christianity is the only universal that can rise above the rubble.

Schaeffer tells us that from the time of the Greeks until around the eighteenth century, all non-Christian Western philosophies went about their quest for a universal in a similar fashion. He identifies three common threads. First, they were all rationalistic. By this Schaeffer means philosophers thought they could start from themselves, without any special revelation, and "gather enough particulars to make [their] own universals."[77] Second, they were rational. They believed that the world is reasonable and antithesis is foundational to our thinking. Without the law of noncontradiction, we cannot begin to think or communicate. This distinction between self-sufficient rationalism and God-ordained rationality is crucial to understanding Schaeffer's overall apologetic. Third, they were romantic or optimistic about what they could achieve. They believed "rationalism plus rationality" could produce a unified field of knowledge to unite all the universals and particulars in our world.[78] So what we find from the Greeks to the eighteenth century is an autonomous rational quest for an all-inclusive paradigm to make sense of the whole world: particulars and universals, the natural universe and the mannishness of man, the external world of mechanics and the internal world of meaning, the lower visible world of physicality and the higher invisible world of spirit and soul. But in each case, starting from the resources of autonomous human reason alone, the quest fell short. Eventually the quest for a rationally discerned unified body of knowledge and meaning was aborted, and modern humanity was born.

Ideas, like literal offspring, do not gestate overnight. In fact, Schaeffer believed it took many centuries for modern thought to reach full term. In keeping with this metaphor, we might liken Schaeffer's historical critique from the thirteenth to the nineteenth century to a series of sonographic snapshots of the developing modern mindset. Below are a few key images from the Schaeffer photo album that reveal his view of how modern thought evolved.

The first trimester. The most important snapshot for Schaeffer during the early stages of development is a picture of Thomas Aquinas (1225-1274). According to Schaeffer, Aquinas opened the door to autonomous Renaissance humanism by placing an inordinate emphasis on human reason and natural theology. Consequently, the authority of the church began to overshadow the authority of the Bible, works righteousness supplanted a Christ-centered soteriology and the pagan classics, especially Aristotle, were synthesized with biblical teaching. Though Aquinas himself remained committed to special revelation, Schaeffer thought the way was paved for an ever-increasing sense of human self-sufficiency, and as the Renaissance progressed, "nature began to 'eat up' grace."[79] Or to put it another way, as nature became increasingly autonomous, severed from the realm of grace and universals, humanity was left with a vast array of meaningless, disjointed particulars.

The second trimester. Our second snapshot focuses on the transition in the seventeenth century from modern science to naturalism, or as Schaeffer calls it, "modern modern science."[80] The early scientists, though not all confessing Christians, operated within a theistic framework. They believed the universe was created by an intelligent being and therefore open to rational investigation. But it was not long before the presupposition of an open, personal universe gave way to the assumption that the universe is closed, impersonal and deterministic. The advent of this new paradigm proved to be a key step toward the eventually divided field of knowledge. From the Newtonians forward, science would no longer limit its study to the universe and its form in subjects like chemistry, astronomy and physics. Now subjects like anthropology and sociology would place "the mannishness of man" under the naturalistic microscope as well.[81] In other words, when the universe shifted from open to closed, everything began to be explained or explained away in naturalistic terms, including the higher realm of universals and grace. The modern-modern scientists romantically believed they could start with a raw objectivity (i.e., positivism) and eventually find a rational, naturalistic explanation for everything in life. Schaeffer tells us that the hope of ever finding a unified body of knowledge was now in grave danger.

The third trimester. Our final snapshot of the developing modern mindset reveals a cluster of key philosophers who vanquished the old rationalistic optimism and ushered in the contemporary world of pessimistic despair. Schaeffer believes the cumulative effect of four men—Rousseau, Kant, Hegel and Kierkegaard—gave birth to our modern epistemological dilemma. Operating from the new base of a closed, impersonal universe—the bequeathal of modern-modern science—the first three men tried in vain to unify the world of grace and nature, and rescue meaning from the heartless clutches of mechanistic determinism. But by the time of Kierkegaard, the flickering hope of a rationally discerned unified body of meaning and knowledge was entirely extinguished.

Schaeffer believes Jean-Jacques Rousseau (1712-1778) was the most important figure during this period, for he reconfigured the nature-grace dichotomy by replacing the spiritual concept of grace with the secularized concept of autonomous human freedom in the upper realm in an attempt to combat autonomous deterministic nature (i.e., naturalism) down below.[82] Rousseau became disillusioned with the triumphalism of the Enlightenment and lost faith in the ideal of progress and the power of human reason. He believed the constraints of society should be eliminated so humanity could return to its natural state of goodness, a state of total, unshackled liberty. Schaeffer tells us that Rousseau played an important role in the formation of Romanticism and later the bohemian ideal of fighting societal norms at every turn. Rousseau's dichotomy furthered the strain between the upper and lower realms of reality, for the concepts of autonomous freedom and autonomous nature are logically incompatible.

After devoting much attention to Rousseau, Schaeffer covers the enormously influential German philosopher Immanuel Kant (1724-1804) in just a few short, unsubstantial paragraphs. Schaeffer believes Kant recognized the universals-particulars problem but labeled the higher realm the "noumenal world" and the lower realm the "phenomenal world." Kant attempted to conjoin these two (Schaeffer does not tell us how), but like Rousseau, he failed. The longing to believe in something was now overwhelming, and many sought to escape the deterministic machine of the closed, impersonal universe at any cost.[83]

This desperate context set the stage for German philosopher Georg Wilhelm Friedrich Hegel (1770-1831). Hegel, like his predecessors, noticed the strain between the upper and lower worlds but decided the locus of the problem was in the realm of methodology. Instead of searching for a unified body of knowledge on the basis of classical logic or antithesis, Schaeffer tells us that Hegel decided to introduce a radically new way of reasoning—the method of synthesis. Hegel saw history as evolutionary and dialectic. A thesis would spring up and then its antithesis would follow. Hegel thought a synthesis of these antithetical theses produced a higher form of truth than previously known. This new synthesis would then, in turn, become a thesis and its corresponding antithesis would emerge. This process would produce another synthesis, which would lead to greater enlightenment, and so on. Schaeffer says that "when Hegel propounded this idea he changed the world."[84] Hegel, like the old philosophers, sought to find a unified body of knowledge, but unlike his predecessors, he did so on the basis of synthesis instead of the classical method of antithesis. The hope of finding a rationally discerned unified field of knowledge was over. As Schaeffer explains, "Truth, as people had always thought of truth, [had] died."[85]

Schaeffer says Hegel was the door into the line of despair, but Danish philosopher Søren Kierkegaard (1813-1855) was the first man under the line, because he gave up hope of finding any type of a unified body of knowledge. Non-Christian philosophers before Hegel had optimistically believed that rationalism plus rationality could produce the unity they desired. Hegel retained the rationalistic optimism of his predecessors but believed that synthesis instead of antithesis was the correct method to achieve the coveted unity. But with Kierkegaard the hope of unity was snuffed out, and a divided field of knowledge, the mark of the modern man, was erected. From this point forward, Schaeffer says, "the line which divides reason from nonreason is as impassible as a concrete wall thousands of feet thick, reinforced with barbed wire charged with 10,000 volts of electricity."[86] The only way to find meaning is to blindly leap from the lower story of reason into the upper story of nonreason.

The main epistemological problem of universals and particulars, despite its different formulations, can be traced through each of these eras. During the Renaissance it was expressed as nature and grace, with Rousseau it changed to nature and freedom, with Kant it was labeled the phenomenal world and noumenal world, and finally with Kierkegaard it was reformulated into a total dichotomy between faith and reason. This is our current dilemma. The quest for a rationally discerned, unified body of knowledge and meaning is dead. Rationality can lead only to pessimistic absurdity. So the modern person is left, as indicated in the beginning of this section, with either grave cynicism or romantic mysticism.

Of course, Schaeffer does not leave his readers in the depths of despair but offers a solution to modern humanity's epistemological problem. He believes that while the Renaissance philosophers were struggling with the nature-grace dilemma, the Reformers simply had no epistemological challenge, for verbal, propositional revelation solves the universals-particulars problem. In Scripture God speaks about himself (grace) and history and the cosmos (nature), providing a unified body of knowledge and meaning.[87] Schaeffer believes "the strength of the Christian system—the acid test of it—is that everything fits under the apex of the existing, infinite-personal God, and it is the only system in the world where this is true."[88] Everything fits, universals and particulars. But as we saw in the previous chapter, Schaeffer thought it was a tactical error to simply expect people to accept such a statement, especially when the majority of moderns hold a set of presuppositions that exclude the claims of Christianity on a priori grounds. He believed "the truth that we let in first is not a dogmatic statement of the truth of the Scriptures, but the truth of the external world and the truth of what man himself is."[89] In other words, we must compare the Christian hypothesis to the external and internal evidence of our world—the universe and its form and the mannishness of man. The big question we must ask is whether, in light of the evidence, the Christian epistemological solution of verbal, propositional revelation is an intellectually credible position to hold.

Schaeffer believes the possibility of divine communication is absurd if one assumes the framework of a closed, impersonal universe. But this framework is hardly beyond dispute; in fact, it is riddled with problems, as we have already seen. On the other hand, given the alternative worldview of the open, personal system, specifically the Christian system, verbal propositional revelation is not only probable but precisely what one would expect. Since one's view of revelation is largely determined by the chosen presuppositional base, the fundamental task is deciding which base best aligns with the internal and external evidence in our world.

Take the phenomenon of communication. Schaeffer tells us that anthropologists believe verbalization is what separates humans from other creatures, but from a naturalistic perspective this phenomenon is mysterious at best. The Christian, on the other hand, has a ready explanation: Christianity tells us that a trinitarian God has created humanity in his own image, and part of being the divine-image bearer is the ability to verbalize. In light of the ability of Christianity to explain the phenomenon of verbalization, Schaeffer then asks, "Is it unthinkable or even surprising that this personal God could or would communicate to man on the basis of propositions? The answer is, no."[90] If God is good we also would expect his communication to be accurate. So the very thing that makes best sense of human verbalization also happens to be the very thing that opens the door to the possibility of verbal, propositional revelation.

Consider also the phenomenon of correlation. Like the phenomenon of communication, we all recognize that, for some reason, things exist in relationships. Things are arranged in a subject-object correlation. Schaeffer affirms that this basic assumption is what made modern science possible.[91] Operating within a theistic framework, the early scientists believed there was a natural relationship between the knower and the known. With the shift to modern modern science, however, this certainty vanished, for in a closed, impersonal, nonteleological universe there is simply no good reason to believe one thing should correlate to another. Given the Christian set of presuppositions, however, the phenomenon of correlation is precisely what one would expect. If a rational God made both the external universe and its form and the internal categories of the human mind, is it surprising to find a correlation between the two? We would expect them to fit.[92] It is worth noting, though Schaeffer does not overtly develop this point, that the phenomenon of correlation leads us to the same type of conclusion we found with verbalization. The very thing that makes best sense of correlation and the scientific enterprise also happens to be the very thing that opens the door to the possibility of occasional divine reordering of the natural world, in other words, miracles.

When we look at the common human experiences of communication and correlation, we find not only that the Christian system makes best sense of these phenomena, but that these phenomena happen to be the very things that open the door to the possibility of both divine communication and divine intervention. As discussed in chapter five, this type of reasoning, what we have called critical rationalism,[93] has a certain circularity to it, but what matters ultimately is its ability to explain the data in question. This it does. The Christian system makes sense of important experiences like communication and correlation, as well as the problem of universals and particulars. Schaeffer also believes that Christianity makes sense of other existential experiences, such as the problem of knowing others and distinguishing between reality and fantasy—experiences unaccounted for by the closed system. In the end it is Schaeffer's contention that Christianity is the only worldview that can answer the big epistemological questions of how we know and how we know we know.

The Greatest Challenge Still Remains

We have now completed a survey of the primary offensive arguments formulated by our apologists and will offer a critical evaluation in chapter nine, but for the moment we must turn our attention to what many have thought to be the greatest challenge to Christianity, namely, the problem of evil. Many atheists have insisted that it does not matter how many offensive arguments are marshaled in favor of theism if the existence of suffering, pain and anguish cannot be rationally explained. If God is all-powerful and perfectly good, why should there be any evil at all? An all-powerful God could obliterate all suffering in an instant, and a perfectly good God would surely want to. Therefore, says the atheist, if God does exist he must be either cruel or impotent. Either way, we are left with a deity who is woefully inferior to the traditional Christian description. So how did Lewis and Schaeffer respond to this powerful challenge? This is the question we must now field.

But suppose that what you are up against is a surgeon whose intentions are wholly good. The kinder and more conscientious he is, the more inexorably he will go on cutting. If he yielded to your entreaties, if he stopped before the operation was complete, all the pain up to that point would have been useless. But is it credible that such extremities of torture should be necessary for us? Well, take your choice. The tortures occur. If they are unnecessary, then there is no God or a bad one. If there is a good God, then these tortures are necessary. For no even moderately good Being could possibly inflict or permit them if they weren't.[1]

C. S. LEWIS

Thus, indeed God can use these things [evil] in our life, even though He did not send them. But that is very different from being cast in the slough of despondency by thinking God sent this to me. Thus I . . . am not left in the cruel grasp of the thinking . . . that if I am sick I either am not a Christian or I do not have sufficient faith. Such teaching is not only wrong but cruel.[2]

FRANCIS SCHAEFFER

On the one hand it would be completely wrong to say that God sends misfortune upon individuals, so that their death, maiming, starvation or ruin is God's will for them. But on the other hand God has set us in a world containing unpredictable contingencies and dangers, in which unexpected and undeserved calamities may occur to anyone; because only in such a world can mutual caring and love be elicited.[3]

JOHN HICK

8

Defensive Apologetics
Guarding the Faith

*T*HE BUILDING WAS DILAPIDATED. THE FOOD NAUSEATING. THE bathrooms rancid. The schoolmaster torturous. C. S. Lewis thought his first boarding school was nothing short of a concentration camp. Week after excruciating week, Jack pleaded with his father to be released from his brutal confinement. When the pardon did finally arrive, however, it was not prompted by his father's mercy but by the school's declining enrollment. Lewis believed this experience stunted any mathematical acuity he might otherwise have developed and nearly "sealed [his] fate as a scholar for good."[4]

Nevertheless, there was one point of light during this dark time at Wynyard: Lewis became an active believer. The young boy began to pray, attend church and nourish his faith with the pure milk of the Word. Unfortunately, Lewis did not advance beyond his dairy diet, and by the time he reached his third boarding school his fledgling faith had completely curdled.

Lewis's physical ineptitude, his mother's untimely demise, the negative disposition of his father, the reading of science fiction and his prepubescent incarceration all converged to undermine Lewis's belief in an all-powerful, perfectly good God. He was equally confounded by the exclusive claims of the Christian faith. It seemed improbable that Christianity could be true if every other religion since the beginning of time was sheer nonsense and heathen superstition. Broadly speaking, the problem of evil and the relationship between Christianity and other religions were the two issues that conspired to sour Lewis's faith.

It is hardly surprising that Lewis would wrestle with these issues and one day dwell on these themes in his apologetic writings, for the problem of evil and the scandal of exclusivity are two of the most formidable intellectual and existential challenges to the faith. In fact, the scandal of exclusivity is really a corollary to the problem of evil, for if some people are eternally damned without a legitimate opportunity to hear the gospel, then the justice and goodness of God certainly appear to be open to dispute. This issue is especially relevant in our day of global awareness and pluralistic sensitivity.

In the next several pages we will consider how Lewis and Schaeffer grappled with the problem of evil and the relationship between Christianity and other religions. But first, it will prove beneficial to familiarize ourselves with the two primary paradigms Christian theologians have adopted in their effort to make sense of the pain, anguish and suffering in our world.

The Augustinian and Irenaean Theodicies

The problem of evil is not a uniquely Christian problem. One need not believe Jesus is the Son of God to find it profoundly disturbing when a mother drowns her two young children by locking them in her car and rolling it into a lake. Even if one does not believe in a good God, acts of terrorism, such as the bombing in Oklahoma City, seem senseless and baffling. One might also find it puzzling that our world is marred by natural disasters that seem to strike at random and diseases that cripple and destroy.

It is not clear, however, why evil should be a problem for those who do not believe in God. If matter and energy are ultimately all that exist and human beings arrived on the scene by a process of blind evolution, there seems to be little reason to complain about evil and suffering. After all, there is finally no one to complain to. If atoms and energy are ultimate reality, presumably they do not hear our protests. They do not hear and they do not care.

Christians, however, claim that the One who is ultimately real does hear and does care. This is why evil poses such a sharp problem for them. Indeed, the higher one's view of God, the more difficult the problem of evil may seem. If one's God is not believed to be very powerful or very good, evil may be relatively easy to account for. But if one believes God is all-powerful and perfectly good, the existence of evil is more difficult to explain.

Many critics of Christianity would go further than this. As they see it, if there really is a God who is all-powerful and perfectly good, there simply would not be any evil at all. For an all-powerful God could eliminate all evil, and if he is also perfectly good, then he would do so. But since there is obviously much evil in our world, there cannot be any such God. Consequently, those who believe in such a God in the face of evil are downright irrational. If there is a God at all, the critic persists, he must be either limited in power or defective in goodness.

This basic argument from evil has been advanced against the Christian conception of God for centuries. It was expressed with great eloquence by the likes of Hume and Voltaire during the Enlightenment. It has been formulated in our time with the tools of modern logic. It remains the main weapon in the atheist's arsenal.

The charge of irrationality is a strong one which thoughtful Christians can hardly ignore, and as often as the charge has been made, Christian thinkers have been faithful to respond to it. The project of answering the charge is called *theodicy*, from the Greek words for "God" and "justice." Theodicy is the attempt to demonstrate the justice of God in the face of evil.

Historically, one of the most important components of theodicy has been the appeal to free will. This move goes all the way back to the church fathers, and it remains an important part of the contemporary Christian response to the problem of evil. The basic idea is very simple, namely, that much of the evil in our world can be attributed to the misuse of freedom. This claim is quite plausible when we survey the kinds of evil that have plagued society down through the ages. War, economic oppression, drug abuse, sexual abuse, murder, deception, treachery—all these and more are instances of evil and suffering that can be traced to bad choices on the part of human beings. God made us free, so the argument goes, and with freedom came the possibility of such choices. It was not his will that we would act in this way, so God is not to blame if we abuse his gift of freedom.

It might be suggested that God could have made a world in such a way that we would always freely choose the right thing. In this case we would have freedom, but there would be no evil in the world. All persons would exercise their freedom in ways that were positive, responsible and constructive. This idealistic scenario is certainly an attractive possibility. It is not so clear, however, that God could have created such a world. If he created us in such a way that we could not actually choose evil, then we would not be really free. If we are truly free, then it is up to us to decide how we shall exercise our freedom. If God knows all of us will make at least some wrong choices, then he cannot create a world in which we are free but there is no evil, even though he is omnipotent.[5]

The heart of the appeal to free will is that freedom is worth the price of evil. Genuine libertarian freedom is essential for real love, real trust, real commitment and real relationships. If we value these, we cannot dispense with libertarian freedom. This is the reason many theologians believe God gave us the ability to choose, despite the fact that it is often abused. It is necessary if we are to have genuine relationships with each other and with God himself. The same freedom that makes it possible to love makes it possible to hate. The same freedom that makes possible a C. S. Lewis also makes possible a Nero. The same freedom that makes possible a Francis Schaeffer makes possible a Hitler. The same freedom that can lead to heaven can also lead to hell.

The appeal to freedom explains many evils in our world, but there are also evils that do not seem to be the result of anyone's bad choices. For instance, what about suffering due to natural disasters like earthquakes, tornadoes, famines, floods and diseases? How are these to be accounted for?

This question brings into focus the difference between the two historically important theodicies we want to sketch out. The first of these is the Augustinian theodicy. This has been the dominant position in Western theology, both Roman Catholic and Protestant. The heart of this position is that Adam and Eve were created morally and spiritually perfect in a world that was also fully perfect. In view of these advantages, the Fall was an act of profound rebellion that deserved severe punishment. So God cursed the world. The Fall, then, was a cataclysmic event that introduced suffering and evil into a previously perfect world. All evil, therefore, is the direct or indirect result of the misuse of freedom.[6]

The other theodicy we want to consider offers a sharply contrasting picture. This is the "soul-making" or Irenaean theodicy, named after Irenaeus, an early Eastern church father whose theology inspired this alternative. It has received increased attention during the past two centuries, especially through the recent contribution of philosopher John Hick.[7]

The heart of this theodicy is the notion that our world was designed by God to be a place of soul-making or character development. Human beings, as originally created, were not fully perfect but rather immature and in need of further growth. In other words, human beings have the raw material for sainthood, but this potentiality must be developed for God's purposes to be achieved.

In this view, the world had a certain amount of adversity and suffering built in as part of God's original plan. It is only by facing and overcoming such difficulties that human potential can be fulfilled. This theodicy also places a strong accent on freedom, for we must freely choose to cooperate with divine grace if we are to experience God's ultimate plan for our lives. The suffering of this world is a tool in his hand to shape and mold us into the likeness of Christ.

This does not mean God specifically sends particular difficulties our way.

However, we live in a world in which we are vulnerable to natural evils, like diseases, accidents and disasters, and all of us must face some variety of hardship and challenge. God will use whatever comes our way to accomplish his purposes of sanctification and character development. None of the natural disasters or sources of suffering can defeat God's purpose if we continue to trust him and cooperate with his grace.

A brief summary should help crystallize these distinct theodicies. The Augustinian account of evil suggests that the first humans were greatly exalted beings who freely fell from a state of moral and spiritual perfection by defiantly rebelling against the known will of God. Because of the great culpability of Adam and Eve, the Fall elicited a grave punishment and extreme curse upon the world. Thus all evil can be traced to the misuse of human freedom. By contrast, the Irenaean account of evil suggests that the first humans were not created morally and spiritually perfect but rather entered this world in a state of innocent immaturity. This theodicy likens the Fall to immature children who failed rather than fully developed adults who rebelled. From this perspective, natural evil is not the result of the Fall but part of God's original design to create an environment of soul-making, a world where true moral development and significant character formation can occur. With these two theodicies in clear view, we can now consider how Lewis and Schaeffer engaged the problem of pain, suffering and evil.

Lewis: The Divine Megaphone of Pain

Lewis thought the key to understanding the problem of evil was in possessing a proper understanding of three concepts: divine omnipotence, divine goodness and human happiness. Given the twentieth-century connotations generally associated with these concepts, it is indeed quite difficult, if not impossible, to make sense of evil in our world, but Lewis argues that our modern perception needs adjustment.

First, he makes it clear, as we discussed in chapter four, that the notion of omnipotence does not mean God can do literally anything. There are logical and moral limits to divine activity. God cannot magically mesh into perfect harmony two logically inconsistent propositions, nor can he by divine edict declare immoral acts virtuous. The notion of omnipotence must be framed by the boundaries of God's character and by that which is logically possible.

In light of this sharpened view of omnipotence, Lewis suggests it is logically impossible to say that "God can give a creature free will and at the same time withhold free will from it."[8] If God has chosen to set humans in an environment where free will is operative, then he cannot be expected to override human freedom or alter the character of the material world whenever an evil choice is about to be made. In fact, a stable, common, predictable world is essential if humans are to make intelligent choices about how to use their freedom and if they are to be held responsible for those choices. Such an environment possesses an unavoidable double-edged quality, for "the permanent nature of wood which enables us to use it as a beam also enables us to use it for hitting our neighbour on the head."[9] A real, significant, sturdy world where humans are culpable for their decisions must include the possibility of abuse. This abuse of human freedom, therefore, can hardly be considered a strike against divine omnipotence, since God cannot perform the logical impossibility of both overriding and preserving human freedom at the same time.[10] Because human freedom is necessary for all that is meaningful in life (e.g., love, relationships, acts of nobility) then God cannot create a meaningful world without letting people exercise their freedom.

Lewis also believes our concepts of divine goodness and human happiness must be revisited. Like many concepts in our society, our notions of goodness and happiness have deteriorated into superficial platitudes. Instead of the traditional robust conception of divine goodness, many in our day "want . . . not so much a Father in Heaven as a grandfather in heaven—a senile benevolence who, as they say, 'liked to see young people enjoying themselves.' "[11] Such a picture suggests a pitiful deity whose only concern is some sappy, insipid, temporal amusement for his creatures instead of their ultimate well-being.

There are things in this world that offer the short-term gain of temporal delight, but the associated price tag is the long-term loss of character formation and profound joy. Coney Island chili dogs and cotton candy might taste good going down, but they are not nearly so tasty on the way back up. On the other hand, spinach and wheat germ might not be what you want to ingest, but in the long run healthy food meets your nutritional needs. God is like a cosmic chef who tailors our diet to our own individual health needs. He is more concerned about clearing out our colon than tantalizing our tastebuds. In other words, God's primary consideration is our eternal health, not our temporal gratification.

This is where Lewis's transformational soteriology becomes evident. God does not want to shield us from the pain, suffering and anguish of the world at all costs so we can divert ourselves with temporary pleasures that have no ultimate redemptive value. God's primary goal is to transform us into healthy beings capable of enjoying the rich, satisfying, lasting pleasures of eternal bliss. God is not like a senile old grandfather whose only concern is the temporal gratification of his grandchildren, but more like a skilled, benevolent surgeon who will do whatever it takes to eradicate the cancer of sin from the character of his creatures, because he knows that ultimate health and happiness are impossible as long as any trace of the malignancy remains. In a fallen world this type of surgery often requires the scalpel of suffering.

In other words, God is loving but his love is tough. Lewis's view of God crystallizes in the Narnian character of Aslan. In *The Lion, the Witch and the Wardrobe* the Pevensie children first hear about Aslan after a hearty meal with a pair of talking Beavers. The Beavers explain that he is "the son of the great Emperor-Beyond-the-Sea .... the great Lion." Susan and Lucy are ambivalent about meeting the King of the Beasts and wonder whether he is safe. Mr. Beaver offers a surprising response: "Who said anything about safe? 'Course he isn't safe. But he's good."[12] The children learn that Aslan is a real lion, with razor-sharp teeth and slashing claws. Fortunately his feral nature is continually guided by an impeccable character.

In the fifth book of the series, *The Horse and His Boy*, a young princess named Aravis learns from firsthand experience how painful the claws of Aslan can be. The princess is fleeing from an abusive home life and has left an innocent servant behind to take the unjust punishment for her departure. During a journey on horseback through the desert, Aravis and a companion are viciously pursued by a lion that slices her back before retreating. Near the end of the story Aslan appears to the children and explains that he was the one who "tore" her. He goes on to reveal his rationale for the injury: "The scratches on your back, tear for tear, throb for throb, blood for blood, were equal to the stripes laid on the back of your stepmother's slave because of the drugged sleep you cast upon her. You needed to know what it felt like."[13] What we learn from this imagery is that Lewis believes God is perfectly willing to hurt us in order to bring about the ultimate healing of our souls.

But why should such excruciating pain be necessary? Lewis believes there are at least two reasons. First, humans are notorious for slipping into patterns of complacency and self-sufficiency when the waters are calm. We all have a tendency to settle into the creaturely comforts of this world and "rest in a shadowy happiness as if it could last for ever."[14] Pain awakens us from our dangerous slumbering drift: "it is His megaphone to rouse a deaf world."[15] It tests our mettle, corrects our wayward attitudes, purifies our motives and helps to set us back on course toward the ultimate goal of Christlike self-surrender. Second, pain and suffering provide opportunities for acts of compassion, nobility and true communal interdependency, which, in turn, build character, forge loving relationships and reflect the glory of God.[16] Lewis believes that God, from the perspective of perfect knowledge and wisdom, uses what is inherently bad—pain and suffering—for instrumental good.

It is important to note, however, that Lewis does not believe pain was part of God's original design. Lewis thinks animal suffering, death and animosity existed before the first humans ever arrived on the scene, but these came into the world through Satan's fall, not by the hand of God. This first fall fractured the natural world and introduced cruelty into the animal kingdom. Humans, therefore, apparently had a redemptive mission right from the start.[17]

Though the natural world had fallen, humans were created pure, without any proclivity toward sin. They possessed "a will wholly disposed, though not compelled, to turn to God."[18] In fact, humans were given all the necessary resources to live a life of uninterrupted communion with God. But at some point, self-will reared its ugly head and human pain, suffering and anguish entered the world through a direct act of defiance and rebellion. Humans became something they were never intended to be: "a new species ... sinned itself into existence."[19] As to how this happened, Lewis sees no need for dogmatism, suggesting "it might have concerned the literal eating of a fruit, but the question is of no consequence."[20] The bottom line is that sin is real and humans are responsible.

God designed us for a smooth relationship with our Creator, but this "very heinous"[21] act of rebellion has whipped up a storm, leaving humanity ship-wrecked. As a result, our voyage back to the harbor must endure gale-force winds, torrential downpours and rough waters. This journey is possible, but it will require the conquering of our selfish inclination, which is constantly pushing us back toward shipwreck. The wind of self-will is no longer at our back softly nudging us toward our Creator, as it was prior to the Fall, but is now flying in our face, furiously driving us away from the One for whom we were made. If Lewis's soteriological vision is true—a vision that requires total self-surrender, complete humility and thorough transformation into selfless, Christlike creatures—then it is imperative that these relentless winds of sinful self-will be stilled at all costs. That is why Lewis believed God sends storms our way. We need a counteracting tempest strong enough to subdue the winds of our self-will and set us back on the correct course. The pain, anguish and suffering we so deeply despise and desperately long to resist prove, in the long run, to be the benevolent tempest that powers us toward the ultimate safety and tranquility of the heavenly harbor.

In summary, what we find with Lewis is a theodicy that is really a synthesis of the Augustinian and Irenaean accounts. Following Augustine, Lewis tells us that the first act of sin was "very heinous" and the consequences were severe. It was an act of intense rebellion and sheer defiance. Humans abused their wonderful gift of freedom and this abuse introduced the pain, suffering and anguish that humanity must now endure. Instead of a strong inclination toward God, humans now possess a strong inclination toward self. The only way back to God, therefore, is through painful self-surrender. This is where the Irenaean vision comes into play. Lewis says our current world has become "a 'vale of soul-making.'"[22] Though God did not originally intend all this anguish, he now employs the raw materials of pain and suffering to chisel us into heavenly works of art. He is the divine dentist who will not stop drilling until the job is done.[23] He is the supernatural surgeon who will not cease cutting until the malignancy is removed.[24] He is the cosmic chef who dishes up victuals that will purge our pallet of all impurities. And it is entirely fruitless to send our plate back to the kitchen, for "if we will not learn to eat the only food that the universe grows—the only food that any possible universe can ever grow—then we must starve eternally."[25]

Schaeffer: The Tomb of Lazarus

Like Lewis, Schaeffer was no stranger to the problem of evil. His son contracted polio as a child, and two of his daughters battled rheumatic fever. But in 1979 the Schaeffers faced their toughest test when Francis was diagnosed with lymphoma cancer. In a cluster of correspondence, nestled within the *Letters of Francis A. Schaeffer,* we catch an intimate glimpse of Schaeffer's attitude toward the intellectual and existential problem of evil.

These letters reveal a man who found his faith capable of withstanding the pressures of a real-life tragedy. Throughout his illness he refused to become embittered, even when it became clear that healing would not come his way. He believed in God's healing touch but was "utterly convinced . . . that the fact that Francis Schaeffer has not been 'cured' and yet is pressing on in the work has been a greater encouragement and blessing to hundreds than if I had been 'cured.' "[26] What was the key to Schaeffer's coping ability? The conviction that we are living in an abnormal world. The natural evil and moral evil that threaten us daily are alien entities, contrary to God's original design and his ongoing desire.[27]

Schaeffer found support for this belief in the reaction of Jesus at the tomb of Lazarus. The original Greek text records that Jesus was not only sorrowful but angry when he discovered Lazarus dead. This suggests a God who is both moved by human suffering and disturbed by the abnormal conditions of our world. Schaeffer finds it particularly significant that Jesus, the sovereign Lord of creation, can be angry at death without being angry at himself. That is why Schaeffer was certain that God was not the source of his cancer.[28] In fact, God "hates the sorrows of the world more than we do—even to the point of sending His Son to die so that eventually there might be healing."[29] Of course, this is not to say that God does not use evil in the world to produce something good, as he did with Schaeffer's illness, yet "that is very different from being cast in the slough of despondency by thinking God sent this [evil] to me."[30]

But if evil is not an intrinsic part of God's creation, then how did it arise? In traditional Augustinian fashion, Schaeffer attributes our current abnormalities to human rebellion. Adam and Eve, who were created in a state of moral and spiritual perfection with no inclination toward sin, made a conscious, space-time choice to disobey God. This wicked act fractured our world and ushered in the enemies of pain, anguish, estrangement, disease, suffering and death. Schaeffer stakes the entire faith on the claim that Adam and Eve possessed the power of contrary choice. If they were determined in any way, then "the whole of Christian theology and every Christian answer falls to the ground."[31] In other words, Schaeffer recognized the necessity of libertarian freedom to advance the free will theodicy. Without the free will theodicy Schaeffer was sure we are stuck with an evil God.

As indicated in chapter seven under the rubric of the moral argument, Schaeffer identified four crucial features that flow from an Augustinian account of evil. First, there is a rational explanation for cruelty in the world without attributing evil to God. Second, this answer to the origin of evil offers the hope of a solution to humanity's moral quandary. Third, since God is not wicked and since sin, pain and suffering are contrary to his will, we can fight injustice and evil in the world without the fear that we are fighting God. Fourth, this position gives us objective moral categories to judge between right and wrong because morality is ultimately grounded in the character of a supremely righteous Being.

On the other hand, Schaeffer did not think the Irenaean theodicy, at least as it is interpreted by John Hick, can provide an adequate solution to the problem of evil.[32] In a lecture delivered during the mid-sixties, Schaeffer challenged Hick, who was then teaching at Cambridge. Hick's *Evil and the God of Love* would eventually earn a reputation as one of the key contributions on the problem of evil during the latter half of the twentieth century.

The heart of Schaeffer's objection to Hick's soul-making theodicy has to do with the notion that the nature of our current world is essentially consistent with God's original design. There were no cataclysmic repercussions when the first sin was committed. The Fall did not fracture the world and introduce pain, suffering and anguish. These elements were an intrinsic part of God's primeval intent, because, as Hick put it, "only in such a world can mutual caring and love be elicited."[33] Hick suggests that character development requires the type of world we now inhabit, so our current conditions are simply the necessary means to God's desired end.

This suggestion strikes at the heart of Schaeffer's central insistence on viewing our current plight as abnormal. Schaeffer believes that if we inhabit a "normal" world, one that matches God's original blueprint, then we are left with an evil God, an intrinsically corrupt humanity with no hope of a solution, no basis for opposing injustice and no ground for an ultimate standard of righteousness. In short, Schaeffer believes Hick's soul-making theodicy undermines the four critical features that naturally flow from the Augustinian account of evil. The only way to answer the problem of evil, therefore, is to insist on a literal, cataclysmic, space-time Fall and radical discontinuity between our current plight and God's original intent.

The Fate of the Unevangelized

With these views in mind, we now turn to a particularly poignant example of the problem of evil, namely, the fate of the unevangelized. One of the central claims of orthodox Christianity is the exclusive assertion that Jesus Christ is the only way to God. In light of this claim, what believer has not wondered what will become of those who die without an opportunity to respond to the gospel? Although some Christians quickly dismiss such ponderings as fruitless theoretical speculation, many reflective believers have realized this topic is not primarily a matter of intellectual curiosity but rather a corollary to the problem of evil. For if some people are eternally damned without a legitimate opportunity to be saved, then it certainly appears we are left with a suspect account of divine justice and goodness.

John Sanders is one scholar who has chosen to engage this subject with philosophical rigor and existential sensitivity. As Sanders points out, this issue can hardly be ignored in our age of increasing pluralism and global awareness. In fact, he tells us that "according to some estimates this is the most asked apologetic question [of our day]."[34] Therefore if we are going to answer the questions our postmodern world is asking, we must be willing to provide a thoughtful response to the pressing inquiry of what happens to those who have not heard.

Christians have answered this question in a wide variety of ways, but most responses can be grouped under one of three general headings. First, there is the position that God will ultimately save everyone; the unevangelized, adherents to other faith systems and even those who explicitly repudiate the gospel in this life will end up in heaven. This position is typically called pluralism or universalism.[35] Second, there is the opinion that only those who explicitly receive the gospel and confess Jesus Christ in this life will be saved. God has provided no other means by which humanity can receive eternal life. Sanders believes this position, which he labels restrictivism, has been the dominant model in fundamentalist and neo-evangelical circles.[36] The third position, however, attempts to chart a via media. Adherents to this model believe salvation can only come through Jesus Christ, but this does not mean one must explicitly embrace the gospel in this life to be saved. Since some people will never hear the gospel or be given a legitimate chance to receive it in this life, God either will provide an opportunity to embrace the truth beyond the grave or will judge people according to the light they have received during their earthly sojourn. Some believe this alternative incorporates the best insights of the two other models without sacrificing the moral and epistemological integrity of the faith. This position is nuanced in a variety of ways under the rubric of "the Wider Hope."[37] We will now attempt to interpret the positions of Schaeffer and Lewis in light of these models, starting with Schaeffer.

Schaeffer: Justice Is Served

The most explicit reference to the fate of the unevangelized in the writings of Francis Schaeffer can be found in the seventh and eighth chapters of *Death in the City*. In these chapters, entitled "The Man Without the Bible" and "The Justice of God," Schaeffer addresses two key questions. First, how will the person who has never heard the gospel be judged? Second, is God just in his judgment?[38]

Schaeffer believes the apostle Paul answers these questions in the opening chapters of the epistle to the Romans. God has provided everyone adequate revelation to discern the existence of a divine Creator. Even those who do not have access to special revelation have the generous testimony of the universe and its form and the "mannishness of man." In addition, the inability of the "man without the Bible" to account for the external and internal states of our world is a "powerful testimony" to the inadequacy of his worldview.[39] In light of all these pointers to the truth, all humanity stands morally culpable and without excuse before a righteous God, whether or not they have heard the gospel.

Everyone is guilty, but that does not mean God will judge everyone the same way. God will judge those who have heard the gospel according to the high standard of Scripture, while those who have never heard the gospel will be judged according to the lower standard of their own God-given conscience or moral code. Schaeffer tells us that everyone has moral motions, whether they admit it or not, and these motions are part of our humanity. Schaeffer concludes that the evangelized will be held to the standard of special revelation, while the unevangelized will be held to the standard of general revelation, particularly their own moral motions.

Schaeffer illustrates the judgment of the person without the Bible accordingly. Imagine that at birth a tape recorder is placed around each person's neck and the record button is pushed. Over time this tape captures all the moral motions, thoughts, words, deeds and judgments of each person's life. When judgment day rolls around, God rewinds the tape and plays it all back, the good, the bad and the ugly, then says, "On the basis of your own words, have *you* kept these moral standards?" Schaeffer tells us that "the whole world will stand totally condemned before God in utter justice, because they will be judged not upon what they have not known, but upon what they have judged others and have not kept themselves. So all men must say, 'Indeed I am justly condemned.' "[40]

In summary, Schaeffer does not believe God will judge the unevangelized according to a form of revelation to which they were never privy, but rather he will judge them according to the very same moral standard to which they held others. Schaeffer insists that this is fully just, for those without the Bible will ultimately condemn themselves, by failing to live up to their own yardstick. According to Schaeffer, this position preserves God's holiness by insisting on judgment for all humanity and underscores the reality of human significance by holding everyone responsible for their actions. The unevangelized therefore stand under the wrath of "the Great Judge,"[41] and "it's up to me [the Christian] in compassion to take the good news to *my kind.*"[42] In other words, those who die without hearing the gospel are destined for eternal damnation. This perspective places Schaeffer firmly within the restrictivist camp.

Lewis: Seek and Ye Shall Find

While Schaeffer rarely addressed this issue in his corpus, the relationship between Christianity and other religions was one of the key themes in the life and literature of C. S. Lewis. This subject helped erode his adolescent faith and also proved to be an important factor in bringing him back many years later. With the assistance of J. R. R. Tolkien and Hugo Dyson, Lewis came to recognize some essential continuities between Christianity and other worldviews. A deep appreciation for myth provided Lewis a lens through which he could see the loving, providential hand of God cultivating his entire creation.

Lewis was certain salvation comes only through Jesus Christ, but this does not mean an overt confession of faith in this life is essential. Millions have lived and died without hearing the gospel or without receiving a legitimate opportunity to respond. For those who are denied such an opportunity, the Holy Spirit secretly guides them to concentrate on pockets of illumination in their respective systems of faith. Since all truth is God's truth, any response to available light is ultimately a response to the Father of lights and a step toward reconciliation. Consequently, Lewis thought someone could be a true follower of Jesus without consciously knowing it.[43]

Lewis found scriptural support for this belief in Matthew 25:30-46. This passage, which describes the final judgment, makes it clear that it is not always possible to distinguish between the sheep and the goats in this life. Every truly good act, despite the religious banner under which it is done, ultimately will be accepted by a holy God. Likewise, every evil act, despite the religious banner under which it is done, ultimately will be rejected by a holy God. This passage reveals the perfectly just and ethical character of a God who does not judge by outward appearance but by inward intent.[44]

This point is illustrated in a famous scene from the final book of the Chronicles of Narnia, *The Last Battle*. The chapter entitled "Further Up and Further In" describes an encounter between Aslan and Emeth, a soldier who has faithfully, though misguidedly, served the lion's archenemy, Tash. When Aslan appears, Emeth immediately recognizes him for who he is—the true Lord. He falls at the lion's glorious feet, expecting execution, but is pleasantly surprised to feel a moist, tender tongue grazing his forehead. Relieved but confounded, Emeth asks how a servant of Tash could possibly find favor with his master's chief nemesis. In the following passage, Aslan reveals the answer:

> Because we are opposites, I take to me the services which thou hast done to [Tash], for I and he are of such different kinds that no service which is vile can be done to me, and none which is not vile can be done to him. Therefore if any man swear by Tash and keep his oath for the oath's sake, it is by me that he has truly sworn, though he know it not, and it is I who reward him.... Dost thou understand, Child? I said, Lord, thou knowest how much I understand. But I said also (for the truth constrained me), Yes, I have been seeking Tash all my days. Beloved, said the Glorious One, unless thy desire had been for me thou wouldst not have sought so long and so truly. For all find what they truly seek.[45]

What we discover with Lewis, then, is a firm belief in a God whose primary requirement of his creatures is not epistemic precision but heart purity. Yet that does not mean all roads lead to heaven, as the universalist insists. Lewis was adamant about Christ's being the exclusive way to God. He simply argued that some people, due to infirmities or circumstances beyond their control, will never hear the gospel, or if they do, they will hear it through a tainted filter of distortion. God takes these factors into account. He knows one's historical and geographical limitations. He knows that someone born prior to the incarnation or beyond the spread of the gospel does not have the same opportunity as the person in Peoria. He knows that a child who has been taught to worship Tash from his father's knee will naturally perceive the teaching of Aslan through a skewed paradigm. God knows all these things and factors them into his dealings with his creatures.[46]

What matters most to a God who is truly just and perfectly good is not the outward formulation of faith but the inward intent to cooperate with the grace that has been given. The Bible assures us that if we will honestly desire and seek the truth, we will find it. Ultimately all light and all truth lead back to their one and only source, the Divine Logos, Jesus Christ. Everyone will have a legitimate opportunity to receive the gospel, either in this life or the next, but salvation will only come through Jesus. This belief clearly places Lewis in the Wider Hope camp on this issue.

Summarizing the Defensive Discord

In this chapter we have noted some significant dissonance between Schaeffer and Lewis. Both men affirmed an Augustinian notion of the Fall, but they viewed our current conditions from contrasting angles of vision. Schaeffer insisted that God hates our sorrows more than we do and that our pain, anguish and suffering are largely the result of living in a fallen world. God can work good out of evil, but that is different from attributing specific bouts of anguish to his direct will. Moreover, we can learn from our present sufferings, but they have no correlation to our ultimate salvation. The imputed righteousness of Christ is our guarantee of eternal life.

Lewis, on the other hand, thought the post-Fall world has become an arena of soul-making. Our self-will is now the chief enemy, and it must be subdued at all costs if we are to be transformed into heavenly beings. This process often requires the raw materials of pain, suffering and sorrow. Though pain is contrary to God's original blueprint and ultimate plan, he is now willing to send direct instances of suffering, if necessary, to achieve the great good of Christlike character formation in a person's life.

Our survey of the fate of the unevangelized has revealed some significant points of tension as well. Schaeffer insists that all are guilty, whether they have heard the gospel or not. God does not judge the unevangelized by the standard of Scripture but rather by the moral standard to which they hold others. Since they do not live up to their own yardstick, and since there is no salvation apart from an overt confession of faith in this life, the fate of the unevangelized is eternal damnation. It is up to Christians to spread the gospel to all corners of the globe if the unevangelized are to have any hope of heaven.

Lewis, on the other hand, believed God distributes his grace throughout the world in a variety of forms and is constantly wooing and drawing all humanity to himself. God's primary concern is internal heart purity, not epistemic precision or external formulations. Since all light and truth flow from God, anyone who sincerely seeks illumination will eventually find its emanating source, whether it is a conscious realization in this life or not. Consequently, Lewis thought it was possible for the unevangelized to be saved apart from an overt confession of faith in this life, but not ultimately apart from Christ.

With our survey of the offensive and defensive arguments complete, we are now prepared to critically evaluate the overall apologetic thrust of these men. We will explore the major points of contrast and contact and devote special attention to how the theological commitments of Lewis and Schaeffer are related to these key apologetic issues. Chapter nine begins where we have left off, with the problem of evil and the fate of the unevangelized.

At the moment, then, of Man's victory over Nature, we find the whole human race subjected to some individual men, and those individuals subjected to that in themselves which is purely 'natural'—to their irrational impulses. Nature, untrammelled by values, rules the Conditioners and, through them, all humanity. Man's conquest of Nature turns out, in the moment of its consummation, to be Nature's conquest of Man.[1]

C. S. LEWIS

Twice [B. F.] Skinner specifically attacked C. S. Lewis. Why? Because he is a Christian and writes in the tradition of the literatures of freedom and dignity. You will notice that he does not attack the evangelical church, probably because he doesn't think it's a threat to him. Unhappily, he is largely right about this. Many of us are too sleepy to be a threat in the battle of tomorrow. But he understands that a man like C. S. Lewis, who writes literature which stirs men, is indeed a threat.[2]

FRANCIS SCHAEFFER

C. S. Lewis put it quite bluntly: Man is being abolished. . . . His abolition has long been overdue. Autonomous man is a device used to explain what we cannot explain in any other way. He has been constructed from our ignorance, and as our understanding increases, the very stuff of which he is composed vanishes. Science does not dehumanize man, it de-homunculizes him, and it must do so if it is to prevent the abolition of the human species. To man *qua* man we readily say good riddance.[3]

B. F. SKINNER

9

Back to Libertarian Freedom and Dignity
Evaluating the Apologetic Arguments

*I*N *THE TAPESTRY* EDITH SCHAEFFER DESCRIBES AN INCIDENT THAT turned out to be both one of the most trying and most valuable experiences she and Francis ever faced. It was moving day. With all their belongings boxed, the Schaeffers were poised to migrate from Philadelphia to Delaware, where Francis was to resume his theological studies at the newly organized Faith Seminary.

During the course of the move, however, one thing after another went wrong. It all started when Francis, who had been given the assignment of purchasing some used furniture and appliances for the new school, was nearly cheated by a merchant. He had carefully selected each item, but when he came back to retrieve them, some of his selections had been replaced with lower-grade merchandise. By the time he returned home to load their personal belongings, he was "most irate."[4]

Francis seemed to get angrier by the minute as he awkwardly maneuvered their cumbersome possessions toward the truck. After a series of mishaps and subsequent outbursts, the family squeezed into the Model A while another man drove the loaded truck in front of them. Fran was joined by Edith, Edith's mother and well-fed newborn Priscilla.

As they drove through the city streets, rain beat down on the hot pavement and steam obscured their view. They lost sight of the truck, took a wrong turn, hit red lights. Each aggravation elicited a louder eruption from Francis. Then their sweet-smelling baby "emitted from both ends at once." Edith describes the unpleasant scene:

A gush of so recently swallowed food came up over my shoulder, down my back and splashed over the seat back, while simultaneously a rush of what could have been mustard leaked forth from both sides of the beautiful white knitted soakers with diapers carefully pinned under them, and covered my lap, my legs, and my shoes. [Fran yelled,] "Can't you even take care of that baby? . . . Don't you know how to put on diapers? WHAT IS THE MATTER WITH YOU?"[5]

Immediately following this latest explosion, Francis lost control of the car on the slick pavement and crashed into another vehicle. Fortunately, no one was hurt, but the two women braced themselves for the climactic tirade. But instead of another outburst, the driver softly uttered a contrite confession: "All right, Lord, I'm sorry; it's enough."[6] At the point of contact with the other car, the words of Hebrews 12:11 had immediately rushed into his mind: "No discipline seems pleasant at the time, but painful. Later on, however, it produces a harvest of righteousness and peace for those who have been trained by it." He was immediately convicted of his behavior and convinced that God had allowed one event after another to take place to chasten him and correct his poor attitude.

Later in the book, Edith describes a time when she was burned in the face by an iron. This accident occurred while she was attempting to carry out a plan that was contrary to God's will. Like Francis in the car, Edith recognized her painful experience as chastening from the Lord—not an arrow directly from the heavenly bow but rather something allowed for the purpose of discipline. Edith is quick to point out that the experience of chastening can be identified only from the inside, by the one going through the anguish of the moment.

It is not for someone else to say to anyone else, "Aha and aha . . . see . . . you are being chastened." I did not say that to Fran when we had the car accident that day in the succession of things when he was getting angrier and angrier. And he did not say that to me although he knew I was being very determined and stubborn about my plan or scheme. We each have recognized our own moments of chastening, and we have stood alone before the Lord to tell Him so, and have personally been "exercised thereby" and have noted some of the peaceable fruits that have resulted. Being chastened is a very private thing.[7]

As we have seen, C. S. Lewis also recognized the value of pain and suffering in the process of correction and character formation. Unlike the Schaeffers, however, Lewis was willing to say some instances of suffering are not simply allowed by God but sent directly from his hand. In the next several pages, under the rubric of apologetic points of contrast, we will evaluate the views of these two apologists on the problem of evil and look specifically at their divergent responses to an existential encounter with cancer. We will then explore a second point of tension, namely, the fate of the unevangelized. (It is interesting that the two major areas of apologetic contrast between these men are both situated in the realm of defensive apologetics.)

After analyzing these topics of tension, we will consider the primary apologetic points of contact: the "mannishness of man" arguments, the charge of superficiality and triumphalism, and the value of cumulative case arguments. Throughout the course of this chapter we will devote special care to the relationship between the apologetic arguments advanced by these men and their respective theological commitments.

The Problem of Evil: The Existential Encounter with Cancer
We start our analysis with the question that opened the last chapter: Why does evil exist if God is both all-powerful and perfectly good? We have seen that both apologists affirmed a cataclysmic Fall in the Augustinian tradition, but significant differences surface when detailing their respective theodicies. These points of contrast are concentrated in two distinct areas: the free-will defense and the subject of soul-making.

In order to develop the first point of contrast, we must highlight an important area of agreement, namely, the utilization of the free-will defense to absolve God from all evil. God has created free beings who possess the power of contrary choice. It is up to each individual to decide how to use this freedom. Therefore, God is not to blame if humans choose to misappropriate this gift. This is probably the most common maneuver employed by theists in combatting the charge that God is culpable for evil.

It is imperative to understand that libertarian freedom is the only model of freedom capable of advancing this particular theodicy, for compatibilism insists that God can determine all things in precise detail without overriding human freedom. Therefore, the compatibilist says that God could have determined everyone to always choose the right thing (e.g., God could have determined Adam and Eve to freely reject the apple), but apparently he has good reasons for not actualizing that type of world. So the compatibilist cannot use the free-will defense to engage the problem of evil but rather must argue that God determined the evil we have to bring about some greater good that would not have been actualized in a world where everyone always chooses to do the right thing.

When confronting the problem of evil, both Lewis and Schaeffer recognized the need for a libertarian kind of freedom to advance the free-will theodicy. Schaeffer, in particular, stakes the entire faith on the claim that

Adam and Eve possessed the power of contrary choice. If they were determined in any way, then "the whole of Christian theology and every Christian answer falls to the ground."[8] Schaeffer insists that God cannot be the ultimate source of evil, even if such evil brings about a greater good, as compatibilism suggests.

We are now in position to see our first point of contrast. Although both apologists blamed humans for the evil in our world, Lewis is the only one with the proper theological apparatus to advance this theodicy with consistency. As our analysis in chapter four revealed, Lewis's view of sovereignty and human freedom can be characterized as an appeal to mystery in some cases and temporary agnosticism in others, but in neither case is he guilty of affirming a self-contradiction. Schaeffer, on the other hand, embraced the incoherent position of paradox. Consequently, he cannot rationally avail himself of the free-will defense to explain evil, for if God has predestined every detail of life there is no possible way Adam and Eve could have chosen otherwise. In short, his belief in total, unconditional predestination negates the suggestion that human freedom is the real source of evil.

As also noted in chapter four, this incoherent paradigm leaves Schaeffer with three options. First, he could tenaciously cling to his belief in libertarian freedom and total, unconditional predestination, but in so doing he would forfeit a rationally discerned, unified body of knowledge, since these claims are logically incompatible. Given total, unconditional predestination, it is impossible for humans to choose other than what God has determined. It does not matter how carefully this claim is framed; one is still left with the fact that Adam and Eve could not have done otherwise, precisely because they were determined to eat the apple and introduce pain, suffering and anguish into our world. There is no escaping this conclusion given total, unconditional predestination.

A second option available to Schaeffer would have been to keep his belief in total, unconditional predestination but adopt a compatibilistic view of freedom. Although Schaeffer was a strict adherent of libertarian freedom, it appears he might have flirted with compatibilism when discussing divine inspiration and biblical inerrancy.[9] As indicated in our analysis in chapter five, Schaeffer was certain that the Bible contains exactly what God desires, down to the very words. He also apparently believed God can precisely control what his human agents write without overriding their freedom. If compatibilism is what Schaeffer had in mind when discussing divine inspiration and inerrancy, then, again, he is left with a theological position from which he cannot successfully advance the free-will theodicy.[10] For if God can accomplish precisely what he wants through humans without overriding their freedom, in this case determine the exact wording of the biblical writers, then he could have determined Adam and Eve and all humans since the foundation of the world to freely choose to do the right thing. In fact, given this model of freedom, God could determine everyone to choose him so no one would need to perish eternally. As indicated earlier, the heart of the problem for the compatibilist is that given the traditional orthodox belief that some will spend eternity in hell, we are left with the thorny conclusion that God could have saved everyone with their freedom intact but for some reason chose not to do so. This appears to be an insurmountable problem for the person who believes in a God who is profoundly good and desires the very best for all his creatures. So the compatibilist is left with the morally confounding problem of reconciling God's goodness and justice with the evil of this world, including the existence of hell, and must do so without the assistance of the free-will defense.[11] If Schaeffer used compatibilism to advance his theory of inspiration, he is left with the unenviable position of accepting the fact that God is ultimately the source of all evil, even if that evil is used to bring about a greater good.

A third option remains, however, and is the only one that can logically advance the free-will theodicy. While keeping his belief in libertarian freedom, Schaeffer must adopt a model of sovereignty that coheres with the power of contrary choice. As previously indicated, Schaeffer overtly refused this option. Yet it is possible that Schaeffer unknowingly nuanced his categories of sovereignty when engaging issues like the problem of evil and inerrancy. If this is true, then Schaeffer is not saddled with the problems of compatibilism but is guilty of slippage between significantly different models of sovereignty.

Now, the model that coheres with libertarian freedom and makes best sense of Schaeffer's view of inerrancy is Molinism.[12] Given this scenario, God, through middle knowledge, identifies those individuals who he knows will freely choose to write precisely what he wants. God does not determine what they will write but rather identifies those who will freely cooperate, in a libertarian sense, with the Holy Spirit in the inspiration process to achieve the exact product God desires. If Schaeffer had this model in mind, however, he has advanced his theory of inerrancy with categories that align easily with an Arminian position but not with Calvinism. But even if he does use a Molinist model when discussing inerrancy, Schaeffer can advance the free-will theodicy only if he adopts a view of God's sovereignty that is compatible with libertarian freedom across the board, not just in one theological area. In short, the only way Schaeffer could have logically utilized the free-will defense, the heart of his theodicy, is if he had adopted an Arminian view of sovereignty in every area of theological discussion, including inspiration, the problem of evil and divine election.

Our second point of contrast concerning the problem of evil centers on the subject of soul-making. As we have seen, Schaeffer offered a strictly Augustinian explanation of evil, but Lewis suggested a synthesis of the Augustinian and Irenaean theodicies. Lewis did not believe the Irenaean account of soul-making was God's original intent, but after the Fall this difficult route became the only way back to our heavenly harbor. God sends storms our way to overwhelm the winds of our stubborn self-will. Pain, suffering and anguish are indispensable tools in this transformational process and "tribulations cannot cease until God either sees us remade or sees that our remaking is now hopeless."[13]

Schaeffer, on the other hand, recognized the value of suffering in the sanctification process but did not believe our salvation is in any way connected to our actual character. The imputation of Christ's righteousness is our ticket to heaven. Consequently, Schaeffer saw no direct correlation between character formation and our fitness for eternity. He did not consider bouts of suffering sent directly from the hand of God to expose our lack of faith or subdue our self-will, although he did believe suffering is sometimes permitted for the purpose of chastening. Most of the pain and suffering we encounter is simply the result of living in an abnormal, fallen world, and no one is immune. God hates our sorrows more than we do, to the point of sending his own Son to the cross. Although God does not directly send every specific instance of pain and suffering, he does creatively work good out of inherently evil and tragic situations.

This contrast is most clearly seen in how these men viewed their respective bouts with cancer. Schaeffer attributed his malady to living in a fractured, fallen world, but Lewis apparently believed his wife's demise was sent directly from the throne of God to show that his faith was a "house of cards."[14] These antithetical paradigms deeply affected their contrasting responses in the face of excruciating circumstances.

While Schaeffer found comfort and encouragement from his vision of an empathetic God weeping over our anguish and despising the death and deterioration of this world, Lewis struggled to keep his faith intact. In a moving existential outpouring just months following Joy's death, Lewis documented his ongoing travail. *A Grief Observed* reveals a man who found little comfort in his time of need: "Talk to me about the truth of religion and I'll listen gladly. Talk to me about the duty of religion and I'll listen submissively. But don't come talking to me about the consolations of religion or I shall suspect that you don't understand."[15] In the throes of despair, Lewis wondered if God is really a "vivisector,"[16] "a Cosmic Sadist,"[17] a "spiteful imbecile"[18] or an evil deity as "a sort of extreme Calvinism" might suggest.[19]

In chapter eight we likened Lewis's description of pain and suffering to God's tempest that pushes us toward the heavenly harbor, but at the height of his angst Lewis wondered if his loved ones, instead of reaching port safely, had been dashed on the rocks.

> The starboard engine has gone. I, the port engine, must chug along somehow till we make harbor. Or rather, till the journey ends. How can I assume harbor? A lee shore, more likely, a black night, a deafening gale, breakers ahead—and any lights shown from the land probably being waved by wreckers. Such was [Joy's] landfall. Such was my mother's. I say their landfalls; not their arrivals.[20]

At the end of the book, however, we find Lewis surfacing from this dark night of the soul with his faith shaken but intact.

A curious irony emerges when we consider these contrasting responses in light of the theological resources available to each man. On the one hand we find Schaeffer, who affirmed total, unconditional predestination, insisting that God did not send his suffering. On the other hand we find Lewis, who held a paradigm of providence that accounts for true contingency, insisting that God did send suffering to him. In other words, the one who could have logically attributed suffering to our abnormal world, Lewis, chose to attribute it to the will of God, while the one who should have logically attributed suffering to the will of God, Schaeffer, attributed it to our abnormal world.

Although this is a strange juxtaposition, we should note that Schaeffer is the only one left with a logical problem. One simply cannot exonerate God from sending suffering if he is the unconditional predestinator of the totality of life. Again, the only way Schaeffer can consistently attribute evil to our abnormal world is to adopt a model of sovereignty that provides for some measure of true contingency and human libertarian freedom. Lewis, however, has no logical problem by attributing suffering to God, given his paradigm of providence, but he does appear to be left with a serious existential predicament. Lewis seemed to believe his transformational soteriology and soul-making theodicy required tracing much of our anguish directly to the hand of God. He certainly seemed to think this was the case with the death of his wife.

It is critical to recognize, however, that one need not attribute individual instances of suffering to the will of God to advance the transformational and

Irenaean theories. Lewis clearly recognized this in some of his other writings on the problem of evil. In one of his letters, for instance, he pointed out that the book of Job shows that not all suffering is punishment and remarks that it would "certainly be most dangerous to assume that any given pain was penal."[21] For the same reason, it would seem to be dangerous to assume that any tragedy or adversity was specifically sent to expose the person involved as having a "house of cards" type of faith. In *The Problem of Pain* Lewis observes that while all Christians must fully absorb, with the help of Christ, the pain of having their self-will corrected, the type and degree of suffering involved vary widely from case to case. Some experience the brutal death of a martyr, while others suffer in ways that show no obvious outward signs. As Lewis remarks with appropriate reserve, "The causes of this distribution I do not know."[22] He does not, in this context, insist that each person receives the precise amount and type of suffering required for transformation. If Lewis had kept this point in mind, it might have spared him some of the existential anguish of concluding that his wife was taken to expose his insufficient faith.

Although it appears that these comments are in tension with his statements in *A Grief Observed*, a closer look might reveal an implicit harmony. Lewis may have believed that the purpose of particular tribulations, though indiscernible from the outside, might in some cases be clear from the inside, that is, to the person going through it. This appears to be the position Lewis advances in *The Horse and His Boy*, the book in which Aslan tears the back of the young princess, Aravis, for the purpose of teaching her a lesson. After the lion explains the reason for this chastening, Aravis asks if the servant she harmed will continue to suffer because of her misdeed. Aslan replies, "Child . . . I am telling you your story, not hers. No-one is told any story but their own."[23] In other words, the only one who can know whether there is a purpose behind a specific bout of suffering is the person who is going through it.

As we saw from our opening vignette in this chapter, the Schaeffers certainly thought that chastening could be safely discerned only from the inside (though they did not believe God directly sends affliction but simply allows it). This position certainly seems reasonable, for if God does chasten us on specific occasions for the purpose of correction, it seems likely that he also would make us aware of why we are being punished. Otherwise the corrective value of the experience is certainly open to dispute. Likewise, it is possible that Lewis rejected the suspect practice of judging the afflictions of others but held open the possibility of receiving enlightenment from the inside. If this is true, there does not appear to be any substantial tension between what Lewis writes in *A Grief Observed* and elsewhere on the problem of pain and suffering.[24]

However we interpret the relationship between Lewis's gut-wrenching encounter with grief and his earlier writings, it is unnecessary to attribute specific instances of suffering to the direct hand of God. To advance the soul-making model one simply needs to say that we live in a world where humans are truly free, in the libertarian sense, and where true contingency exists. Such a world is required for real loving relationships and significant acts of nobility. Given these variables, everyone is vulnerable to pain, suffering and evil. God does not necessarily send individual bouts of suffering but rather takes whatever comes our way and uses it redemptively to deepen our character and transform us into Christlike beings.

Lewis's belief that some, but not all, of our suffering is sent directly to us also poses the awkward practical dilemma of not knowing whether or not we are challenging the very messenger of God if we try to fight natural afflictions. How do we know that a particular malady is not the prescribed medicine for our ultimate healing? By resisting the tonic, we might be resisting our only cure.[25]

One could suggest that such a dilemma is averted if we receive inside knowledge, as we just considered. God reveals the purpose of the pain to the subjective sufferer, and this knowledge allows one to know whether or not God is behind the affliction. But this does not provide an adequate solution, for experience seems to show that such moments of subjective revelation are the exception, not the rule. God does not always tell people "their story." In fact, it appears that most people who encounter the tragedies of life are left without answers. They do not know if God is teaching them a particular lesson or if they have simply been caught in the spokes of life. The mystery remains, and that is one reason that coping with tragedy is so difficult. If God does not always tell us the reason behind our suffering, then we still seem to be left with the awkward dilemma of not knowing whether we are fighting God by resisting a particular ailment.

Schaeffer was certainly concerned about this epistemological dilemma. He believed the only way we can oppose evil without the fear of opposing God is to be certain that God is not the source of our sorrows, at least not directly.[26] The only way we can be sure of this is to insist on radical discontinuity between our current conditions and God's original creation. This can be achieved only by insisting on a literal, cataclysmic, space-time Fall as recorded in the opening chapters of Genesis. It was Schaeffer's contention that this formula alone can provide a basis for fighting suffering without the fear that we are fighting God.

Schaeffer is on to an important point, namely, that God is perfectly good and opposes all forms of evil. But it is unnecessary to insist on an Augustinian formula of radical discontinuity and a literal reading of Genesis to advance this insight. Contrary to Schaeffer's belief, the Irenaean teaching of essential continuity between God's original design and our current environment need not impugn God's character or undermine our objective moral categories. It is fully intelligible to suggest that a profoundly good God created a world where his creatures are vulnerable to pain, anguish and evil, because such a world is the best kind of environment to produce the great good of true loving relationships and significant beings. God does not want humans to abuse their freedom, nor does he directly will calamities upon his creatures, but unfortunately such evils are part and parcel of a world where unprogrammed choices are made and true contingency exists.

It is possible, then, to have a profoundly good God, objective moral categories and a base from which to challenge evil in our world, apart from an Augustinian theodicy and a literal reading of Genesis.

The Fate of the Unevangelized: Tough Love or Tough Luck?

We now turn our attention to the second major point of contrast, namely, the destiny of those who die without hearing the gospel. This issue, probably more than any other contemporary apologetic topic, crystallizes the fundamental theological differences between these two men.

Before we can hone in on the heart of this conflict, however, we must first identify three key points of agreement. First, both believed that God is perfectly holy and cannot tolerate sin of any kind. Second, both affirmed that all humans are sinners and fall short of God's perfect standard. Third, both insisted that Christ is the only solution to humanity's moral dilemma. Schaeffer and Lewis both believed an adequate response to the fate of the unevangelized must account for all three of these key orthodox commitments.

Yet despite these common core beliefs, these apologists diverged sharply on this issue. From the angle of restrictivism, Schaeffer suggested that it is entirely just for God to condemn the unevangelized because he does not judge them on the basis of what they do not know but rather on the basis of their own moral motions. Since general revelation has no salvific power, Christians have the enormous responsibility of spreading the gospel to all parts of the globe. While Lewis certainly believed in the importance of the Great Commission, he embraced the wider hope that a profoundly good God would somehow provide a legitimate opportunity for all humanity to respond to the gospel. The question we must ask, then, is which perspective best does justice to the character of God, the significance of humans and the uniqueness of Christ? We will start with Schaeffer's position.

Schaeffer has no problem accounting for the uniqueness of Christ, since he believes no one will be saved apart from an overt confession of faith in this life. But when we turn to the significance of humans and the character of God, Schaeffer's case appears to falter. Let us reconsider the heart of his argument. Schaeffer tells us that God is fully just because "the man without the Bible" will not be judged on the basis of Scripture but rather on the basis of his own moral motions, specifically, the standards to which he has held others. He claims that this position honors God's character because all will be judged according to the degree of revelation they have received. In addition, human significance is secured, for every action is taken seriously and no sin will go unpunished.

Yet Schaeffer's insistence on God judging the unevangelized on the basis of what they know simply misses the mark. Any meaningful notion of judgment presupposes not only the knowledge of what is expected but also the capability of meeting those expectations. Imagine a father taking his toddler out to a basketball goal and commanding him to slam-dunk the ball on a ten-foot rim. This particular father is a perfectionist who demands one hundred percent success, so even one failed attempt will elicit wrath. The child knows what is expected, but does this mean he possesses the requisite ability to accomplish the assigned task? No matter what effort the boy puts forth, he is bound to fail. The toddler trips, tumbles and falls woefully short time and again, only to find his father berating him for not performing this impossible feat.

The same is true with Schaeffer's account of the unevangelized. "The man without the Bible" receives general revelation in the form of his own moral motions. He lives as if some things are right and others are wrong but does not live consistently with what he knows to be correct. But if the doctrine of total depravity is true, and Schaeffer clearly believed it to be, then the man without the Bible cannot possibly live up to the standard of his own moral motions. And if he is incapable of living up to this standard, then how can this standard possibly serve as a just gauge for judgment?

But this is not the only problem for Schaeffer. He has also painted a picture of a God who has provided a solution to this moral dilemma but has not made this solution universally accessible. Let us return to our vignette. After being banished for failing to meet his father's unreasonable expectations, the boy learns later that his father had another son, a secret offspring who is capable of dunking like Michael Jordan every time he touches the ball. The child is told that his father would have lifted his wrath if only the toddler had allowed this other secret son to do the dunking for him. But he was unaware of this solution. To make matters worse, the boy then discovers that his father had let some of his siblings in on the secret from which he had been excluded. All the children were equally incapable of dunking the ball, but some were told the secret solution and others were not. The boy is confounded, first by the impossible expectations of his father and second by the disproportionate distribution of the secret solution.

The fundamental problems with Schaeffer's proposal should now be apparent. Would a good and just father really judge his child by a standard that is clearly beyond the child's capability? Would a good and just father really allow the knowledge of this solution to be distributed disproportion-ately? If this father treats some of his children this way, then the integrity of this parent and worth of these children are certainly open to question. In short, Schaeffer's position appears to undermine the character of God and the value of unevangelized persons.

We now turn our attention to Lewis. While Schaeffer could satisfactorily account for only one core belief, the uniqueness of Christ, we find Lewis offering an angle of vision that does justice to all three. His assertion that all humans, the evangelized and unevangelized alike, will receive a legitimate opportunity to receive the gospel honors the justice and goodness of God. God is not like the father who holds his children to a standard without providing the necessary resources. Of course, his children can choose whether or not to access those resources, but they are available to all. Consequently, the value and significance of all humanity is preserved because the "Father of lights" wants everyone to embrace the universal solution of Jesus Christ, though not every believer will do so consciously in this life.[28]

What we find with Lewis's position, then, is a balanced alternative to both narrow restrictivism, which impugns the character of God and undermines the significance of the unfortunate unevangelized, and open-ended univer-salism, which dilutes the uniqueness of Christ by insisting upon the equal validity of all truth claims. With characteristic concision, Lewis articulates an attractive via media near the conclusion of his essay "Christian Apologet-ics":

> Of course it should be pointed out that, though all salvation is through Jesus, we need not conclude that He cannot save those who have not explicitly accepted Him in this life. And it should (at least in my judge-ment) be made clear that we are not pronouncing all other religions to be totally false, but rather saying that in Christ whatever is true in all religions is consummated and perfected. But, on the other hand, I think we must attack wherever we meet it the nonsensical idea that mutually exclusive propositions about God can both be true.[29]

How could two men who were equally committed to the core orthodox beliefs of God's holiness, humanity's significance and the uniqueness of Christ, offer such divergent responses on this pressing issue? The answer to this question will not only shed light on why these men approached the fate of the unevangelized in distinctly different ways, but it will also explain some of the key theological rifts we have unearthed in earlier chapters.

Many of these rifts, including the nature of the atonement, the issue of divine election, the scope and purpose of revelation and the fate of the unevangelized, are merely symptomatic of a much deeper divide. Simply put, the foundational distinction between these two apologists is rooted in contrasting visions of God. Schaeffer viewed God fundamentally as a judge and naturally interpreted many of these issues with legal categories and imagery, while Lewis saw God primarily as a father and consequently viewed reality predominantly through a relational grid.

Let us recall their contrasting views of the atonement. While Schaeffer frequently spoke about the relational and present aspects of salvation, the logical priority in his soteriological scheme was the legal act of justification: if we have not been pardoned through a conscious decision to accept Christ as Savior, then we are still under the wrath of "the Great Judge."[30] It is simply impossible to enter into a relationship with the heavenly Father until the legal issue is settled and the Judge is appeased. Lewis, on the other hand, rejected a forensic model of the atonement, emphasizing instead a model of enablement. This paradigm highlights the need for true repentance, imparted righteousness and thorough cooperative transformation. Lewis did not see God primarily as a Judge focused on punishment but as a Father focused on rehabilitation. For Schaeffer, salvation was first and foremost a matter of procuring forensic forgiveness from the Divine Magistrate, but for Lewis salvation was essentially a matter of being rightly related to our heavenly Father.

These guiding legal and relational grids are equally apparent when we consider the issue of divine election. Schaeffer believed God unconditionally elects some for salvation and others for eternal damnation. All humanity is under the judgment of God's gavel, but some are fortunate enough to receive mercy, while others receive their just deserts for breaking God's holy law, even though they could not have done otherwise. This doctrine of unconditional election is necessarily advanced with legal categories, for it is difficult, at best, to imagine a loving father operating in this fashion.[31] This is precisely why Lewis rejected this doctrine. He believed God is a profoundly good and fair Father who is doing everything within his power to save all his creatures, and the notion of a loving Father passing over some of his children, whom he could just as easily saved, is inconceivable.

One's soteriological grid is organically connected to the subject of revelation as well, for if one believes salvation is limited to the unconditionally elect, then it is fully consistent to expect God's revelation to be limited too. This is precisely what we find with Schaeffer, who believed general revelation does not provide enough light to save but does provide enough to condemn.

Schaeffer appeared to have at least two considerations in mind when discussing general revelation. First, he believed special revelation alone can save. As we saw from his critique of Aquinas, Schaeffer staunchly rejected the belief that natural theology was capable of leading people to saving faith. Second, since some people will never have access to special revelation, general revelation must be clear enough to hold everyone accountable to God's righteous law. In short, the trick is to make general revelation sufficiently opaque to safeguard the salvific necessity of special revelation but sufficiently transparent to declare the unevangelized guilty. The following two examples show how Schaeffer tried to pull this off.

First, in *The God Who Is There* Schaeffer tells us that revelation is like a torn monograph. General revelation, the universe and its form and the mannishness of man, is like a mutilated book with "just one inch of printed matter on each page." This is enough revelation to know that the indiscernible print on the pages did not come about by chance, but it would "be impossible to piece together and understand the book's story."[32] Obviously the only way to understand the story is to find the missing fragments and reattach them to the proper pages in the mutilated book. Of course, the missing fragments represent the Bible. Not only does this vignette underscore the importance of how these different forms of divine disclosure cohere, but it also reveals the extremely limited role to which Schaeffer consigns general revelation. In other words, general revelation is sufficiently murky to secure the salvific necessity of special revelation.

Yet when Schaeffer turns his attention to the fate of the unevangelized in *Death in the City*, the clarity of general revelation crystallizes significantly. Instead of one-inch scraps of incomplete type, we are told that the "man without the Bible" has received enough general revelation to be held accountable. In fact, the inability of the unevangelized person to make sense of this generous general revelation is a "powerful testimony" to the inadequacy of his worldview. The implication is that if the "man without the Bible" would just follow this revelation to its logical conclusion, he would arrive at the truth. Of course Schaeffer tells us that the unevangelized person will not do this, because he is an autonomous sinner who suppresses the truth in unrighteousness. In other words, general revelation is sufficiently transparent to declare the unevangelized guilty.

So when Schaeffer discusses the importance of Scripture, general revelation is reduced to one-inch, unintelligible scraps of printed matter, but when he discusses the accountability of the unevangelized, general revelation suddenly becomes sufficiently clear to consign people to eternal hell. But how could one-inch, unintelligible scraps possibly be a just standard of judgment? Even if the unevangelized are only held accountable to these scraps, what type of meaningful revelation can be discerned from such confusion? Schaeffer would surely respond by saying that these fragments are sufficiently clear to tell us that life did not come about by chance, that there is an author behind our world. Surely this is true, but how does this help the person who is left without the bulk of the book? Even if the unevangelized person acknowledges an author, this person is still left with the impossible task of discerning some type of coherent, propositional message from the available mutilated text. Even if some semblance of order could be discerned, would it be possible for the unevangelized person to respond in perfect obedience to this limited revelation and achieve salvation? And if it is not possible to live up to the revealed standard, then how can that standard be a just gauge?

We have placed these two examples side by side to highlight the tension in Schaeffer's thinking. Schaeffer probably never intended these vignettes to show up next to one another, for his position can maintain some measure of plausibility only if the unevangelized have been given a reasonable amount of revelation. But one-inch scraps of indiscernible type are hardly reasonable. It appears then that Schaeffer is subtly shifting between two distinctly different views of general revelation.

We might compare him to a photographer who allows the context of the situation to dictate what kind of filter he will affix to his camera lens. When focusing on the salvific necessity of Scripture, he attaches a filter that makes general revelation substantially opaque. But when he fills the viewfinder with the fate of the unevangelized, Schaeffer replaces this opaque filter with one that is significantly more transparent. Suddenly general revelation is considerably enhanced, so much so that the unevangelized person has enough clarity to be condemned. The one constant in both cases, however, is that general revelation is never sufficient by itself to offer the hope of salvation. It is limited in scope and function. Consequently, those who are never exposed to special revelation are necessarily among the nonelect.

Again, what fallen earthly father, let alone a perfect heavenly Father, would provide some of his children enough light to be condemned but not enough to be saved? It is even difficult to imagine a fallen earthly judge doing such a thing. In contrast to Schaeffer's disjunctive view of revelation, Lewis insisted on essential continuity between all forms of divine disclosure. Since our heavenly Father is both Creator and Redeemer of the entire world, it stands to reason that he would provide sufficient revelation not only to hold all humanity accountable but to provide a legitimate opportunity for everyone to be saved.

This is precisely where Lewis's views of the Moral Law and myth become integral. God has embedded the Moral Law (what Lewis calls the Tao in *The Abolition of Man*) into the universe and also has sprinkled "good dreams" or mythical patterns of the truth throughout his creation. Consequently, everyone is given some measure of illumination, and whoever cooperates with God's grace and follows this luminosity to its source will find the eternal Logos of Jesus Christ and the "Father of lights."[33]

The issues just discussed—the atonement, unconditional election and the nature of revelation—have a direct bearing on the fate of the unevangelized. The cumulative force of Schaeffer's forensic perspective leaves those who die without hearing the gospel in the merciless hands of the Great Judge who has ordered the world in such a way that these unfortunate persons are not privy to God's salvific solution.[34] In short, two words describe the plight of the unevangelized: *tough luck.* You were born in the wrong place. You were born at the wrong time. You were passed over. You did not get a chance, but you get what you deserve—even though you could not have done otherwise.[35]

Lewis, by contrast, did not think God is a Judge who demands some external epistemic expression from someone who could not possibly offer such a formulation; instead God is a loving Father who sees the heart and judges according to intent. He is like a parent who recognizes the difference between a child who accidentally spills her milk and a child who deliberately smashes her glass. A loving father does not ignore the mess, but he takes the intent into account. A judge, on the other hand, simply declares that spilled milk is spilled milk, and demands a reckoning, whatever the intent. This is the sharpest distinction between a legal and a relational view of God. The legal paradigm focuses on the external expression of faith for one to be saved, while the relational paradigm insists that a profoundly good and fair Father will examine the heart, factor in infirmities and disadvantages, and ultimately gauge each person against the precise amount of light and resources that has been provided. Of course, given Lewis's soteriology, there will need to be a comprehensive cooperative plan of transformation before one is fit for heaven, whether one has heard the gospel in this life or not.[36] Our Father is good, but he is not soft. Still, tough love is better than tough luck any day.

We conclude this section by anticipating one possible objection. Some might insist that we have distorted the positions of our apologists. After all, did not Schaeffer consistently discuss issues like human significance, sanctification and libertarian freedom, topics that are best understood through a relational lens? And did not Lewis say that Christianity does not begin to speak until we realize we are guilty before a Lawgiver? Did not both men use a vast array of verbal pictures for God in their respective writings? Would it not then be a distortion to attempt to cleanly organize all the theological and apologetic perspectives of these men under two neat headings?

There is no question that both men recognized the rich diversity of divine imagery embedded in Scripture, and that ignoring any of this imagery can lead to a truncated vision of God. Nevertheless, it is our contention that each apologist filtered all of reality through a fundamental grid. Schaeffer possessed a Reformed paradigm, which emphasizes the judicial and regal qualities of God, while Lewis operated within an Anglican/Arminian framework, which highlights the relational and ethical qualities of God. It is important to realize that both traditions view God as a Father, Judge and King; the difference comes in terms of emphasis. Yet as we have seen, contrasting points of emphasis can lead to radically divergent visions of God.

What we find particularly with Schaeffer is a man who, despite confident claims to a unified field of knowledge, lived with a significant degree of theological tension. His training equipped him with Reformed categories, but his writings consistently revealed strong Arminian intuitions.[37] He wrote frequently about the power of contrary choice, human significance and sanctification but could never cleanly reconcile his views on these issues with his Reformed understanding of providence. He claimed to hold first-cause human freedom and total, unconditional predestination in perfect balance, but when push came to shove his Reformed convictions prevailed. This is evidenced by the clear organic connection between his views on soteriology, divine election, scope of revelation and the fate of the unevangelized. In each case, God is seen fundamentally as "the Great Judge."

It simply is not enough to look at the proportion of Schaeffer's writings to determine the guiding grid he used. If sheer proportion could settle the issue, Schaeffer's consistent emphasis on first-cause freedom and sanctification, coupled with his conspicuous silence on predestination, could easily lead the less informed reader to declare Schaeffer an Arminian who occasionally flirted with Calvinism.[38] What is ultimately necessary to identify Schaeffer's guiding grid is to see how his views on key theological and apologetic issues cohere. When this is done we see that what binds them together is a forensic adhesive.

Tough Luck or Tough Love? Contrasting Angles of Vision

	Schaeffer	Lewis
1. *Fundamental role of God*	Judge	Father
2. *Guiding grid*	Legal	Relational
3. *Soteriological emphases*	Punishment	Rehabilitation
	Justification	Moral transformation
	Pardon	Enablement
	Imputed righteousness	Imparted righteousness
	External epistemic expression	Internal heart purity
4. *God's salvific intent*	Unconditional election	Universal accessibility
5. *Relationship between natural and special revelation*	Natural revelation provides enough light to condemn but not enough to save. Special revelation is God's only salvific form of disclosure.	Essential continuity between all forms of revelation. The Tao provides a universal standard to which all are accountable, and myth reveals universal patterns of truth which anticipate and point to the fullest revelation in Christ.
6. *Fate of the unevangelized*	Different from those who have heard—tough luck	Same as those who have heard—tough love

Mannishness of Man Arguments: Back to Freedom and Dignity

In the first half of this chapter we have considered some key areas of contrast between Schaeffer and Lewis. We now turn our attention to the first significant point of apologetic contact, namely, the employment of "mannishness of man" arguments. If you recall, Schaeffer divided common ground with nonbelievers into two areas: the external world, or the universe and its form, and the internal world, or the mannishness of man.[39] Though Lewis and Schaeffer were committed to holistic apologetics, both clearly concentrated on this latter realm in their books. In the next few pages we will identify the reason for this emphasis and see how these apologists shared a common concern, challenged a common foe, employed a common strategy and accessed a common resource in an effort to advance many of these internally focused arguments.

The Complete Works of Francis A. Schaeffer comprises twenty-one titles and more than two thousand pages. Within this five-volume set, Schaeffer cites C. S. Lewis a total of eight times in four books: *No Final Conflict, Back to Freedom and Dignity, How Should We Then Live?* and *Whatever Happened to the Human Race?* Interestingly, every reference but one relates to a portion of Lewis's space trilogy.

In *No Final Conflict* Schaeffer considers a thesis Lewis advances in *Out of the Silent Planet* and *Perelandra*. In these books Lewis suggests that the earth was fractured by the fall of Satan, so there was a degree of abnormality already on the scene by the time the first humans arrived. As noted in chapter five, Schaeffer considered this theory scripturally suspect. When we turn to *How Should We Then Live?* and *Back to Freedom and Dignity*, however, we find Schaeffer citing Lewis with deep appreciation. In both books he references the epic conclusion to Lewis's space trilogy, *That Hideous Strength*. In *How Should We Then Live?* Schaeffer includes this science-fiction thriller in a chronological index that traces key events, persons and literature that have helped shape and interpret Western culture. In *Back to Freedom and Dignity* Schaeffer encourages believers "to read carefully this prophetic piece of science fiction. What Lewis casts as a warning in the form of fantasy and science fiction is much closer today."[40]

It is hardly surprising to find Schaeffer resonating with this work, for it is a gripping preview of where a world without objective morality is heading. *That Hideous Strength*, the imaginative counterpart to *The Abolition of Man*, paints a picture of naturalistic conditioners who are set on controlling the fate of the human race. Lewis envisions a world where genetic engineering and psychological and chemical manipulation will dominate society in an attempt to eradicate all that is uniquely human. The absence of absolute, objective boundaries will allow a select few to condition humanity according to their personal preferences. In one telling scene, a member of this inner ring explains the group's raison dêtre:

> Man has got to take charge of Man. That means, remember, that some men have got to take charge of the rest . . . sterilization of the unfit, liquidation of backward races (we don't want any dead weights), selective breading. . . . We'll get on to biochemical conditioning in the end and direct manipulation of the brain.[41]

Lewis believed naturalistic determinism, if allowed to chart its own deadly course, would eventually lead to the abolition of humanity. Schaeffer pursued this very same theme in *Back to Freedom and Dignity*, which, as the wordplay in the title suggests, is a rebuttal to B. F. Skinner's classic work *Beyond Freedom and Dignity*. In this book Schaeffer sounds a clarion call that bears a striking resemblance to the words of Lewis:

> We are on the verge of the largest revolution the world has ever seen—the control and shaping of men through the abuse of genetic knowledge, and chemical and psychological conditioning. Will people accept it? I don't

think they would accept it if (1) they had not already been taught to accept the presuppositions that lead to it, and (2) they were not in such hopelessness.[42]

Clearly, both men shared a passionate concern—the safeguarding of human freedom and dignity. This joint concern is the chief point of resonance between them. Both recognized the increasing dehumanization of the twentieth century and the susceptibility of society to manipulating influences. As can be seen from the above citation, Schaeffer thought people would reject manipulation and conditioning if it were not for their inculcated presuppositions and utter lack of hope. But what type of presuppositional base has produced this state of dismal despair? Quite simply, presuppositions grounded in an impersonal worldview.

In a chapter entitled "The Basis for Human Dignity" from *Whatever Happened to the Human Race?* Schaeffer makes it clear that he and Lewis were battling the same common foes: "C. S. Lewis pointed out that there are only two alternatives to the Christian answer—the humanist philosophy of the West and the pantheist philosophy of the East. We would agree."[43] Although these two worldviews might seem very different on the surface, Schaeffer goes on to identify the fundamental similarity between them, namely, the belief that ultimate reality is impersonal. In the West, everything is ultimately reduced to matter; in the East, everything is ultimately reduced to spirit. In both cases, everything is ultimately reduced to the impersonal plus time plus chance. If the impersonal is the backdrop for all reality and humans are products of chance, then in the grand scheme of things personality appears to be a puzzling anomaly that is finally meaningless and unfulfillable. The words of Bertrand Russell that we considered in chapter seven are a chilling reminder that if the world is ultimately reduced to impersonal matter or energy, then all human hopes, loves, beliefs, heroism, devotion, inspiration and genius someday will "be buried beneath the debris of a universe in ruins."[44] This is the inevitable implication of naturalism—hopeless despair.

This common concern for human significance in the face of these common impersonal foes seems to explain why Lewis and Schaeffer did little by way of traditional historical apologetic arguments and natural theology. Instead of focusing on the integrity of the New Testament documents and detailed cosmological and teleological arguments, both men set their sights on the prime area of weakness for these impersonal worldviews, namely, the realm of personality.[45] The genius to this common strategy is its economy. An apologetic focused on human personality offers two features for the price of one, for impersonal presuppositions just happen to be most vulnerable precisely where Christian resources can most readily instill hope. In other words, a "mannishness of man" apologetic undermines the presuppositions of the dominant impersonal worldviews, while simultaneously providing a rational basis for human hope, the two things Schaeffer thought most necessary to combat "the largest revolution the world has ever seen"—the naturalistic conditioning of the human race.

In the third chapter of *Miracles*, entitled "The Cardinal Problem of Naturalism," we find Lewis targeting his opponent's Achilles' heel. He tells us that "if Naturalism is true, every finite thing or event must be (in principle) explicable in terms of the Total System." If something exists that cannot be explained in naturalistic terms, "then Naturalism would be in ruins."[46] Of course, Lewis believed rationality is one such phenomenon that does the trick. But rationality is not the only soft spot. An impersonal worldview is hard-pressed to account for any facet of personality. In addition to reason, human freedom, moral motions, aesthetic sensitivities, aspirations and love are all puzzling phenomena in a universe that is ultimately impersonal. Since few naturalists and pantheists are willing to deny the existence of these important human qualities, at least when it comes to their daily lives, this was the logical apologetic entry point for both Lewis and Schaeffer. In fact, seven of the offensive arguments considered in chapter seven are concentrated in this realm, and as we have already seen, both men also employed the free-will defense to engage the problem of evil.

So instead of external teleological arguments, we find Lewis and Schaeffer focusing their energy on assembling a cluster of internal teleological arguments designed not only to combat the impersonal systems of naturalism and pantheism but also to provide a plausible and hopeful alternative to these despairing worldviews. God has designed humanity for a purpose and each facet of personality has a proper function and corresponding satisfaction. Since Christianity can account for every facet of personality, it offers a plausible explanation for the confounding existential question of why humans are a mixed bag of virtue and evil. The majority of the offensive arguments marshaled by these men (e.g., morality, rationality, desire, agape) are geared to explain the positive side of humanity, how people are capable of rising to great heights of grandeur and nobility. The primary defensive argument, the free-will defense, explains the negative side of humanity, how people can descend to the dismal depths of perversion and depravity. So we see that these offensive and defensive arguments work together to offer a satisfying, well-rounded explanation for the total human experience.

A final point is important. Throughout this book, we have consistently emphasized the relationship between theology and apologetics. Apologetic arguments are not neutral resources that can be employed equally by all theological traditions. One's apologetic must naturally cohere with and emerge from one's worldview. Consequently, arguments in favor of human personality will be most convincing if they flow from a theology that is fundamentally relational and personal. This will necessarily include a view of human freedom that provides for rational insight, moral judgment and true relational response. In short, many of these arguments focused on personality are advanced with libertarian fuel.

As we have seen, the power of contrary choice is essential to secure the claim that humans are valuable and responsible beings. Any form of determinism, whether it is naturalistic, behavioristic or theistic, undermines human significance. Both apologists emphasized this essential point. Schaeffer repeatedly insisted that the entire Christian system hinges on a nondetermined humanity. In his view, total determinism reduces people to machines. This is the great plight for twentieth-century humanity: all facets of personality have been flattened by the steamroller of "modern modern" science.

Lewis, likewise, recognized the ravaging effects of naturalistic determinism. In the argument from rationality, he makes it clear that the proper Christian position declares that human reason "is set free, in the measure required, from the huge nexus of non-rational causation; free from this to be determined by the truth known."[47] In other words, true rational insight requires some degree of indeterminacy.

In *The Abolition of Man* we find Lewis scoring a similar point. He tell us that the naturalistic manipulators, who are so intent on demolishing the constraints of absolute truth and objective morality, promise a vision of unfettered freedom and utopian control but deliver universal bondage and dehumanization.

> At the moment, then, of Man's victory over Nature, we find the whole human race subjected to some individual men, and those individuals subjected to that in themselves which is purely 'natural'—to their irrational impulses. Nature, untrammelled by values, rules the Conditioners and, through them, all humanity. Man's conquest of Nature turns out, in the moment of its consummation, to be Nature's conquest of Man.[48]

In other words, the essence of man's abolition is ultimately the loss of true human freedom.

In the end, libertarian freedom is also essential for deep, meaningful relational response. In *Mere Christianity* Lewis points out that profound Christian love is not some sort of involuntary wave of emotion but rather "an affair of the will."[49] The deepest kind of love is a matter of choice. Consider the following thought experiment. Suppose you are single and you have met the person of your dreams. Unfortunately, this person will have nothing to do with you. However, suppose a romance pill had been invented that would make any person to whom you give it fall in love with you. If you could somehow slip this "cupid capsule" into this person's drink, this person would love you devotedly forever. With the pill, you will be loved; without it, you will continue to be ignored. Would you want the cupid capsule?

Though some might stoop to such desperate manipulative measures, we know in our heart of hearts that such a "relationship" would not be truly meaningful and satisfying. It would be a hollow, artificial experience. What this shows is that genuine libertarian freedom, the power of contrary choice, is essential for real love, real trust, real commitment and real relationships. In short, a profoundly meaningful relationship requires the ability to walk away.

Superficiality and Triumphalism: The Supreme Snares of Popular Apologetics

As indicated earlier in this study, not all readers have embraced Lewis and Schaeffer with outstretched arms. In fact, these men tend to evoke extreme responses. In some circles cult-like followings have emerged, while in other settings these men are ridiculed and dismissed as sophomoric and superficial. Of course, this latter group is largely composed of scholars who have aired their opinions, in varying degrees of disapprobation, through a host of journal articles and a handful of monographs. Lewis has been challenged most notably by the somewhat caustic pen of John Beversluis in *C. S. Lewis and the Search for Rational Religion*, while Schaeffer has received his most serious critiques from Thomas Morris in *Francis Schaeffer's Apologetics* and from a cross-section of scholars in *Reflections on Francis Schaeffer*.[50] Although it would take us far afield to rehash the detail of these critiques, our study would be less than complete if we did not highlight two charges that have been consistently leveled against these apologists: superficiality and triumphalism.

Both men covered vast amounts of apologetic territory in rapid fashion. Consider Schaeffer's sweeping flow of history. In *Escape from Reason* he traces the development of Western culture from Thomas Aquinas until the 1960s in approximately seventy pages. Much of this same material is repeated in other books, such as *The God Who Is There, He Is There and He Is Not Silent* and *How Should We Then Live?*

Lewis, likewise, was known to move the reader through immensely complex material at a breakneck pace. The philosophical and theological ground covered in the first sixty pages of *Mere Christianity* is astounding. Beversluis points out that Lewis deals with only the most simplistic alternative accounts for morality, ignoring a whole range of subjectivist and objectivist ethical theories en route to the controversial Trilemma.[51]

These brief examples are sufficient to substantiate the charge that each man, at least on occasion, offered sketchy treatments of highly complex subject matter. Although this is surely true, there are three points we ought to keep in mind when considering the charge of superficiality. First, we must remember that neither man claimed to be a professional philosopher, despite being occasionally billed by their publishers as such. Schaeffer consistently made it clear that his area of interest was not academic apologetics or philosophy but frontline evangelism. It should also be noted that Lewis, though teaching philosophy for a brief stint early in his career, was frequently careful to qualify the scope of his philosophical and theological prowess. In fact, Basil Mitchell points out that one should not regard Lewis as a philosopher in the first place but rather as a "lively independent thinker." If Mitchell had been asked to produce a list of the philosophers at Oxford, "Lewis wouldn't have been mentioned among them."[52] So the first thing we should realize is that when we come to Lewis and Schaeffer we should not come expecting the philosophical rigor of a Plantinga or Swinburne. Those who come with such expectations are sure to be disappointed.

The second thing we should keep in mind is that these men were not writing specifically to a scholarly crowd but were making a broad appeal to the masses. Both apologists were in the business of communicating what Dick Keyes has termed "intermediate knowledge."[53] They rejected the notion that weighty metaphysical matters are the exclusive property of trained philosophers, and they recognized a dire need to translate this lofty material into language and imagery that would be more readily accessible to the common person.

In light of such a purpose, these men should not be discredited for failing to spell out every detail of an argument if the argument satisfactorily persuades the intended audience. In fact, if some of these arguments were wound any tighter they might become too tedious and stringent for many to follow. The obvious result would be counterproductive in view of the apologetic and evangelistic focus of these men. J. I. Packer makes this same point in a vivid way:

> [Schaeffer's] communicative style was not that of the cautious academic who labors for a complete coverage that never exaggerates or gets proportions wrong. It was rather that of the crusading "cartoonist" whose simple sketches leave behind photographic rectitude and embrace a measure of the grotesque in order to ram home a judgment. Academics censured Schaeffer for communicating this way, but his informal cartoonist's style was apt enough for what he was trying to do.[54]

The third consideration we should mention is that even if these men were nonprofessional philosophers engaging a general audience, that does not mean their arguments are necessarily unsound. They simply may be under-developed or in need of finetuning. In a critique of Beversluis's book, Thomas Morris suggests "that there are very interesting considerations to be mar-shaled in the direction Lewis was heading."[55] Morris offers the same sort of appreciative point in his evaluation of Schaeffer's apologetics. In other words, sketchy arguments can be fortified by those inclined to take on such a task. In fact, in an appendix to *The Complete Works* version of *The God Who Is There*, we find Schaeffer perfectly willing to let the "more academically oriented philosopher . . . deal with more of the necessary details."[56]

Interestingly, Oxford philosopher John Lucas did precisely what Schaeffer is suggesting. During the sixties, Lucas proposed the idea of reenacting the famous Lewis-Anscombe debate of 1948. Only this time, Lucas would stand in for Lewis and attempt to advance his line of reasoning. Anscombe agreed to the reenactment. Following the debate, there was wide agreement that Lucas had successfully defended Lewis's position. In fact, Basil Mitchell suggests that "if one were to think in terms of winners or losers, I think maybe that Lucas was the winner on points."[57]

This is not the only example of a trained philosopher fortifying a Lewisian argument. Consider also Peter Kreeft's creative attempt to illuminate and strengthen the Trilemma. In *Between Heaven and Hell* Kreeft suggests that all humanity can be divided into two categories: those who claim to be God and those who do not. He then suggests that everyone can be divided into two further categories: those who are sagacious and those who are not. By sagacious, Kreeft means a person universally recognized as a great moral teacher. Consequently, we all fit into one of the following four classifications: (1) nonsagacious, do not claim to be God—most of humanity, (2) nonsa-gacious, profess to be God—lunatics and liars, (3) sagacious, do not claim to be God—Moses, Plato, Aristotle, Buddha, Muhammad, etc., (4) sagacious, professes to be God—Jesus of Nazareth.

In this fascinating reformulation, Kreeft illustrates precisely what Lewis was getting at. There are people who have claimed to be God, but they clearly do not deserve the venerable title of a sage. There are also those who are sagacious, but they never claimed to be God. But there is only one person in the history of the world who both claimed to be God and is universally considered profoundly sagacious, namely, Jesus of Nazareth.[58] It is also worth noting that in an important book on New Testament scholarship, philosopher C. Stephen Evans has offered the Trilemma a vote of confidence, suggesting that this argument remains a viable apologetic option provided the necessary care is taken to exhibit the reliability of the gospel accounts.[59]

Of equal signficance, philosophers Victor Reppert and Basil Mitchell have identified strong similarities between some of Lewis's central arguments and those advanced by two of the leading Christian intellectuals of our time. Reppert identifies congruence between Lewis's work in *Miracles* and Alvin Plantinga's rigorous challenge to naturalism,[60] while Mitchell draws a parallel between *The Abolition of Man* and the widely influential writing of ethicist Alasdair MacIntyre. Mitchell sums it up well by saying, "Lewis had a sort of intuitive vision of the kind of arguments that in a more philosophically sophisticated way MacIntyre marshals in [his] books."[61]

In light of these three considerations—the nonprofessional philosophical status of Lewis and Schaeffer, their intended popular audience and the underdeveloped yet promising direction of many of their arguments—the charge of superficiality might not have as much force as initially suspected.

But Lewis and Schaeffer are not out of the woods yet. For at this point the critic might say that it is not brevity and oversimplification that is the most bothersome feature of these apologetic arguments but rather the fact that these men led their uninformed readers to believe that they were more comprehensive and conclusive than they really were. In other words, the primary problem with these men is their triumphalistic tone.

Take Schaeffer's consistent claim that the Christian is not left with merely probable answers. In his apologetic trilogy he repeatedly makes statements like "It is not that [Christianity] is the best answer to existence; it is the only answer."[62] And when discussing the value of formal philosophy, Schaeffer expresses the belief that "if the total course does not give answers so that the students are left with more than probability in regard to Christianity, it is much less than a course in philosophy can and should be."[63]

These are confident claims from a man who in his most focused philosophical treatment covers the highly complex subjects of metaphysics, morality and epistemology in a total of seventy pages. Moreover, throughout his corpus Schaeffer focuses almost exclusively on the impersonal systems of naturalism and pantheism but rarely engages other theistic worldviews like Islam and Judaism. The point here is that not even the most rigorous Christian philosophy, let alone the loosely constructed arguments Schaeffer marshals, is capable of producing the type of intellectual certitude that is being suggested. It appears that Schaeffer would have benefited from distinguishing between complete intellectual certitude of the Cartesian variety and the more modest claim of psychological certitude to which believers are entitled when the preponderance of evidence points in the direction of Christian truth claims.

Lewis, likewise, has been accused of using a tone that far exceeds the philosophical merit of his arguments. This is nowhere more evident than in the early pages of *Mere Christianity,* where Lewis rather tersely dismisses the major alternatives to the Christian faith and tops his argument off with the rhetorically charged Trilemma. In his pointed critique, John Beversluis makes it clear that his "complaint about the Broadcast Talks is not that Lewis fails to be as thorough as his subject matter demands, but that he gives the impression of being thorough."[64] Beversluis repeatedly accuses Lewis of setting up straw men, posing the false dilemma and leaving his audience with the perception that the essential issues have been settled and the primary foes waylaid.

This point certainly has some force. It does appear that Lewis is guilty of this charge on occasion, particularly in *Mere Christianity.* Nevertheless, it is hardly fair to label him consistently triumphalistic in tone, for as we have already noted, Lewis frequently qualified the scope of his theological and philosophical expertise and often submitted his reasoning to those who were more learned in a given area. In fact, although both our apologists succumbed to triumphalism at times, it appears that on the whole Lewis tended to be more guarded, judicious and cautious in his claims than did Schaeffer.

A brief comparison of *Escape from Reason* and Lewis's inaugural address "De Descriptione Temporum" might illuminate this assertion. Colin Duriez points to "some striking parallels" between these two essays, including the joint belief that "the greatest challenge in the history of the West took place around the beginning of the nineteenth century and ushered in a characteristically modern mentality."[65] Without question, there are some notable similarities. It is fascinating to see how both apologists trace the development of Western culture across a variety of disciplines and cite many of the same factors that have led to the epistemological and moral upheaval of the twentieth century.

But despite significant congruence, there is a decidedly different tone in these works. While Schaeffer's bold ideational critique of Western history has been labeled "pretentious" by Clark Pinnock[66] and likened to "outright myth-making" by Richard Pierard,[67] Lewis's modest overview is characterized by careful qualification and admirable reserve. He recognizes that the "dating of such things must of course be rather hazy and indefinite."[68] Thus he does not claim to nail down the epistemological shift with precision but merely states that the gulf runs "somewhere between us and the Waverly Novels, somewhere between us and *Persuasion.*"[69] Moreover, at the beginning of his lecture he offers his work "to continual attack and speedy revision"[70] and says his modest project is "less like a botanist in a forest than a woman arranging a few cut flowers for the drawing-room."[71] In other words, we see

Lewis, a first-rate student of history, exhibiting a healthy respect for the enormously difficult and highly controversial task of historical reconstruction. In so doing Lewis successfully avoided, at least in this instance, the prime pitfall of triumphalism.

Constructing a Majestic Manor: The Value of Cumulative Case Arguments

We may conclude that both Lewis and Schaeffer were, in varying degrees, susceptible to triumphalism, or what Stephen Davis has called "hard apologetics."[72] According to Davis, a "hard apologetic argument" is one that seeks to demonstrate the irrationality of rejecting Christian truth claims, while a "soft apologetic argument" seeks to demonstrate the rationality of embracing Christian truth claims without insisting that all other worldviews are irrational positions to hold. The tendency of both our apologists to gravitate toward "hard apologetics" should be obvious. Schaeffer passionately insisted that Christianity offers "the only answer" to all the major philosophical questions, while Lewis certainly thought his argument from rationality had successfully exposed the irrational position of the naturalist, leaving this worldview "in ruins."[73]

Hard apologetic claims like these are highly suspect. Even the most tightly constructed and carefully refined versions of these arguments are open to dispute. There are simply too many questionable premises and alternative possibilities to nail down these issues with absolute certainty. But if this is true, does this mean the only option available to the Christian is soft apologetics? Must this enterprise be reduced to simply exhibiting the rationality of Christian claims without challenging the intellectual basis of other worldviews? We do not think so. While the hard apologist tends to overestimate the power of these arguments, the soft apologist is inclined to underestimate the force of Christian truth claims. In short, we believe there is a third alternative that strikes a proper balance. We shall call it *firm apologetics*. The proponent of firm apologetics does not present the Christian position as the only answer but rather as the most probable or most rational response given all relevant evidence and considerations. Such a view avoids the polarized pitfalls of claiming too much for these arguments on the one hand and too little on the other. In this section, we want to consider one promising way in which a firm apologetic can be advanced, namely, through the employment of a cumulative case argument.

Cumulative case arguments have recently received a good deal of attention as a philosophically viable alternative to traditional natural theology. Such an alternative is certainly worth considering, since it is widely believed that traditional arguments simply do not succeed as deductively valid proofs, which is the way natural theology has typically employed them. The proponent of the cumulative case approach, however, suggests that while these traditional arguments might fail as deductively valid proofs, they can still be valuable when grouped together in such a way that they reinforce one another and offer a satisfying vision of reality.

Some philosophers, however, strongly reject such a reformulation, insisting that since these arguments individually fail as formal proofs, they are altogether useless for supporting the rationality of religious belief. Antony Flew, for instance, has remarked, "A failed proof cannot serve as a pointer to anything, save perhaps to the weaknesses of those who have accepted it. Nor, for the same reason can it be put to work along with other throwouts as part of an accumulation of evidences. If one leaky bucket will not hold water that is no reason to think that ten can."[74]

Advocates of cumulative case arguments, however, take exception to this claim. Richard Swinburne, a contemporary proponent, points out that arguments that are not deductively valid can still be inductively useful. Indeed, Flew's analogy of the buckets "is a particularly unhappy one for his purpose. For clearly if you jam ten leaky buckets together in such a way that holes in the bottom of each bucket are squashed close to solid parts of the bottoms of neighboring buckets, you will get a container that holds water."[75]

Some critics of Lewis and Schaeffer have treated their apologetic work as deductive arguments and have subjected each individually to critical scrutiny, and in the end found them wanting. In fact, this is precisely the approach of Beversluis. Such an approach is not altogether unfair given the fact that both apologists tended to claim more for their arguments than was warranted, at times even suggesting they were conclusive proofs. But noting this does not dispose of their efforts altogether, for the question remains whether their arguments might be recast more effectively in a cumulative case mode. This is especially appropriate since both Lewis and Schaeffer, despite periodic forays into hard apologetics, showed signs of occasionally employing cumulative case principles. Gordon Lewis has even suggested that this is precisely what Schaeffer was doing throughout his apologetic in an informal way.[76] In addition, William Abraham has identified Lewis as a popular proponent of this method.[77]

Although cumulative case arguments can be advanced in a variety of informal ways, it is important to note that they can also be deployed with considerable technical dexterity. Swinburne is an excellent example of this approach. He employs probability calculus in a rather formal manner, while marshaling various arguments. Others, such as Basil Mitchell, have employed the same basic strategy less formally but with no less philosophical sophistication. Mitchell's approach, according to Abraham, is "self-consciously modest." The modesty is a function of recognizing the multifaceted complexity involved in rationality. "Given the nature of the case, the balance of probabilities and considerations is too fine, circuitous, numerous, and various to be captured by any explicit formulation of the argument."[78]

This point deserves emphasis. Otherwise it may be wrongly thought that cumulative case arguments are, at best, a poor cousin to serious, rigorous philosophical arguments of the deductive and formal variety. That is, they may be seen as an ad hoc ploy when more substantive efforts fail. But the point is that in many academic disciplines and other areas of investigation, the evidence and relevant considerations simply will not yield to a deductive or formal approach. Nevertheless, these can be rationally assessed and evaluated. The plausibility of this suggestion is much enhanced when we consider such disciplines as history, literature, law and the physical sciences. In each of these disciplines, competing claims are advanced and defended by marshaling the relevant lines of evidence. Yet in each of these, the various strands of evidence are too complex to be reduced to formal argument forms.

The essential insight of cumulative case arguments is that the various considerations accumulate, pile up and together make a strong case, a case that none of the individual pieces of evidence make in isolation. The various factors can accumulate in this fashion because they cohere in a certain pattern. They mutually reinforce and relate to one another. They are not random bits of evidence, but as noted in chapter four, they are like scattered pieces of a jigsaw puzzle. As the various pieces come together and interlock, a distinct pattern emerges, a pattern that is at best only partially revealed by individual pieces. Schaeffer offers this same sort of imagery when discussing one facet of general revelation, the "universe and its form":

> The universe around us is like an amazing jigsaw puzzle. We see many details, and we want to know how they fit together. This is what science is all about. Scientists look at the details and try to find out how they all cohere. So the first question that has to be answered is: how did the universe get this way? How did it get this form, this pattern, this jigsaw quality it now has?[79]

Lewis also displayed a keen awareness of the subtle and sometimes elusive nature of rationality when dealing with a subject as complex as religious belief. In particular, Lewis made this point in his case for believing in the central miracles of Christianity. In his discussion of the probability of these miracles, he argued that what is needed is a different criterion for judging the intrinsic probability of alleged miracles than is usually offered. The criterion Lewis suggested is our "innate sense of the fitness of things."[80]

Such a suggestion is bound to raise eyebrows, for it may seem far too vague and subjective to be of much help. In the concluding paragraph of the same chapter, Lewis admitted the difficulty of what he would be attempting in the following chapters as he tried to demonstrate the positive probability of the Christian miracles on his proposed criterion. "I shall not, however, proceed by formally setting out the conditions which 'fitness' in the abstract ought to satisfy and then dovetailing the Miracles into that scheme. Our 'sense of fitness' is too delicate and elusive a thing to submit to such treatment."[81] At the beginning of the following chapter, Lewis employs the illustration (which we have cited in chapter six) of possessing portions of a novel or symphony while missing the central part. How would we judge someone's claim to have found the key missing element? "Our business would be to see whether the new passage, if admitted to the central place which the discoverer claimed for it, did actually illumine all the parts we had already seen and 'pull them together.' "[82]

Notice the mutually confirming and interlocking nature of the pieces of data if things really fit as proposed. The central piece is offered tentatively and accepted or rejected on the basis of whether it coheres with the other pieces. But the pieces do not stand absolutely without it, for the central chapter is what makes sense of them, thus the circuitous and delicate nature of the reasoning involved. Recall the example of the champion weightlifter that we cited in chapter five to help make sense of Schaeffer's tripartite case for inerrancy. There is a certain circularity in this reasoning but it is not a vicious circularity.

Much the same point is suggested later in *Miracles*. There Lewis is discussing miracle accounts in other religions. While not prepared to deny all such miracles, Lewis nevertheless says, "But I claim that the Christian miracles have a much greater intrinsic probability in virtue of their organic connection with one another and with the whole structure of the religion they exhibit."[83] Notice the two directions in which the miracles are organically connected. First, the miracles are connected in this fashion with each other and the rationality of believing in them is strengthened by their mutual support. Second, there is also an organic connection between the miracles and "the whole structure of the religion they exhibit." The structure supports the miracles, and the miracles in turn support the structure.

The structure Lewis has in mind includes the conception of God proposed by Christianity. As he notes, some religions have a conception of God such that miracles would seem out of place or inappropriate. For instance, religions that consider nature an illusion or otherwise devalue it would not seem to be likely to value God's miraculous involvement in the natural realm. "But in

Christianity, the more we understand what God it is who is said to be present and the purpose for which He is said to have appeared, the more credible the miracles become."[84] Again, the plausibility of the Christian conception of God is confirmed by the miracles just as the miracles may be likely, given what Christians believe about God.

Alleged miracles that have no such supporting structure are another matter altogether. Of such an isolated miracle Lewis writes, "Nothing comes of it, nothing leads up to it, it establishes no body of doctrine, explains nothing, is connected with nothing."[85] The implication is obvious, though Lewis does not make it fully explicit: A great deal came of the Christian miracles, just as a great deal of purported revelation led up to them and was fulfilled by them; they established a remarkable body of doctrine and they explain a great deal that is otherwise odd. In short, their connection with so many other important claims and facts gives them a strong claim to being the missing chapter of the human story.

Now, we suggest that all the arguments marshaled by Lewis and Schaeffer have most philosophical force when presented in this sort of way. There is an organic connection between the various considerations to which they appeal in their arguments, and these considerations are, in turn, connected in a fitting and persuasive manner with the large framework of theism. Reflect on the close connection between the various components of the "mannishness of man," which as we have seen play such a prominent role in the respective apologetic systems of these men. Our apologists have shown that morality and rationality are not easily explained by naturalistic premises. Likewise, the value we place on the human loves, coupled with our recognition of their vulnerability to corruption, point to the need for a deeper kind of love if our longing for love is to be satisfied. These are the very things that make us distinctively human beings and endow our lives with meaning. They are integrally interconnected, and each makes best sense if we are creatures of a personal God. Our pervasive desire for a deep happiness that cannot be satisfied by anything in this world points in the same direction and reinforces the other pieces of evidence.

Lewis's Trilemma naturally closes the circle. It gives definition to God and shows that he is a being who cares for us enough to come among us to provide for salvation, a salvation that can satisfy our deepest desires and answers our search for an indestructible love. The belief that Jesus really was the Son of God incarnate adds credence to the alleged miracles he performed and accounts for the remarkable impact he made on subsequent history, including the body of doctrine that developed and the founding and success of the Christian church. Again, there is an accumulation of evidence that coheres, interlocks and fits a distinct and persuasive pattern.

While Lewis's Trilemma argument is undoubtedly one of his most famous, it is worth emphasizing again that he and Schaeffer both focused primarily on "mannishness of man" considerations. Although Schaeffer appealed to the "universe and its form" as part of his total case, it is striking that neither of our apologists gave serious attention to classical cosmological and teleological arguments. It is further remarkable that neither developed a substantive historical case for the resurrection of Jesus.[86] This is striking, since an impressive case can be made for it, and it has been a central pillar in much apologetic work. Moreover, both Lewis and Schaeffer recognized the importance of history for orthodox Christianity as well as the importance of the reliability of the New Testament documents.

We suggest that an even more sturdy cumulative argument can be made if these kinds of considerations are properly integrated into the overall case. Recent developments in cosmology, physics and biology have contributed to the revival of cosmological and teleological arguments, and refurbished versions that are both scientifically and philosophically sophisticated are readily available. Likewise, the case for Jesus' resurrection has been made in a way that is both historically and philosophically informed. Adding these sorts of arguments to the rest makes an even more complete and convincing case.

In conclusion, let us note one other advantage of cumulative case arguments. Not only does this mode of reasoning and rational justification do justice to the complexity of the considerations we must often deal with, but it is also a promising alternative to the classical foundationalism that has dominated epistemology for centuries but is now widely repudiated and discredited. Classical foundationalism seeks to build the edifice of belief from an entirely secure foundation of beliefs that are self-evident, evident to our senses or otherwise beyond dispute. The entire structure is to be built up from this solid foundation by careful deductions, inferences and so on. Thereby a sturdy house was thought to be constructed.[87]

The cumulative case approach also seeks to build a solid dwelling but makes no pretense of starting from foundational beliefs that all rational persons would accept or find compelling. It is the total structure, beauty and elegance of the house that is inviting and offers itself as preferable to other houses on the street. This is a majestic manor of which our apologetic butlers, C. S. Lewis and Francis Schaeffer, could be proud.

When the real hope for Heaven is present in us, we do not recognize it. Most people, if they really learned to look into their hearts, would know that they want, and want acutely, something that cannot be had in this world.[1]

C. S. Lewis

It is not more spiritual to believe without asking questions. It is not more biblical. It is less biblical and eventually it will be less spiritual, because the whole man will not be involved. . . . It must be the whole man who comes to understand that the gospel is truth and believes because he is convinced on the basis of good and sufficient reason that it is truth.[2]

Francis Schaeffer

If even only a *few* Christians do begin to practice the holiness and love of God on a moment by moment basis . . . Schaeffer believed that the Holy Spirit would move in a mighty way throughout the church. . . . In this we are reminded of the early church Fathers' conviction and the conviction of C. S. Lewis "that holiness is actually to be practiced by the Christian and . . . that if only ten percent of the world's population had holiness the rest of the people would be converted quickly."[3]

Lane Dennis

10

21 Lessons for the 21st Century

Holism, Holiness and the Hope of Heaven

W ITH OUR COMPARATIVE ANALYSIS COMPLETE, WE ARE NOW IN position to address the question posed at the beginning of this book—namely, what can C. S. Lewis and Francis Schaeffer offer the apologetic enterprise on the eve of the third millennium and beyond? Though we have suggested some answers along the way, this final chapter is designed to tackle this question head on.

At the outset we proposed that the needs and desires of our pluralistic, fragmented, postmodern world can be met best by excavating the ancient riches of paleo-orthodoxy. With this in mind, it is our contention that the essential embryonic insights for forging a compelling and compassionate apologetic for the twenty-first century are embedded in the classic apologetic text 1 Peter 3:15-16: "But in your hearts set apart Christ as Lord. Always be prepared to give an answer to everyone who asks you to give the reason for the hope that you have. But do this with gentleness and respect, keeping a clear conscience, so that those who speak maliciously against your good behavior in Christ may be ashamed of their slander."

This text is often marshalled by those who advocate a rational apologetic. Indeed, such an interpretation is thoroughly warranted, for Peter makes it clear that Christians must be ready to offer a reasoned account of their faith. But an intelligent, thoughtful explanation, as important as that is, is only part of Peter's charge. Peter is calling us not simply to a rational, one-dimensional response that addresses the intellect of the listener, but rather to a full-orbed apologetic that engages the entire person: mind, will and emotions.

The emphasis on the rational component in this passage is obvious. We are to prepare a case and offer a defense, an *apologia* for our beliefs. (This is of course the Greek word from which our term *apologetics* comes.) But Peter also is addressing the affective, emotional dimension, because we are not defending simply a system of doctrines or a set of propositions but also the "hope" that is lodged within the heart of every believer. Indeed, it is this very hope that Peter assumes will arrest the attention of nonbelievers and prompt them to inquire about the faith. In the opening verses of this epistle, Peter tells us that Christians have a "living hope" grounded in the resurrection of Jesus Christ and focused on heaven. In other words, this is not some vague, nebulous, contentless brand of hope, something akin to mere wishful thinking. On the contrary, the Christian should possess a profound expectation of glory that is firmly rooted in a cognitively discerned space-time event. And since the Christian hope is open to rational verification, our minds are capable of fully endorsing it.

Peter also tells us that the manner in which this hope is presented is of prime importance. The gospel should be defended and preached in a way that conveys full respect for the dignity of those who listen. Apologetics should be done with gentleness and respect, and the message should be backed up by lives of moral integrity. This allows the conscience to join the mind in fully endorsing the hope produced by the living Christ.

In sum, what Peter offers us here in the classic apologetic text is a vision of a thoroughly integrated, holistic apologetic. Since genuine faith requires a response to the gospel at all levels of our being, our apologetic efforts should appeal to all levels as well. In short, we should offer an apologetic that seeks to engage the mind, enchant the emotions, empower the will and restore relationships.

As we have seen throughout our study, Schaeffer and Lewis were both sensitive to the holistic character of the apologetic endeavor. Schaeffer envisioned the Christian system as "a view of truth that involves the whole person"[4] and accordingly emphasized the importance of bringing every facet of the human experience under the banner of Christ's lordship. Lewis likewise recognized the full-orbed nature of the Christian journey and was careful to avoid a truncated presentation of the gospel. In *Mere Christianity* he offered the following caution: "If you are thinking of becoming a Christian, I warn you you are embarking on something which is going to take the whole of you, brains and all."[5]

In what follows we want to offer twenty-one lessons for the twenty-first century, or to put it another way, a twenty-one-gun salute to the most influential apologists of our time. In light of the holistic focus of these men, we have grouped these lessons under the four headings listed above. We should also note that the epigraphs at the outset of this chapter signal the direction of the complete apologetic we want to recommend. Such an apologetic will be thoroughly holistic, grounded in holiness and focused on the desire that resides in every human heart, namely, the hope of heaven.

Engaging the Mind

1. Objective reality and absolute truth. Lewis and Schaeffer never tired of emphasizing the crucial importance of objective reality and absolute truth. While neither lived to see deconstructionism and other distinctly postmodern forms of radical relativism in full bloom, neither apologist would be surprised by such trends. The seeds of these developments had already been sown when they wrote. Each of our apologists had a prophetic sense of where relativism would lead. It is our conviction that their emphasis on objective reality and absolute truth is one of their most important and lasting contributions to theology and apologetics.

A number of Christian leaders have rightly recognized that the postmodern mindset has little use or appreciation for the notion of objective truth and rational argument, and have gone on to propose that we should play these down in contemporary apologetics and evangelism, preferring instead the personal, the relational, the emotional and the aesthetic.

We believe Lewis and Schaeffer would sound a caution at this point to those who are jumping on the postmodern bandwagon. While there is certainly nothing wrong with understanding and engaging a culture on its own terms and shaping our apologetic accordingly, this can easily slip into cultural accommodation. Moreover, while objective truth may not be the most fruitful point of entry in contemporary apologetics, it cannot be ignored or soft-pedaled in the long run without disastrous consequences. No matter which point of entry is used, the important thing is finally to convert whole persons—heart, soul, mind and strength.

A glance back at the recent history of evangelicalism can make the point. Recall that in the early days of evangelicalism, the major point of emphasis was on doctrinal purity and integrity. The cognitive dimensions of the faith were front and center. The mind was the focus, and the stress was on correct belief. It is not surprising that the next generation of young evangelicals began to emphasize social action and ministry, a dimension of the Christian life they saw as neglected by their immediate forebears. They discovered that such social engagement was an important part of their heritage as practiced by their grandparents and great-grandparents in the faith.[6] More recently, the evangelical church and the church at large have witnessed a strong emphasis on the emotional and experiential dimensions of the faith. Again, this area was often lacking when the main accent was on correct belief.

Clearly, if any dimension of our personality is neglected in Christian teaching and apologetics, it will not be long suppressed. Lewis observed that "famished nature will be avenged and a hard heart is no infallible protection against a soft head."[7] While Lewis was concerned in this passage with famished emotions, the point holds equally for a famished intellect. If it is not satisfied by persuasive rational considerations, it will take its revenge as surely as repressed emotions and feelings will eventually exact a price. If apologists of this generation neglect a proper emphasis on objective truth and rational argument, the church will surely pay the toll in the next generation.

2. Honest answers to honest questions. One hallmark of Schaeffer's ministry was his willingness to provide honest answers to honest questions. He realized that many young people during his era had been told by their parents and church leaders that spiritual questioning is a sign of weak faith. Schaeffer did not buy this for a minute. He passionately rejected such fideistic counsel, insisting that "it is not more spiritual to believe without asking questions. It is not more biblical. It is less biblical and eventually it will be less spiritual, because the whole man will not be involved."[8] Schaeffer keenly recognized that a spirituality without an intellectual grounding is a mere shadow of the rich, robust, satisfying faith that God desires for all his children. Such a faith is also dangerously vulnerable to the inevitable challenges of life, whether it be the loss of a loved one or the teaching of a false prophet.

The Christian community should joyfully follow Schaeffer's lead by encouraging honest inquiry. Candid intellectual inquiry is not a sign of spiritual weakness but rather a quest for the ultimate integration point that will bring coherence and meaning to the human experience. If we really believe that Jesus Christ is not only the way and the life but also the truth, then we can enthusiastically encourage seekers to probe the depths of the Christian claims with full confidence that a sincere search will culminate in ultimate satisfaction.

3. The big questions of life. For every seeker who came to L'Abri in a state of focused inquiry, Schaeffer realized there were countless others indifferent toward the big questions of life. For those people, it is not merely a matter of providing honest answers to honest questions, but rather it is helping them see why they ought to care about ultimate issues at all. In a world of growing specialization, fragmentation and skepticism, Schaeffer recognized that people were becoming increasingly proficient at diverting themselves from the big questions of life: "People are playing many, many games instead of thinking the big questions. Their game can be knocking one tenth of one second off a downhill run on the Swiss Alps. It also can show up in a highly disciplined science where one focuses on a very small area of reality and then never thinks of the big question."[9]

Though the art of diversion is an age-old craft, it is easy to understand its proliferation in a day of widespread relativism. This is the logical outcome for a world that has lost its faith in ever achieving a rationally discerned unified body of knowledge and meaning. If we are incapable of discerning any objective verities in life, then why engage the traditional big questions? Is it not more sensible to eat, drink and be merry, or to focus on more manageable subject matter during our brief time here on this planet?

Given the assumption of epistemological relativism, this does seem sensible, but only if we arrive at this view by honestly grappling with the big questions of life, for how else can we have any intellectual assurance that relativism is the ultimate context? Though some surely have embraced relativism after honestly engaging the big questions, Schaeffer and Lewis recognized that most people in our society simply have been carried along by the cultural consensus. These are the people whom our apologists often attempted to reach, and we must do the same. We must show those who have carelessly embraced a set of assumptions that there is too much at stake in life to buy into any worldview, including Christianity, without adequate reflection. Our perception of the ultimate context frames everything we care about, from downhill skiing to scientific minutia. On that basis, nothing should be more important than engaging the big questions of life.

4. A unified body of knowledge and meaning. A leading motif in the Schaeffer corpus is the divided field of knowledge and meaning. It was Schaeffer's staunch conviction that the twentieth century ushered in an age of fragmentation. Reason and faith, intellect and imagination, matter and meaning all have been shoved into mutually exclusive compartments. In fact, a young C. S. Lewis serves as a prime example of this type of dichotomized existence: "The two hemispheres of my mind were in the sharpest contrast. On the one side a many-islanded sea of poetry and myth; on the other a glib and shallow 'rationalism.' Nearly all that I loved I believed to be imaginary; nearly all that I believed to be real I thought grim and meaningless."[10]

Recognizing that everyone possesses a natural aversion to dissonance, Schaeffer deftly and compassionately nudged people to the point of tension in their own lives and then offered the self-consistent, comprehensive, livable worldview of historic, biblical Christianity as a hopeful alternative. We suggest that this method of "taking the roof off" and the commitment of both our apologists to a unified body of knowledge and meaning are important examples for the church today.

Some would insist, however, that the charge of intellectual inconsistency has lost its leverage in an age that devalues reason. Consequently, this notion of pushing people to the point of tension is no longer a viable apologetic maneuver. Dick Keyes is one contemporary L'Abri leader who is unwilling to discard the method altogether but does believe we ought to replace the term *consistency* in our apologetic vernacular with *honesty*.[11] After all, many postmodern people do not care about the notion of cognitive consistency, but there is widespread agreement that we ought to be true to ourselves or sincere about our own beliefs.

Keyes has accurately identified the popular sympathies of our postmodern age, and we applaud his attempt to adapt this method accordingly. But it is not clear that such a maneuver is altogether desirable. If *honesty* is simply used as a more palatable synonym for *intellectual consistency*, a case can be made. But if the nonbeliever is led to think that a self-consistent vision of reality is not an integral part of the Christian faith, then a grave loss has been suffered. Our goal is not to simply usher people into the faith but to see them thoroughly transformed into entirely integrated beings, and this includes a view of reality that is self-consistent, comprehensive and livable. We would also do well to remember that an integrated worldview necessarily will include a commitment to true but inexhaustive truth and, as noted in chapter four, a willingness to think deeply and carefully about the subject of mystery.

5. The historical texture of the Christian faith. What would you say if you picked up the newspaper tomorrow morning and the lead headline screamed, "Bones of Jesus Found: Scholars Refute Resurrection"? Your first reaction might likely be grave skepticism and a quick glance through the body of the story to identify the names of these radical revisionists. But suppose upon reading the opening paragraph you discovered that the academicians who made this pronouncement are not of the Jesus Seminar variety but rather a battery of the most respected evangelical New Testament scholars in the world. The article indicates that these venerable professors had secretly gathered at an archaeological site in Jerusalem to examine a new find and that the whole group, much to their chagrin, concluded that these were the actual bones of Jesus of Nazareth. In light of this startling revelation, would you give up your Christian faith?

As emotionally and psychologically devastating as it might be to discard the faith, we would have to side with the apostle Paul, who said that "if Jesus has not been raised, you are still in your sins." Unlike most of the religions of the world, Christianity is rooted in space-time history and is therefore open to both verification and falsification. Schaeffer made this point well when he wrote, "If the tomb was not empty—so that a camera crew could have recorded the absence of Jesus' body at the same time that they could have filmed the linen strips and headcloth in which his body had been wrapped—we have no hope."[12]

Although Lewis and Schaeffer differed concerning the historicity of some Old Testament accounts, they both tenaciously affirmed the historical texture of the New Testament narrative. Using keen literary discernment, Lewis confidently asserted that there are only two possible interpretations of the Gospel records, either eyewitness accounts or "modern, novelistic, realistic" fiction.[13] Since the latter did not surface until many centuries after the time of Christ, there is good reason to believe that the events recorded in the Gospels are descriptions of true history.

The Bible is a record of God's salvific activity in human history. This revelatory account, which crystallizes in the passion of Christ, is a clear, concrete, tangible expression of God's loving compassion for his entire creation. To denude the Gospels of their historic content is to strip away the very heart and hope of the faith. In an age marked by grave historical skepticism and widespread gnosticism, Christian apologists must follow the example of Schaeffer and Lewis by insisting on the objective, space-time character of the Christian faith. As we argued in chapter five, if the Son of God did not enter the world as a little baby in Bethlehem, live a sinless life in Jewish flesh, die a terrible death on Calvary and leave an empty tomb on Easter morning, then the whole Christian faith falls to the ground.

6. Cultural engagement. It is surely significant that the two most influential spokesmen for orthodox, evangelical Christianity in the twentieth century were both apologists. Both spent much of their time and energy engaging ideas and challenging the prevailing wisdom of the age. Ironically, much of modern culture, including the church, is heavily pragmatic and has little patience with such issues as whether or not naturalism is a coherent worldview or whether it can adequately account for personality. The immediate pragmatic cash value of such discussions and distinctions is not always apparent. At first glance they may seem almost irrelevant to the urgent needs of people in a hurting society. Much of the church is driven by what has been called "the tyranny of the urgent," matters of immediate concern that call for action now.

Lewis and Schaeffer both realized that our society did not arrive at its lost condition overnight, and they recognized that the root problems are much deeper than can be addressed by immediate action. That is why they engaged ideas. Ideas have consequences, and the consequences are not always felt instantly. Deep and long-term social change requires insightful analysis of root issues.

Richard John Neuhaus has remarked that evangelicals have been very good at personal evangelism but not very good at cultural evangelism.[14] That is, they have not been nearly as effective in engaging culture at the level of the ideas and practices that shape our common life. Such engagement does not typically produce dramatic results that can be measured instantly and in obvious ways. Cultural evangelism is a more subtle operation, and it can be measured only with the benefit of years of hindsight.

Schaeffer called for such broad engagement as follows: "If we are going to join the battle in a way that has any hope of effectiveness—with Christians truly being salt and light in our culture and society—then we must do battle on the entire front."[15] Both by example and instruction, Schaeffer encouraged his fellow Christians to join the battle on a wide range of intellectual, cultural, social and moral issues. With both Schaeffer and Lewis, hindsight reveals a legacy of lasting impact, which is still being measured and is likely to be so for years to come.

7. *Critical rationalism and cumulative case argumentation.* In chapter nine we suggested that Lewis and Schaeffer occasionally employed the principles of cumulative case argumentation, an attractive alternative to classical foundationalism. Now we want to propose further that this mode of reasoning and marshaling of arguments has considerable apologetic promise because it can respond to some of the central themes of postmodernism without falling into the relativism that is characteristic of postmodern epistemology. Postmodernism is difficult to define precisely, and its correct contours remain a matter of (perhaps interminable) controversy. This alone is a good reason for Christian apologists to exercise appropriate reserve before assuming the whole world has gone postmodern for now and forever. At any rate, a central postmodern theme is the claim that all fundamental beliefs and commitments are arbitrary and thus impervious to reason and evidence. Given this notion, there is no basis for thinking a rational conversion from one fundamental commitment to another is possible. Thus Stanley Fish characterizes the breach between believer and nonbeliever as follows: "The difference between a believer and a nonbeliever is not that one reasons and the other doesn't, but that one reasons from a first premise the other denies; and from this difference flow others that make the fact that both are reasoning a sign not of commonality but of its absence."[16] Given one's commitment to one's first premise, one can absorb any and all evidence and interpret it to fit one's fundamental belief.[17]

Consider in this light the much-publicized mass suicide of the members of the Heaven's Gate cult in California. In an essay in *Time* magazine, Pico Iyer argued that the incident raised the question "When does a 'cult' become a faith?" The essence of the essay is that there is no clear answer to this question and, moreover, no way to rationally adjudicate competing religious claims. "The leap of faith is—and has to be—a plunge into the unrational (which to skeptics seems 'unreasonable'), and by its nature it is a move that leaves the rest of us behind. Every religion is a different language that, to those outside it, makes as little sense as Mandarin dialogue or Cyrillic characters do to me."[18] This is an example of a typically postmodern comment, which Stanley Fish would enthusiastically endorse.

It may be that a verificationist methodology, crafted along cumulative case lines with a sensitive feel for the various facets of evidence, has a better chance than any other approach of engaging and converting the postmodern mind. This approach recognizes that we do indeed reason from some fundamental hypothesis, presupposition, paradigm or first premise. Moreover, we do so unavoidably. But such fundamental commitments are subject to verification and confirmation or, on the other hand, disconfirmation or falsification. This is not to deny that a sufficiently ingenious person may not be able to interpret virtually any piece of data to fit his of her first premise. However, not all such hypotheses and first premises are created equal, and not all account equally well for the various and multifaceted data that need to be explained in a satisfying worldview.[19] Demonstrating this is the key to avoiding relativism. Doing so creatively and persuasively is the ongoing task of the Christian apologist.

Enchanting the Emotions

8. Emotional redemption. A central point of *The Abolition of Man* is that true virtue is impossible without trained emotions. Without the support of such trained emotions, we are powerless to do what is right in a consistent fashion, even if we know intellectually what we ought to do. The key to real character, then, is for the emotions to be trained so they follow the lead of the intellect. This requires that our heart, our "chest" as Lewis put it, must be shaped and schooled by the perception of objective truth and value as surely as our intellect grasps it.

This point is of particular relevance for our culture, which has still not recovered its balance after the age of Romanticism. Our culture is unhealthily preoccupied with the emotional, the experiential and the affective, at the expense of the rational and the moral. The answer is not to suppress emotion or to minimize its significance; rather, it is to recover the notion that there are both appropriate and inappropriate emotional responses just as there are true and false beliefs. Which is which is determined by what is objectively true and valuable. The church needs to help train the emotions and recognize the role of emotion in holistic faith. The answer is not to restrain emotion but to train it.

It is worth remarking here that part of the appeal of Schaeffer's writings is his palpable passion. The reader senses that Schaeffer feels deeply what he is saying and writing and that his emotion is fully commensurate with the matters he is addressing. As he stated explicitly, "If we fight our philosophic battles, our artistic battles, our scientific battles, our battles in sociology, our battles in psychology, our battles in literature, our battles in drama coolly, without emotional involvement, do we really love God?"[20] In short, emotional deserts are no more to be preferred than emotional floods that recognize no boundaries.

9. The marriage of myth and fact. The myth of progress has given way to the progress of myth. This is one way of describing the transition from the optimistic Age of Reason into our current Age of Imagination. As C. Stephen Evans has aptly noted, "there is considerable fascination with mythology in our culture."[21]

Evans suggests a number of reasons for the appeal of myth in our postmodern age. Chief among them is the belief that "myth is in many ways living water for a dry culture."[22] As we suggested earlier, humans are created for a thorough integration of all faculties, and whenever one is stressed beyond its proper limits the pendulum will swing out of balance in the opposite direction. Such is the case today. Enlightenment rationalism has parched the soul of the West, and our culture has turned with a vengeance to imaginative reservoirs like myth to quench its thirst.

Although this intense affair with the imagination may seem temporarily exhilarating, without a proper corrective the postmodern world is in danger of exchanging one plague for another. The drought-stricken farmer who is initially thrilled to watch the cool showers saturating his cracked soil is eventually dismayed if his crops are swept away by a flood. Only the proper balance of sun and rain can yield a healthy harvest.

In this connection, Lewis's understanding of the Christian story as the marriage of "Perfect Myth and Perfect Fact" might provide some promising resources in keeping these polarized plagues at bay. His commitment to the historical texture of the New Testament narrative provides the appropriate epistemological grounding for the faith, giving the mind its proper due, while his emphasis on the mythical quality of the Gospels offers, as Lewis put it, "the vital and nourishing element" that satisfies our imaginative and affective cravings.[23] This is an integrated vision that appeals to the whole person, "claiming not only our love and our obedience, but also our wonder and delight, addressed to the savage, the child, and the poet in each one of us no less than to the moralist, the scholar, and the philosopher."[24]

10. Subversion by surprise. Lewis and Schaeffer did some of their best evangelistic and apologetic work with those who were resistant to a direct presentation of the gospel. Years of compassionate conversation and an attentive ear enabled Schaeffer to "smoke out" incongruities with remarkable finesse. Lewis, likewise, was adept at catching his audience with its guard down. One way he went about doing this was by turning the tables on the skeptic. Consider how he responded to the charge that Christianity is discredited by its similarity to other religions. Instead of seeing similar motifs as a strike against the faith, Lewis persuasively insisted that this is precisely what we ought to expect if God is really the Creator and Sustainer of the entire world. Lewis was exceptionally proficient at offering an angle of vision that shifted a negative charge into a positive proof. It is in these moments of surprise that many are most vulnerable to the truth.

Yet Lewis employed this subversive approach most effectively through his imaginative writings. In the sacrifice of Aslan we are moved by the depth of divine kenosis. In the transformation of the beastly Eustace we are repulsed by the stubborn, scaly quality of sin. In the battle between Ransom and Weston we are gripped by the epic struggle between good and evil.[25] In each instance, the reader is subtly encountering the contours of Christianity whether it is consciously realized or not. Once the skeptic has touched, tasted and gazed upon the truth, the chance for a rational response is immeasurably increased.

Such an approach holds great promise in a day of widespread resistance to traditional, direct, rational appeals. As Christian apologists in a visually oriented culture, we must engage our audience by using concrete and captivating imagery and a whole array of imaginative means. As William Abraham has noted, "the use of narrative, allegory, drama, fantasy, poetry and the like, may prove extremely important in the articulation of the Christian faith and in opening up the heart and the mind to the depth and simplicity of the gospel. ... Lewis's heart may prove more lasting than his head at this point."[26] Or to put it another way, it will take all the ingenuity we can muster to successfully steal past those ever-watchful dragons.

11. The attraction of agape. Perhaps no culture more than modern and postmodern Western culture has been more obsessed with love, and has celebrated it more, while gleaning less real satisfaction from it. Naturalism tells a story in which love is a relative newcomer on the stage of history, emerging late in the evolutionary scheme from impersonal and loveless sources. But according to Christian theism, love is the eternal and highest reality. Human loves are an image of Love himself and thus have a more secure grounding in ultimate reality.

As Lewis argued so powerfully, a proper relation to Love is what can redeem and preserve the human loves. The central Christian doctrines of Incarnation and atonement are a powerful and moving account of Love offering that relationship to human beings. There is good reason to believe, then, that when love is credibly demonstrated by Christians in the context of a relationship to a God of overwhelming love, our culture will be prepared to listen to our story of how Love is reaching out to them. Schaeffer put the point as follows: "Because every man is made in the image of God and has, therefore, aspirations for love, there is something that can be in every geographical climate—in every point of time—which cannot fail to arrest his attention."[27]

The notion of agape, of a love that needs nothing and is pure gift, is a powerful resource for confronting the attitude of suspicion that pervades the postmodern mindset. As many postmoderns see it, behind every truth claim is an unacknowledged bid for control and power. Therefore all such claims need to be exposed and deconstructed. But according to Christianity, God is all-powerful and thus has no needs of any kind, least of all the need to grasp power through deceit and manipulation. Because he is all-powerful and utterly self-sufficient, he can love perfectly, with no hidden springs of dubious motivation. The very claim that such a God exists is a frontal challenge to the pervasive suspicion that is so rampant in our day. Of course, the insistently suspicious can choose to see the very idea of agape as a remarkably subtle attempt at control and manipulation. But the notion of such a love, credibly demonstrated, has as much chance as anything at breaking down the walls of suspicion within which many postmoderns have chosen to shelter themselves.

12. The hope of heaven. In their fascinating book *Heaven: A History*, Colleen McDannell and Bernhard Lang observe that even among conservative Christians "eternal life has become an unknown place or a state of vague identity."[28] A recent article in *Time* magazine made the same point, although it reported that 81 percent of those they polled professed to believe in heaven as a place "where people live forever with God after they die." While they still believe in heaven "their concept of exactly what it is has grown foggier, and they hear about it much less frequently from their pastors."[29]

The attitude of many people toward heaven is reflected in the 1990s movie *Michael.* John Travolta in the title role plays an angel who is permitted one more visit to earth before he must go to heaven forever. The implicit message is that earth is better than heaven. Thus Michael wants to partake of the sinful pleasures of earth before submitting to the eternal boredom of life with God. This point was made in a student paper that went on to compare Lewis's writings on heaven with those of a contemporary theologian. While their formal beliefs about heaven were essentially the same, the student remarked that the description of heaven by the noted theologian gave him no desire to go there. Reading Lewis's account of heaven, however, stirred in him a deep sense of joy and excitement and awoke the longing for heaven.[30]

The three most profound pages in *Mere Christianity* may be Lewis's brief discussion of the Christian virtue of hope and its relation to the longing for heaven. This longing is precisely the longing for deep and lasting happiness that all human beings have felt stirring in their hearts. Heaven is about happiness and joy, and if we do not understand this and believe it heartily, then the desire to love God and be properly related to him will be correspondingly weak and vague. Apologetics cannot succeed in making a relationship with God desirable without at least a glimpse of the hearty delights of heaven. Nor is the real terror of hell really understood until it is grasped that sin is the destruction of joy and satisfaction.

If our deepest longing is really for God, then that longing is a desire for heaven. At the heart of our apologetic task is the charge of helping people name their deepest longings.

Empowering the Will

13. The highway to happiness. Holiness. In our age, this term conjures up a whole array of bizarre, outdated images. Thoughts of sour-faced, cannot-do-anything-fun legalists are surely what comes to mind for many. This is unfortunate. In a day when society is desperately searching for unshakable happiness and sturdy ethical moorings, the very thing understood least is that which is needed most—a renewed appreciation for the biblical concept of holiness.

Even within Christian circles, holiness has all too often been construed as a relatively marginal matter or a doctrinal distinctive of certain sectarian denominations, as Schaeffer frequently discovered when delivering his powerful lectures on sanctification and true spirituality. Lewis, likewise, challenged the popular notion that holiness should be relegated to the periphery. In fact, in a book about "mere Christianity," the classical faith of the church, Lewis insists that Christianity is about nothing other than God's offer to make us like Christ. Moreover, he explains the great doctrines of the Trinity and the Incarnation in just these terms. Holiness is not a sideline issue or the concern of only those with esoteric interests, but rather it is the heart of the faith.

Now, the notion of holiness will be properly understood only if we view it through a relational lens. If interpreted through a fundamentally forensic grid, this doctrine will naturally appear to be heavily lacquered with a thick tar of legalism. Holiness cannot be reduced to a set of rigid rules without slipping into a tedious and repellent moralism. Unfortunately, this legal view of holiness pervades the contemporary mindset both inside and outside the church, which largely explains this doctrine's widespread neglect.

Lewis's view of holiness, by contrast, is richly relational, which opens up a whole new dimension of splendor. Certainly this doctrine includes the moral renewal we so desperately need, but it is more than that. It is also a vision of the beauty and meaning of life that answers to our deepest longings for settled satisfaction. Holiness is not an oppressive burden meant to beat us down but rather a pathway of purity designed to lead us "further up and further in," to the unfathomable delights of the celestial city and the everlasting arms of our holy heavenly Father. When reflecting on his initial encounter with MacDonald's *Phantastes,* Lewis contrasted the truncated forensic view of holiness with the real thing.

> I should have been shocked in my teens if anyone had told me that what I learned to love in *Phantastes* was goodness. But now I know, I see there was no deception. The deception is all the other way around—in that prosaic moralism which confines goodness to the region of Law and Duty, which never lets us feel in our face the sweet air blowing from "the land of righteousness," never reveals that elusive Form which if once seen must inevitably be desired with all but sensuous desire—the thing "more gold than gold."[31]

One of the most pressing assignments for the twenty-first century apologist is to strip away the deception that keeps people from seeing the heart of the Christian faith—the biblical doctrine of holiness—in all its golden glory and spectacular splendor. This means we must consciously reject today's dominant, stifling legal grid in favor of one that is profoundly liberating and richly relational.

14. True moral guilt. Closely connected to the need for a renewed appreciation for holiness is the need to recapture the biblical concept of sin. Schaeffer and Lewis both recognized the difficulty of awakening a sense of sin in a culture saturated with psychological techniques designed to explain away the notion of true moral guilt. Nevertheless, both apologists insisted that a cure cannot be administered until people recognize they are sick. Schaeffer made it clear that the unbeliever must realize "that we are talking about *real guilt* before God, and we are not offering him merely relief for his guilt-feelings."[32]

Lewis recognized three aspects of morality: interpersonal human relationships, individual character and our relationship to God. He pointed out that most modern people focus their attention on the first dimension, while largely ignoring the other two. He likened the ethical life to a fleet of ships attempting to reach a destination. To have any hope of a successful journey the ships must not only avoid colliding into one another, but each vessel also must remain seaworthy and stay headed in the right direction.[33]

The interesting thing about this metaphor is its relational quality. Instead of contextualizing sin within a legal framework, which considers deviant behavior a violation against some abstract law or lawgiver, we see Lewis interpreting sin as a matter of relational failure. When we consider morality in this way, suddenly the other two neglected ethical dimensions are illuminated. Every act of sin, whether it directly violates a fellow human being or not, is a relational breach because it diminishes one's own character, which in turn has an important bearing on future relationships. Ultimately all sin, whether or not it has immediate earthly interpersonal ramifications, grieves our heavenly Father, who knows his children will never be truly happy if they are not holy. Understanding sin and true moral guilt in a relational sense is both the most biblical model and most promising approach in our highly relational age. The apologetic task in the twenty-first century is to challenge the prevailing moral relativism by insisting that morality is grounded not in some abstract law or the will of an arbitrary Judge but rather in the character of the perfectly good and profoundly loving, infinite-personal God of the Bible.

15. Libertarian freedom. One of the central themes of this book has been the insistence upon maintaining a self-consistent, comprehensive, livable vision of reality that does justice to the character of God and the significance of humans. This means there is no escaping the reality that apologetics is tightly connected to systematic theology. In fact, apologetic activity should emerge naturally from one's theological assumptions and commitments. That is why we have devoted so much space in this study to issues like soteriology, free will and determinism, divine election, and biblical inspiration. These are not peripheral matters that can be easily brushed aside, for our views on these subjects form our bedrock perceptions of reality and will invariably influence our approach to the apologetic task. To put it another way, apologetics is not a theologically neutral enterprise. If one is to maintain intellectual integrity, the arguments marshaled and methods employed must cohere with one's espoused worldview.

One of the most important theological lessons we can learn from both Lewis and Schaeffer is the necessity of insisting upon a libertarian form of freedom. If we are to offer a self-consistent, comprehensive, livable worldview that accounts for God's impeccable character and human dignity, then libertarian freedom must be an essential part of the equation. As we have clearly seen, compatibilism simply will not do. This view of freedom is riddled with problems. It undermines God's justice, glory and goodness and fails to offer a satisfying account for the enigmatic mixture of nobility and wretchedness in the human heart.

Arguably, the most damaging strike against compatibilism is its utter inability to explain why God has not predestined everyone to freely choose him if freedom is really compatible with determinism. In our estimation, this is the mortal blow to the compatibilist. If this question cannot be answered convincingly, then compatibilists can hardly expect their position to be taken seriously by those who firmly believe in a profoundly loving and richly relational God.

Lewis and Schaeffer both recognized the need for a libertarian form of freedom to advance many of their apologetic arguments. But it is critical to note here that the success of such arguments does not hinge upon human effort. As indicated earlier, a commitment to libertarian freedom is not an endorsement of works-righteousness or sinful self-autonomy. Scripture makes it clear that we can do nothing in our own strength. We cannot emphasize too strongly the necessity of divine grace, the empowerment of the Holy Spirit, the importance of prayer and a clear understanding of dual agency in the apologetic endeavor. We affirm that God is always the primary agent and the sole initiator in calling his sheep back to the fold. The job of the apologist and potential convert is to simply cooperate with the grace of God and rely on the resources that only he can provide.

16. Moral intuitions. In *The Problem of Pain* Lewis noted that we face a dilemma when we try to relate God's goodness to our own notion of goodness. On the one hand, since God is wiser than we are, and his ways higher than our ways, what seems good to us may not really be good, and what seems evil may not really be evil. On the other hand, if this is true, then calling God good is meaningless, and if he is not good in our sense, then we shall obey him not on moral grounds but through fear. Such obedience to God would be no different from submitting to a powerful tyrant.

According to Lewis, the way to avoid this dilemma is to recognize that our moral judgments are indeed different from God's, but not radically so. Given this perspective, God's goodness "differs from ours not as white from black but as a perfect circle from a child's first attempt to draw a wheel. But when the child has learned to draw, it will know that the circle it then makes is what it was trying to make from the very beginning."[34] Given this perspective, our basic moral intuitions and judgments are sound but in need of further refinement, training and correction from revelation. In other words, revelation fulfills and completes our best moral instincts instead of rejecting or undercutting them. Moreover, this means that Scripture should be interpreted in ways that cohere with our deepest moral intuitions, just as it should be interpreted in ways that accord with the basic laws of logic.

Of course, this is not to say that Scripture should be subordinated to human reason and moral judgment. It is to say that God is the ultimate source of human reason and moral judgment, just as he is the source of Scripture. So there is good reason to think that our best reason and moral judgment will be compatible with Scripture, properly interpreted. To set Scripture against our clearest logical and moral intuitions is to promote fideism at best and skepticism at worst.

Our discussion earlier about unconditional election and the fate of the unevangelized illustrates how moral intuitions interact with biblical interpretation and theological formulation. Lewis's position on these issues flows naturally from his belief that our sense of goodness is fundamentally consistent with divine goodness. This commitment is crucial for an apologetic that is morally satisfying, as well as morally challenging. This is the sort of apologetic that will engage our will and empower us to advance to higher moral achievements.

17. Virtue epistemology. A few lessons back, we made the point that holiness is nonnegotiable for deep, settled satisfaction. Now we want to insist that holiness is equally essential for true epistemological insight and profound discernment. In other words, personal character has a direct bearing on one's ability to apprehend the nature of ultimate reality.

As noted in chapter five, Lewis thought one reason God has not provided unambiguous revelation is because such a message might have engaged only the mind instead of "the whole man." God's primary purpose is not to satisfy our curiosity but rather to transform us into holy beings. With this goal in mind, it seems quite plausible that the ambiguity found in Scripture and in the world at large is necessary to elicit the holistic response God desires. If we approach the truth in holistic integrity, we can trust God to supply ever-increasing insight and psychological certitude.

This conviction, which has been advanced under the rubric of virtue epistemology in recent times, is woven throughout the Lewisian corpus. In *Prince Caspian* virtuous Lucy can perceive the guidance of Aslan, while the rest of the children are oblivious to his presence. In *Till We Have Faces* the undefiled Psyche can see an invisible palace, while her sister is blinded by the perversion of possessive love. In *The Magician's Nephew* Digory and Polly can understand Narnia's talking animals, while devious Uncle Andrew can only hear beastly inarticulate utterings.[35]

The bottom line is that epistemological insight is more than a cognitive operation. It takes the whole person, including a purified will. Paul Holmer, author of *C. S. Lewis: The Shape of His Faith and Thought*, has made this point well: "What we know depends upon the kind of person we have made of ourselves. The world's infinite riches, its values and worths, its pleasures and depths can be found only if we are qualified subjects."[36]

Restoring Relationships

18. Pastoral apologetics. Jerry Jenkins, former editor of *Moody Magazine*, tells of a time when he heard Francis Schaeffer speak in Chicago. After presenting his *How Should We Then Live?* material, Schaeffer fielded questions from an audience of more than four thousand. Jenkins recalls one gentleman who "began a question in a halting, nearly incoherent growl. Clearly, he suffered from cerebral palsy." Schaeffer pressed his eyes firmly shut and listened intently as the questioner offered a lengthy, garbled inquiry. Jenkins admits to grasping only about a quarter of the question, but Schaeffer discerned all but the final three words, which the man reiterated. Schaeffer responded, "Forgive me . . . the last word again, please." With the full question grasped, Schaeffer verbalized a summary and responded "with the time and dignity he had accorded all the other questions." When this same man followed up with another tedious question, Schaeffer "repeated the process, being sure he understood every word and answering fully."[37] While many in the audience were frustrated by this, Schaeffer displayed remarkable patience and compassion—vintage Francis Schaeffer, the pastor.

Lewis also displayed a shepherd's heart. In one of the most moving passages in all of *Mere Christianity*, one can almost imagine the author placing his hand on the shoulder of a despairing soul, while offering the following keen and compassionate psychological advice:

> But if you are a poor creature—poisoned by a wretched up-bringing in some house full of vulgar jealousies and senseless quarrels—saddled, by no choice of your own, with some loathsome sexual perversion—nagged day in and day out by an inferiority complex that makes you snap at your best friends—do not despair. He knows all about it. You are one of the poor whom he has blessed. He knows what a wretched machine you are trying to drive. Keep on. Do what you can. One day (perhaps in another world, but perhaps far sooner than that) he will fling it on the scrapheap and give you a new one. And then you may astonish us all—not the least yourself: for you have learned your driving in a hard school.[38]

Lewis displayed an uncommon balance and sensitivity when discussing psychological issues. He insisted vigorously that humans are responsible beings yet at the same time recognized the widespread infirmities that plague much of humanity through no fault of their own. His solution was to place his trust in the wisdom and goodness of our heavenly Father, who will one day separate our true character, that for which we are properly responsible, from the psychological, emotional, environmental and physiological baggage we have involuntarily inherited. This is a profoundly compassionate and balanced perspective that avoids the all-too-common extremes of our day: a rigid moralism on the one hand, which largely ignores the influence of infirmities, and different forms of psychological and behavioristic determinism on the other, which downplay or altogether deny the existence of moral responsibility. Lewis provides a characteristically appealing via media that strikes just the right balance.

Schaeffer and Lewis show us in their own distinctive ways that apologetics must be saturated with compassion and pastoral wisdom if our message is to be attractive. All too often apologetic arguments are marshaled with polemical venom and little apparent concern for the ultimate well-being of the listener. Our apologists, by contrast, are excellent models of how a keen mind and warm heart can combine for a powerful apologetic presence.

19. Flexibility and versatility. John Frame, professor of apologetics and systematic theology at Westminster Theological Seminary in California, believes Schaeffer's most important contribution was his ability to bring the full spectrum of reality into the apologetic arena.[39] From biology to business, philosophy to physics, ecology to engineering, Schaeffer consistently displayed remarkable flexibility and versatility in his quest to meet a wide range of people on their own turf.

Schaeffer firmly believed that apologetics must be a person-relative enterprise. Each individual is unique, so no single argument will work with everybody. This is undoubtedly a poignant word in light of our highly diverse culture. We can be sure that a canned apologetic that largely ignores personal considerations will stall more often than not. What we need now more than ever is a nonmechanical method, one that can be tailored to the specific needs and interests of each individual.

Here again, the cumulative case approach is well-suited to meet this need. It is an inherently flexible model that provides for a good deal of creativity and adaptation. As we have seen, this approach is much like assembling a jigsaw puzzle. There is only one ultimate pattern, but a variety of angles from which construction can begin. With one person we might start at the bottom, in which case a landscape will naturally emerge first. With someone else we might start from above, in which case a cluster of clouds and a vivid blue sky will initially appear. Ultimately, however, despite the direction from which we start, all the pieces will need to be set in place if we are to be thoroughly converted and the complete picture is to crystallize. Such a model clearly offers the flexibility and versatility needed to forge a compassionate, person-relative apologetic for the twenty-first century.

20. The final apologetic. While Schaeffer's apologetic arguments and cultural commentary have elicited a wide variety of responses throughout evangelicalism, there is one feature of his ministry that has evoked nearly unanimous favor, namely, his captivating emphasis on community. Even Jack Rogers, one of Schaeffer's stiffest critics, has noted that he finds the Schaeffers' "arguments exasperating, but the description of life at L'Abri exhilarating."[40] The L'Abri community is in many ways a microcosm of what the church ought to be. It combines spiritual formation, intellectual stimulation, holy living, ethnic diversity, shared responsibility and mutual interdependency. It is a fertile context for engaging the whole person.

Some of Schaeffer's most passionate writing revolved around this topic. He boldly challenged his readers to open their homes in hospitality. He explained that most of his and Edith's wedding presents were destroyed during L'Abri's first three years. Their linens were ripped. Cigarettes seared their rugs. Diseased teenagers slept in their beds. It was this bank of real-life authenticity that enabled Schaeffer to speak with such force on these issues. Consider his rebuke to white evangelical complacency: "In the past year, how many blacks have you fed at your dinner table? How many blacks have felt at home in your home? And if you haven't had any blacks in your home, shut up about the blacks."[41]

Schaeffer was convinced that Christians are called to be a counterculture, a revolutionary organism that faithfully models individual and corporate spirituality that is radically different from what the secular world has to offer. If the world does not see this in the Christian community, then our claims to credibility will have very little force. In fact, Schaeffer tells us on the basis of John 13 that if the world does not see profound loving relationships among the brethren, they have the right to judge not only the faith of those believers but the truth claims of Christianity as well. The final apologetic for Schaeffer was the beautiful exhibition of Christian community. This is a model worth emulating.

21. The final reality. Love is the final apologetic. Schaeffer made it utterly clear that this kind of love is of a distinctly Christian variety. It is not a mere "humanistic, romantic oneness among men in general."[42] Rather, it is the same kind of love that Jesus showed his followers. For Christians this is nothing less than the same kind of love demonstrated by the Son of God incarnate. But there is more. The love Christians are to demonstrate and exemplify is ultimately the same kind of love that the Father had for his Son from all eternity. This love should produce a unity among Christians that is nothing less than an image of the unity of the Trinity. Schaeffer cited in this connection John 17:21, a part of Jesus' high-priestly prayer: "that all of them may be one, Father, just as you are in me and I am in you. May they also be in us so that the world may believe that you have sent me."

The flow of love is as follows. From all of eternity, there was love and unity among the Persons of the Trinity. Then, the Son of God incarnate loved his disciples with the same kind of love with which his Father loved him before the world was created. Next, the disciples are commanded to love each other as Christ loved them. Thus, their love should model and display the eternal love of the Trinity. The final apologetic is finally nothing less than the breathtaking notion that the ultimate reality of Trinitarian relationship and love should be on display among Christians.

Indeed, the Trinitarian resources for making sense of personality is another important part of Schaeffer's apologetic. In *The God Who Is There* Schaeffer argued with great vigor that human personality could not be adequately explained if ultimate reality is impersonal. The impersonal plus time plus chance simply do not provide a plausible explanation for the existence of personality. By contrast, Christianity has a satisfactory answer to this otherwise mysterious phenomenon: "Within the Trinity, before the creation of anything, there was real love and real communication. Following on from this statement, the Bible states that this God who is personal created man in His own image. . . . He is the image of this kind of God, and so personality is intrinsic to his makeup. God is personal, and man is also personal."[43]

Not surprisingly, the same sort of emphasis is in Lewis. Indeed, the fourth book of *Mere Christianity* is entitled "Beyond Personality: or First Steps in the Doctrine of the Trinity." Lewis makes it immediately clear that what he means by going beyond personality is not reverting to impersonality, as is often the case when people say they do not believe in a personal God because they believe God is beyond personality. If God is impersonal, then he is less than we are. In Lewis's argument, the Christian view of God is the only option that explains how God can be beyond personality, that is, more than a person in the ordinary sense, without being impersonal. According to Christianity, there is only one God, but he exists in three eternal persons.

This conception of God makes sense of how human persons can be united to God while retaining their individual identity. By contrast, when pantheists try to explain how they are absorbed into God, it is like a drop of water falling into the ocean. All personal and individual identity is lost. "It is only the Christians who have any idea of how human souls can be taken into the life of God and yet remain themselves—in fact, be very much more themselves than they were before."[44]

Moreover, Lewis points out that the great idea that God is love is an implicitly trinitarian claim: for God's very nature to be love, he must contain at least two persons. "If God was a single person, then before the world was made, He was not love."[45] But Christians believe God did not only begin loving when the world was created. Rather, love is his eternal, essential nature. Christians "believe that the living, dynamic activity of love has been going on in God for ever and has created everything else."[46]

Lewis goes on to expound Christian life and experience in trinitarian terms. The whole offer of Christianity for Lewis is to share in the life of Christ, in fact to become "little Christs."[47] This means that the ultimate goal of the Christian life is to be taken up into the fellowship of the Trinity. This is salvation and this is eternal life. Lewis makes this point in his characteristically inviting way:

> The whole dance, or drama, or pattern of this three-Personal life is to be played out in each of us: or (putting it the other way round) each one of us has got to enter that pattern, take his place in that dance. There is no other way to the happiness for which we were made. . . . If you want joy, power, peace, eternal life, you must get close to, or even into, the thing that has them. . . . They are a great fountain of energy and beauty spurting up at the very center of reality. If you are close to it, the spray will wet you: if you are not, you will remain dry.[48]

In short, the joy of eternal life is to partake of the joyous life of the source of life himself, the triune God. The doctrine of the Trinity not only explains where we came from (personality), it also tells us where we are going.

Thus in the Christian view, love, communication, personality and relationship go down to the very bottom of reality. They are not newcomers that emerged accidentally from an impersonal source. We earlier stressed the power of a relational model for theology and apologetics. The ultimate reason for this emphasis has now emerged. The Trinity is relational. A relational apologetic flows naturally from a theology that is fully and consciously Trinitarian. This is the radiant vision we must communicate to our age. Nothing less will illuminate the shadowlands of this shrouded world. Nothing less will disclose the breathtaking final reality of the infinite-personal, triune God who is there.

Notes

Introduction

[1]C. S. Lewis, "Learning in War-Time," in *The Weight of Glory and Other Addresses* (New York: Collier, 1980), p. 28.

[2]Francis Schaeffer, *The God Who Is There*, vol. 1, bk. 1 of *The Complete Works of Francis A. Schaeffer* (Westchester, Ill.: Crossway, 1982), p. 11.

[3]John G. Stackhouse, "By Their Books Ye Shall Know Them," *Christianity Today* 40, no. 10 (September 16, 1996): 59.

[4]C. S. Lewis, "De Descriptione Temporum," in *They Asked for a Paper* (London: Geoffrey Bles, 1962), p. 25.

[5]Personal communication from Chris Mitchell, director of the Marion E. Wade Center at Wheaton College, Wheaton, Ill., April 1996.

[6]Two of the most intriguing Lewis web sites are "C. S. Lewis and the Inklings Home Page" (http://ernie.bgsu.edu/~edwards/lewis.html) and "Into the Wardrobe: The C. S. Lewis WWW Page" (http://c.s.lewis.cache.net).

[7]Bruce Edwards, "Lewis Redux: A Postmodern Dialogue," posted on the "C. S. Lewis and the Inklings Home Page."

[8]Michael Maudlin, "1993 Christianity Today Book Awards," *Christianity Today* 37, no. 4 (April 5, 1993): 28.

[9]J. I. Packer, foreword to *Reflections on Francis Schaeffer*, ed. Ronald W. Ruegsegger (Grand Rapids, Mich.: Zondervan, 1986), p. 16.

[10]Personal communication from Dick Keyes, Wilmore, Ky., July 26, 1996.

[11]Personal communication from James Albritton, April 1996.

[12]Personal communication from Lane Dennis, Wheaton, Ill., April 1996.

[13]Michael S. Hamilton, "The Dissatisfaction of Francis Schaeffer," *Christianity Today* 41, no. 3 (March 3, 1997): 22.

[14]Jeff Jordan, "Not in Kansas Anymore," in *God and the Philosophers*, ed. Thomas V. Morris (New York: Oxford University Press), p. 132.

[15]See Jerry L. Walls, "On Keeping the Faith," in *God and the Philosophers*, ed. Thomas V. Morris (New York: Oxford University Press), pp. 102-12.

[16]Thomas V. Morris, "Suspicions of Something More," in *God and the Philosophers*, ed. Thomas V. Morris (New York: Oxford University Press), p. 14.

[17]Thomas Oden has coined the term *paleo-orthodoxy* to distinguish those who adhere to historic Christian orthodoxy in the "ancient (paleo) ecumenical sense" from "the modern (Bultmannian-Tillichian-Niebuhrian) theological tradition of neo-orthodoxy" (*The Challenge of Postmodernism* [Wheaton, Ill.: Victor, 1995], p. 398). It is our suspicion that Lewis would have resonated with this terminology. In an interview with David Soper, which appeared in *Zion's Herald* magazine in 1948, Lewis first learned of the term *evangelical*. When Soper explained why American leaders had developed the term (to distance themselves from rigid fundamentalism on the right and extreme liberalism on the left), Lewis replied by saying a better term would have been "Classical Christianity." For our purposes, *paleo-orthodoxy* and *Classical Christianity* are synonymous terms. Both refer to a Christian orthodoxy that is grounded in Scripture and summarized by the ancient ecumenical creedal statements of the patristic church

(e.g., the Apostles', Nicene and Athanasian creeds).

[18]The front line of theistic philosophy was so thin in the fifties that well-known atheist Antony Flew felt compelled to engage the popular philosophy of C. S. Lewis in a significant, groundbreaking volume entitled *New Essays in Philosophical Theology*, ed. Antony Flew and Alasdair MacIntyre (New York: Macmillan, 1964).

[19]Stackhouse, "By Their Books," p. 59.

[20]Richard John Neuhaus, "The Schaeffer Legacy," *First Things*, no. 34 (June/July 1993): 64. Prison Fellowship founder Charles Colson, who teamed with Neuhaus to produce the highly acclaimed *Evangelicals and Catholics Together* (Dallas: Word, 1995), is one such evangelical friend indebted to both apologists. Colson, who was voted "favorite living author" by *Christianity Today* readers in 1993, was deeply affected by Lewis's *Mere Christianity* during his Watergate imprisonment and has called Schaeffer "one of the great prophets of the twentieth century" (*Evangelicals and Catholics Together*, p. 29).

[21]The shunning of Schaeffer by evangelical academicians stretches across a wide variety of disciplines, while the ambivalence toward Lewis is primarily contained to philosophical and theological circles. The words of James L. Sauer, a librarian by trade and an editor of the journal *Touchstone*, illustrate the embarrassment of many evangelical scholars to acknowledge their indebtedness to Schaeffer: "I hesitate to mention the effect that Francis Schaeffer's work had on my worldview. (He's out of favor with some brainy evangelicals—too simplistic, too right wing.)" On the other hand, Sauer has no problem praising Lewis: "I cannot say enough about the influence of C. S. Lewis on my mind and imagination. (I guess I join the throngs of Lewisian Evangelicaland, with membership card and Narnia decoder ring.) I was let into a world of books, ideas, apologetics, romanticism, mere Christianity, creativity, redeemed rationalism, and freedom in Christian thought" (*Touchstone* 9, no. 2 [Spring 1996]: 48).

[22]Thomas V. Morris, review of *C. S. Lewis and the Search for Rational Religion* by John Beversluis, *Faith and Philosophy* 5, no. 3 (July 1988): 319.

[23]Bob Fryling detailed the shift from modernity to postmodernity in a helpful paper delivered to the International Fellowship of Evangelical Students World Assembly in 1995.

[24]See J. Richard Middleton and Brian J. Walsh, *Truth Is Stranger Than It Used To Be* (Downers Grove, Ill.: InterVarsity Press, 1996), pp. 69-79, for a fuller explication of the postmodern incredulity toward metanarratives.

[25]William J. Abraham, "C. S. Lewis and the Conversion of the West," in *Permanent Things*, ed. Andrew A. Tadie and Michael H. Macdonald (Grand Rapids, Mich.: Eerdmans, 1995), p. 271.

[26]See Timothy R. Phillips and Dennis L. Okholm, eds., *Christian Apologetics in the Postmodern World* (Downers Grove, Ill.: InterVarsity Press, 1995), and David S. Dockery, ed., *The Challenge of Postmodernism: An Evangelical Engagement* (Wheaton, Ill.: BridgePoint/Victor, 1995).

[27]William Lane Craig, *Reasonable Faith* (Wheaton, Ill.: Crossway, 1994), p. xv.

[28]C. S. Lewis, "Christian Apologetics," in *God in the Dock* (Grand Rapids, Mich.: Eerdmans, 1970), p. 92.

Chapter 1: The Biographical Foundation

[1]C. S. Lewis, *Surprised by Joy* (New York: Harcourt Brace, 1956), pp. 228-29.

[2]Francis A. Schaeffer, preface to *True Spirituality*, vol. 3, bk. 2 of *The Complete Works of Francis A. Schaeffer* (Westchester, Ill.: Crossway, 1982), pp. 195-96.

[3]Edith Schaeffer, *The Tapestry* (Waco, Tex.: Word, 1984), p. 37.

[4]"The Nation," *Time* 82, no. 22 (November 29, 1963): 38.

[5]George Sayer, *Jack: C. S. Lewis and His Times* (San Francisco: Harper & Row, 1988), p. 17.

[6]Lewis, *Surprised by Joy*, p. 6.

[7]Ibid.

[8]Ibid., p. 7.

[9]Ibid.

[10]Ibid., p. 12.

[11]Ibid., p. 10.

[12]Ibid., pp. 14-15.

[13]Readers of *Surprised by Joy* might be unfamiliar with these boarding-school names since Lewis felt it necessary to use fictitious names in many cases. Consequently, Belsen is really Wynyard, Chartres is Cherbourg House, and Wyvern is Malvern.

[14]Lewis, *Surprised by Joy*, p. 61.

[15]Ibid., p. 62.

[16]Ibid., pp. 63-65.

[17]Ibid., p. 133.

[18]According to Paul F. Ford, Digory Kirke is a combination of Kirkpatrick and Lewis himself. See *Companion to Narnia* (New York: HarperCollins, 1994), p. 142. This would explain the professor's commitment to reason within a supernatural framework.

[19]C. S. Lewis, *The Lion, the Witch and the Wardrobe* (New York: Collier, 1970), p. 45.

[20]Lewis, *Surprised by Joy*, p. 170.

[21]Ibid., p. 181.

[22]When Lewis joined the Cambridge faculty, he chose to commute rather than sell his home in Oxford.

[23]Lewis was not only inept with tools, he was also woeful in mathematics. He passed all his Oxford entrance exams with flying colors, except the one dealing with basic math. His stint in the service proved to be the saving grace. Upon his return to Oxford, after two years of service during World War I, he learned that veterans would not be required to take "Responsions," the exam he had failed. If it were not for this exemption, Lewis most likely would have never finished at Oxford.

[24]Lewis, *Surprised by Joy*, pp. 207-8.

[25]Ibid., p. 207.

[26]Ibid., pp. 208-9.

[27]Ibid., p. 225.

[28]Ibid., pp. 228-29.

[29]Ibid., p. 237.

[30]Sayer, *Jack*, pp. 134-35.

[31]Bruce L. Edwards, "A Modest Literary Biography and Bibliography," posted on the "C. S. Lewis and the Inklings Home Page."

[32]Lyle W. Dorsett, *The Essential C. S. Lewis* (New York: Collier, 1988), p. 8.

[33]Ibid., p. 3.

[34]C. S. Lewis, *The Pilgrim's Regress* (Grand Rapids, Mich.: Eerdmans, 1992), p. 200.

[35]C. S. Lewis, *Letters of C. S. Lewis*, ed. W. H. Lewis (London: Geoffrey Bles, 1966), p. 167.

[36]See an exchange between Sherwood Wirt of the Billy Graham Evangelistic Association and C. S. Lewis in *God in the Dock* (Grand Rapids, Mich.: Eerdmans, 1970), p. 267.

[37]Although Lewis has often be criticized for his lack of philosophical acumen, Thomas Talbott is one professional philosopher who offers Lewis high praise. In reference to *The Problem of Pain*, Talbott writes, "I have yet to encounter a more convincing piece of Christian philosophy written during the first half of this century; it anticipates John Hick's 'soul-making' theodicy and sets forth clearly some of the assumptions behind Alvin Plantinga's Free Will Defense" (from "C. S. Lewis and the Problem of Evil," *Christian Scholar's Review* 17, no. 1 [September 1987]: 37).

[38]For an interesting philosophical discussion on the debate between Anscombe and Lewis, see Victor Reppert, "The Lewis-Anscombe Controversy: A Discussion of the Issues," *Christian Scholar's Review* 19, no. 1 (September 1989): 32-48.

[39]Sayer, *Jack*, p. 189.

[40]Those who doubt the stability of Lewis's faith at the end of his life are encouraged to read *Letters to Malcolm: Chiefly on Prayer* (New York: Harcourt, Brace and World, 1964), written

the year of his death and published posthumously.

[41]Peter Kreeft, C. S. Lewis for the Third Millennium (San Francisco: Ignatius, 1994), p. 9.

[42]E. Schaeffer, Tapestry, p. 37.

[43]Ibid.

[44]Ibid., pp. 42-43.

[45]Ibid., p. 51.

[46]Ibid., p. 52. See also Lane T. Dennis, "Conversion in an Evangelical Context: A Study in the Micro-sociology of Religion," Ph.D. diss., Northwestern University, 1980, pp. 125-49, for some interesting parallels between Schaeffer's conversion and Thomas Kuhn's theory of paradigm shifts.

[47]Ibid., p. 54.

[48]Ibid., p. 62.

[49]Ibid., pp. 122-23.

[50]Ibid., pp. 131-32.

[51]Ibid.

[52]This denomination later became known as the Orthodox Presbyterian Church.

[53]E. Schaeffer, Tapestry, p. 200.

[54]Jerram Barrs, St. Louis and the Beginnings of Children for Christ, audiotape of a lecture presented at Covenant Theological Seminary, September 21, 1989 (St. Louis: Covenant Seminary Electronic Media Ministries, 1992).

[55]The International Council of Christian Churches was a fledgling separatist movement that sought to preserve the purity of fundamentalist Reformed doctrine.

[56]F. Schaeffer, preface to True Spirituality, pp. 195-96.

[57]In Letters of Francis A. Schaeffer (Westchester, Ill.: Crossway, 1985), Schaeffer describes this hayloft experience as seeing "a little blazing glory of God" (p. 14). These words are reminiscent of an experience Blaise Pascal once called his "Night of Fire." Coincidentally, both men were thirty-nine years old at the time of their respective illuminations. Schaeffer, however, was extremely cautious when he spoke of this experience. He did not want his Reformed colleagues to think he was proclaiming a second work of grace or some sort of mystical experience. He simply came to see the power of the reality of Christ in his day-to-day existence.

[58]E. Schaeffer, Tapestry, p. 387.

[59]Michael S. Hamilton, "The Dissatisfaction of Francis Schaeffer," Christianity Today 41, no. 3 (March 3, 1997): 25.

[60]Francis A. Schaeffer, Introduction to Francis Schaeffer (Downers Grove, Ill.: InterVarsity Press, 1974), p. 36.

[61]Hamilton, "Dissatisfaction of Francis Schaeffer," p. 25.

[62]Ibid., p. 26.

[63]Cal Thomas, "Francis August Schaeffer: Crusader for Truth," Fundamentalist Journal 3, no. 7 (July/August 1984): 47-48.

[64]Francis A. Schaeffer, "Concerning the Books by Francis and Edith Schaeffer," in Genesis in Space and Time (Downers Grove, Ill.: InterVarsity Press, 1972), p. 163.

[65]E. Schaeffer, Tapestry, p. 106.

[66]Richard John Neuhaus, the 1997 Asbury Theological Seminary Theta Phi lecturer, made this assertion during a lecture in Asbury's Estes Chapel in Wilmore, Ky., March 6, 1997.

[67]The Mark of the Christian was originally published in 1970. The inclusion of this piece in The Great Evangelical Disaster was simply a reaffirmation of Schaeffer's longstanding commitment to speaking the truth in love.

[68]Thomas, "Francis August Schaeffer: Crusader for Truth," p. 49.

[69]Vernon C. Grounds, "A Friend of Many Years Remembers Francis Schaeffer," Christianity Today 28, no. 9 (June 15, 1984): 62.

[70]Philip Yancey, "Schaeffer on Schaeffer, Part 2," Christianity Today 23, no. 13 (April 6, 1979): 25-26.

[71]Peter van Inwagen, "Quam Dilecta," in *God and the Philosophers*, ed. Thomas V. Morris (New York: Oxford University Press), p. 33.

[72]Despite these points of contrast in the realm of family life, there are a few interesting similarities under this rubric as well. First, Schaeffer and Lewis, who are known to many for their cerebral apologetic, were both extremely effective at reaching children. The Schaeffers worked extensively with youngsters during their early ministry, and Lewis skillfully crafted the influential Narnia tales and carried on correspondence with many precocious readers.

A few geographical connections between Lewis and Schaeffer are worth mentioning as well. Edith traces her roots on her father's side back to County Down, Ireland, the stomping grounds of C. S. Lewis. Also, one of Schaeffer's daughters, Susan, used to live on the same street as Lewis during a stint in Oxford. Today she and her husband, Ranald Macaulay, a Cambridge graduate, direct the English L'Abri. They have a daughter who, at a Cambridge high school, teaches English literature and Shakespeare—subjects another Cambridge instructor once taught quite admirably. (From Edith Schaeffer, letter to one of the authors, January 17, 1997.)

Chapter 2: The Nature of Salvation

[1]C. S. Lewis, *Mere Christianity* (New York: Macmillan, 1960), p. 176.

[2]Francis A. Schaeffer, *Basic Bible Studies*, vol. 2, bk. 4 of *The Complete Works of Francis A. Schaeffer* (Westchester, Ill.: Crossway, 1982), pp. 358-59.

[3]The Westminster Confession of Faith (PCA) 17.1, 2a.

[4]Lewis, *Mere Christianity*, p. 6.

[5]Ibid., p. 8.

[6]Francis A. Schaeffer, *The Great Evangelical Disaster* (Wheaton, Ill.: Crossway, 1984), p. 72.

[7]Ibid., p. 74.

[8]Lewis, *Mere Christianity*, p. 57.

[9]Schaeffer, *Great Evangelical Disaster*, p. 46.

[10]Clark Pinnock, "Assessing the Apologetics of C. S. Lewis," *The Canadian C. S. Lewis Journal*, Spring 1995, p. 13.

[11]C. S. Lewis, "Christianity and Literature," in *Christian Reflections* (Grand Rapids, Mich.: Eerdmans, 1967), p. 10.

[12]Ibid., p. 14.

[13]Os Guinness, conversation with the authors, Wilmore, Ky., November 21, 1996.

[14]Francis A. Schaeffer, *True Spirituality*, vol. 3, bk. 2 of *The Complete Works of Francis A. Schaeffer* (Westchester, Ill.: Crossway, 1982), p. 268.

[15]Ibid., p. 235.

[16]Schaeffer, *Basic Bible Studies*, p. 348.

[17]Ibid., p. 349.

[18]Schaeffer, *True Spirituality*, p. 267.

[19]Ibid.

[20]Francis A. Schaeffer, *Doctrinal Series: Justification*, audiotape, catalog no. 109.3 (Michigan City, Ind.: L'Abri Cassettes).

[21]Schaeffer, *Basic Bible Studies*, p. 349.

[22]Francis A. Schaeffer, *Letters of Francis A. Schaeffer*, ed. Lane T. Dennis (Wheaton, Ill.: Crossway, 1985), p. 127.

[23]Ibid., p. 126.

[24]Schaeffer, *True Spirituality*, p. 268.

[25]Schaeffer, *Basic Bible Studies*, p. 361.

[26]Ibid., p. 363.

[27]Ibid., pp. 350-54.

[28]Schaeffer, *True Spirituality*, p. 295.

[29]Ibid. Schaeffer thought Wesley's aspiration for sanctification was on target but "his theology

in this area was mistaken and he used wrong terminology." It is not clear that Schaeffer understood Wesley's teaching on the subject of entire sanctification and Christian perfection. Wesley's teaching on this subject will inevitably be misunderstood when interpreted through a legal lens instead of an ethical one. Wesley did not believe we can reach an outward state of perfection in this life. This will never be the case since fallen humans are saddled with a variety of emotional, psychological and physical infirmities. Complete perfection will come only at glorification. But Wesley did believe the Holy Spirit could and does purify and perfect the heart of the believer by faith in this life, enabling the entirely sanctified Christian to live a life of perfect love in terms of intent but not outcome. For further study on Wesley's teaching on entire sanctification, see Thomas C. Oden, *John Wesley's Scriptural Christianity: A Plain Exposition of His Teaching on Christian Doctrine* (Grand Rapids, Mich.: Zondervan, 1994), and Kenneth J. Collins, *A Faithful Witness: John Wesley's Homiletical Theology* (Wilmore, Ky.: Wesley Heritage, 1993).

[30]Schaeffer, *True Spirituality*, p. 244.

[31]Schaeffer, *Basic Bible Studies*, p. 365.

[32]Lewis, *Mere Christianity*, p. 8.

[33]C. S. Lewis, *Letters of C. S. Lewis*, ed. W. H. Lewis (London: Geoffrey Bles, 1966), p. 198.

[34]In *Iustitia Dei: A History of the Christian Doctrine of Justification* (London: Cambridge University Press, 1986), 2:1-3, Alister McGrath points out that the formal distinction between justification and sanctification grew out of the Protestant Reformation. McGrath argues that Augustine did not make this distinction but rather considered sanctification an essential component of justification. It is worth noting that Lewis appears to be articulating a perspective that resonates with the classical, catholic perspective of Augustine, while Schaeffer insists on the distinctly Protestant formulation.

[35]Lewis certainly believed that divine forgiveness is a part of salvation, but he did not believe that it is God's primary purpose. He thought the purpose of salvation is to transform sinful humans into holy creatures capable of relating to their Creator and enjoying the eternal bliss of heaven.

[36]C. S. Lewis, *The Problem of Pain* (New York: Macmillan, 1962), p. 61.

[37]Lewis, *Mere Christianity*, p. 59.

[38]Ibid., p. 172.

[39]Edgar William Boss, "The Theology of C. S. Lewis" (Th.D. diss., Northern Baptist Theological Seminary, 1948). Boss misrepresents Lewis's view of the atonement by calling it an "Example Theory."

[40]Lewis, *Mere Christianity*, p. 129.

[41]Ibid., p. 59.

[42]Ibid., p. 60.

[43]C. S. Lewis, *Letters to Malcolm: Chiefly on Prayer* (New York: Harcourt, Brace and World, 1964), pp. 108-9.

[44]Lewis, *Mere Christianity*, p. 59.

[45]Ibid., p. 60.

[46]C. S. Lewis, *The Great Divorce* (New York: Macmillan, 1946), pp. 99-100.

[47]Ibid., p. 100.

[48]Ibid., pp. 104-5.

[49]It is worth noting that Lewis paints a picture of the ransom theory of the atonement in *The Lion, the Witch and the Wardrobe,* but the transformational model is threaded throughout his overtly theological and apologetic works.

[50]Schaeffer, *Basic Bible Studies*, pp. 358-59.

[51]Lewis, *Mere Christianity*, p. 176.

Chapter 3: God's Sovereignty and Human Significance

[1]C. S. Lewis, *Letters of C. S. Lewis*, ed. W. H. Lewis (London: Geoffrey Bles, 1966), p. 252.

[2]Francis A. Schaeffer, *True Spirituality*, vol. 3, bk. 2 of *The Complete Works of Francis A. Schaeffer* (Westchester, Ill.: Crossway, 1982), p. 305.

[3]The Westminster Confession of Faith (PCA) 3.1.

[4]Edith Schaeffer, *The Tapestry* (Waco, Tex.: Word, 1984), pp. 189-90.

[5]William Hasker, *Metaphysics: Constructing a World View* (Downers Grove, Ill.: InterVarsity Press, 1983), p. 40.

[6]The paradigms of hard determinism, soft determinism (compatibilism) and libertarianism are commonly accepted categories of thought in contemporary philosophy of religion. William Hasker's definitions are cited throughout this chapter, but comparable discussion of this subject can be found in a host of basic texts, including Richard Taylor, *Metaphysics*, 4th ed. (Englewood Cliffs, N.J.: Prentice-Hall, 1992), and William Halverson, *A Concise Introduction to Philosophy* (New York: Random House, 1972).

[7]Hasker, *Metaphysics*, p. 32.

[8]Ibid.

[9]See Stewart C. Goetz, "A Noncausal Theory of Agency," *Philosophy and Phenomenological Research* 49, no. 2 (December 1988): 303-16, and "Libertarian Choice," *Faith and Philosophy* 14, no. 2 (April 1997): 195-211.

[10]Hasker, *Metaphysics*, p. 33.

[11]Hard determinism and libertarian freedom are both examples of "incompatibilism," since each position affirms the mutual exclusivity of complete determinism and freedom. Soft determinism, on the other hand, is often called "compatibilism," since this paradigm harmonizes a notion of complete determinism with a form of freedom.

[12]Francis A. Schaeffer, *Our System of Doctrine*, adapted from a paper read at the General Synod of the Bible Presbyterian Church (Philadelphia: Publications Committee of the Bible Presbyterian Church, 1942), p. 1.

[13]Francis A. Schaeffer, *God's Sovereignty and Man's Significance*, audiotape, catalog nos. 101.1 and 101.2 (Michigan City, Ind.: L'Abri Cassettes).

[14]Francis A. Schaeffer, *No Little People*, vol. 3, bk. 1 of *The Complete Works of Francis A. Schaeffer* (Westchester, Ill.: Crossway, 1982), p. 146.

[15]Schaeffer, *God's Sovereignty and Man's Significance*.

[16]Ibid.

[17]Ibid.

[18]The Westminster Confession of Faith (PCA) 3.3.

[19]Ibid., 3.7.

[20]James B. Hurley, "Schaeffer on Evangelicalism," in *Reflections on Francis Schaeffer*, ed. Ronald W. Ruegsegger (Grand Rapids, Mich.: Zondervan, 1986), p. 272.

[21]Francis A. Schaeffer, *Doctrinal Series: Assurance*, audiotape, catalog no. 112.1 (Michigan City, Ind.: L'Abri Cassettes).

[22]Schaeffer, *God's Sovereignty and Man's Significance*.

[23]A quick glance at the index to *The Complete Works of Francis A. Schaeffer* reveals more than fifty references to freedom but no references to predestination or election.

[24]Schaeffer, *God's Sovereignty and Man's Significance*.

[25]Francis A. Schaeffer, *The God Who Is There*, vol. 1, bk. 1 of *The Complete Works of Francis A. Schaeffer* (Westchester, Ill.: Crossway, 1982), p. 113.

[26]Schaeffer, *True Spirituality*, p. 305.

[27]It should be noted that Schaeffer and Lewis never used the terms *libertarian freedom* and *compatibilism*. Consequently, some might suggest that we are thrusting categories of thought upon these men. Though we are sensitive to such concerns, in this instance such a charge can hardly stick. All that is meant by "libertarian freedom" is the power of contrary choice, and Schaeffer's insistence on a nondetermined, first-cause choice makes it quite clear that libertarianism is the type of freedom he has in mind, even if he was not acquainted with the term.

[28]Schaeffer, *God's Sovereignty and Man's Significance*.

[29]Ibid.

[30]Ibid.

[31]Ibid.

[32]C. S. Lewis, *Surprised by Joy* (New York: Harcourt Brace, 1956), p. 32.

[33]C. S. Lewis, *Mere Christianity* (New York: Macmillan, 1960), pp. 177-80.

[34]Ibid., p. 178.

[35]Ibid., p. 179.

[36]Indeed, this is further proof that Lewis was a libertarian. A soft determinist would not see complete foreknowledge as a threat since compatibilistic freedom does not require the power of contrary choice. Those who challenge the notion of complete foreknowledge generally do so on the grounds that it somehow precludes the possibility of choosing otherwise.

[37]C. S. Lewis, *The Screwtape Letters* (New York: Bantam, 1982), p. 80.

[38]For a more detailed discussion of this point, see Lewis's *The Discarded Image* (London: Cambridge University Press, 1964), pp. 88-89.

[39]Lewis, *Screwtape Letters*, p. 81.

[40]Lewis traces the "Eternal Now" position to Boethius (*Screwtape Letters*, p. 81), but Thomas Morris identifies the roots of this position with pre-Christian philosophical sources like Plotinus, the Neo-Platonists and Parmenides. See *Our Idea of God* (Notre Dame, Ind.: University of Notre Dame Press, 1991), p. 121.

[41]C. S. Lewis, *Miracles* (New York: Macmillan, 1978), p. 175.

[42]Ibid., p. 181.

[43]Lewis, *Letters of C. S. Lewis*, pp. 251-52.

[44]C. S. Lewis, *Letters to Malcolm: Chiefly on Prayer* (New York: Harcourt, Brace and World, 1964), pp. 49-50.

[45]C. S. Lewis, *Surprised by Joy*, p. 224.

[46]Ibid., pp. 224-25.

[47]Lewis, *Letters of C. S. Lewis*, p. 252.

[48]Ibid.

[49]Ibid., p. 245.

[50]Ibid., p. 252. Though Lewis does not explicitly indicate what he means by the "other view," it appears he has some form of Arminianism in mind.

Chapter 4: Evaluating the Mystery Maneuver

[1]C. S. Lewis, *The Problem of Pain* (New York: Macmillan, 1962), p. 28.

[2]Francis A. Schaeffer, *The God Who Is There*, vol. 1, bk. 1 of *The Complete Works of Francis A. Schaeffer* (Westchester, Ill.: Crossway, 1982), p. 121.

[3]David Basinger, "Biblical Paradox: Does Revelation Challenge Logic?" *Journal of Evangelical Theological Education* 30, no. 2 (June 1987): 213.

[4]Frank Schaeffer, *Portofino* (New York: Berkley Books, 1996), pp. 128-29.

[5]Ibid., pp. 129-30.

[6]Ibid., p. 131.

[7]Ibid., p. 132.

[8]Ibid.

[9]Frank Schaeffer, letter to one of the authors, November 23, 1996.

[10]Schaeffer, *The God Who Is There*, p. 100.

[11]Basinger, "Biblical Paradox: Does Revelation Challenge Logic?" p. 205.

[12]For a collection of rigorous essays concerning the logical coherence of key Christian doctrines, see Ronald J. Feenstra and Cornelius Plantinga Jr., eds., *Trinity, Incarnation and Atonement* (Notre Dame, Ind.: University of Notre Dame Press, 1989). For an excellent book-length treatment of the Incarnation in particular, see Thomas V. Morris, *Logic of God Incarnate* (Ithaca, N.Y.: Cornell University Press, 1986).

[13]Richard P. Feynman, *QED: The Strange Theory of Light and Matter* (Princeton, N.J.: Princeton

University Press, 1985), p. 37.

[14]Dick Keyes, director of the Southborough (Massachusetts) branch of L'Abri, indicated in a conversation with the authors (Wilmore, Ky., July 26, 1996) that Schaeffer never rejected any portion of the Westminster Confession. Keyes did, however, say that Schaeffer was uncomfortable with the "overly mechanical" language the divines used at times. This might explain why Schaeffer endorsed the Synod Statement of the International Presbyterian Church (July 11, 1981), a document designed to supplement, but not contradict, the teaching of the Westminster Confession. The statement reads:

1. We believe that the existence and character of the infinite and personal God is the only basis for affirming human responsibility.
2. We reject any statement of the doctrine of God's sovereignty which makes it seem that an emphasis on the real significance of man's choice is a denial of God's sovereignty or vice versa.
3. We believe that the difficulty of this question is one which is true of all of our knowledge. For example, in science, even though our understanding increases with increased information, we will never comprehend the infinite. Similarly in thinking about God and man we have simply to affirm that man is fully responsible and that God is fully sovereign.
4. We reject all statements that affirm or imply that God is the author of evil, or wills human sin, or that history is the unrolling of a divine determinism.

Though this statement was designed to clarify the work of the Westminster divines, it clearly reflects Schaeffer's paradoxical position—a definite departure from the compatibilistic teaching of the Westminster Confession.

[15]The Westminster Confession of Faith (PCA) 3.1.

[16]Schaeffer made a distinction between predestination and determinism. Presumably he thought a personal cause was somehow less problematic than an impersonal cause. But it does not matter if the sufficient cause is personal or impersonal; if one cannot choose otherwise, the choice has been determined. In other words, there are important differences between theological determinism and naturalistic determinism. In the latter, impersonal laws of nature determine all events in an unbroken web. For the theological determinist, a personal God determines all things according to his will. But the point of emphasis is that each believes one can consistently affirm both freedom and complete determinism.

[17]William J. Abraham, *An Introduction to the Philosophy of Religion* (Englewood Cliffs, N.J.: Prentice-Hall, 1985), pp. 142-45.

[18]John Calvin, *Institutes of the Christian Religion*, ed. John T. McNeill, trans. Ford Lewis Battles (Philadelphia: Westminster Press, 1960), p. 957, as quoted in Abraham, *Introduction to the Philosophy of Religion*, p. 144.

[19]Prominent defenders of libertarian freedom in Christian philosophy include Alvin Plantinga, Richard Swinburne, Eleonore Stump, John Lucas, Peter van Inwagen, Stewart Goetz, Philip Quinn, William Lane Craig, Alan Donagan, Thomas Flint, Alfred Freddoso, Timothy O'Conner and William Hasker.

[20]Abraham, *Introduction to the Philosophy of Religion*, p. 146. Harry Frankfurt has recently, and ingeniously, argued that the power to choose otherwise (what he calls the Principle of Alternate Possibilities) is not required for moral responsibility. His interesting counterexamples to this principle do not bear on our case, for they have to do with unactualized potentialities that would have influenced the outcome of an event but in fact do not. In the Calvinistic view of predestination, people are unable to do otherwise than they do because they have in fact been determined by God. For an interesting discussion of Frankfurt, see Peter van Inwagen, *An Essay on Free Will* (Oxford: Clarendon, 1983), pp. 161-82. Van Inwagen argues that Frankfurt's counterexamples do not show that determinism and moral responsibility are compatible. The sort of freedom required for moral responsibility is such that when agents are "faced with having to choose among various incompatible courses of action, *each* of these courses of action is such that they can (are able to, have it within their power to) choose *it*" (p. 180).

[21]Ibid.

[22]Ibid., pp. 150-51.

[23]Francis A. Schaeffer, *True Spirituality*, vol. 3, bk. 2 of *The Complete Works of Francis A. Schaeffer* (Westchester, Ill.: Crossway, 1982), p. 305.

[24]R. K. McGregor Wright, *No Place for Sovereignty* (Downers Grove, Ill.: InterVarsity Press, 1996), p. 53.

[25]Ibid., p. 54.

[26]Cornelius Van Til, "The Apologetic Methodology of Francis A. Schaeffer" (unpublished paper, Westminster Theological Seminary Library, 1974), p. 31.

[27]For a philosophically informed view of why Calvinism requires some form of compatibilism or a rejection of human freedom altogether, see John S. Feinberg, "God, Freedom and Evil in Calvinist Thinking," in *The Grace of God, the Bondage of the Will*, ed. Thomas R. Schreiner and Bruce A. Ware (Grand Rapids, Mich.: Baker Book House, 1995), 2:459-83.

[28]Walter Hollenweger, *Evangelism Today: Good News or Bone of Contention?* (Belfast: Christian Journals, 1976), pp. 73-74.

[29]Francis A. Schaeffer, *God's Sovereignty and Man's Significance*, audiotape, catalog nos. 101.1 and 101.2 (Michigan City, Ind.: L'Abri Cassettes).

[30]Schaeffer, *The God Who Is There*, p. 121.

[31]Francis A. Schaeffer, *Escape from Reason*, vol. 1, bk. 2 of *The Complete Works of Francis A. Schaeffer* (Westchester, Ill.: Crossway, 1982), p. 231.

[32]Ibid.

[33]Schaeffer, *The God Who Is There*, p. 122.

[34]According to Richard Muller, an endorsement of middle knowledge would entail a concession on the part of the Reformed believer on "virtually all of the issues in debate" and would necessitate the adoption of an Arminian perspective. See *The Grace of God, the Bondage of the Will*, vol. 2, p. 265.

[35]C. S. Lewis, *Surprised by Joy* (New York: Harcourt Brace, 1956), p. 224.

[36]Ibid., pp. 224-25.

[37]C. S. Lewis, *God in the Dock* (Grand Rapids, Mich.: Eerdmans, 1970), p. 261.

[38]Schaeffer, *God's Sovereignty and Man's Significance*.

[39]Lewis, *Surprised by Joy*, pp. 224-25.

[40]Ibid., pp. 232-33.

[41]See *The Personal Heresy: A Controversy* (London: Oxford University Press, 1965). This work was jointly authored by Lewis and E. M. W. Tillyard.

[42]Lewis, *Surprised by Joy*, p. 224.

[43]Lewis, *Problem of Pain*, p. 28.

[44]C. S. Lewis, *Miracles* (New York: Macmillan, 1978), pp. 12-24.

[45]For a discussion of different theories of God's omniscience and omnipotence, see chapters 2 and 3 of Jerry L. Walls, *Hell: The Logic of Damnation* (Notre Dame, Ind.: University of Notre Dame Press, 1992).

[46]Os Guinness pointed out Schaeffer's pastoral strategy during a conversation with the authors, Wilmore, Ky., November 21, 1996.

[47]Schaeffer, *The God Who Is There*, p. 151.

[48]Of course we do not mean to suggest that apologetics is simply a game where the goal is to "outscore" or "outwit" the person with whom you are conversing.

[49]Schaeffer, *The God Who Is There*, p. 119.

[50]James Sire, telephone conversation with one of the authors, April 1996.

Chapter 5: Biblical Authority and Divine Inspiration

[1]Francis A. Schaeffer, *The Great Evangelical Disaster* (Wheaton, Ill.: Crossway, 1984), pp. 25-26.

[2]C. S. Lewis, *Letters of C. S. Lewis*, ed. W. H. Lewis (London: Geoffrey Bles, 1966), p. 287.

[3]The Chicago Statement on Biblical Inerrancy, Article 13, the Articles of Affirmation and Denial.

[4]Schaeffer, *Great Evangelical Disaster,* pp. 43-44.

[5]Ibid., p. 44.

[6]The defense of inerrancy is a common thread that binds the Schaeffer corpus. All five volumes of his *Complete Works* contain references to biblical inspiration. The second volume, entitled "The Christian View of the Bible as Truth,"offers an extensive treatment of the subject. *Great Evangelical Disaster,* his concluding commentary on the issue, was completed during the final weeks of his bout with cancer, two years after *The Complete Works* were published.

[7]It is worth noting that Lewis does not discuss the subject of biblical inspiration in *Mere Christianity,* the work many consider the definitive twentieth-century defense of the core tenets of historic Christian orthodoxy. When Lewis wrote this book, he asked four clergymen (Anglican, Presbyterian, Methodist and Roman Catholic) to critique the manuscript of book 2. In the preface he wrote, "The Methodist thought I had not said enough about Faith, and the Roman Catholic thought I had gone rather too far about the comparative unimportance of theories in explanation of the atonement. Otherwise all five of us were agreed" (p. 8). None of the clergy mentioned Lewis's silence on the issue of inspiration.

[8]For a brief introduction to Schaeffer's historical perspective on this issue, see Schaeffer's foreword to *The Foundation of Biblical Authority,* ed. James Montgomery Boice (Grand Rapids, Mich.: Zondervan, 1978), pp. 15-20. See also Forrest Baird, "Schaeffer's Intellectual Roots," in *Reflections on Francis Schaeffer,* ed. Ronald W. Ruegsegger (Grand Rapids, Mich.: Zondervan, 1986), pp. 45-67.

[9]Francis A. Schaeffer, *He Is There and He Is Not Silent,* vol. 1, bk. 3 of *The Complete Works of Francis A. Schaeffer* (Westchester, Ill.: Crossway, 1982), p. 305.

[10]Ibid., p. 345. It is interesting that throughout this appendix Schaeffer uses the term *infallibility* instead of *inerrancy. He Is There and He Is Not Silent* was originally published in 1972, a time when Schaeffer apparently still had confidence in the term communicating what he intended. Schaeffer eventually believed the term was co-opted by neo-evangelicals who accepted what he believed to be an inferior theory of inspiration. (See *Great Evangelical Disaster,* p. 57.) Though Schaeffer modified other portions of his original writings for the *Complete Works* edition, it is curious to note that he does not qualify the use of *infallibility* in this appendix.

[11]Ibid., p. 349.

[12]An Anselmian conception of God envisions a divine being who exhibits the greatest conceivable qualities to the fullest possible extent (e.g., all-powerful, all-loving, all-knowing). For a contemporary explication of perfect being theology, see chapter two of Thomas V. Morris, *Our Idea of God* (Notre Dame, Ind.: University of Notre Dame Press, 1991).

[13]Schaeffer, *He Is There and He Is Not Silent,* p. 347.

[14]Ibid.

[15]Francis A. Schaeffer, *No Final Conflict,* vol. 2, bk. 2 of *The Complete Works of Francis A. Schaeffer* (Westchester, Ill.: Crossway, 1982), p. 124.

[16]Schaeffer, *He Is There and He Is Not Silent,* p. 348.

[17]Ibid, p. 349.

[18]Schaeffer, *No Final Conflict,* p. 125.

[19]William J. Abraham, *Divine Revelation and the Limits of Historical Criticism* (New York: Oxford University Press, 1982), p. 39.

[20]Ibid.

[21]C. S. Lewis, "Modern Theology and Biblical Criticism," in *Christian Reflections* (Grand Rapids, Mich.: Eerdmans, 1967), p. 152.

[22]Ibid., p. 163.

[23]C. S. Lewis, *Reflections on the Psalms* (New York: Harcourt Brace, 1958), pp. 109-10.

[24]Harold Lindsell, *The Bible in the Balance* (Grand Rapids, Mich.: Zondervan, 1979),

pp. 286-87.

[25]Harold Lindsell, foreword to *The Best of C. S. Lewis* (Washington, D.C.: Canon, 1974), pp. vi-vii.

[26]Harold Lindsell, letter to *The Wittenburg Door,* no. 65 (February-March 1982): 15.

[27]Lewis, "Modern Theology and Biblical Criticism," p. 161.

[28]See Jerry L. Walls, "C. S. Lewis and Evangelical Ambivalence," *The Wittenburg Door,* no. 62 (August-September 1981): 20.

[29]C. S. Lewis, *The Problem of Pain* (New York: Macmillan, 1962), p. 118.

[30]Lewis, *Reflections on the Psalms,* p. 112.

[31]C. S. Lewis, *Letters to Malcolm: Chiefly on Prayer* (New York: Harcourt, Brace and World, 1964), p. 59.

[32]Lewis dispels any question about his commitment to biblical consistency when he writes, "I take it as a first principle that we must not interpret any one part of Scripture so that it contradicts other parts" (from *Letters of C. S. Lewis,* p. 251).

[33]C. S. Lewis, "Why I Am Not a Pacifist," in *The Weight of Glory and Other Addresses* (New York: Collier, 1980), p. 35.

[34]C. S. Lewis, *The Literary Impact of the Authorised Version* (London: Athlone, 1950), p. 25.

[35]Lewis, "Modern Theology and Biblical Criticism," p. 153.

[36]C. S. Lewis, *The World's Last Night and Other Essays* (New York: Harcourt Brace, 1960), pp. 98-99.

[37]C. S. Lewis, *Surprised by Joy* (New York: Harcourt Brace, 1956), p. 227.

[38]Lewis, *Reflections on the Psalms,* p. 114.

[39]Lewis, *The Problem of Pain,* p. 23.

[40]Lewis, *Reflections on the Psalms,* p. 110.

[41]Ibid., pp. 85-89.

[42]C. S. Lewis, *Miracles* (New York: Macmillan, 1978), p. 113.

[43]Ibid., p. 134.

[44]C. S. Lewis, "The Grand Miracle," in *God in the Dock* (Grand Rapids, Mich.: Eerdmans, 1970), p. 86.

[45]Lewis, *Letters of C. S. Lewis,* pp. 286-87.

[46]Ibid., p. 287.

[47]Lewis, *Reflections on the Psalms,* p. 116. This statement clearly reflects Lewis's commitment to a principle he called "Transposition"—the "adaptation of a richer to a poorer medium" (see *The Weight of Glory and Other Addresses,* pp. 60-61).

[48]Lewis, *Letters of C. S. Lewis,* p. 247.

[49]Lewis, *Reflections on the Psalms,* p. 111.

[50]Ibid., p. 113.

[51]Lewis, "Dogma and the Universe," in *God in the Dock,* p. 43.

[52]C. S. Lewis, *An Experiment in Criticism* (Cambridge: Cambridge University Press, 1961), p. 19.

[53]Lewis's high view of literature and his sensitivity to interpreting the text according to authorial context and intent has led Michael Christensen to characterize Lewis's perspective as a "literary view of inspiration" (see *C. S. Lewis on Scripture* [Waco, Tex.: Word, 1979], p. 93). We should also point out, however, that Lewis did not believe authorial intent can settle every issue cleanly. In fact, he believed that some important truths can work their way into the text apart from the author's knowledge. The important hermeneutical principle to recognize here is that the biblical text can mean more than the author intends but it cannot mean something other than or contrary to the author's original intent. This is especially the case with the multivalent imagery used in apocalyptic literature.

[54]Lewis, *Reflections on the Psalms,* p. 112.

[55]Ibid.

[56]Schaeffer, *Great Evangelical Disaster,* p. 187.

[57]Lewis, *Reflections on the Psalms,* p. 112.

[58]Ibid.

[59]William J. Abraham, *The Divine Inspiration of Holy Scripture* (New York: Oxford University Press, 1981), pp. 16-17.

[60]In "The God of Abraham, Isaac and Anselm" (*Faith and Philosophy* 1, no. 2 [April 1984]: 177-87), Thomas V. Morris underscores the importance of taking both a priori and a posteriori considerations seriously when doing philosophical theology. Such an approach allows deductive assumptions and inductive observations to engage in dynamic interaction. The end result is an emergent theory that often requires mutual modification in order to do justice to all the relevant data.

[61]Blaise Pascal, *Pensées* (London: Penguin, 1966), no. 234, p. 101.

[62]An interview with Alister McGrath and George Hunsinger, "Evangelicals and Postliberals: Shall the Twain Meet?" *Academic Alert* 5, no. 2 (Spring 1996): 4.

[63]Kent Hill, "Francis Schaeffer (1912-84): An Evaluation of His Life and Thought," in *Faith and Imagination,* ed. Noel Riley Fitch and Richard W. Etulain (Albuquerque, N.M.: Far West Books, 1985), p. 159.

[64]Ibid., p. 160.

[65]Schaeffer, *No Final Conflict,* p. 124.

[66]See Richard Burridge's excellent comparative study of the Gospels with Graeco-Roman biography, *What Are the Gospels?* (Cambridge: Cambridge University Press, 1992).

[67]Jack Rogers, "Francis Schaeffer: the Promise and the Problem, Part 2," *Reformed Journal* 27, no. 6 (June 1977): 17. Rogers attributes Schaeffer's resistance to cultural, historical and linguistic considerations to assumptions that are largely conditioned by Scottish common sense realism.

[68]Schaeffer, *He Is There and He Is Not Silent,* p. 347.

[69]Such an account might be defended using a Molinistic or middle knowledge notion of divine-human interaction. That is to say, God would choose as authors of Scripture those persons whom he infallibly knew by way of middle knowledge would write exactly what he wanted. As was pointed out in the previous chapter, however, Schaeffer would almost certainly have repudiated such a position. He affirmed the Westminster Confession, which roots God's foreknowledge in the predestining will of the Divine. Molinism reverses this causal sequence.

[70]Francis A. Schaeffer, *Genesis in Space and Time,* vol. 2, bk. 1 of *The Complete Works of Francis A. Schaeffer* (Westchester, Ill.: Crossway, 1982), p. 87.

[71]The Chicago Statement on Biblical Inerrancy, article 13, the Articles of Affirmation and Denial.

[72]Clark H. Pinnock has suggested that under the banner of the Chicago Statement many inerrantists end up affirming positions that are strikingly similar to those held by many of the noninerrantists they so vehemently oppose. See "The Inerrancy Debate Among the Evangelicals" (no data), as cited by Robert M. Price in "Inerrant the Wind: The Troubled House of North American Evangelicals," *The Evangelical Quarterly* 55, no. 3 (July 1983): 132.

[73]For a thoughtful critique of naturalistic bias in science, see Phillip E. Johnson, *Reason in the Balance* (Downers Grove, Ill.: InterVarsity Press, 1995).

[74]Schaeffer, *No Final Conflict,* p. 138.

[75]Ibid., p. 133.

Chapter 6: Strategic Apologetics

[1]C. S. Lewis, *Miracles* (New York: Macmillan, 1978), p. 109.

[2]Francis A. Schaeffer, *Whatever Happened to the Human Race?* vol. 5, bk. 3 of *The Complete Works of Francis A. Schaeffer* (Westchester, Ill.: Crossway, 1982), p. 359.

[3]G. K. Chesterton, *Collected Works of G. K. Chesterton,* ed. George Marlin et al. (San Francisco: Ignatius, 1986), pp. 380-81.

[4]Edith Schaeffer, letter to one of the authors, January 17, 1997.

[5]Francis A. Schaeffer, *The God Who Is There*, vol. 1, bk. 1 of *The Complete Works of Francis A. Schaeffer* (Westchester, Ill.: Crossway, 1982), p. 110.

[6]John Duns Scotus, *Philosophical Writings*, trans. Allan Wolter (Indianapolis: Bobbs-Merrill, 1962), p. 10. Scotus quotes Avicenna, *Metaphysics I.*

[7]It should be noted that these three methodologies are not exhaustive; there are other important approaches that do not fit neatly into any of these three categories. Alvin Plantinga's argument that belief in God is properly basic is one good example.

[8]Gordon R. Lewis, "Schaeffer's Apologetic Method," in *Reflections on Francis Schaeffer*, ed. Ronald W. Ruegsegger (Grand Rapids, Mich.: Zondervan, 1986), p. 70.

[9]Ibid., pp. 70-71.

[10]Ibid., p. 71.

[11]Thomas V. Morris, *Francis Schaeffer's Apologetics: A Critique* (Grand Rapids, Mich.: Baker Book House, 1987), p. 17.

[12]Jerram Barrs, *A Review of a Review, Part 2*, audiotape of a lecture presented at Covenant Theological Seminary, October 19, 1989 (St. Louis: Covenant Seminary Electronic Media Ministries, 1992).

[13]Kenneth C. Harper, "Francis A. Schaeffer: An Evaluation," *Bibliotheca Sacra* 133 (April 1976): 138.

[14]Os Guinness, conversation with the authors, Wilmore, Ky., November 21, 1996.

[15]Robert L. Reymond, *The Justification of Knowledge* (Nutley, N.J.: Presbyterian & Reformed, 1976), p. 147.

[16]G. Lewis, "Schaeffer's Apologetic Method," p. 86.

[17]Colin Brown, *Philosophy and the Christian Faith* (London: Tyndale, 1969), p. 265.

[18]Lane Dennis, conversation with one of the authors, Wheaton, Ill., April 1996.

[19]Jack Rogers, "Francis Schaeffer: The Promise and the Problem, Part 1," *Reformed Journal* 27, no. 5 (May 1977): 12-13.

[20]Nearly forty references to the term *presuppositions* can be found in the index to Schaeffer's complete works.

[21]Schaeffer, *Whatever Happened to the Human Race?* p. 353.

[22]Schaeffer, *God Who Is There*, p. 6.

[23]Ibid., p. 7.

[24]Ibid.

[25]Ibid., p. 9.

[26]Ibid., p. 45.

[27]Os Guinness, conversation with the authors, Wilmore, Ky., November 21, 1996.

[28]William Edgar, "Two Christian Warriors: Cornelius Van Til and Francis A. Schaeffer Compared," *The Westminster Theological Journal* 57, no. 1 (Spring 1995): 59.

[29]This anonymous poem, entitled "Presuppositionalism," appeared in an issue of *The Bible Today* (n.d.).

[30]Francis A. Schaeffer, "A Review of a Review," *The Bible Today*, May 1948, pp. 7-8.

[31]Edith Schaeffer, *The Tapestry* (Waco, Tex.: Word, 1984), p. 314.

[32]Cornelius Van Til, "The Apologetic Methodology of Francis A. Schaeffer," typescript, Westminster Theological Seminary Library, 1974, p. 11.

[33]Schaeffer, *Whatever Happened to the Human Race?* p. 359.

[34]Schaeffer, *The God Who Is There*, p. 60.

[35]Ibid., pp. 140-41.

[36]Van Til, "Apologetic Methodology of Francis A. Schaeffer," pp. 8-9.

[37]Schaeffer was notorious for giving his own distinctive definitions to technical philosophical terminology. This is surely one major reason why so many capable philosophers have misinterpreted his method. Even InterVarsity Press editor James Sire struggled with Schaeffer's message until he figured out how Schaeffer was defining his terms (James Sire, telephone conversation with one of the authors, April 1996).

[38]Morris, *Francis Schaeffer's Apologetics*, p. 18.

[39]Schaeffer, *The God Who Is There*, p. 38.

[40]Ibid., p. 39.

[41]Ibid., p. 34.

[42]Schaeffer, *Whatever Happened to the Human Race?* p. 366.

[43]Schaeffer, "Review of a Review," p. 8.

[44]Schaeffer, *The God Who Is There*, pp. 78-79.

[45]Ibid., p. 69.

[46]As we detailed in chapter four, Schaeffer's paradoxical view of libertarian freedom and unconditional predestination undermines his claim to a fully self-consistent, comprehensive and livable worldview. Consequently, Schaeffer himself was vulnerable to having his own roof removed.

[47]Schaeffer, *The God Who Is There*, pp. 138-39. After the roof is removed and the person moves to an open position, Schaeffer thought three things need to be understood before one can become a Christian: real truth, real guilt and real history. These points correspond to what Schaeffer often called the three bows: the metaphysical bow, the moral bow and the epistemological bow. In other words, we must realize God is really there, that our problem is not just guilt feelings but true moral guilt, and that faith is rational and based on objective truth—it is not a mystical, subjective leap in the dark.

[48]Francis A. Schaeffer, "The Mark of the Christian," in *The Great Evangelical Disaster* (Wheaton, Ill.: Crossway, 1984), pp. 160-61.

[49]Ibid., p. 163.

[50]Ibid., p. 171.

[51]Ibid., p. 173.

[52]Ibid., p. 176.

[53]Ibid., p. 165.

[54]We should note that this series of balanced assertions poses no logical problem for Schaeffer.

[55]Peter Kreeft and Ronald K. Tacelli, *Handbook of Christian Apologetics* (Downers Grove, Ill.: InterVarsity Press, 1994), pp. 22-23.

[56]C. S. Lewis, "Why I Am Not a Pacifist," in *The Weight of Glory and Other Addresses* (New York: Collier, 1980), p. 41.

[57]Os Guinness, conversation with the authors, Wilmore, Ky., November 21, 1996.

[58]Cornelius Van Til, *The Defense of the Faith* (Philadelphia: Presbyterian & Reformed, 1955), p. 77.

[59]C. S. Lewis, "Christian Apologetics," in *God in the Dock* (Grand Rapids, Mich.: Eerdmans, 1970), p. 101.

[60]C. S. Lewis, *Mere Christianity* (New York: Macmillan, 1960), p. 39.

[61]C. S. Lewis, "Man or Rabbit?" in *God in the Dock*, pp. 108-9.

[62]Lewis, "Christian Apologetics," p. 91.

[63]C. S. Lewis, "Religion: Reality or Substitute?" in *Christian Reflections* (Grand Rapids, Mich.: Eerdmans, 1967), p. 41. See also p. 189 of *The Discarded Image* (London: Cambridge University Press, 1964) for a related discussion of medieval epistemology.

[64]See "On Obstinacy in Belief," in *They Asked for a Paper* (London: Geoffrey Bles, 1962), p. 183.

[65]Lewis, *Mere Christianity*, p. 123.

[66]It should be noted that Lewis thinks we are called to hold to our beliefs in the face of some apparent contrary evidence. After all, Christians are engaged in a relationship, and it is going to take a significant amount of contrary evidence to undermine our trust in and love for a person who has proven to be reliable. In "On Obstinacy in Belief," Lewis makes an important distinction between apologetic argument and personal assent: "You are no longer faced with an argument which demands your assent, but with a Person who demands your confidence" (p. 193).

[67]Lewis, *Mere Christianity*, p. 123.

[68]Lewis, "Religion: Reality or Substitute?" p. 43.

[69]Lewis, *Miracles*, p. 3.

[70]Ibid.

[71]C. S. Lewis, "Bulverism," in *God in the Dock*, p. 273.

[72]Ibid.

[73]Ibid., p. 274.

[74]In "On Obstinacy in Belief," Lewis writes, "I do not admit that a hypothesis is a belief" (p. 190). It is important to understand what Lewis means by this. In an apologetic setting, believers compare the Christian hypothesis to other competing theories to see which worldview makes best sense, but in the realm of spiritual devotion, once a Christian commitment has been made, the believer does not speak in scientific terms but rather in relational terms. Lewis puts it like this: "Assent, of necessity, moves us from the logic of speculative thought into what might perhaps be called the logic of personal relations" (p. 196).

[75]Lewis, *Miracles*, p. 33.

[76]Lewis, "Religion: Reality or Substitute?" p. 41.

[77]Lewis, *Miracles*, p. 114.

[78]Ibid., p. 109.

[79]C. S. Lewis, *Surprised by Joy* (New York: Harcourt Brace, 1956), p. 223.

[80]G. K. Chesterton, *Collected Works of G. K. Chesterton*, ed. George Marlin et al. (San Francisco: Ignatius, 1986), pp. 380-81.

[81]Schaeffer, *Whatever Happened to the Human Race?* p. 359.

[82]William Strunk and E. B. White, *The Elements of Style*, 3rd ed. (New York: Macmillan, 1979), p. xvi.

[83]Lewis, *Mere Christianity*, p. 123.

[84]Lewis, "Christian Apologetics," p. 93.

[85]Ibid., p. 98.

[86]Ibid., p. 93.

[87]Ibid.

[88]Os Guinness, Asbury College Staley Lecture Series, Wilmore, Ky., November 20, 1996. Some might be uncomfortable with this method, viewing it as a form of manipulation. But according to Guinness "subversion by surprise" simply puts people in position to see the truth; it does not coerce them to accept it.

[89]Lewis, *Surprised by Joy*, p. 179.

[90]Ibid., p. 181.

[91]C. S. Lewis, *Letters of C. S. Lewis*, ed. W. H. Lewis (London: Geoffrey Bles, 1966), p. 167. There appears to be tension between Lewis's comments in this context and that which he accuses Gaius and Titius of doing in *The Abolition of Man* (New York: Macmillan, 1955), namely, smuggling their philosophical assumptions into a book on English composition. Lewis writes, "The very power of Gaius and Titius depends on the fact that they are dealing with a boy: a boy who thinks he is 'doing' his 'English prep' and has no notion that ethics, theology, and politics are all at stake" (p. 16). It seems we could equally say, "The very power of C. S. Lewis depends on the fact that he is dealing with a boy: a boy who thinks he is reading science fiction and has no notion that ethics, theology, and politics are all at stake." So far as we can tell, Lewis never explains why his practice is legitimate whereas theirs is not.

[92]C. S. Lewis, "Sometimes Fairy Stories May Say Best What's to Be Said," in *Of Other Worlds: Essays and Stories*, ed. Walter Hooper (New York: Harcourt, Brace and World, 1966), p. 37.

[93]Quoted by Colin Duriez, *The C. S. Lewis Handbook* (Grand Rapids, Mich.: Baker Book House, 1994), pp. 203-4.

[94]C. S. Lewis, *Letters to Children*, ed. Lyle W. Dorsett and Marjorie Lamp Mead (New York: Touchstone, 1995), p. 52.

[95]C. S. Lewis, *An Experiment in Criticism* (Cambridge: Cambridge University Press, 1961), p. 41.

[96]Ibid., pp. 43-44.
[97]C. S. Lewis, "Myth Became Fact," in *God in the Dock*, p. 65.
[98]Ibid., p. 66.
[99]See Peter Schakel, *Reason and Imagination in C. S. Lewis* (Grand Rapids, Mich.: Eerdmans, 1984).
[100]Lewis, *Letters of C. S. Lewis*, pp. 270-71.

Chapter 7: Offensive Apologetics
[1]Francis A. Schaeffer, *The God Who Is There*, vol. 1, bk. 1 of *The Complete Works of Francis A. Schaeffer* (Westchester, Ill.: Crossway, 1982), p. 14.
[2]C. S. Lewis, *Mere Christianity* (New York: Macmillan, 1960), p. 56.
[3]Colin Duriez, *The C. S. Lewis Handbook* (Grand Rapids, Mich.: Baker Book House, 1994), p. 46.
[4]We have taken poetic license to fictitiously flesh out an actual experience recorded by George Sayer. See *Jack: C. S. Lewis and His Times* (San Francisco: Harper & Row, 1988), p. 278. The Lewis quotations in this paragraph can be found in *Mere Christianity*, p. 25.
[5]C. S. Lewis, "Christian Apologetics," in *God in the Dock* (Grand Rapids, Mich.: Eerdmans, 1970), p. 95.
[6]Lewis, *Mere Christianity*, p. 39.
[7]Lewis, "Christian Apologetics," p. 96.
[8]Lewis, *Mere Christianity*, pp. 17-18.
[9]Ibid., p. 21.
[10]Ibid., p. 22.
[11]Ibid.
[12]Ibid., p. 23.
[13]Ibid., p. 24.
[14]Ibid.
[15]Lewis believed the words of great religious and ethical leaders such as Zarathustra, Jeremiah, Socrates, Gandhi and even Jesus are really quite similar in spirit. The heart of their teaching is on the same trajectory, though some are more profound and vivid formulations of the same insight. Lewis devoted a twenty-five-page appendix at the end of *The Abolition of Man* to illustrating this common core morality, what Lewis in this particular book calls the Tao.
[16]C. S. Lewis, "On Ethics," in *Christian Reflections* (Grand Rapids, Mich.: Eerdmans, 1967), p. 52.
[17]Lewis, *Mere Christianity*, p. 19.
[18]Ibid., p. 26.
[19]Ibid., p. 25.
[20]Ibid.
[21]Ibid., p. 28.
[22]Ibid., p. 29.
[23]Ibid., p. 30.
[24]Ibid., pp. 31-32.
[25]Ibid., p. 34.
[26]Ibid.
[27]Ibid., p. 54.
[28]Ibid., p. 55.
[29]Ibid., p. 56.
[30]C. S. Lewis, *Miracles* (New York: Macmillan, 1978), p. 12.
[31]Ibid., p. 16.
[32]Ibid., p. 15.
[33]Ibid., p. 16.
[34]Ibid., p. 17.

[35]Ibid., pp. 22-23.
[36]Lewis, *Mere Christianity*, p. 119.
[37]Ibid.
[38]Ibid.
[39]Ibid., p. 120.
[40]Ibid.
[41]C. S. Lewis, *The Weight of Glory and Other Addresses* (New York: Collier, 1980), pp. 8-9.
[42]C. S. Lewis, *The Four Loves* (New York: Harcourt Brace, 1960), p. 9.
[43]Ibid., p. 6.
[44]Ibid., p. 115.
[45]Ibid., p. 133.
[46]Ibid., p. 134.
[47]C. S. Lewis, *The Great Divorce* (New York: Macmillan, 1946), p. 93.
[48]Francis A. Schaeffer, *He Is There and He Is Not Silent*, vol. 1, bk. 3 of *The Complete Works of Francis A. Schaeffer* (Westchester, Ill.: Crossway, 1982), p. 277.
[49]Ibid., pp. 277-78.
[50]Ibid., p. 279.
[51]Ibid., p. 281.
[52]Ibid., p. 282.
[53]Ibid.
[54]Ibid., p. 283.
[55]Ibid., p. 278.
[56]Ibid., p. 283.
[57]Ibid., p. 291.
[58]Schaeffer, *The God Who Is There*, pp. 95-96.
[59]Schaeffer, *He Is There and He Is Not Silent*, p. 294.
[60]Ibid.
[61]Ibid., p. 296.
[62]Ibid., p. 295.
[63]Ibid.
[64]Ibid., p. 294.
[65]Ibid., p. 295.
[66]Ibid., pp. 298-99.
[67]Ibid., p. 302.
[68]Ibid., pp. 301-2.
[69]Francis A. Schaeffer, *Escape from Reason*, vol. 1, bk. 2 of *The Complete Works of Francis A. Schaeffer* (Westchester, Ill.: Crossway, 1982), pp. 233-34.
[70]Schaeffer, *He Is There and He Is Not Silent*, p. 332. In a glossary at the end of *The God Who Is There*, Schaeffer defines the term *romantic* as "a view of life that has no base in fact, being the product of an exaggerated optimism" (p. 202).
[71]Bertrand Russell, *Why I Am Not a Christian* (New York: Simon & Schuster, 1957), p. 107.
[72]For some classic expressions of the connection between the loss of meaning and suicide, see E. D. Klemke, ed., *The Meaning of Life* (New York: Oxford University Press, 1981). See especially the selections by Tolstoy and Camus.
[73]These figures are from the reprinted versions in *The Complete Works of Francis A. Schaeffer*.
[74]Schaeffer, *He Is There and He Is Not Silent*, p. 305.
[75]Ibid., p. 306.
[76]Ibid.
[77]Francis A. Schaeffer, *How Should We Then Live?* vol. 5, bk. 2 of *The Complete Works of Francis A. Schaeffer* (Westchester, Ill.: Crossway, 1982), p. 166.
[78]Schaeffer, *Escape from Reason*, p. 229.
[79]Ibid., p. 212.

[80]Schaeffer, *He Is There and He Is Not Silent,* p. 310.
[81]Schaeffer, *How Should We Then Live?* pp. 167-68.
[82]Ibid., pp. 172-73.
[83]Ibid., p. 178.
[84]Schaeffer, *The God Who Is There,* p. 14.
[85]Schaeffer, *How Should We Then Live?* p. 179.
[86]Ibid., p. 188.
[87]Schaeffer, *He Is There and He Is Not Silent,* p. 324.
[88]Ibid., p. 339.
[89]Schaeffer, *The God Who Is There,* pp. 140-41.
[90]Schaeffer, *He Is There and He Is Not Silent,* p. 327.
[91]Ibid., p. 329.
[92]Ibid.
[93]"Critical rationalism" should not be confused with Schaeffer's notion of autonomous, sinful rationalism.

Chapter 8: Defensive Apologetics

[1]C. S. Lewis, *A Grief Observed* (New York: Bantam, 1976), p. 50.
[2]Francis A. Schaeffer, *Letters of Francis A. Schaeffer,* ed. Lane T. Dennis (Westchester, Ill.: Crossway, 1985), p. 158.
[3]John Hick, "Soul-Making Theodicy," in *Philosophy of Religion: Selected Readings,* ed. Michael Peterson, William Hasker, Bruce Reichenbach and David Basinger (New York: Oxford University Press), p. 292.
[4]C. S. Lewis, *Surprised by Joy* (New York: Harcourt Brace, 1956), p. 34.
[5]See Alvin Plantinga, "Free Will Defense," in *Philosophy of Religion: Selected Readings,* pp. 254-80.
[6]It is doubtful that Augustine had a sufficient notion of freedom to adequately advance the free-will defense. See John Hick's *Evil and the God of Love,* rev. ed. (San Francisco: Harper & Row, 1977), pp. 64-69, and Rowan Greer's "Augustine's Transformation of the Free Will Defence," *Faith and Philosophy* 13, no. 4 (October 1996): 471-86.
[7]See Hick, *Evil and the God of Love.*
[8]C. S. Lewis, *The Problem of Pain* (New York: Macmillan, 1962), p. 28.
[9]Ibid., p. 33.
[10]Ibid., pp. 33-34.
[11]Ibid., p. 40.
[12]C. S. Lewis, *The Lion, the Witch and the Wardrobe* (New York: Collier, 1970), pp. 75-76.
[13]C. S. Lewis, *The Horse and His Boy* (New York: Collier, 1970), p. 194.
[14]C. S. Lewis, "Answers to Questions on Christianity," in *God in the Dock* (Grand Rapids, Mich.: Eerdmans, 1970), p. 52.
[15]Lewis, *The Problem of Pain,* p. 93.
[16]Ibid., p. 110.
[17]Ibid., p. 136.
[18]Ibid., p. 81.
[19]Ibid., p. 83.
[20]Ibid., p. 80.
[21]Ibid.
[22]Ibid., p. 108.
[23]Lewis, *A Grief Observed,* p. 38.
[24]Ibid., p. 50.
[25]Lewis, *Problem of Pain,* p. 54.
[26]Schaeffer, *Letters of Francis A. Schaeffer,* p. 171.
[27]Francis A. Schaeffer, *He Is There and He Is Not Silent,* vol. 1, bk. 3 of *The Complete Works of*

Francis A. Schaeffer (Westchester, Ill.: Crossway, 1982), p. 300.

[28]Schaeffer, *Letters of Francis A. Schaeffer*, p. 155.

[29]Ibid., p. 156.

[30]Ibid., p. 158.

[31]Francis A. Schaeffer, *True Spirituality*, vol. 3, bk. 2 of *The Complete Works of Francis A. Schaeffer* (Westchester, Ill.: Crossway, 1982), p. 305.

[32]Francis A. Schaeffer, *On the Problem of Evil and Good—God of Love*, audiotape, catalog no. 82.1s (Michigan City, Ind.: L'Abri Cassettes).

[33]Hick, "Soul-Making Theodicy," p. 292.

[34]John Sanders, "Evangelical Responses to Salvation Outside the Church," *Christian Scholar's Review* 24, no. 1 (September 1994): 45. For fuller treatment, see Sanders's *No Other Name* (Grand Rapids, Mich.: Eerdmans, 1992). Note particularly the section on Lewis, pp. 251-57.

[35]Michael Peterson, William Hasker, Bruce Reichenbach and David Basinger, eds., *Reason and Religious Belief* (New York: Oxford University Press, 1991), p. 223.

[36]Sanders, "Evangelical Responses to Salvation Outside the Church," pp. 45-46.

[37]Ibid., pp. 50-52.

[38]Francis A. Schaeffer, *Death in the City*, vol. 4, bk. 4 of *The Complete Works of Francis A. Schaeffer* (Westchester, Ill.: Crossway, 1982), p. 277.

[39]Ibid., p. 278.

[40]Ibid.

[41]Ibid., p. 267.

[42]Ibid., p. 284.

[43]C. S. Lewis, *Mere Christianity* (New York: Macmillan, 1960), p. 176.

[44]C. S. Lewis, *Letters of C. S. Lewis*, ed. W. H. Lewis (London: Geoffrey Bles, 1966), pp. 251-52.

[45]C. S. Lewis, *The Last Battle* (New York: Collier, 1970), pp. 164-65.

[46]See "Man or Rabbit?" in *God in the Dock*, p. 110. In this essay, Lewis discusses the possibility of people like Socrates, Confucius and atheist John Stuart Mill becoming believers once their "honest ignorance" or "honest error" has been corrected.

Chapter 9: Back to Libertarian Freedom and Dignity

[1]C. S. Lewis, *The Abolition of Man* (New York: Macmillan, 1955), pp. 79-80.

[2]Francis A. Schaeffer, *Back to Freedom and Dignity*, vol. 1, bk. 4 of *The Complete Works of Francis A. Schaeffer* (Westchester, Ill.: Crossway, 1982), pp. 382-83.

[3]B. F. Skinner, *Beyond Freedom and Dignity* (New York: Alfred A. Knopf, 1971), p. 200.

[4]Edith Schaeffer, *The Tapestry* (Waco, Tex.: Word, 1984), p. 198.

[5]Ibid.

[6]Ibid., p. 199.

[7]Ibid., pp. 228-29.

[8]Francis A. Schaeffer, *True Spirituality*, vol. 3, bk. 2 of *The Complete Works of Francis A. Schaeffer* (Westchester, Ill.: Crossway, 1982), p. 305.

[9]It is possible that Schaeffer simply affirmed his paradoxical position in this context as well, but compatibilism is the only rationally self-consistent Calvinistic model to make sense of this view of inerrancy. It is also possible that Schaeffer thought God just overrode the freedom of the biblical authors to achieve his purposes. This, however, seems unlikely in light of Schaeffer's high view of human freedom and significance. Such a view also leaves us with the problematic question of why God, if he is willing to override human freedom to bring about his desired ends, did not prevent the first humans from falling. Moreover, we must wonder why God would override the freedom of the biblical authors to preserve inerrancy in the original autographs, yet allow errors to slip in during the transmission process. And as we have seen, Schaeffer freely admitted corruption in the transmitted text.

[10]For an interesting discussion on the relationship between inerrancy and the free-will defense, see the exchange between Randall and David Basinger and Norman L. Geisler in the July

1983 (55, no. 3), October 1985 (57, no. 4) and October 1986 (58, no. 4) issues of *The Evangelical Quarterly*.

[11]See chapter 3 of Jerry L. Walls, *Hell: The Logic of Damnation* (Notre Dame, Ind.: University of Notre Dame Press, 1992).

[12]A Molinist view of strict inerrancy is not without its own problems, however. In fact, such a position seems suspect on the same grounds mentioned in note 9. For if God, through middle knowledge, selected those writers who would freely cooperate with the Holy Spirit in the writing of the Holy Scriptures, then why would he not do the same during the transmission process?

[13]C. S. Lewis, *The Problem of Pain* (New York: Macmillan, 1962), p. 107.

[14]C. S. Lewis, *A Grief Observed* (New York: Bantam, 1976), p. 61.

[15]Ibid., p. 28.

[16]Ibid., p. 46.

[17]Ibid., p. 43.

[18]Ibid., p. 35.

[19]Ibid., p. 36.

[20]Ibid., p. 39.

[21]C. S. Lewis, *Letters of C. S. Lewis*, ed. W. H. Lewis (London: Geoffrey Bles, 1966), p. 237.

[22]Lewis, *Problem of Pain*, p. 104.

[23]C. S. Lewis, *The Horse and His Boy* (New York: Collier, 1970), p. 194.

[24]Obviously we do not mean to suggest that Lewis's shaken faith and grief-induced anger are consistent with his writing elsewhere. Rather, the consistency we are pointing out is the view that God directly sends specific bouts of suffering our way for the purpose of transforming us into Christlike creatures and the purpose of our specific suffering can be known only from the inside.

[25]Lewis sought to address this dilemma in *Problem of Pain*, pp. 107-14.

[26]Schaeffer attempted to draw a sharp distinction between what God allows and what God directly sends, but it is hard to see how such a distinction is truly meaningful if God is ultimately the unconditional predestinator of every aspect of life, including our sufferings.

[27]Peter van Inwagen, "Quam Dilecta," in *God and the Philosophers*, ed. Thomas V. Morris (New York: Oxford University Press), p. 47.

[28]C. S. Lewis, *Reflections on the Psalms* (New York: Harcourt Brace, 1958), p. 80.

[29]C. S. Lewis, "Christian Apologetics," in *God in the Dock* (Grand Rapids, Mich.: Eerdmans, 1970), p. 102.

[30]Francis A. Schaeffer, *Death in the City*, vol. 4, bk. 4 of *The Complete Works of Francis A. Schaeffer* (Westchester, Ill.: Crossway, 1982), p. 267.

[31]In our estimation it is also difficult to imagine a just judge acting this way, as we have already detailed.

[32]Francis A. Schaeffer, *The God Who Is There*, vol. 1, bk. 1 of *The Complete Works of Francis A. Schaeffer* (Westchester, Ill.: Crossway, 1982), p. 119.

[33]It is worth noting that Schaeffer clearly rejected the natural law tradition (see *How Should We Then Live?* vol. 5, bk. 2 of *The Complete Works of Francis A. Schaeffer* [Westchester, Ill.: Crossway, 1982], p. 176), and it seems likely that he was uncomfortable with Lewis's belief that a significant core morality can be traced across cultures and religions. Schaeffer was leery of any view that might appear to diminish the unique claims of Christianity and deemphasize the necessity of biblical revelation. This can be seen in his own discussion of moral motions. Instead of siding with Lewis in the belief that an essential moral law is built into the fabric of the universe, Schaeffer makes the much more modest claim that all people simply believe some things are right and others are wrong. He seems unwilling to suggest that there are any specific, concrete moral principles that are universally shared, for again, this might leave the impression that one can discern Judeo-Christian morality apart from special revelation. Another example of Schaeffer's disjunctive view of revelation in contrast to Lewis's idea of essential continuity

is Schaeffer's discomfort with Lewis's use of the Tao. This might explain why he favorably cites the relatively obscure *That Hideous Strength* more than once in his writings but is totally silent when it comes to the widely influential *The Abolition of Man*, a book that deals with the same basic topic as this science-fiction fantasy but does so with an overt commitment to the natural law.

[34]This point is readily acknowledged by Reformed theologian Loraine Boettner, who offers a description that is both forthright and chilling: "Those who are providentially placed in the pagan darkness of western China can no more accept Christ as Savior than they can accept the radio, the airplane, or the Copernican system of astronomy, things concerning which they are totally ignorant. When God places people in such conditions we may be sure that He has no more intention that they shall be saved than He has that the soil of northern Siberia, which is frozen all the year round, shall produce crops of wheat. Had he intended otherwise He would have supplied the means leading to the designed end." Loraine Boettner, *The Reformed Doctrine of Predestination* (Grand Rapids, Mich.: Eerdmans, 1954), p. 120, as quoted in John Sanders, *No Other Name* (Grand Rapids, Mich.: Eerdmans, 1992), pp. 50-51.

[35]We do not intend the reader to interpret the phrase "tough luck" in a literal sense, especially since Schaeffer did not believe in luck. We are simply using this phrase in its commonly accepted figurative sense. For a philosophically informed discussion of this topic, see Linda Zagzebski's "Religious Luck," *Faith and Philosophy* 11, no. 3 (July 1994): 397-413.

[36]In addition to contrasting guiding grids, we should point out that Lewis possessed richer theological resources to engage this key apologetic issue. The particular resource we have in mind is the doctrine of purgatory. Such a doctrine not only provides for postmortem purification, the necessary implication of a cooperative transformational soteriology, but also provides a place where those who were denied a legitimate opportunity on this side of the grave can hear the truth of the gospel. This seems to be the type of picture we find Lewis developing in *The Great Divorce*. Incidentally, this doctrine of purgatory is also best understood through a relational lens. It is reasonable to believe a loving, patient heavenly Father would provide everyone an adequate opportunity to receive the gospel and the proper conditions to reach a state of full transformation. For a defense of how some people could choose hell over heaven following a postmortem encounter with the truth, see chapter 5 of Walls, *Hell: The Logic of Damnation*.

[37]Dick Keyes tells of a time when he essentially laid out the wider hope position to Schaeffer, pointing out specifically the logical necessity of a good, loving God's providing not only enough light to condemn but also enough light to save. According to Keyes, Schaeffer was sympathetic to such a proposal but responded by saying, "Dick, I hope you are right, but I never would dare teach it because everyone would understand me to be teaching relativism" (Dick Keyes, conversation with the authors, Wilmore, Ky., July 26, 1996). We would suggest this as another example of Schaeffer's sound relational intuitions, but they simply were not strong enough to overcome his predominantly legal paradigm.

[38]We do not mean to suggest that Schaeffer never referenced Calvinism or the Reformation in his books. He clearly did, particularly in his historical critiques. But when he discussed theology, his consistent emphasis was on subjects such as libertarian freedom, holiness and human significance. As noted in chapter three, the index to Schaeffer's *Complete Works* reveals more than fifty references to freedom but not a single reference to predestination or election.

[39]It is worth noting that in chapter five of *Whatever Happened to the Human Race?* Schaeffer also mentions that we have a point of contact through the Bible in history because it is open to verification.

[40]Schaeffer, *Back to Freedom and Dignity*, p. 371.

[41]C. S. Lewis, *That Hideous Strength* (New York: Macmillan, 1947), pp. 37-38.

[42]Schaeffer, *Back to Freedom and Dignity*, p. 381.

[43]Francis A. Schaeffer, *Whatever Happened to the Human Race?* vol. 5, bk. 3 of *The Complete Works*

of Francis A. Schaeffer (Westchester, Ill.: Crossway, 1982), p. 361.

[44]Bertrand Russell, *Why I Am Not a Christian* (New York: Simon & Schuster, 1957), p. 107.

[45]It is not entirely surprising that these two apologists did not focus more on traditional cosmological and teleological arguments, given Schaeffer's aversion to Thomistic natural theology and the fact that Lewis's adolescent faith in God was partially undermined by what he calls the "Argument from Undesign," an argument based on the apparent flaws of the natural world.

[46]C. S. Lewis, *Miracles* (New York: Macmillan, 1978), p. 12.

[47]Ibid., pp. 22-23.

[48]Lewis, *Abolition of Man*, pp. 79-80.

[49]C. S. Lewis, *Mere Christianity* (New York: Macmillan, 1960), p. 117.

[50]See John Beversluis, *C. S. Lewis and the Search for Rational Religion* (Grand Rapids, Mich.: Eerdmans, 1985); Thomas V. Morris, *Francis Schaeffer's Apologetics: A Critique* (Grand Rapids, Mich.: Baker Book House, 1987); and Ronald W. Ruegsegger, ed., *Reflections on Francis Schaeffer* (Grand Rapids, Mich.: Zondervan, 1986).

[51]Beversluis, *C. S. Lewis and the Search for Rational Religion*, p. 40.

[52]Andrew Walker, "Reflections on C. S. Lewis, Apologetics and the Moral Tradition: Basil Mitchell in Conversation with Andrew Walker," in *A Christian for All Christians*, ed. Andrew Walker and James Patrick (Washington, D.C.: Regnery Gateway, 1992), p. 14.

[53]Dick Keyes, conversation with the authors, Wilmore, Ky., July 26, 1996.

[54]J. I. Packer, foreword to *Reflections on Francis Schaeffer*, ed. Ronald W. Ruegsegger (Grand Rapids, Mich.: Zondervan, 1986), p. 10.

[55]Thomas V. Morris, review of *C. S. Lewis and the Search for Rational Religion* by John Beversluis, *Faith and Philosophy* 5, no. 3 (July 1988): 320.

[56]Schaeffer, *The God Who Is There*, p. 186.

[57]Walker, "Reflections on C. S. Lewis," p. 9.

[58]When presenting this argument we must be careful to offer one key qualification in relation to category number two (nonsagacious, profess to be God), for many New Age adherents would take exception to the assertion that they are either lunatics or liars. What we must point out is that the God we have in mind here is not of an Eastern pantheistic variety but rather the monotheistic deity of the Judeo-Christian tradition. To claim to be this kind of deity would indeed qualify one to be either a lunatic or a liar. See Peter Kreeft, *Between Heaven and Hell* (Downers Grove, Ill.: InterVarsity Press, 1982), and chapter 7 of Peter Kreeft and Ronald K. Tacelli, *Handbook of Christian Apologetics* (Downers Grove, Ill.: InterVarsity Press, 1994), for further reflection on how the Trilemma can be strengthened to meet the challenges of our day.

[59]C. Stephen Evans, *The Historical Christ and the Jesus of Faith* (New York: Clarendon, 1996), p. 351.

[60]See Alvin Plantinga, *Warrant and Proper Function* (New York: Oxford University Press, 1993), p. 237, n. 28 .

[61]Walker, "Reflections on C. S. Lewis," pp. 16-17.

[62]Francis A. Schaeffer, *He Is There and He Is Not Silent*, vol. 1, bk. 3 of *The Complete Works of Francis A. Schaeffer* (Westchester, Ill.: Crossway, 1982), p. 288.

[63]Schaeffer, *The God Who Is There*, p. 187.

[64]Beversluis, *C. S. Lewis and the Search for Rational Religion*, p. 42.

[65]Colin Duriez, *The C. S. Lewis Handbook* (Grand Rapids, Mich.: Baker Book House, 1994), p. 46.

[66]Clark Pinnock, "Schaefferism as a World View," *Sojourners* 6, no. 8 (July 1977): 33.

[67]Richard Pierard, "Schaeffer on History," in *Reflections on Francis Schaeffer*, p. 212.

[68]C. S. Lewis, "De Descriptione Temporum," in *They Asked for a Paper* (London: Geoffrey Bles, 1962), p. 17.

[69]Ibid.

[70]Ibid., p. 11.

[71]Ibid., p. 12.

[72]Stephen T. Davis, *Risen Indeed: Making Sense of the Resurrection* (Grand Rapids, Mich.: Eerdmans, 1993), p. 1.

[73]Lewis, *Miracles*, p. 12.

[74]Richard Swinburne, *The Existence of God* (Oxford: Clarendon, 1979), note on p. 14.

[75]Ibid.

[76]Gordon R. Lewis, "Schaeffer's Apologetic Method," in *Reflections on Francis Schaeffer*, pp. 88-89.

[77]William J. Abraham, "Cumulative Case Arguments for Christian Theism," in *The Rationality of Religious Belief*, ed. William J. Abraham and Steven Holtzer (Oxford: Clarendon, 1987), p. 18.

[78]Ibid., p. 27.

[79]Schaeffer, *Whatever Happened to the Human Race?* p. 357.

[80]Lewis, *Miracles*, p. 106.

[81]Ibid., p. 107.

[82]Ibid., p. 109.

[83]Ibid., p. 133.

[84]Ibid.

[85]Ibid.

[86]Lewis gestured in this direction in some of his comments in *Miracles* (see pp. 145-48). It is also worth noting that Lewis showed sympathy for this sort of argument in a letter addressed to John Warwick Montgomery, published in *History and Christianity* (Downers Grove, Ill.: InterVarsity Press, 1976), pp. 6-7.

[87]See Alvin Plantinga, *Warrant: The Current Debate* (New York: Oxford University Press, 1993), and Alvin Plantinga and Nicholas Wolterstorff, eds., *Faith and Rationality* (Notre Dame, Ind.: University of Notre Dame Press, 1983), for some formidable assaults on classical foundationalism.

Chapter 10: 21 Lessons for the 21st Century

[1]C. S. Lewis, *Mere Christianity* (New York: Macmillan, 1960), p. 119.

[2]Francis A. Schaeffer, *Two Contents, Two Realities*, vol. 3, bk. 4 of *The Complete Works of Francis A. Schaeffer* (Westchester, Ill.: Crossway, 1982), p. 408.

[3]Lane T. Dennis, introduction to *Letters of Francis A. Schaeffer* (Westchester, Ill.: Crossway, 1985), p. 11.

[4]Francis A. Schaeffer, *Whatever Happened to the Human Race?* vol. 5, bk. 3 of *The Complete Works of Francis A. Schaeffer* (Westchester, Ill.: Crossway, 1982), p. 392.

[5]Lewis, *Mere Christianity*, p. 75.

[6]For example, see Donald Dayton, *Discovering an Evangelical Heritage* (Peabody, Mass.: Hendrickson, 1976).

[7]C. S. Lewis, *The Abolition of Man* (New York: Macmillan, 1955), p. 24.

[8]Schaeffer, *Two Contents, Two Realities*, p. 408.

[9]Philip Yancey, "Schaeffer on Schaeffer, Part 2," *Christianity Today* 23, no. 13 (April 6, 1979): 25.

[10]C. S. Lewis, *Surprised by Joy* (New York: Harcourt Brace, 1956), p. 170.

[11]Dick Keyes, conversation with the authors, Wilmore, Ky., July 26, 1996.

[12]Schaeffer, *Whatever Happened to the Human Race?* p. 402.

[13]C. S. Lewis, "Modern Theology and Biblical Criticism," in *Christian Reflections* (Grand Rapids, Mich.: Eerdmans, 1967), p. 155.

[14]Richard John Neuhaus, the 1997 Asbury Theological Seminary Theta Phi lecturer, made this assertion at the Theta Phi induction banquet, Lexington, Ky., March 6, 1997.

[15]Francis A. Schaeffer, *A Christian Manifesto*, vol. 5, bk. 4 of *The Complete Works of Francis A. Schaeffer* (Westchester, Ill.: Crossway, 1982), p. 445.

[16]Stanley Fish, "Stanley Fish Replies to Richard John Neuhaus," *First Things*, no. 60 (February 1996): 35.

[17]Ibid., pp. 36-38. Alert readers may see here shades of Van Til.

[18]Pico Iyer, "Our Days of Judgment," *Time* 149, no. 14 (April 7, 1997): 94.

[19]It is noteworthy that the following response to Fish from Richard John Neuhaus is congruent with the suggestions we are recommending: "One reason I am a Christian is that Christianity makes more sense of more facts than any other way of construing reality that I know of " (*First Things*, no. 60 [February 1996]: 30).

[20]Francis A. Schaeffer, *Death in the City*, vol. 4, bk. 4 of *The Complete Works of Francis A. Schaeffer* (Westchester, Ill.: Crossway, 1982), p. 245.

[21]C. Stephen Evans, "The Incarnational Narrative as Myth and History," *Christian Scholar's Review* 23, no. 4 (1994): 387.

[22]Ibid., p. 403.

[23]C. S. Lewis, "Myth Became Fact," in *God in the Dock* (Grand Rapids, Mich.: Eerdmans, 1970), p. 64.

[24]Ibid., p. 67.

[25]See chapter 14 of C. S. Lewis, *The Lion, the Witch and the Wardrobe* (New York: Collier, 1970); chapter 7 of *The Voyage of the Dawn Treader* (New York: Collier, 1970); and *Perelandra* (New York: Macmillan, 1958).

[26]William J. Abraham, "C. S. Lewis and the Conversion of the West," in *Permanent Things*, ed. Andrew A. Tadie and Michael H. Macdonald (Grand Rapids, Mich.: Eerdmans, 1995), p. 275.

[27]Francis A. Schaeffer, "The Mark of the Christian," in *The Great Evangelical Disaster* (Wheaton, Ill.: Crossway, 1984), p. 164.

[28]Colleen McDannell and Bernhard Lang, *Heaven: A History* (New York: Vintage, 1990), p. 352.

[29]David Van Biema, "Does Heaven Exist?" *Time* 149, no. 12 (March 24, 1997): 73.

[30]Jason Leininger, paper written in the C. S. Lewis Seminar at Asbury Theological Seminary, Wilmore, Ky., June 1997.

[31]C. S. Lewis, introduction to George MacDonald, *Phantastes and Lilith* (Grand Rapids, Mich.: Eerdmans, 1964), p. 12.

[32]Francis A. Schaeffer, *The God Who Is There*, vol. 1, bk. 1 of *The Complete Works of Francis A. Schaeffer* (Westchester, Ill.: Crossway, 1982), p. 139.

[33]Lewis, *Mere Christianity*, pp. 70-71.

[34]C. S. Lewis, *The Problem of Pain* (New York: Macmillan, 1962), p. 39.

[35]See chapters 9-11 of C. S. Lewis, *Prince Caspian* (New York: Collier, 1970), chapters 10-15 of *Till We Have Faces* (New York: Harcourt Brace, 1956) and chapter 10 of *The Magician's Nephew* (New York: Collier, 1970), where Lewis writes, "For what you see and hear depends a good deal on where you are standing: it also depends on what sort of person you are" (p. 125).

[36]Paul L. Holmer, *C. S. Lewis: The Shape of His Faith and Thought* (New York: Harper & Row, 1976), p. 90.

[37]Jerry Jenkins, letter to the editor, *Christianity Today* 41, no. 5 (April 28, 1997): 8.

[38]Lewis, *Mere Christianity*, pp. 181-82.

[39]Dick Keyes, *Francis Schaeffer's Contribution to Apologetics*, audiotape 2908 (Michigan City, Ind.: L'Abri Cassettes).

[40]Jack Rogers, "Francis Schaeffer: The Promise and the Problem, Part 2," *Reformed Journal* 27, no. 6 (June 1977): 19.

[41]Francis A. Schaeffer, *The Church at the End of the Twentieth Century*, vol. 4, bk. 1 of *The Complete Works of Francis A. Schaeffer* (Westchester, Ill.: Crossway, 1982), p. 92. For another resource that deals with Schaeffer's commitment to racial reconciliation, see Sylvester Jacobs, *Born Black* (London: Hodder & Stoughton, 1977).

[42]Schaeffer, "Mark of the Christian," p. 162.
[43]Schaeffer, *The God Who Is There*, pp. 93-94.
[44]Lewis, *Mere Christianity*, p. 141.
[45]Ibid., p. 151.
[46]Ibid.
[47]Ibid., p. 153.
[48]Ibid.

Author, Name and Subject Index

"Khazna"—he laughed—"Mufaddi's blood is lost . . . lost."

"Lost!"

"Woman, you should ask whose blood is next."

"Ours is a long story, Abu Othman."

"Long. How much longer?"

"Trust in God, man. All is well with the world."

"God only knows." He laughed sadly. "Hope for the best. No one can read the future."

ABOUT THE AUTHOR

Dr. Abdelrahman Munif was born in Jordan circa 1933 into a trading family of Saudi Arabian origin. He was stripped of his Saudi citizenship for political reasons. He earned a license in law from Baghdad and Cairo Universities, and his Ph.D. in oil economics from the University of Belgrade. During his career in the field of oil, he served as Director of Planning in the Syrian Oil Company and later as Director of Crude Oil Marketing. In Baghdad he was editor-in-chief of *Al-Naft wal Tanmiya (Oil & Development)*, a monthly periodical. He now devotes his time solely to the writing of novels. *Cities of Salt*, the first novel of a trilogy, was written during his stay in France.

Among his other novels are *Sharq Al Mutawasit (East of the Mediterranean)*, *Heen Tarakna Al-Jisr (When We Left the Bridge)*, and *Alam Bila Kharait (A World Without Maps)*, written with Jabra Ibrahim Jabra.

ABOUT THE TRANSLATOR

Peter Theroux was born in Boston in 1956, and was educated at Harvard and the American University of Cairo. He has lived and traveled in Iraq, Syria and Saudi Arabia, and is the author of *The Strange Disappearance of Imam Moussa Sadr* (Weidenfeld & Nicolson, London). He lives in Long Beach, California.